VICTIMOLOGY

VICTIMOLOGY

A Study of Crime Victims and Their Roles

JUDITH M. SGARZI, Ph.D.
Mount Ida College

JACK McDEVITT, M.P.A.
Northeastern University

Editors

Prentice Hall

Upper Saddle River, New Jersey 07458

Library of Congress Cataloging-in-Publication Data

Victimology : a study of crime victims and their roles / Judith M. Sgarzi and Jack
McDevitt, editors.
   p.   cm.
Includes bibliographical references and index.
ISBN 0-13-437286-7
   1. Victims of crimes. I. Sgarzi, Judith M. II. McDevitt, Jack

HV6250.25 .V53 2002
362.88—dc21

2002016996

Publisher: Jeff Johnston
Executive Editor: Kim Davies
Assistant Editor: Sarah Holle
Production Editor: Hilary Farquhar, Stratford Publishing Services
Production Liaison: Barbara Marttine Cappuccio
Director of Production and Manufacturing: Bruce Johnson
Managing Editor: Mary Carnis
Manufacturing Buyer: Cathleen Petersen
Creative Director: Cheryl Asherman
Cover Design Coordinator: Miguel Ortiz
Marketing Manager: Jessica Pfaff
Cover Designer: Miguel Ortiz
Formatting and Interior Design: Stratford Publishing Services
Printing and Binding: Phoenix Book Tech Park

Pearson Education LTD, *London*
Pearson Education Australia Pty. Limited, *Sydney*
Pearson Education Singapore, Pte. Ltd.
Pearson Education North Asia Ltd., *Hong Kong*
Pearson Education Canada, Ltd., *Toronto*
Pearson Educación de Mexico, S.A. de C.V.
Pearson Education—Japan, *Tokyo*
Pearson Education Malaysia, Pte. Ltd

10 9 8 7 6 5 4
ISBN   0-13-437286-7

Crime victims even today are too often overlooked, and their pain too often minimized. We hope this book helps to describe the broad set of consequences that crime has on all those who identify themselves as victims. We would like to see this book become an educational learning experience as well as an instrument for change for all who read it.

Contents

Acknowledgments   xi

About the Authors   xiii

"Victim's Song: And Freedom Rings"   xvii

Introduction   1

PART I   Targets of Predators   7

Chapter 1   Victims of Serial Killers
             The "Less-Dead"   9
                 Kim and Steve Egger

Chapter 2   Perceived Risks of Date Rape   33
                 Michael Shively

Chapter 3   In Harm's Way
             *The Client in Professional Sexual
             Misconduct*   55
                 Jennifer Eastman

Chapter 4   The Media's Influence on Behavior and Violence
            Is Society the Victim of the Media?   69
            Judith M. Sgarzi

PART II   Victims of Political or Identity Status   87

Chapter 5   Major Problems Facing Victims
            of Child Abuse   89
            Patricia Smith and Judith M. Sgarzi

Chapter 6   The Role of Victimization in Criminal
            Offending of Female Youth Gangs   101
            Dana M. Nurge and Michael Shively

Chapter 7   Victims of Domestic Violence   117
            Gwen P. DeVasto

Chapter 8   Treatment and Recognition for
            Victims of Terrorism   159
            Jeremy Spindlove

Chapter 9   Hate Crimes Victimization
            *A Comparison of Bias- and Nonbias-
            Motivated Assaults*   189
            Jack McDevitt and Jennifer Balboni

Chapter 10   Victims of Racial Profiling   205
            Amy Farrell and Deborah Ramirez

PART III   Victims in Organizational Contexts   219

Chapter 11   Straight Time
            *Inmates' Perceptions of Violence and
            Victimization in Prison*   221
            Craig Hemmens and James W. Marquart

Chapter 12   Victims of School Violence   238
            April J. Berry-Fletcher and John D. Fletcher

Chapter 13   Victims of Campus Violence   258
            April J. Berry-Fletcher

Chapter 14   Workplace Violence
The Sexual Assault and Rape of Jane Doe   281

Norman F. Lazarus

Chapter 15   Victims of Victimless Crimes   309

John D. Fletcher

PART IV   Responses to Victimization   331

Chapter 16   A Constitutional Amendment for Victims
The Unexplored Possibility   333

Jennifer Eastman

Chapter 17   Police and Victims of Domestic Violence   347

Michael E. Buerger

Chapter 18   Balanced and Restorative Justice
*Reengaging the Victim in the
Justice Process*   370

Jennifer M. Balboni

Index   385

Acknowledgments

I thank first and foremost my co-editor, Jack McDevitt, for agreeing to do this book with me and for all of his help throughout.

I also extend my deepest thanks to all of the chapter authors, who were patient and diligent in their work. For each of us it was a labor of love. Without the expertise and varied knowledge of each of the authors, who contributed long hours and hard work, this book would not have come together in the way it did.

Jack McDevitt and I also thank the following reviewers for their helpful comments and insight: Dr. Lucien Lombardo, Old Dominion University; Lee E. Ross, University of Wisconsin; and Rebecca Nathanson, Housatonic Valley Community College.

I thank Mount Ida College for the support it gave me for this project and its belief in me. I particularly want to thank several people who never stopped gently moving me in the right direction through their faith, love, and support: Dr. James Martin, Dr. Susan Holton, and my friend and favorite colleague, Ellen Goldberger, J.D. Without their continued gentle pressure I might not have moved forward to complete the book.

Last but above all, I thank my family—my husband, Peter (my biggest fan and supporter); my son Christopher and his wife, Colleen; my son Jason-Arthur; his wife, Aimeé; and their son, Julian-Arthur—who brought me the greatest joy throughout this process. I also thank my mother, Fran; she has always known this would come to pass.

A special thanks to my dear friend Pamela Parsons, who helped me at every stage of this book's development.

Judith M. Sgarzi, Ph.D.

I would like to thank Judie Sgarzi for inviting me to participate in this project. Although sometimes it seemed as if it would never end, Judie's care and good humor kept the project on track.

I would also like to thank the College of Criminal Justice at Northeastern University and in particular Dean Jack Greene and Dean Robert Croatti for their continued support both intellectually and personally.

I would like to thank the staff of the Center for Criminal Justice Policy Research—Jen Balboni, Susan Bennett, Shea Cronin, Amy Farrell, Michael Buerger, Carli DeMari, and Marion Sullivan—for their professionalism, their remarkable research expertise, and, most important, the support they showed me during a difficult period. It meant more than I can say.

Most important, I would like to thank my family: my sons, Sean and Brian, and my wife, Jan, the love of my life. Their patience, support, and insights have enhanced this book and all my work, and most important, my life.

Jack McDevitt

About the Authors

Jennifer M. Balboni is a doctoral candidate in the Law, Policy and Society Program at Northeastern University, as well as senior research associate at the Center for Criminal Justice Policy Research. She has worked at the CCJPR since 1997 researching hate-crime reporting and victimization processes. Ms. Balboni has published several articles, reports (including *Improving the Academy of Bias Crime Reporting Nationally,* coauthored with Jack McDevitt and released by President Clinton in September 2000), and book chapters (forthcoming), as well as op-ed pieces in the *Boston Globe* about hate crime and juvenile justice.

April J. Berry-Fletcher, M.S.W., LICSW, is currently the director of counseling services at Mount Ida College. She is also a visiting instructor at Boston College Graduate School of Social Work, Salem State College, Fisher College, and Mount Ida College.

Michael E. Buerger, Ph.D., is an associate professor and the graduate coordinator for the Criminal Justice Program at Bowling Green State University, Ohio. Following nine years as a police officer, he received a doctorate in criminal justice from Rutgers University in 1993. He was the field director for the RECAP Experiment and the Hot Spots of Crime Experiment for the Crime Control Institute, and was a visiting fellow with the National Institute of Justice. A wide range of police-related topics defines his research interests, most recently community and problem-oriented policing, police handling of domestic violence, and the resistance of the police culture to administratively imposed reform.

Gwen Park DeVasto, M.Ed., L.C.S.W., has worked in the field of domestic and workplace voilence for 23 years as a social worker and educator. DeVasto, recently retired form the Quincy, Massachusetts, Model Domestic Violence Program, has trained in or consulted with professionals from 45 states and 17 countries. As a violence prevention expert, DeVasto was invited to the White House and appeared on various news programs, including *60 Minutes.* She continues her passion for educating about this subject not only in schools and colleges, but also in training seminars for businesses, government and private agencies, and criminal justice settings nationally and internationally as a private consultant.

Jennifer Eastman is a visiting lecturer in law at Framingham State College. She has written numerous articles on law and psychology, and psychohistorical studies of Albert Camus and Paul Cezanne. She is currently working on a book about Freud and Sophocles.

Kim Egger holds a B.S. in psychology from the University of Illinois at Springfield and is currently pursuing a master's degree in law and psychology. For the past 10 years she has been developing a database of over 1,300 serial killers from 1900 to 2000. She has lectured at Purdue University, the University of Illinois at Springfield, and Brazosport College, Texas.

Steve Egger, Ph.D., professor of criminal justice at the University of Illinois at Springfield, has been conducting research on serial murder since 1983. In 1985, he wrote the first dissertation on serial murder and has since written three books on the subject. He has worked as a police officer, homicide investigator, police consultant, law enforcement academy director, and was interim dean of the College of Health and Human Services at the University of Illinois at Springfield.

John D. Fletcher, Ed.D., is currently the statewide director of Family Counseling Centers, Massachusetts Society for the Prevention of Cruelty to Children.

Craig Hemmens, J.D., Ph.D., is an associate professor in the Department of Criminal Justice Administration at Boise State University. He has written 2 books and more than 80 articles on a variety of criminal justice topics, including corrections, criminal procedure, and juvenile justice.

Amy Farrell is research coordinator at the Institute on Race and Justice and a senior research associate at the Center for Criminal Justice Policy Research at Northeastern University. Her research focuses on disparate treatment of individuals within the criminal justice system. In addition to her work on police practice, she is conducting research to help clarify the influence of defendant characteristics on downward departure decisions in federal sentencing. She has recently completed a study examining the interactive roles of race and gender on departure decisions, which was supported by a graduate research fellowship awarded by the National Institute of Justice.

Norman F. Lazarus, Attorney at Law, is currently in private practice. He is experienced in all phases of complex civil and criminal litigation, and in sexual harassment, employment, and discrimination law. He briefed and argued a landmark case in this area before the full bench of the Massachusetts Supreme Judicial Court.

James W. Marquart, Ph.D., is professor of criminal justice at and director of the Institute for Victimization Studies at Sam Houston State University, Texas. He has written several books and a number of articles, mostly focusing on corrections issues.

Jack McDevitt, M.P.A., is associate dean for Research and Graduate Studies in the College of Criminal Justice at Northeastern University, where he also directs the Institute for Research on Race and Justice. Jack is the coauthor, with Jack Levin, of *Hate Crimes: The Rising Tide of Bigotry and Bloodshed.* He is a coauthor of numerous governmental reports, including *Improving the Quality and Accuracy of Bias Crime Statistics Nationally* for the Department of Justice. He has been teaching and conducting research at Northeastern for the past 18 years.

Dana M. Nurge, Ph.D., is an assistant professor in the College of Criminal Justice at Northeastern University. She has recently completed a book manuscript based on a qualitative study of female gangs in Boston, and is currently conducting applied research on programming for "at-risk" adolescent girls. Her primary research interests relate to juvenile justice policy, juvenile corrections, and youth violence/gang prevention and intervention programming.

Deborah Ramirez, Ph.D., is a professor of law with Northeastern University's Asa S. Knowles School of Law. Most recently, Professor Ramirez has coauthored *Promising Practices: A Resource Guide for Racial Profiling Data Collection* for the Department of Justice Resource. She specializes in issues of race and criminal justice, racial profiling and jury selection, and has spoken nationally on issues of race, ethnicity, and discrimination.

Judith M. Sgarzi, Ph.D., is currently the program director for criminal justice at Mount Ida College. Dr. Sgarzi is a forensic criminologist who also writes and teaches in the area of criminal thinking patterns and their development. She is a general specialist and has written and presented papers in a wide variety of areas of criminal justice. Currently she is coauthoring a book with Jack McDevitt on police corruption titled *The Thin Blue Line.*

Michael Shively is a research associate at Abt Associates, Inc., in Cambridge, Massachusetts. His most recent publications include "Male self-control and sexual aggression," featured in *Deviant Behavior,* and the second edition of *Elementary Statistics in Criminal Justice* (Addison-Wesley), written with colleagues James Fox and Jack Levin (Addison-Wesley). His research interests include corrections and sexual assaults.

Patricia Smith is a pen name for a chapter author who wishes to remain anonymous.

Jeremy Spindlove is a former British police officer and aviation security specialist. He has worked in many countries in the Middle East and Africa and has seen the horrors and suffering of terrorism victims at first hand. He is the coauthor of a book on terrorism titled *Terrorism Today: The Past, the Players, and the Future* (Prentice Hall, 2000).

"Victim's Song: And Freedom Rings"

Don't be silenced when you hear the thunder's roar,
Don't stand aside; stand in place, silent and tall,
And listen to Freedom Ringing above the whispered words.

When their fists are raised like hammers and strike
for deadly blows,
Let your lips quiver, but no tears shed.
As blood flows out from wounds not healed,
Speak out the truth from silent shouts,
And hear again from history's song,
Let Freedom Ring.

Exchange their bullets, swords, and broken trust,
For hands of steady support.
Entwined within the promise of fairness true.
While cymbals clang and noisy chatter is hushed,
In whispers of joy and verse of Freedom Rings.

Let not their stinging words of hate and malice grind you down.
Hold fast to roots of pride long placed,
From loving families' dreams bequeathed.
And turn to glory's colors flown on high for all to see,
And hear the echoed song of hope as sung while Freedom Rings.

Judith M. Sgarzi, Ph.D.

Judith Sgarzi would like to dedicate this poem to all the victims' families of the devastating events that occurred on September 11, 2001, especially to her neighbors Mr. and Mrs. Lawrence Hunt in memory of their son, William Christopher Hunt, and to his family: wife Jennifer and daughter Emma, and brother Daniel Hunt and his wife Jean.

Introduction

The concept of victim dates back to ancient cultures and civilizations. Its original meaning was rooted in the exercise of sacrifice—the taking of a life of a person or animal to satisfy a deity (Karmen, 1990).

Karmen (1990) defined victimology as

> The scientific study of victimization, including the relationships between the victims and the offenders, the interactions between victims and the criminal justice system—that is, the police and courts, and corrections officials—and the connections between victims and other societal groups and institutions, such as the media, businesses, and social movements. (p. 3)

Today the word *victim* is used to refer to many different people: victims of domestic violence, victims of hate crime, victims of workplace violence, and so on. Not only do we recognize victims today, but also we recognize that there are many differences in the ways individuals become victimized in our society.

Over the past decade, legislatures and agencies involved in criminal justice have begun to pay much more attention to the victims of criminal behavior. Historically, the victims of crime were an afterthought within the criminal justice system, sometimes even seen as a necessary evil. Police interacted with victims primarily to find out if they could identify a suspect, prosecutors dealt

1

with victims only as trial witnesses, and the courts frequently ignored the victim entirely. Almost all the emphasis was placed on the offender, first on identifying and arresting the offender and then on punishing and/or rehabilitating the offender. There was scant concern about the impact of the crime on the victim.

The crime victim's movement initially focused most of its attention on the needs of victims of violent crime. The study of victimology has expanded in recent years to include those who experience harm firsthand, for example, victims of domestic violence, hate crime, and police brutality, as well as those who experience secondary victimization, such as the families and friends of the victims.

During the past couple of decades the problems associated with the practice of "victim blaming" also began to receive much attention. The authors in this book believe that victim blaming has been one of the biggest impediments to meaningful reforms in the criminal justice system. In the areas of rape and sexual assault, criminal justice authorities initially looked for things the victim might have done to bring the crime upon herself. Questions were asked such as, Why was she dressed that way? What was she doing in that area at that time of day? Was she drinking? We believe that blaming victims removes the blameworthiness of the offender, revictimizes the victim, and is unacceptable and destructive to moving toward resolution of solving the problems of victimization in our society.

In 1982, the President's Task Force on Victims of Crime made a series of recommendations for improving services to victims. Since this report, the focus of the criminal justice system in many states has been broadened to include more programs and services for victims. The agencies of criminal justice have begun to realize that victims are their constituents, and these constituents need their assistance. Initial efforts to include victims in the process developed in variety of forms, including allowing victims to make a victim impact statement at trial, informing victims about the progress of their case, and providing financial compensation for certain categories of victims. At present, approximately 45 states have passed some version of a victims' bill of rights, which guarantees victims a number of rights similar to those mentioned above.

Although these efforts have been positive steps forward for crime victims, they have in many cases delivered less than supporters had hoped. For example, the idea behind victim impact statements is that victims, by discussing the pain they endured, might help judges set a more appropriate sentence for a crime, but the statements have been less effective in this regard than original supporters intended. It is true that many victims are now afforded an opportunity to speak before sentencing, but too often the sentencing judge has already made up her mind (or a sentence has been dictated by a plea bargain or an existing mandatory sentence) and the victim's words have little impact on the sentence to be handed down. Although the opportunity to make a statement to the court and, often, to the offender, may have a cathartic value for the victims, if it has no impact on the sentence, it is a hollow gesture. It has also become apparent to court officials that this opportunity is more important for some victims than for others. Some victims find standing up in court and making a statement about their victimization traumatizing and they want no part of it, while others feel it plays an important part in the healing process. We have begun to recognize that victims of crime cope with their victimization in many different ways and that strategies for victim support must reflect these differences.

This problem has plagued many of the initial reforms implemented to assist victims, in that most reforms treat victims of crime as if they are all the same. It is as if the rape victim and the store owner who has been robbed have had similar experiences. True, both are victims of crime, but that is where the similarity ends. The aftermath of a rape is much different from the aftermath of a shoplifting incident. The problem with most victims' support policies and programs is that they treat all victims the same. It is important to understand that victims experience the crime and its aftermath differently, depending on the context of the event. Factors that may affect how a victim perceives the incident include the severity of the crime, the relationship of the victim to the offender, the setting of the crime, and the support system available to the victim.

We are glad to report that more recent research on victim-related issues and shared responsibility has taken a new focus, studying the characteristics of crime victims and risk factors in order to better understand victimization in the context in which it occurred.

The term *victim* has evolved to one commonality, which can be applied to all victims: Victims are individuals who have suffered injury and harm by forces beyond their control and not related to their personal responsibility (Karmen, 1990).

In this book we provide information on a wide array of crimes in their individual contexts, with the goal of demonstrating to the reader some of the range of victimization experiences that crime victims are forced to deal with. We believe this methodology offers a richer and more realistic approach to understanding the process of victimization and the broad range of coping mechanisms that victims use to deal with their particular experience. In addition, we believe this approach allows the reader to understand in more depth the issues facing the agencies of criminal justice that are attempting to service victims in our society.

As mentioned, one of the factors that influences how victims will deal with their victimization is whether they have a relationship to the offender. As we discuss in Part I, it is clearly different if a crime is committed by someone a victim has known and trusted, such as a co-worker or a fellow student on campus, than if the crime is committed by a total stranger. When people are victimized by someone close to them, they have to deal with a loss of personal trust as well as with overcoming the crime itself. This is less the case if the crime is perpetrated by a stranger. In this case there is no prior relationship to be dealt with; however, this kind of victimization offers its own set of issues to overcome. In stranger crimes, particularly the most serious, such as serial killing, rape, and hate crimes, the broader community as well as the targeted individual becomes a victim of these crimes. The terror that these crimes evoke can spread across an entire community. Take, for example, the reaction of communities when there is a suspicion that a serial killer is in the area.

When we hear that a horrendous crime has occurred in our area, many of us go through the same process. We listen to the details to see if it could happen to us. We hear that the killing was a result of a bad drug deal or that the rapist targeted certain individuals, for example, prostitutes, and we feel better. We feel less frightened because we feel these perpetrators will not be looking for us since we do not engage in those behaviors. In contrast, if a crime is truly random and we cannot distance ourselves from it, our level of fear increases significantly. If the victims are truly random, any one of us could be the next one. These crimes are among the most terrifying for the broader community.

A final context of victimization is the victim's political or identity status, which we discuss in Part II. In these crimes the victim is chosen not because the offender sees an opportunity for financial gain, such as in a robbery, but because she is perceived to be a member of a group. In terrorism and hate crimes, for example, victims are chosen because the offender believes the victims represent a particular political or racial or ethnic group. These crimes offer a unique set of challenges for victims to overcome. Since they were attacked because of who they are, and not what they did, they can't alter their behavior to reduce the chance that this kind of crime will happen again. These crimes can affect an entire community and increase the pool of victims in ways that many other crimes cannot. After a terrorist incident, entire communities become fearful and in many cases alter their normal behavior, for fear of becoming a target. That is most often the goal of the offender.

Another contextual factor is the setting where the victimization occurred, and in Part III we examine crimes in which the setting was an important element. For example, if a crime occurs on a college campus or in a workplace, the dynamic of the victimization changes. Frequently, these crimes take the form of harassment. Since the offender is in regular proximity to the victim, a disagreement can sometimes escalate to a long-term harassment situation. In addition, the victim's ability to distance himself from his attacker is reduced, since often the victim has to deal with not only the offender but also his friends. Sometimes the only way to deal with the crime is for the victim to leave the setting, again dramatically altering his ability to overcome the impact of the crime.

Finally, in Part IV we look at some specific remedies intended to improve the ability of victims to deal with their experience. Recommendations such as the victim bill of rights and the use of restorative justice programs realize the uniqueness of each victim's experience and attempt to provide support for victims that is tailored to their particular context.

One of the first books entirely devoted to victims was *The Crime Victim's Book* (Bard and Sangrey, 1979), and it addressed the question, Who is the victim? Bard and Sangrey stated,

> Every victim of personal crime is confronted with a brutal reality: the deliberate violation of one human being by another. The crime may be a murder or a rape, a robbery or a burglary, the theft of an automobile, a pocket picking, or a purse snatching—but the essential internal injury is the same. Victims have been assaulted—emotionally and sometimes physically—by a predator who has shaken their world to its foundation. (National Victim Assistance Academy, 1998, p. 3)

Why should the criminal justice system concern itself with helping victims of crime? Because if nothing is done to assist victims, the psychological trauma they face will often impair their ability and/or willingness to cooperate with the police and courts (Karmen, 1990). The President's Task Force Report on Victims of Crime (1982) stated that victims must be treated better, because the criminal justice system will not work without their help.

At every key stage, from filing a police report to attending a parole hearing, interactions can be stressful for the victims, and often the process exacerbates crime-related psychological trauma (President's Task Force on Victims of Crime, 1982).

We cannot get the help we need to facilitate the operations of the criminal justice system if we do not assist the very individuals it was designed to serve.

It is the editors' hope that this book will give the reader a better understanding of the experiences of victims, including ways to assist those in our society who are victims of crime.

References

Bard, M., and Sangrey, D. (1979). *The Crime Victim's Book.* New York: Basic Books.

Karmen, A. (1990). *Crime Victims: An Introduction to Victimology.* Belmont, CA: Wadsworth.

National Victim Assistance Academy. (1998). Theoretical perspectives of victimology and critical research. Available at http://www.ojp.usdoj.gov/ovc/assist/nvaa/ch03.htm.

President's Task Force on Victims of Crime. (1982). *Final Report.* Washington, DC: U.S. Department of Justice, Office for Victims of Crime.

PART 1

TARGETS OF PREDATORS

CHAPTER 1

Victims of Serial Killers
The "Less-Dead"

Kim and Steve Egger

> *"I were just cleaning up the streets."*
> PETER SUTCLIFFE, *the Yorkshire Ripper*

Introduction: The "less-dead"

When the novel *The Silence of the Lambs* was published, it became a best-seller. When the movie was made, it packed the theaters and received numerous Academy Awards. People flocked to the cinema to see the riveting performances of Sir Anthony Hopkins and Jodie Foster. The character of Dr. Hannibal Lecter was suddenly known everywhere, parodied on television comedy programs and the talk of the town. Hannibal Lecter, as portrayed by Hopkins, captured the public's imagination.

Why? Americans, Brits, and Russians, along with nearly all of the rest of the world, have made heroes out of not only fictional serial killers but the real serial killers among us. While their numerous victims lie in their graves, serial killers can still send the press into high gear. They are still remembered years after their crimes. Books, articles, and the press continue to produce copious amounts of ink, hanging on every word these killers say, every court action that is held on their behalf, and every excuse they make for their behavior.

Why? Why is it that we are so fascinated by these aberrations of the human race while ignoring their victims? Part of the answer may be, particularly in American society, that we secretly admire the "cowboys," who are part of the myth of the American West, and the "bad boys" who are being produced by our modern society.

The so-called bad boys and cowboys of the United States helped settle this country. Even in the earliest days of U.S. history the serial killers were there, except they were not recognized for what they truly were; instead, they became the heroes of the new nation. Perhaps, then, the key to this problem lies not within the serial killer, but rather, within the victims whom he or she generally chose. Throughout our country's history, serial killers have murdered the people who were the least powerful. Some killers had the official sanction of their communities (searching out and murdering Native Americans and so-called witches), and others worked without sanction (murdering undesired settlers, outcasts, and those who deviated from societal norms), but with praise nonetheless. We still can hear the ballads of Billy the Kid and Bonnie and Clyde (Newton, 1992). It is the *victim's status* in society that gives us *part* of the answer to the question of why we continue to make serial killers heroes. The fictional Dr. Lecter is only the latest in a long line of heroes.

It was not only the brilliant acting of Hopkins as Lecter that transformed this fictional serial killer from a cruel, sadistic animal into a hero. The public is preprogrammed to identify with or even laud the role of the serial killer in our society and to forget the victim. The victims, who are viewed when alive as a devalued stratum of humanity, become "less-dead," since for most of society they were "less-alive" before their death and now become the "never-were." Their demise becomes a ritual of social cleansing by those who dare to wash away these undesirable elements. Just as the psychopathic serial killer depersonalizes his victims, society dissociates these victims from the human race because of the irritant symbols they represent. Victims become those who "had it coming" or whose fate was preordained.

The serial killer is seen by many as possessing courage, individuality, and a unique cleverness lacking in general society. His skill in eluding police for a long time transcends the very reason he is being hunted, overshadowing the killer's trail of grief and horror.

It is only when the "less-dead" are perceived as above the stature of prostitutes, homosexuals, street people, runaways, or the elderly that our own at-risk vulnerability becomes a stark reality that we can no longer ignore. Even as we begin to identify with the killer's prey, we shrug off such feelings and intellectualize the precipitant behavior of the victims and their lifestyles as the reason for their demise.

Once caught, the serial killer doesn't look abnormal on our television screens or the front pages of our newspapers, and his "less-dead" victims become less and less real. Their similarity to our own lives and their demise, which should alert us to our own risk, loses clarity as our self-manufactured reality excludes us from ever being a victim of a serial killer.

Our ability to feel compassion for serial murder victims is diminished by the excessive brutality displayed on Hollywood movie screens. The wide-screen realism and appeal of a serial killer becomes a metaphor of our future morality, whereby the "less-dead" victims are dropped from perceived reality.

Serial Murder Victims

In most cases, *the victims are selected solely because they crossed the path of the serial murderer* and became a vehicle by which hypo-arousal occurred for his pleasure at a particular point in time (S. Egger, 1984). Victims are self-selecting only inasmuch as they happened to be in a certain place and point in time, or because of their symbolic significance to the killer. These are the only known precipitating factors. Unlike in other homicide cases, the presence and availability of the serial killer's victims are the only reasons they are chosen; they have little responsibility for their victimization.

There are, however, some strong commonalities among victims of serial killers. There is generally no prior relationship between victim and killer. If there is a prior relationship, it is one in which the victim has a subjugated role. Victims may have symbolic value for the killer and/or be perceived as prestigeless and, in most instances, unable to defend themselves or alert others to their plight. In many instances, the victims are perceived by the killer to be powerless because of their situation in time, place, or status within their immediate surroundings. Examples of serial killers' most common victims are prostitutes, vagrants, the homeless, migrant workers, homosexuals, missing children, single women (out by themselves), elderly women, college students, and hospital patients. Levin and Fox (1985) appear to concur: "Serial killers almost without exception choose vulnerable victims—those who are easy to dominate. . . . The serial killer typically picks on innocent strangers who may possess a certain physical feature or may just be accessible" (pp. 75, 231). They list as examples of these vulnerable and frequent victims of the serial murderer prostitutes, hitchhikers, children, derelicts, and elderly women (pp. 75–78).

In discussing the susceptibility and vulnerability of victims, Karmen (1983) states,

> The vulnerability of an individual or group to criminal depredations depends upon an opportunity factor as well as an attractiveness factor. People who appear at the "right time" and the "right place," from the offender's point of view, run extreme risks. Hence certain lifestyles expose individuals and their possessions to greater threat and dangers than others. (p. 241)

Karmen provides examples of these high-risk lifestyles: homosexuals cruising downtown areas and public rest rooms; cult members soliciting funds on sidewalks and in bus stations; and released mental patients and skid row alcoholics wandering the streets at odd hours (pp. 241–242).

Maghan and Sagarin (1983), in discussing homosexuals as victimizers and victims, note that "the offender's rage against society is deflected and targeted on those who are victimized as the offender is. . . . Victimization appears to produce a rage that feeds an offender mentality, and offenders then choose victims who are the most vulnerable, closest (spatially and socially), and offer the greatest opportunities" (p. 160).

If Karmen's (1983) discussion of vulnerability and Maghan and Sagarin's (1983) discussion of victim–victimizer are combined, an extrapolation is possible in examining the victims of the serial murderer. If many serial murderers were victimized in childhood, as case studies and research suggest, and vulnerable because of their childhood situation, they may in fact choose victims like their earlier selves or from the same general lifestyle. Karmen states, "One common thread that emerges from most victim/offender studies is that both parties are usually drawn from the same group or background" (p. 242). However, it must be noted that there are no empirical studies of victim–offender relationships in serial murders in the literature, other than anecdotal material or conclusions based on a very few cases. Therefore, no valid conclusions can be drawn from the literature regarding victim–offender relationships in this context. The literature does suggest, however, that many of these killers have been abused, neglected, and victimized in their childhood and indicates the possibility that some serial killers may victimize persons who remind them of themselves as children.

Some blame the mobility of U.S. society for making victims more available to serial murderers. "It's not unusual for people—especially if they're drug users—to just up and leave home," says Commander Alfred Calhoun of the Ouachita Parish Sheriff's Office in Monroe, Louisiana. "Many become victims because they're hitchhiking or wandering in deserted places" (Gest, 1984, p. 53). Robert Keppel contends that since many serial murderers are charismatic, they can convince their victims to go with them using some pretext. "They pick people they can have power and control over, small-framed women, children and old people" (Lindsey, 1984, p. 7).

Psychiatrist Helen Morrison contends that the look of the victims is significant. She states, "If you take photos, or physical descriptions of the victims, what will strike you is the similarity in look." The physical appearances of the victims of some serial killers do bear a striking resemblance to one another, but this may hold few implications for investigators. Morrison also theorizes that some nonverbal communication exists between victim and killer: "There's something unique in that interaction" (McCarthy, 1984, p. 10). Morrison believes that the victims of serial murderers were symbolic of something or someone deeply significant in the murderers' lives. Some psychologists contend that the victims represent cruel parents on whom some murderers feel they cannot directly take revenge (Berger, 1984).

Morrison believes serial murderers do not distinguish between human beings and inanimate objects (Berger, 1984). In this way they may be similar to contract killers, whom Dietz (1983, p. 115) describes as depersonalizing their victims. Lunde (1976) found that sexual sadist murderers dehumanize their victims or perceive them as objects. He concludes that this "prevents the killer from identifying with the victims as mothers, fathers, children, people who love and are loved, people whose lives have meaning" (p. 61).

Hickey (1997) analyzed the cases of 2,526 to 3,860 serial murder victims between the years 1800 and 1995. He found a marked increase in the number of victims between 1975 and 1995. The annual rate of victims during the time between 1975 and 1995 was 0.02 per 100,000, compared to the annual homicide rate of 9.6 per 100,000 population for the same time period. He notes, "We run a greater risk of being a victim of domestic homicide and an even greater risk of being a victim of other violent crimes than we do of dying at the hands of a serial killer" (p. 102). However, we must remember that these statistics represent the deaths of human beings.

As S. Egger (1984) observed, if one loses a family member, loved one, or friend as a result of a killing in which victim and attacker had a prior relationship, the relationship tends to mitigate the loss for survivors in that it provides some sense of rationality for the act. In other words, some form of interaction between the victim and attacker has taken place prior to the point of fatal encounter. When the relational distance is great, as is the case in most serial murders, no sense of rationality can be found for the act, and the tolerance levels of survivors or society at large approach zero.

To kill a stranger not only defies an understanding of the rationality for such an act but accentuates a general level of fear because of the apparent randomness of victim selection. Lundsgaarde (1977) states the problem for the survivors succinctly: "The killer who chooses a stranger as his victim overtly threatens the preservation of social order" (p. 140).

Hickey's (1997) data reveals that between 1800 and 1995, population density rather than regionality accounted for the numbers of victims of serial killers, except in California, which had double the number of cases with multiple victims than occurred in New York, which ranked second in victim count. In 337 serial murder cases that occurred between 1800 and 1995, the number of victims was between 2,526 and 3,860, depending on how the researchers or police count the victims. This means that the average number of victims of each serial murderer is between seven and eleven. Hickey's data further reveals that in 19 of America's most populous states, the number of victims per case was six or more victims. In the remaining 31 states, Hickey found a range of one to five cases in which one or more victims were killed.

Serial killers seem to instinctively recognize the vulnerabilities of the individuals they select. The runaway teenager, the homeless man, or the woman who sells her body on the street all share several distinct characteristics: They are vulnerable, available, and easy for the serial killer to target without incurring the wrath of society. In 1994, S. Egger conceptualized the idea of the "less-dead" (K. Egger, 1996) to account for the majority of the victims of serial killers. It seems as if the would-be serial killer is aware of the public disdain for these people, the most vulnerable in American society. It is not a strictly American choice, however. Across international boundaries, the weakest members of society are the most frequently targeted by serial killers.

Society's Throwaways: A Low Priority for Law Enforcement

Unfortunately, there is a great deal less pressure on the police when the victims of a serial murder come from the marginal elements of a society or a community. People are much less incensed over a serial murderer operating in their area when they have little or no identification with the victims. The victims seem unreal, and little attention is paid to their demise.

As can readily be seen from press reports in newspapers and on television news programs, victims and survivors receive little attention in mass media accounts of crime. Unless the victims are well-known celebrities or people of power and wealth, the central focus of the media is on the crime and the offender.

PROSTITUTES: VICTIMS OF CHOICE

The data available on serial murder investigations indicate that one of the most common victims of a serial killer is the female prostitute. Seventy-eight percent of all victims of serial killers in the United States from 1960 to 1995 were prostitutes (K. Egger, 1999). From the killer's perspective, these women are simply available in an area that provides anonymity and adequate time in which to make a viable selection. It is highly probable that the serial killer selects prostitutes most frequently because they are easy to lure and control during the initial stages of what becomes abduction. Potential witnesses of this abduction see only a pickup and transaction prior to paying for sex. They are programmed to see what they expect to see when a woman gets into a car with a john. The attitude of society also makes the prostitute a desirable target. Women who are prostitutes are perceived by society as drug-addicted, friendless failures. They are viewed as "less-dead" because few see them as human beings and even fewer as the daughters and sons or mothers and brothers of people who love them. And after all, who will miss one less prostitute plying her trade on the streets?

A search of major newspaper reports of prostitutes as victims in serial murders cases that were either unsolved or under active investigation between October 5, 1991, and October 5, 1993, revealed that 198 prostitutes were identified as victims of serial killers involving 21 distinct serial murder patterns (S. Egger, 1998, p. 79). This is an average of more than nine prostitutes as victims per serial murder case. No other group was as frequently identified as victims of serial murders during that period. For the female prostitute, lifestyle most certainly plays a part in her being at-risk prey for a serial killer.

A careful selection of vulnerable victims does not mean the serial killer is a coward; it means that he or she has the street smarts to select victims who will not resist, will be relatively easy to control, and will not be missed. Such careful selection protects the killer from identification and apprehension. In many cases, selection of prostitutes ensures that the killing may never be revealed, and may not even be identified as a related series of crimes, and that the perpetrator may go on killing, fueling the need to kill again. Or if such a victim's remains are found, she will be difficult for the police to identify, given her lifestyle and lack of close ties to family, relatives, or the community.

The "less-dead," as applied to the victims of serial murder, can be defined as follows:

> The "less-dead" comprise most of the victims of serial killers. They are referred to as the "less-dead" because they were "less-alive" before their violent demise and now become "never-were." These victims are the devalued and marginalized groups of society or community. They are the vulnerable and the powerless. For example, prostitutes, migrants workers, the homeless, homosexuals, institutionalized persons, and the elderly who are frequently the victims of serial killers are considered the "less-dead." These groups lack prestige and in many instances are unable to alert others to their plight. They are powerless given their situation in time, place, or their immediate surroundings. (K. Egger, 1996, p. 15, and S. Egger, 1998, p. 6)

The prostitute, marginalized and devalued by society, is the "victim of choice" for the average serial killer. This choice can be traced to numerous sources, fundamentalist religious attitudes toward women and sexuality being two of the most prominent.

The "grandfather of serial murder" is Jack the Ripper (Caputi, 1987). Jack the Ripper chose prostitutes as his victims for sound reasons. The socioeconomic status of his victims greatly affected his choice. The murders attracted attention because of the nature of the crimes, not the victims. The Ripper murders in Victorian England caused an uproar because of their heinous nature, but the deaths of today's victims of modern-day Jack the Ripper fail to cause the same response. Because society has placed little value on their lives, law enforcement officials often follow suit. The public outcry for justice may be loud when the killings are first recognized, but regardless of the initial reaction, the "less-dead" can expect to be forgotten in death just as they were forgotten in life.

The Green River killings took place between 1982 and 1984, in Seattle, Washington, and heralded the beginning of the present-day slaughter of prostitutes. The total number of victims may never be known. Authorities know that at least 50 women met their deaths at the hands of the yet-unidentified Green River Killer. However, there may still be bodies around Seattle and in other areas that have yet to be found and attributed to this killer.

The *Seattle Times* coverage of the Green River killings fueled the investigation and propelled the case to national prominence. In their coverage of the killings, Tomas Guillen and Carlton Smith had to fight the attitudes of law enforcement officials and the public to push police officers to "do their jobs"(Griffiths, 1993). In Seattle it became a battle for public sentiment and will to pay for the costly investigation that would span decades. It is, after all, the public who pays for a serial murder investigation, and the public had to be continually convinced that the deaths of prostitutes were worth the cost. Although they worked to educate and inform the public, after the reporters moved on to other endeavors, the case fell slowly into obscurity.[1]

Asked about the role of the media in the investigation of the Green River Killer, Guillen responded,

> Briefly, police would say they investigate every case in the same manner. I believe otherwise. The less coverage a case gets, the easier it is for police to cut back. We go into this issue in our book, *The Search for the Green River Killer.* Kraske, who ran the first task force, clearly said the media played a role on police response. I still can't believe the task force was dismantled. The task force still had plenty of work to do. I have to think the task force would have continued if the victims were outstanding citizens. We tried to humanize the victims by writing a feature about their lives when they were found dead. We wanted to mention that they were children once and had dreams. I have to be honest, though, I think journalistic practices routinely brought out the negative side of the victims. *I still can't believe the public—Seattle and the Pacific Northwest—let police and the politicians scale down the investigation to one investigator. There was no outcry. There were no protests. Nothing. Everyone just went home. What a sad commentary!* (Tomas Guillen, personal communication with K. Egger, November 2000, emphasis added)

Joel Rifkin was another man who preyed on prostitutes. His arrest, like that of his predecessor, Ted Bundy, was the result of a patrol officer's routine traffic stop, and his instinct that something was not right after he spoke to the driver. That something turned out to be the body of one of the prostitutes Rifkin had killed, which he had placed in the back of his station wagon and was taking to dump somewhere in New York. CNN reporter Jeanie Moos, reporting in 1993 after Joel Rifkin was convicted and sent to prison, made this observation about Rifkin's most common victim, the prostitute:

Time after time, serial killers have zeroed in on prostitutes. Forty-nine dumped along the Green River in Washington; 11 killed by this man in the Rochester, New York, area; a string of murders of truck-stop prostitutes; even six red-headed prostitutes strangled in five states. Every prostitute you talk to knows of others who are missing. (CNN News, July 2, 1993, reporting from New York)

After the Rifkin conviction, the *New York Times* also looked at the problem of prostitutes being victimized by violent criminals.

Many prefer to ignore it. Even as the authorities were sorting out Mr. Rifkin's murderous stories, prostitutes were going about their business throughout the city, in force, as usual. For them, serial killers are just another occupational hazard. Violence is the nature of the beast. And working girls, as prostitutes like to be called, often disappear, never to be heard from again.

"The women we see are resourceless," said Allannah Thomas, a project manager for the Foundation for Research on Sexually Transmitted Diseases, which distributes condoms, conducts H.I.V. testing and provides other outreach services to prostitutes throughout New York City. The women are hurt by dates, by their personal partners and in the course of drug transactions. A lot of times people come up to us and ask us to dress wounds.

Richard Ayala, an outreach worker for the foundation, said that in the two years since he began driving the foundation's van, distributing condoms and testing women for H.I.V., he has noticed that many women simply disappear.

"Sometimes the girls tell us about the ones that disappear," he said. "They tell us this woman moved, this one died, this one was killed. But you never really know." ("Easy Prey," 1993, p. 23)

When the killer is preying on prostitutes in poor or minority communities, the people in the community may be the first to recognize that a serial killer is at work, while the law enforcement community does not. It is sad that the public is sometimes aware of a serial killer at work in their community long before the police are. A case in point is that of Hubert Geralds Jr., who was killing in the Englewood area of Chicago, Illinois. In 1995 the community organized to present local law enforcement officers with information to support their contention that a serial killer was at work in their neighborhoods. Law enforcement officials denied it. They had sent the cases in question to the FBI, who failed to find any connection between the murders. A call from the sister of Geralds, however, led to his arrest for the murder of six women, all of whom were prostitutes and drug users and all of whom were strangled in the same way. He was tried, convicted, and later sentenced to death.

Working at the same time and in the same area of Chicago was Gregory Clepper, a black man who had killed 14 women beginning in 1991. He managed to remain undetected; it was only because he confessed that the murders were finally linked to him. Because his crimes were linked to drugs, police failed to see what the neighborhood already knew—a serial killer was at work, targeting young, black women who used drugs and sometimes worked as prostitutes.

Chicago authorities finally admitted that there were at least three serial killers working in the area in the 1990s, all targeting young, black women who sometimes worked as prostitutes and were using drugs. However, this admission came only after the arrests of two suspects, one of whom was Geralds. The community felt that because they were black, poor, and living in a high crime area, the cases were not given the attention they merited ("Serial slaying scandal," 1995, p. 1).

These crimes have forced law enforcement agencies to confront one of the most commonly accepted myths of serial killers: that they are white, middle-aged, middle-class men who prey on victims much like themselves. This myth has probably allowed many serial killings in the black community to go undetected by law enforcement. As the number of black and minority males who are arrested and charged with serial murder continues to rise, this misconception will have to change. When black people in predominately black neighborhoods start turning up dead, police need to take a closer look at these crimes. If you don't look for the connections, you cannot find them. Black-on-black crime includes serial murder and probably always has. Racism, bigotry, and ignorance have almost certainly allowed a number of black serial killers to kill with impunity over the past century. Hickey (1999) agrees that black serial killers are simply not as readily acknowledged by law enforcement or the public. "We just don't talk about them as much. They're killing their own, often killing black prostitutes, and they just don't get the attention" ("Southside slayings defy myths about serial killers," 1999, p. 1). This lack of knowledge gives black serial killers unprecedented freedom to kill repeatedly without fear of apprehension.

By the official FBI count, the black serial killer is a rarity. Only Hickey (1997) has recognized that black serial killers are actively killing in the United States and have been doing so all along. The sad fact is that when a serial killer's work is detected, it is nearly automatically assumed that the killer is a white male. The black serial killer can remain undetected, particularly when he preys on those in his own community. The Atlanta, Georgia, child killings were thrust into national prominence only because of the public's natural sympathy for children and because many people believed that a white supremacist was at work in the neighborhoods of Atlanta. Preying on black prostitutes is nearly always a sure way of getting away with murder.

In our nation's history, the status of African Americans has progressed from being little more than that of a possession, to struggling to be recognized in the 1950s and 1960s, to fighting the systemic racism of U.S. society today. It was only in the last 50 years that the presence of black serial killers was noted and in the past 10 years that researchers recognized that the number may be higher than originally thought.

This is true not only for the African American community in the United States, but for all minority communities.

Prostitutes of all backgrounds seem to bring out the worst in the serial killers who routinely target them. The fact that their deaths are often seen as a result of their own making makes them the victim of least risk to the serial killer and thus puts them at high risk of becoming prey. When prostitutes are killed, the public perception is that they are responsible for their own deaths. The flurry of arrests in the 1990s is evidence of the atrocities being committed against them.

Even more recently, Eric Armstrong, a 26-year-old white male and former sailor on the U.S.S. *Nimitz,* was arrested for the deaths of three prostitutes in and around Detroit, Michigan. His arrest resulted not from police work but from a mistake by the killer: He came to the attention of local authorities when he reported seeing a body. It was the body of his latest victim, and DNA evidence linked Armstrong to her death. In addition to the 3 Detroit-area deaths, police say the suspect has confessed to committing at least 11 other killings since 1992: 3 in the Seattle area, 2 in Hawaii, 2 in Hong Kong, and 1 each in North Carolina, Virginia, Thailand, and Singapore. He may also be linked to the deaths of several prostitutes in Japan, Korea, and Israel.

Robert Yates Jr. killed at least 11 prostitutes in the Pacific Northwest. His brutal assaults began in 1996, and it was not until two years later that Spokane authorities admitted they were dealing with a serial killer. Yates, the father of five, was seen by all, including his wife and father, as simply living the American dream, and then he was identified by the police as a serial killer. Yates was arrested in April 2000 because of the long, hard work of Spokane detectives and the help of his potential victims, the prostitutes of Spokane. In addition to these murders, Yates pled guilty to two killings in Walla Walla, Washington, in 1975 and another killing, that of Stacy Hawn, in 1988. The first case, the murder of a college couple, had remained unsolved for a quarter of a century. The case of Stacy Hawn had also gone unsolved. No one, including the police, suspected the involvement of Robert Yates Jr., and his admission to these killings came as a shock to the relatives of the victims, who had never imagined that the Spokane prostitute-killer they had read about in local newspapers for many months had been their family member's killer. The authorities suspect that the modus operandi of these early crimes may have established Yates's pattern of future killings ("Yates whet his taste . . ." 2000, p. 1).

It was only because Yates admitted to the three prior murders that the Spokane County prosecutor allowed him to be sentenced to life in prison without parole ("Authorities are shocked . . ." 2000, p. 1). His father, his wife, and the families of the victims still don't know why he killed.

How long could Yates have continued his killings? After a quarter of a century, he was finally caught. Caught because in the final two years of killing he made mistakes that police recognized and were able to use to identify him as a serial killer, and these led to his apprehension and conviction.

CHILDREN

The "less-dead" are also often children. Serial killers typically target runaway, homeless, and/or minority children in the United States, and in other countries. This is particularly true in countries where many children have to resort to begging to survive. Street children in South America are often left to their own devices by families that can't support them and societies that don't acknowledge them. These children are forced to prostitute their bodies or abilities to survive. Two cases that illustrate this are those of Pedro Lopez in South America and, more recently, Javed Iqbal in Pakistan.

In January 2000, Javed Iqbal was arrested in Lahore, Pakistan, for killing 100 young boys, ages 6 to 16, and dissolving their bodies in a vat of acid. All of his victims were street children, or children turned out on the streets by their parents to beg. What brought Iqbal to the attention of the Pakistani authorities was a letter that he sent to the newspaper bragging about his crimes.

Pakistan is a predominately Islamic country where prostitution is for all intents and purposes nonexistent because of religious law. Thus instead of the prostitutes who are selected in other countries, young male street children are often targeted by serial killers.

The *BBC World News* described the situation of the young boys:

> And one pundit has taken Pakistan's conservative sexual mores to task as a trigger for the murders. "The abuse of young boys is an unspoken but rampant aspect of everyday life," the pundit writes. "This is one result of the gender segregation prevalent in traditional societies like ours that nobody wants to talk about." (*BBC World News*, 2000)

The case in South America remains one of the most unimaginable on record in modern times. In this particularly gruesome case, Pedro Lopez, nicknamed the "Monster of the Andes," killed at least 400 children in Colombia, Peru, and Ecuador beginning in the late 1970s. His self-confessed killings were viewed with skepticism until he began taking authorities to the graves of his victims. Lopez finally quit talking to authorities when informed that he could be sentenced to death for the murders of the Colombian girls. Ecuador convicted Lopez of 110 murders and sentenced him to life. In Ecuador, the usual life term amounts to 16 years, making Lopez eligible for parole in 1990. Because of the Ecuadorian law, Colombia awaited his release and planned to try him for the murders of at least 100 girls and to seek the death penalty. Frighteningly, Lopez was released in the summer of 1998 ("Pedro Lopez freed," 1998, p. 19). Despite the best efforts of Colombian authorities to take him into custody to stand trial, Lopez disappeared into the Ecuadorian rainforest without a trace. He has since seemingly vanished from the face of the earth. Is he still killing? If he is still alive, it is almost certain that he has claimed as yet unidentified victims.

Other countries are not alone in offering their children for victims. One of the most terrible homicide cases in U.S. history is that of Dean Corll in Texas. In the 1970s, a serial killer was at work in the Houston suburb of Pasadena. Young boys of the working-class poor began disappearing. The police wrote off the disappearances as runaways and were not inclined to investigate further, despite the attempts of alarmed parents to make them do so. This continued throughout the early 1970s, as the number of missing young men rose to 27. The mystery of their disappearances was solved on August 8, 1973, when police received a frantic phone call from Elmer Wayne Henley, saying that he had just killed Dean Corll. What followed was the discovery of the work of a serial killer who had systematically murdered at least 27 young boys in three years. Henley insisted that there were more bodies buried in the Houston area, but police were no longer interested in pursuing the case when they exceeded the victim count of the Californian serial killer Juan Corona, who was convicted of killing 25 migrant workers (Olsen, 1974).

And there is a new trend developing in the war-torn countries of the world: Children who prey on other children. Recently the BBC reported the arrest of a nine-year-old boy in Rwanda for the crime of serial murder. There are three known victims, all children (BBC Worldwide Monitoring, January 28, 2000). This may be only the beginning of a new tide of very young serial killers, created by the unstable politics and socioeconomic devastation of the Third World.

Amnesty International recently called for the end of torturing children. Children in war-torn and Third World countries are the most at risk: "Armed opposition groups also must be encouraged not to further their causes by abusing children. By allowing violence against children to continue, we put at risk our futures" (Amnesty International, 2000, p. 35). Politics, religion, and poverty are combining to create potentially deadly behaviors in many underprivileged populations. North America and Europe have been fortunate to date, but as violence and poverty spread, Western countries may find themselves under siege by people with nothing to lose by violence.

HOMELESS PERSONS

The homeless are also often targeted by serial killers as victims of low risk. Cases involving the homeless that have been solved have occurred in California and New York. The names Michael Player, Patrick Kearney, Joseph Danks, and Charles Sears are included in any list of serial killers who murdered the homeless and were apprehended. The sad fact remains, however, that many other cases involving the homeless are unsolved and unnoticed by the public.

One of the most recent happened in Denver, Colorado, where it was reported in October 1999 that five homeless men had been beaten to death by an unknown assailant. Even when the body count rose to five, authorities were still reluctant to admit that there was a serial killer at work in their midst. "We can't rule it out—a serial killer—but we don't have enough evidence to say that it is," said Detective Steve Shott. "It's obvious whoever's responsible for this is targeting the homeless." Even a former FBI agent was hesitant to say that there was a serial killer at work. Former FBI profiler Gregg McCrary agreed on the possibility of a serial killer—but cautioned against jumping to conclusions. "It's suspicious, just on the face of it," he said. But a researcher in the area of serial murder for many years was unambiguous in his assessment of the killings: "Clearly it seems that there is little chance otherwise," said James Alan Fox of Northeastern University, the author of three books on serial killers. "You have five people killed in a short period of time in a similar fashion in the same general area fitting the same general description. It's far too similar to be coincidence" ("Transient deaths linked? 5 slayings," 1999, p. B1).

To this date, the case remains unsolved.

PATIENTS

Patients in hospitals, clinics, and nursing homes are also likely to be targeted by serial killers. Their vulnerability and helplessness seem to bring out the "killer instincts" in medical personnel who use their patients to exorcise their personal demons. Patients of the so-called angel of death are frequently the elderly. Doctors, nurses, and even nursing assistants have all found victims close at hand.

A number of these cases have been reported in the past 25 years. One recent case was in Indiana. Orville Lynn Majors was linked to at least 130 deaths in the Vermillion County hospital in which he worked, although he was tried and convicted on only 6 of those deaths. He was sentenced to 360 years. His reign of terror lasted from 1993 until a nursing supervisor finally realized what he was doing in 1995. The deaths of his patients were not easy deaths.

> Prosecutors said Majors gave his victims fatal overdoses and that some of the injections were witnessed by their loved ones. Investigators said he

used the potentially heart-stopping drug potassium chloride, vials of which were found in his home and car. During the trial a former room-mate, Andy Harris, testified that Majors told him he hated old people and said "they should all be gassed." (*BBC World News*, 1999)

Patients become members of the "less-dead" because of their power-lessness and the absolute and unquestioning trust people place in medical personnel. The serial murderer who is also a physician is even more difficult to detect than nurses. The medical community is a closed society and protects its own.

The year 2000 saw the end of a career of murder by a physician who had been killing in the United States and in Zimbabwe, when Michael Swango was finally arrested in New York, on his way to Saudi Arabia to practice medicine. Swango was sentenced to life imprisonment on October 18, 2000, for the deaths of four persons. Authorities believe that the victim count is much higher.

Swango has pleaded guilty to killing four people: McGee at Ohio State University Hospital and three men who were patients at a Veterans Affairs hospital in Northport, N.Y., where Swango was a resident in 1993. But Swango long had been suspected in a number of deaths involving patients at hospitals since he was dismissed from a residency program in neurology at Ohio State University Hospital—now OSU Medical Center—in early 1984. After leaving Columbus, Swango was imprisoned in 1985 in Illinois for the nonfatal poisonings of several paramedics. Upon his release in 1987, he worked at hospitals and clinics in Virginia, South Dakota and New York and abroad in Zimbabwe, often using false names and histories and leaving suspicious deaths in his wake. Local authorities had investigated the death of McGee, as well as four other suspicious deaths that had occurred at OSU Hospital in the mid-1980s. But they said there was never enough evidence to charge Swango. "If they really knew how many he has killed, I think he'd be recognized as one of the biggest mass murderers of all time." In fact, according to author James B. Stewart, who wrote a recent investigative history of Swango called *Blind Eye*, the "evidence suggests" that Swango killed at least 35 people. ("Swango admits," 2000, p. 1A)

The FBI says McGee may be one of some 60 victims of Swango's, which would make him the most prolific serial killer of the past century. But in court in New York, where Swango was sentenced to life without parole, he showed no remorse or emotion. "It was like all this suffering meant nothing to him," says Stewart. "I've never encountered a human being like that." ("Rx: Life behind bars," 2000, p. 74)

The Killing Fields:
Where Are the Victims Found?

Serial killers are found in the peaceful neighborhoods of the affluent; in the popular bars of cities; at bus stops; public parks, and shopping malls; and simply roaming the interstate highways of the nation. Serial killers hunt in all these places and more. They are in our colleges, hospitals, and workplaces. They live among us and kill, all while continuing to be the husbands, fathers, and friends we trust. None of us is guaranteed of safety, just as none of us can truly know the mind of another. Their hunting grounds are everywhere.

The hunting grounds vary a great deal among serial killers, but many select their victims from the same general areas, where they feel comfortable, have control over those frequenting the area, or know that the area is infrequently patrolled by local police. They hunt in areas where they will not be noticed or appear different from others. They seek anonymity.

Hickey (1997) developed a mobility classification of three types of serial killers. The first is the place-specific killer, who murders within his or her own home, place of employment, or other sites. An example of this type is Jeffrey Dahmer, who killed 16 of his 17 victims in Milwaukee. Fourteen of these victims were killed in his apartment. A second type is the localized serial killer, who seeks his victims within a state or urbanized area. An example of a local serial killer is Robert Yates Jr., who recently admitted to killing 16 people in the Spokane, Washington, area. All of his victims were abducted from a red light area of the city. The third type is the traveling serial killer who kills while traveling through or relocating to other areas of the country. An example is Andrew Cunanan, who began his killing spree in May 1997, and committed murders from Minnesota to Florida.

Using his mobility classification, Hickey found that 20–23% of victims were killed in specific places, 36–43% of victims were killed by local killers, and 36–42% of victims were killed by traveling killers. Further, Hickey found that men and women who generally stayed close to home killed 59–63% of all victims in his database. However, the victims of these serial killers were more likely to be killed away from home. Hickey also found that place-specific serial killers were responsible for the smallest percentage of victims but had the highest number of victims per case.

Most victims from Hickey's (1997) database were women and children. This group could certainly be considered weak, helpless, and without power and control. Hickey found that "in general, serial killers have victimized female adults (65%) consistently more than male adults, but half of all offenders surveyed had killed at least one male adult" (p. 112). Hickey also noted an increase in the number of elderly victims per case. However, this could simply be the result of our aging population.

There appear to be a number of favored hunting grounds for the serial killer. The different areas in which serial killers search for their prey reflect the different types of victims sought out by the killer. The red light areas of the larger urban areas are probably the most favored hunting grounds for the serial killer, given the large number of prostitutes who are victimized each year. Here, the killer can blend in with all the other johns, and have relatively little fear of drawing attention. Another urban area where these killers hunt is where homosexuals cruise for sex. Many serial killers have lured and abducted their victims from business establishments that provide short-term services to people in transit, such as convenience stores or service stations near interstate highways. These locations appear to provide very attractive hunting grounds to the serial killer, given the almost guaranteed anonymity of the stranger-to-stranger interaction that occurs there and the likelihood that witnesses remember little of their brief time there. One unique and attractive characteristic of these points of prey, from the killer's perspective, is that stranger-to-stranger interaction is the norm and to be expected. No one takes any notice.

The Quick Dismissal of the Investigative Value of Victim Information

U.S. criminal law defines a criminal offense as an offense against the state and specifies that it is the state, rather than the victim, who prosecutes the charged offender. The criminal justice system focuses on the crime and the criminal offender. Little formal attention is paid to the victim, other than as a source of evidence to strengthen the state's efforts in prosecuting the offender. The needs, comfort, and convenience of victims (in the case of serial murder, the surviving relatives and loved ones of the victims) become insignificant in a system that emphasizes crime control and prosecution.

Criminologists have only recently turned their attention to crime victims. Much of this research has focused on lifestyle and victimization, victim characteristics, and victim precipitation (the ways victims contribute to their own victimization). Seldom has criminology studied victims' or survivors' responses or ways to provide assistance to them.

Ironically, the criminal investigation literature depicts a similar disinterest in the victims or survivors. Once the physical evidence and other information gathered begin to point toward a suspect or a type of suspect, the victims or survivors quickly become only names on a police report for entry into a master name index file, to be retrieved at a later date only if they are considered valuable in the prosecution of the defendant.

In the investigation of a number of homicides believed to have been committed by the same individual, victim information may be the most important information collected by criminal investigators. For in many serial murder investigations, physical evidence from the crime scene is scarce or nonexistent. In most of these homicides (as noted earlier), the victim and killer previously had not been acquainted. In other words, the victims may be the only major source of information on which the investigation can proceed.

As sociologist David Ford has indicated, in the investigation of gay murders committed in the Indianapolis, Indiana, area in the early 1980s, the Central Indiana Multiagency Investigative Team initially discounted the value of a victimological approach to the investigation (Egger, 1990). Ford argues that this early exclusion of a valuable investigative strategy was a major problem for the team's effectiveness.

Early attention by investigators to the targeted victims is essential in serial murder investigations, which typically reveal a very elusive killer. Sufficient analysis of targeted victims and their networks will inevitably yield greater insight into the victim's role in the crime setting, and permit inferences regarding the killer's decision-making process in selection of intended victims.

Ford argues that an applied victimological approach consists of five general tasks to assemble social characteristics of victims and circumstances of the crimes.

1. Identify the category or type of victim.
2. Delineate the victim's social networks.
3. Determine the personal factors contributing to risk.
4. Describe the situational factors affecting risk.
5. Identify routine victim activities and expected behaviors related to contact with predators (Egger, 1990, p. 116, adapted).

Ford, a sociologist and the only non-sworn member of the Indiana investigative team, argues for the importance of analyzing the ecology of possible contact settings (between killer and potential victims) to help narrow the focus of the investigation to promising areas for locating witnesses, including surviving victims.

Much of the research on serial murder has concentrated on finding similarities among these murders. With few exceptions, the victims of serial killers have been ignored. However, one of the greatest similarities among serial killers is their consistent choice of victims. As discussed earlier, many of the victims of serial murderers are vagrants, the homeless, prostitutes, migrant workers, homosexuals, missing children, single women out by themselves, elderly women, college students, or hospital patients. In other words, the serial killer preys on people who tend to be vulnerable or those who are easy to lure and dominate.

Part of these victims' vulnerabilities may be that they frequent certain locations, or that they are powerless, or that they are considered the throwaways of our society. Many are not missed or reported missing. A good example of this, noted earlier, is the arrest of Joel Rifkin in New York on June 28, 1993. After a lengthy interrogation, Rifkin confessed to killing 17 prostitutes during the previous three years. After his confession, the police investigation concentrated on finding and identifying Rifkin's victims. This was indeed difficult, since it was found that few of these victims had been reported missing. In instances where victims had been found, they were yet to be identified when Rifkin was arrested. No one had missed these women until Rifkin stumbled into the hands of a New York state trooper.

Little else is known regarding the victims of serial murderers other than that they are almost always a stranger to the murderer. In a preponderance of cases, the victims are young females, presumably chosen to satisfy the dominance craving of the mostly male serial murderers. The victims are sometimes young males, as in the serial murder cases of John Wayne Gacy, Dean Corll, and Jeffrey Dahmer. It has been estimated that 50% of unidentified bodies in county morgues or medical examiners' offices across the country are young children or adolescents (Wingo, personal communication, July 1983). Unfortunately, we don't know how many of these bodies represent victims of serial murder.

In a number of cases it appears that the victims were selected solely because they crossed the path of the serial murderer and became a vehicle for his hypo-arousal and pleasure (S. Egger, 1984). Victims may be self-selecting only in that they existed at a certain place and point in time. This and possibly the physical appearance of the victim, which may hold some symbolic significance for the killer, are the only known precipitating factors for their selection. Lack of prestige, powerlessness, and membership in a lower socioeconomic or minority group are common characteristics of serial murder victims. Levin and Fox (1985) seem to agree that "serial killers almost without exception choose vulnerable victims—those who are easy to dominate" (p. 75). "The serial killer typically picks on innocent strangers who may possess a certain physical feature or may just be accessible" (p. 231).

Predatory stranger offenses may be particularly dependent on the availability of vulnerable victims at a particular geographic location. Also, victim precipitation, the extent to which the victim's actions contribute to his or her demise, is considered a major cause or certainly a contributing factor of homicide by many criminologists. However, the extent to which victim precipitation occurs in serial murder can only be speculated on since little information is usually available regarding the interaction between the killer and the victim prior to the point of fatal encounter.

There are a number of high-risk lifestyles that make a person prone to becoming a victim: homosexuals cruising downtown areas and bathrooms; cult members soliciting funds on sidewalks and in bus stations; and released mental patients and skid row alcoholics wandering the streets at odd hours (Karmen, 1983). In some instances, it may simply be that an individual is alone. Females out by themselves are particularly vulnerable, given the high proportion of female serial murder victims. Prostitutes are almost certainly at risk. But for most women, there appears to be strength in numbers in reducing the risk of a serial murderer attack.

In many cases, serial murderers may be attacking mirror images of themselves. If sexual child abuse and neglect are contributing factors in the production of a serial killer, the killer may be choosing victims like his earlier self or from the same general lifestyle. Many victim–offender studies indicate that both parties are usually from the same group or background (Maghan & Sagarin, 1983).

Some blame the mobility of American society for making victims more available to serial murderers. We are indeed a transient culture. Robert Keppel, chief investigator, Attorney General's Office in Washington state, contends that since many serial murderers are charismatic, they can convince their victims to go with them for some reason: "They pick people they can have power and control over, small-framed women, children and old people" (Lindsey, 1984, p. 7).

Many psychiatrists and psychologists believe that the victims of serial murderers are symbolic of something or someone deeply significant in the murderers' lives. Some psychologists have said that the victims represent cruel parents against whom some murderers feel they cannot directly take revenge. The alternative for the serial murderer is to indirectly take revenge, by killing others who resemble or represent this parent.

Typically the serial killer doesn't think much about his victims, has little empathy for loved ones of the victims, and exhibits no remorse. When asked about his victims, Ted Bundy responded, "What's one less person on the face of the earth anyway?" Australian serial killer James Miller, charged with the murder of seven young girls and women, stated while testifying, "They weren't worth much. One of them even enjoyed it" (Wilson, 1983, p. 81).

A number of researchers have found that children and young women are the prime targets for serial killers. These groups are certainly considered victim prone, primarily as a result of their vulnerability. Hickey (1997) found 93 serial killers, 24% of those he studied, who had killed at least one child, and as indicated earlier, young females comprise a majority of serial murderers' victims.

Conclusion and Future Implications

Law enforcement agencies and their homicide investigators must begin to realize that by allowing victims of serial killers to remain "less-dead," they are in effect placing a lower value on victims' differences. The more "less-dead" a victim is, the less emphasis will be placed on identifying and apprehending the killer. After a short time the police will simply move on to other cases, unless they receive pressure for resolution from politicians or the news media. Without an outcry from the survivors (in many cases involving the "less-dead," there are no survivors), little pressure is placed on law enforcement agencies to solve these cases. The cases rapidly become cold and personnel move on to other homicide investigations. This is an indictment not of law enforcement but of how we as a society view certain segments of our society. Law enforcement is a part of that society and provides a service to it. The intentional killing of a human being, whether she or he is identified as belonging to a specific group in that society, is still a death that must be addressed.

One tool of law enforcement that must be enhanced is the psychological profile, which is an attempt to provide investigators with more information about an unidentified serial killer. The purpose of this tool, sometimes referred to as investigative profiling, is to develop a behavioral composite, combining sociological and psychological assessments of the offender. Profiling is generally based on the premise that accurate analysis and interpretation of the crime scene and other locations related to the crime can indicate the type of behavioral patterns; knowledge and an understanding of the patterns can lead investigators to potential suspects. The problem with profiling is that it frequently overlooks or places little emphasis on the victims. The focus is on the offender, and the victim seems to be lost in the analysis.

One remedy for enhancing the psychological profile is to conduct a psychological autopsy on serial murder victims. Psychological autopsies are used to determine the reasons and rationale of individuals who commit suicide. We suggest that the technique in determining why a person commits suicide be adapted to an analysis of the victims of a serial killer. This would require an investigative analysis of the last hours or days of the victim prior to his or her point of fatal encounter with the serial killer. Such an analysis might tell criminal investigators why the serial killer selected the victim, or whether the serial killer had stalked the victim because of the victim's lifestyle or actions.

Another area that needs to be immediately addressed is educating the public about the value of *all* the members of our society, including the "less-dead." No chain is stronger than its weakest link, and no society is stronger than its most disadvantaged members. The "less-dead" are devalued for a number of reasons, including their lack of education, economic resources, and social resources necessary to live in a manner acceptable to most citizens. Are we going to continue to justify their deaths out of our own fear and loathing for these, our fellow human beings? Is it because of these deficiencies that we continue to rationalize and ignore these cases and have low expectations of law enforcement to solve them? We need to honestly look at the role that prejudices play in the public's and law enforcement's response to serial killers. We, as a society, need to stop sending subtle signals to serial killers that as long as they choose victims in the category of the "less-dead," their murders are somehow more acceptable and we will continue to accept their victims' deaths with little note. Does the public perception of these victims and their lifestyles account for the treatment that their deaths receive in the popular media? Are we going to ignore the horrible waste of human life and potential while allowing the serial killers to continue to become the "heroes" of tomorrow?

Victims of serial killers are for the most part ignored by investigators and society. This appears to be the case whether the victim falls in the category of the "less-dead," or could be classified as "more-dead," on the basis of her or his higher socioeconomic standing in the community. We must remember that when victims are ignored, the survivors are also ignored.

Robert Yates's wife, Linda, sent a Spokane newspaper a public letter, asking for forgiveness and understanding, when her husband was arrested. ("Yates' wife," 2000). In Augusta, Georgia, the wife of another man charged with serial murder publicly apologized and begged the families of her husband's victims for forgiveness and understanding for herself and her children ("Wife's letter," 2000). The parents, siblings, spouses, and children of serial killers are also victims. Their initial disbelief and final horrified acceptance of his or her crimes are in some ways more devastating than the trauma of the victim's families. The person they thought they knew is still alive, breathing, and imprisoned, with the answers to all their questions locked away, inside his or her mind. The man or woman they loved, shared a life with, looked to as a parent, has suddenly become a stranger, a monster in the eyes of the world, and they are left to attempt to reconcile the two. And the children are once again victimized. They are left with all the questions and doubts, without the maturity and understanding of their adult counterparts. Without the assistance, love, and support of their families, friends, and society, they are alone, filled with questions, and left to grow up to exorcise their own demons; they are also the victims of their loved one who is a serial killer.

In the future we need to change the way we treat these families. The relatives and loved ones of the victims must also be considered victims and treated accordingly. As can be seen in numerous media accounts of serial murder cases, the survivors are almost never mentioned and quickly forgotten by society and the criminal justice system. The survivors of a serial killer's acts should be afforded the same consideration that his or her victims deserve but too often do not get. This means that survivors should be offered grief counseling and victim compensation, and be made aware of their rights as victims.

Endnote

[1]At the time of this writing (December 2001), an arrest has been made in several of the Green River killings. Guillen and Smith continue to follow and comment on the case for the *Seattle Times*.

References

Amnesty International report calls for end to torture of children. (2000, December 9). *Houston Chronicle*, p. A35.

BBC World News. (1999, November 15). *http://news.bbc.co.uk/hi/english/world/americas/newsid 52100/521904.stm.*

Berger, J. (1984, September 8). Mass killers baffle authorities. *New York Times*, p. 1.

Caputi, J. (1987). *The Age of Sex Crime.* Bowling Green, OH: Bowling Green State University Popular Press.

Dietz, M. L. (1983). *Killing for Profit.* Chicago: Nelson Hull.

Easy prey for a violent criminal: Prostitutes view murder as just one more occupational hazard. (1993, July 5). *New York Times*, Section 1, p. 23.

Egger, K. (1996). *The sociological implications of serial killers and their victims.* Unpublished paper.

————. (1999). Preliminary database on serial killers from 1900 to 1999. Unpublished manuscript.

Egger, S. (1984). A working definition of serial murder and the reduction of linkage blindness. *Journal of Police Science and Administration,* 12(3): 348–357.

————. (1990). *Serial Murder: An Elusive Phenomenon.* New York: Praeger.

————. (1992). *Serial Killing the Lambs of Our Dreams.* Essay presented at the annual meeting of the Academy of Criminal Justice Sciences, Pittsburgh, PA.

————. (1998). *The Killers Among Us: An Examination of Serial Murder and Its Investigation* (1st ed.). Upper Saddle River, NJ: Prentice Hall.

Gest, T. (1984, April 30). On the trail of America's "serial killers." *U.S. News & World Report,* p. 53.

Hickey, E. (1997). *Serial Murderers and Their Victims* (2nd ed.). Belmont, CA: Wadsworth.

————. (1999, August 10). Southside slayings defy myths about serial killers. *Chicago Tribune,* p. 1.

Karmen, A. (1983). Deviants as victims. In D. E. MacNamara, and A. Karmen (Eds.), *Deviants: Victims or Victimizers?* (pp. 237–254). Thousand Oaks, CA: Sage.

Levin, J., Fox, J. (1985). *Mass Murder.* New York: Plenum Press.

Lindsey, R. (1984, January 21). Officials cite a rise in killers who roam U.S. for victims. *New York Times,* pp. 1, 7.

Lunde, D. T. (1976). *Murder and Madness.* Stanford, CA: Stanford Alumni Association.

Lundsgaarde, H. P. (1977). *Murder in Space City.* New York: Oxford University Press.

Maghan, J., Sagarin, E. (1983). Homosexuals as victimizers and victims. In D. E. McNamara and A. Karmen (Eds.), *Deviants: Victims or Victimizers?* (pp. 147–162). Thousand Oaks, CA: Sage.

McCarthy, K. (1984, June 28). Serial killers: Their deadly bent may be set in the cradle. *Los Angeles Times,* p. 1.

Murder by Number (videotape). (1993). R. Griffiths, prod. and dir. Atlanta, GA: CNN.

Newton, M. (1992). *Serial Slaughter.* Port Townsend, WA: Loompanics.

Olsen, J. (1974). *The Man with the Candy.* New York: Simon & Schuster.

Pedro Lopez freed. (1998, December 6). *Scotland on Sunday,* p. 19.

Puzzling case may be solved. (2000, October 18). *Seattle Times*. Available at http://archives.seattletimes.nwsource.com

Rx: Life behind bars; Dr. Michael Swango avoids the death sentence he chose for his patients. (2000, October 9). *People*, p. 74.

Serial killer scandal: Ten black women died on the streets of Chicago but police saw no link until the alleged killer's sister turned him in. (1995, June 27). *The Guardian (London)*, p. 13.

Swango admits to slaying. (2000, October 19). *Columbus [Ohio] Dispatch*, p. 1A.

Transient deaths linked? 5 slayings. (1999, October 27). *The Denver Post*, p. B1.

Wife's letter expresses sorrow. (2000, October 19). *Augusta [Georgia] Chronicle*. Available at http://augustaarchives.com.

Wilson, C. (1983). *The Encyclopedia of Mass Murder, 1962–1982*. New York: Putnam.

Yates whet his taste for murder with pair of college students. (2000, October 18). *Seattle Times*. Available at http://archives.seattletimes.nwsource.com.

Yates' wife thanks people for support. (2000, June 14). *Spokane Spokesman-Review.com*.

CHAPTER 2

Perceived Risks of Date Rape

Michael Shively

Introduction

Before the 1970s, sexual aggression was considered a rare crime committed by a relatively small number of pathological men. Studies of convicted rapists fueled speculation that rape was primarily the act of a person suffering from various personality disorders or other psychological problems (e.g., Ellis and Brancale, 1956; Gebhard et al., 1965).

Research since then has established that rape and other sex offenses are more common than previously thought. Estimates vary a great deal, depending on how and from whom the information is gathered, but the weight of the evidence strongly suggests that 10–25% of women in the United States will be the victim of a completed or attempted rape during their lifetime (e.g., Brener et al., 1999; Spitzberg, 1999; Tjaden and Thoennes, 1998). In addition, the typical rapist is a relatively normal man with little or no criminal record and no evidence of serious psychological problems to indicate that he is at risk of committing sex crimes (e.g., Alder, 1985; Kroner and Mills, 1998; Oliver et al., 1993; Spaccarelli et al., 1997). Furthermore, many studies show that rather than being the stereotypical deranged stranger leaping from the bushes to attack his female prey, the rapist more often than not is known to his victims (Koss, 1988; Silverman et al., 1988; Sorenson et al., 1987). Often, he is someone the woman knows intimately, such as a current or former boyfriend (e.g., Johnson and Sigler, 2000; Tyler et al., 1998).

Given that most rape occurs between men and women who know one another, often in the context of dating situations (e.g., Koss, 1988), it is crucial to understand the dynamics of such situations if effective intervention and prevention strategies are to be developed. In this chapter, I examine one important aspect of such scenarios: how different kinds of dating situations affect women's perceptions of the risk of rape. If women do not perceive as threatening certain situations in which they are at greater risk, it is unlikely that they will be able to take action to avoid an attempted sexual assault. A recent study examining this issue is described in this chapter, and potential uses of the information gained through this research are discussed. First, it is helpful to have an understanding of the definitions of some of the terminology used and to describe the context of the study.

DEFINITIONS OF SEXUAL AGGRESSION, DATE RAPE, AND ACQUAINTANCE RAPE

For a behavior to be legally defined as rape or another form of sexual assault, it must involve sexual contact, and this contact must occur without the consent of one of the people involved. *Sexual aggression* is a more general term, referring to a variety of crimes that are considered sexual in nature. For example, a man who exposes himself in public is usually guilty of "lewd conduct" or "indecent assault" according to state criminal laws. This offense involves no physical contact but does entail an interaction that is unwelcome to the victim and has a sexual component. Thus, it is regarded as sexual aggression. Other types of behaviors considered sexual aggression include indecent assault and battery (which can include fondling or sexually touching someone against his or her wishes), various kinds of sexual contact between adults and children, and rape.

The term *rape* refers to a particular kind of sexual aggression. Most state rape laws consider rape to be penetration of any part of a person's body by any part of another person's body or by an object. Clearly, conventional sexual intercourse meets the sexual contact requirement, as does oral or anal penetration of a person's body by any other body part or object. Other types of contact, such as touching someone's breast, can be considered sexual contact, but are classified as less serious kinds of sex offenses (such as "indecent assault and battery" or "third-degree sexual assault") and not as rape.

The second part of the definition is concerned with consent. Ultimately, determinations of consent require one to make a judgment about the potential victim's state of mind. Some victims do not offer overt resistance, such as screaming, physically fighting, or pleading with the offender in an attempt to make him stop, but this does not necessarily mean that they are consenting. Some victims are so intimidated by their assailant, because of his size and strength or the presence of a weapon, for example, that they believe it useless to fight. Victims may fear that their screaming or fighting would only serve to anger the offender, who might severely beat or kill them in addition to sexually assaulting them. In these cases, it is incorrect to say that the person was a consenting sexual partner, even if she or he were not overtly forced or threatened and did not physically resist or cry for help.

It is cases such as these that make it useful to distinguish between a legal and a clinical definition of rape. A clinical definition is concerned primarily with the state of the victim. Only victims truly know their state of mind at any given moment, and if they believe that sex occurred without their consent, that is enough to regard them as a victim of sexual aggression. Legal definitions have a different focus and different standards that must be met. The U.S. criminal justice system is constitutionally bound to presume the innocence of the accused, and the standard of evidence required to override this presumption ("beyond a reasonable doubt") is quite high. In rape cases, once sexual contact has been established (through physical evidence or testimony), the main concern is whether the behavior of the alleged victim would be interpreted by a reasonable person as communicating nonconsent (for an excellent discussion of this issue, see Estrich, 1987). In rape trials, consent is often the most difficult thing to determine. For a rape conviction, it must be demonstrated that the woman's behavior signaled nonconsent and that the man overcame her resistance through the use or threat of force. In some cases, of course, this is quite clear: Kicking, screaming, and yelling "no" and "stop" are unambiguous communications of resistance. In other instances, however, a legal determination of nonconsent is difficult to meet. For example, a woman may initially say "no" or "wait" in response to a man's sexual advances, but may at some point stop overtly resisting because of fear, fatigue, or the belief that resistance is ineffective. While a woman in these circumstances would be a victim of sexual assault, in criminal trials her discontinuation of resistance would be portrayed by the defense as behavior that a reasonable person (their client, the accused) would interpret as consent. If it cannot be proven beyond a reasonable doubt that her ceasing to resist was due to the alleged offender's use or threat of force (or due to some form of incapacitation of the woman, such as extreme intoxication), it is unlikely that the accused would be convicted of rape or sexual assault.

Other factors can be taken into account in defining sexual aggression. For example, a person with a psychological disability such as a profound cognitive impairment or developmental disorder may not be considered competent to make the determination of consent, and a person who has sex with such an individual would be guilty of rape. Similarly, a physical disability can render a person incapable of consenting or communicating consent, and someone who has sex with such an individual would be guilty of rape. A recent case in Massachusetts serves as an example. A woman had been in a coma for several years, was completely unresponsive, and was in the care of a nursing home. At one point, a physical examination revealed that she was six months pregnant. It is clear that her physical and mental condition made it impossible for her to be a consenting partner in any sexual activity. The man found to have impregnated her had sexual intercourse with a person unable to provide consent, and was therefore charged with rape.

The same logic applies to people who are profoundly intoxicated with drugs or alcohol: Although they may normally be competent, their extreme intoxication can render them temporarily unable to provide consent or to offer resistance indicating nonconsent. A fairly common form of rape occurs when someone at a party drinks to the point of passing out, and an offender takes advantage of the person's condition by having sex with him or her.

In some cases it is easy to determine that a crime is a case of sexual assault. For example, a woman may be sleeping in her bedroom when a burglar, holding a knife to her throat and threatening to kill her if she fights or screams, holds her down and physically forces her to have sexual intercourse. This event clearly involves sexual contact, and, just as clearly, the contact occurred as the result of the use and threat of force and was not an act of consensual sex. Many other events are not so easy to categorize. For example, a couple may be on a date and may engage in some level of sexual foreplay. At some point the man may try to engage the woman in oral sex, and she may initially say no and resist his advances. He may persist in his attempts, verbally pressuring her but not using force or overtly threatening her in any way. Eventually, she performs oral sex on him. Is this sexual aggression? Most states' criminal justice systems would probably determine that it is not. Although she was initially reluctant, none of the evidence presented conclusively shows that at the moment sexual contact occurred, she was resisting and the man overcame this resistance through the use or threat of force. What she does to communicate nonconsent and what he does in response are the important factors in legal cases. To determine whether the case meets a clinical definition, one would have to determine the woman's state of mind at the time of the act. If she had stopped resisting and was engaging in the sexual act out of fear, the event would meet a clinical definition of sexual assault. If she had stopped resisting because she truly wanted to engage in sex, this would be an instance of consensual sex.

Another definition is important for understanding the issues discussed in the rest of this chapter. The term *date rape* refers to rape that occurs in the context of dating situations. It is sometimes used to describe a rape that occurs between people who are currently (or have previously been) in a dating relationship, even if the rape did not occur on a date. This term has evolved to distinguish such incidents from those occurring in other contexts, such as rape during a burglary. However, most state rape laws make no distinction between date rape and other types of rape. There is good reason for this: The relationship between people has little direct relevance for determining whether a rape has occurred. If both sexual contact and the lack of consent can be demonstrated, it matters not whether the two people are strangers, on a date, or married. The term *acquaintance rape* is sometimes used to distinguish incidents that occur between people who know one another from those that occur between strangers.

Finally, it is worth noting that nearly all clinical and legal definitions of sex crimes are, appropriately, gender neutral. That is, they do not assume that only males can be offenders or that only females can be victims. Research shows that both victims and offenders can be of either gender (e.g., Greenfield and Snell, 1999; Mezey and King, 1992; Waldner-Haugrud and Magruder, 1995). However, the research described in this paper examined date rape with men as offenders and women as victims. There were several reasons for restricting the study to this combination. The main reason was that the vast majority of rapes (and date rapes in particular) are committed against women by men. Another was that college students were studied (the majority of whom identify themselves as heterosexual), and in trying to assess how people might react to real situations by presenting them with hypothetical situations, it is critical that the situations presented are relevant to the people surveyed. For example, asking heterosexual students to assess the risk of date rape in a homosexual dating situation would be problematic.

THE IMPACT OF RAPE ON VICTIMS

The novelist John Irving once described rape as the most serious crime that the victim survives. The scientific evidence supports this characterization. There are very serious negative consequences for rape victims. When overt force is used, victims are usually left with cuts and bruises, and sometimes broken bones and other severe traumas. This can be true of any assault victim, but sexual assaults carry other, unique physical consequences. For example, female victims of forced intercourse may become pregnant, and victims of most kinds of rape are at risk of contracting sexually transmitted diseases.

In addition to the physical toll, there are serious emotional, psychological, and social consequences that, when compared to the effects on victims of other violent crimes, are often unusually severe. Among the symptoms documented in rape victims are depression, sleep disorders, anxiety attacks, generalized fear, and withdrawal from social interaction (e.g., Ferraro, 1996; Kilpatrick et al., 1985). Effective indicators of personal distress are seriously considering and attempting to commit suicide. Rape victims have been found to attempt and seriously consider suicide at more than three times the rate of victims of other types of violent crime, such as aggravated assault and robbery (Kilpatrick et al., 1985; see also Vannatta, 1996).

While many people regard date or acquaintance rape as slightly less serious than other kinds of rape, there is overwhelming evidence that its impact on victims is at least as severe as that of rape committed by a stranger (e.g., Stermac et al., 1998). For example, the degree of post-rape depression, fear, and problems with social adjustment is no less for acquaintance rape than for stranger rape (e.g., Kilpatrick et al., 1985; Koss et al., 1988). Researchers have even found some symptoms to be *more* severe in victims of acquaintance rape. For example,

Katz (1991) found that victims of acquaintance rape have longer recovery time, view themselves more negatively, and place more blame on themselves for their incident.

Even sexual harassment, which typically occurs between acquaintances and which many people (and most laws) regard as a less serious offense than rape or other kinds of physical sexual assaults, has serious consequences. Many studies of sexual harassment victims find high levels of anxiety, depression, and post-traumatic stress disorder (PTSD) (e.g., Murdoch and Nichol, 1995; Petrocelli and Repa, 1992). Others have found increased alcohol and drug abuse (e.g., Richman et al., 1992) and a higher lifetime risk of suicide attempts (Davidson et al., 1996). A study of female Army personnel found that sexual harassment and assault resulted in more severe PTSD than did combat exposure in the Persian Gulf War (Wolfe et al., 1998).

RISK FACTORS

Clearly, rape is a crime that occurs frequently and has severely negative consequences for victims. Accordingly, there has been a great deal of work by victim advocates, educators, public health and criminal justice professionals, and others directed toward rape prevention. In an attempt to gather information that may help in the development of effective prevention strategies, researchers over the past 20 years have learned a great deal about risk factors associated with sexual aggression. One of the more robust findings is that alcohol increases risk. For example, Koss (1988) found that 74% of perpetrators and 55% of victims had consumed alcohol prior to sexual assault and these results are supported elsewhere (e.g., Abbey et al., 1996; Schwartz and Pitts, 1995). Victimization surveys also find that different kinds of force or coercion used by perpetrators pose different degrees of risk (e.g., Koss, 1988; Muehlenhard and Linton, 1987; Tyler et al., 1998; Waldner-Haugrud and Magruder, 1995), with more forceful methods resulting in a greater chance that the attempted sexual assault will be completed. The kinds of resistance offered by potential victims (e.g., Koss, 1988; Quinsey and Upfold, 1985; Ullman and Knight, 1992, 1995) also affect risk, with vigorous and forceful forms of resistance (such as biting and screaming) being more successful in thwarting an attack than passive kinds of resistance, such as crying and begging for the man to stop. Similarly, location (e.g., Koss, 1988; Ullman et al., 1999) and the prior relationship between the parties involved (e.g., Abbey et al., 1996; Coker et al., 1998) have been identified as risk factors.

PERCEIVED RISK

Less well documented is how women *perceive* the risk of sexual aggression in dating scenarios. This information may be very valuable in rape prevention efforts. For example, if we know that the consumption of alcohol on dates places women at greater risk, but we discover that women do not perceive it as doing so, it would tell us that women are missing an important risk cue. If so, it would be beneficial to stress the risks associated with alcohol in educational programs designed to help women lower their risk of rape victimization.

A few studies have attempted to find out how women respond to risk factors in dating scenarios. For example, Norris et al. (1996) conducted focus groups and a survey to examine how women view the risk of date rape. They concluded that women significantly underestimate the threat, particularly in high-risk situations such as parties involving alcohol. However, women did indicate that alcohol may reduce their ability to resist sexual advances, by both interfering with their ability to read risk cues and reducing their physical ability to resist. In addition, alcohol consumption was found to impose a psychological barrier to resistance: The women studied indicated that their drinking may be perceived by their male dates as a signal of sexual availability and that it would diminish their right to resist sexual advances.

Cook (1995) asked women whether they believed that sexual aggression would occur in any dating situation, and then whether it would be expected in dates involving a list of separate conditions (such as the woman's being stoned or drunk and the couple's having dated for a long time). About 10% of those surveyed expected rape or attempted rape to occur in unspecified dating situations, but the percentage rose to as high as 38% under certain conditions. Rape was expected most often when the couple had dated for a long time and when the woman was described as "leading the man on."

Cue et al. (1996) presented women with vignettes describing dating scenarios and changed the content of some of the vignettes to determine the impact of different situations on the perceived likelihood of sexual aggression. Two variables were examined: the type of man on the date (defined as either high or low in "rape congruence," or how well he fit the profile of a man likely to rape) and whether alcohol was consumed on the date (either coffee or beer was described as being consumed). They concluded that the likelihood of the man's sexually assaulting his date was rated higher for rape-congruent men, but was not affected by the consumption of alcohol. The latter finding conflicts with the results of the study by Norris et al. (1996).

One of the most thorough attempts to assess women's recognition of threat in dating scenarios was recently conducted by Norris et al. (1999). Participants were presented with vignettes varying several situational factors and were asked to rate how they would feel in the situations described. They concluded that the elements that were varied across the different scenarios, including their drinking alcohol and the physical isolation of the physical setting, were not strongly related to perceptions of risk. This suggests that women may sometimes fail to recognize that certain situations place them at greater risk than others. That is, if women were accurately perceiving risk cues, their ratings of the relative risk involved in situations should have been strongly related to the variations in the situations, especially since the researchers varied differences in the use of alcohol and the physical isolation of the location.

Although Norris et al. (1999) is one of the best assessments of how women perceive situational risk and addresses several other important issues, the way the analyses and results are presented does not allow one to assess the relative contribution of each situational element to women's perceptions of threat. For example, nine different vignette elements were varied, but their independent contributions to perceived risk were not presented. Instead, the variables were grouped into two risk categories: "clear" and "ambiguous" risk. In addition, the dependent measures examined feelings of threat but did not assess women's perceptions of the likelihood that a sexual assault would be attempted or completed.

These ongoing studies and others (see Breitenbacher, 1999; Cue et al., 1996) have made great contributions to our understanding of how women assess risk in certain situations. The research methods used have some important limitations, however. The main drawback to the studies is that only a few of the features of the scenarios could be examined for their effect on risk judgments. Again, this does not render their results meaningless, and sometimes it is appropriate to look at a few variables at a time in building an understanding of certain kinds of situations. However, real-life dating situations are complex, and vary in a multitude of ways, both subtle and obvious. Any number of differences from situation to situation could significantly affect women's perceptions of threat. Given this, it is important to study these kinds of situations with methods that capture more of this real-life complexity. The methods used in the study described in this chapter allow many different situational elements to be examined at the same time. The technical details of this approach, called the factorial survey method, have been described by Rossi and Anderson (1982), Jacoby and Cullen (1999), and Shively (2001), among others.

A Survey of Women's Perceptions of the Risk of Date Rape

In the present study, people were presented with brief vignettes describing dating situations in which the prior relationship between a man and woman is established, their date on a particular evening proceeds until they are alone, he attempts to have sexual intercourse with her, and she resists. The man then considers using one of several means of overcoming the woman's resistance in order to have intercourse with her. Respondents were asked to rate the likelihood that the man would continue his attempts to have sex and, if so, the likelihood that he would succeed.

SURVEY CONTENT

The vignettes contained 10 variables, each suggested by prior research to affect the risk of date rape. Three variables addressed the prior relationship between the man and woman: a qualitative description of the type of the relationship, the length of the relationship, and whether they had had sex with each other. Also described in the vignette were the consumption of alcohol by the man and woman, the location where he attempts to have sex with her, consensual foreplay, descriptions of the woman's verbal and physical resistance, and the means of coercion the man considers using to overcome the woman's resistance. Each respondent read a set of 15 different vignettes, each of which was followed by the two rating scales. The complete set of dimensions and levels comprising the vignettes can be seen in Table 2.1, and a sample vignette and its accompanying rating scales are presented in Box 2.1.

BOX 2.1
Sample Vignette and Rating Scale

She was his girlfriend for about six months. They had had sex together before. That night they went out to dinner, where he had a lot to drink and became very drunk, and she did not have any alcohol. After dinner, they went to a party at his house. After a while they went to a bedroom where they were alone, and they sat and talked. After doing this for some time he tried to have intercourse with her, and she said no. She also told him to stop, and physically fought to stop him. At this moment he considers holding her down and continuing.

(1) How likely is it that he would continue trying to have intercourse with her?

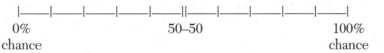

    0%   50–50   100%
  chance   chance

(2) If he did continue trying to have intercourse with her, how likely is it that he would succeed in having intercourse with her?

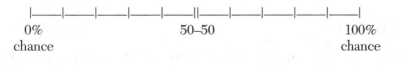

    0%   50–50   100%
  chance   chance

     Although the vignettes consisted mainly of the variables described, a piece of text appeared as a constant in all the scenarios and described the hypothetical woman as saying no in response to the man's initial sexual advance. This statement was included to ensure that all the vignettes contained the minimal pre-conditions for sexual aggression: an attempt at sex that is resisted.

Each respondent was asked to imagine that the man in the scenarios was more or less like the men they know at the university, and to imagine what such men would do in the situations described. The purpose of the instructions was to set some parameters for judging the situations and the behavior of the people in them. After reading each scenario, respondents were asked to indicate the likelihood that the male would continue his attempts at intercourse with the resisting woman and, if so, the likelihood of his succeeding, on a 0–100% chance scale.

Conventional survey items used to measure respondent characteristics were included in the questionnaire packets to develop more complete models for understanding threat judgments. Nine questions from Burt's (1980) Rape Myth Acceptance (RMA) scale were included to measure general attitudes toward sexual aggression on a positive to negative dimension. Other questions asked for information about respondents' sexual experience, past relationships with people of the opposite sex, experience with alcohol, and age. Since they were not found to substantially affect judgments, data on the individual traits are not discussed further in this chapter.

DATA COLLECTION

The following analyses are based on self-administered survey data collected from 330 women enrolled at the University of Massachusetts at Amherst. Given that dating and sexual encounters provide the context for sexual aggression between dating partners, the population from which the sample was drawn is particularly well suited for this research: Most college students are simultaneously unmarried and sexually active. Of course, generalizations from classroom samples are tenuous. Although efforts were made to ensure that the sample was representative of the student population, such as using classes meeting general education requirements taken by all students, the usual limitations of such samples remain. However, for a survey on sexual aggression, the practical benefits of classroom samples (such as high response and completion rates and control over the survey administration environment) balance well against their limitations.

METHOD OF ANALYSIS

As previously mentioned, the technical details of how the data gathered by the vignette survey are described elsewhere (see Applegate et al., 2000; Jacoby and Cullen, 1999), and only a brief overview is necessary here. In Table 2.2, the coefficients (the numbers listed under the headings "Likelihood of Continuing Attempts" and "Likelihood of Succeeding") listed next to each of the pieces of vignette information can be interpreted as expressing how a rating was affected by the presence of a particular level in the vignette. In factorial survey terminology, each vignette variable is called a "dimension" and each of the possible values of each dimension that may be included in the vignettes is called a "level." The effect of the independent variable on the rating is assessed in reference to the omitted level and is net of the effect of the other levels.

An example should help to explain the information in Table 2.2. As seen in this table, Dimension D contains information about the man's use of alcohol. Each of the vignettes included one of the four different descriptions of the man's drinking listed as levels within this dimension: He had "a lot to drink and became very drunk," "several drinks and became drunk," "a few drinks and had a mild buzz," or "did not have any alcohol." The numbers listed next to the top three levels of Dimension D indicate how the ratings changed when the particular level was included, compared to when the reference level (did not have any alcohol) was in the vignettes. For example, when the man in the vignettes was described as having a lot to drink and becoming very drunk, the rated likelihood of his continuing his attempts to have sex with the woman was over 4.5 points higher (on the 100-point rating scale) than when the vignettes described the man as not having any alcohol (the reference level).

Results

From the 330 women surveyed, ratings of 4,943 vignettes were obtained. Table 2.1 presents the descriptive statistics and distributions of the two risk ratings. Overall, women saw these scenarios as containing high risk: The average rating of the likelihood that rape would be attempted was 73%, and the average rated chance that rape would be completed was 62%.

To determine the effects of the vignette variables on judgments of risk, the two ratings were regressed on the 10 vignette dimensions. The results were verified using HLM, a computer program for multilevel statistical modeling (Bryk et al., 1996). The only individual-level variable of theoretical interest having significant effects on this rating task was rape myth acceptance (RMA), so these scores were incorporated in the model. The other individual-level variables explained little variance and were not considered further.

The prior relationship between the man and woman was described along three separate dimensions (type, length, and prior sex) and independently varied in the vignettes. Only the "prior sex" dimension affected perceived risk. Ratings of the likelihood of both attempted and completed rape increased by about three points on the 0–100% chance scales when the couple was described as having had prior sex, compared to scenarios when they were described as not having had sex before.

Men who consumed alcohol were considered more likely to continue their coercive attempts to have sex, but were not considered more likely to succeed.

TABLE 2.1 Distribution of Perceived Likelihood That the Male Would Continue and Succeed in Attempts to Have Intercourse with His Resisting Female Dating Partner in the Vignette*

Rating	Likelihood of Continuing Attempts	Likelihood of Succeeding
100	7.3 %	3.4 %
95	14.9	7.3
90	9.0	6.1
85	14.4	10.4
80	6.9	5.9
75	9.6	9.6
70	4.5	4.7
65	6.3	7.0
60	3.6	4.2
55	3.3	5.0
50	7.3	12.0
45	2.4	3.9
40	1.5	2.8
35	2.2	4.0
30	1.1	2.0
25	1.9	3.4
20	.8	1.7
15	1.0	3.0
10	.7	1.6
5	.9	1.4
0	.3	.8
Mean rating	73.1	62.4
Median rating	80.0	65.0
Standard deviation	22.5	25.0
Number of vignettes rated	4,940	4,943

* The percentages refer to the percent of the vignettes that received each rating. For example, respondents said there was a 100% chance that the man would continue his attempts to have intercourse in 7.3% of the vignettes.

When the hypothetical woman consumed alcohol, the rated likelihood that the man would continue the attempt increased only slightly, but the rated likelihood of his succeeding increased significantly. Surprisingly, location, sexual foreplay, and the woman's verbal resistance had no effect on risk judgments.

The two remaining vignette variables, the woman's physical resistance and how the man considers trying to overcome it, significantly affected ratings. The man's slapping or threatening to hurt the woman increased the perceived

TABLE 2.2 Impact of Vignette Variables and Rape Myth Acceptance Scale Score on the Perceived Risk of Sexual Aggression

Vignette Dimension and Level	Change in Women's Ratings	
	Likelihood of Continuing Attempts	Likelihood of Succeeding
Dimension A: Relationship Between Man and Woman		
She was his girlfriend.	.3060	.7067
She was a close friend of his.	−.4896	.7401
She was a friend of his.	.1956	−1.4382
Reference: She was an acquaintance of his.		
Dimension B: Length of Relationship		
Over one year.	−.4641	.6134
About one year.	.2071	.1615
About six months.	−1.0376	−.4600
About one month.	−.8159	−.1580
Reference: A couple of weeks.		
Dimension C: Prior Sex		
They had had sex together before.	**2.4860****	**3.4597****
Reference: They had never had sex together.		
Dimension D: Man's Use of Alcohol		
A lot to drink, became very drunk.	**4.5806****	.2627
Several drinks, became drunk.	**4.7158****	.0991
Few drinks, had a mild buzz.	**3.4409****	.4372
Reference: Did not have any alcohol.		
Dimension E: Woman's Use of Alcohol		
A lot to drink, became very drunk.	1.9371*	**8.0398****
Several drinks, became drunk.	2.0581*	**8.5182****
Few drinks, had a mild buzz.	.7290	**4.2820****
Reference: Did not have any alcohol.		
Dimension F: Location		
His apartment.	.4910	1.9295
Her apartment.	.4575	2.1205
His house.	.2849	2.2372
Her house.	.2445	1.0849
A party at his house.	−.1623	1.8979
A party at her house.	.4890	−.3956
Reference: A party at a friend's house.		

(continued)

TABLE 2.2 (continued)

Vignette Dimension and Level	Change in Women's Ratings	
	Likelihood of Continuing Attempts	Likelihood of Succeeding
Dimension G: Consensual Foreplay		
They kissed.	1.5417°	1.0486
They kissed while he touched her breasts.	1.1206	1.2683
Reference: They sat and talked.		
Dimension H: Her Verbal Resistance		
She told him to stop.	1.1757	1.9906°
She told him very firmly to stop.	–0.0688	–.2941
She threatened to yell for help.	–1.7126	–2.0952°
Reference: She asked him to stop.		
Dimension I: Her Physical Resistance		
She physically resisted his attempts.	**–3.4676°°°**	**–5.7394°°°**
She physically fought to stop him.	**–2.5741°°°**	**–4.0347°°°**
Reference: She did not physically resist him.		
Dimension J: His Threat or Force		
Telling her he will hurt her.	**6.6472°°°**	**9.1147°°°**
Holding her down and continuing.	1.2852	**6.1028°°°**
Slapping her and continuing.	**5.0460°°°**	**8.1391°°°**
Reference: Trying to persuade her to continue.		
RMA	**.1072°°°**	**.1659°°°**
Constant	**65.4644°°°**	**49.9772°°°**
R^2	.0378	.0677
Sig. F	.0000	.0000
Number of vignettes rated	4,940	4,943

Figures in bold show a statistically significant impact of vignette level on ratings, using both ordinary least squares (OLS) regression and hierarchical linear modeling (HLM) techniques.
° $p \leq .05$.
°° $p \leq .01$.
°°° $p \leq .001$.

likelihood of both attempted and completed assault. The man's holding the woman down did not affect the perceived risk of the man continuing his attempts, but did increase the rated likelihood of his succeeding.

RMA scores were weakly but statistically significantly related to risk judgments. Women with higher RMA scores rated both attempted and completed rape as slightly more likely than did women with lower scores.

Discussion of Survey Results

Although many studies have examined contextual variables associated with the *objective* risk of sexual aggression, relatively little is known about how these variables affect *perceived* risk. This information is needed since effective avoidance or resistance strategies are not likely to be activated by potential victims if they do not perceive a threat. The research described in this chapter (see also Shively, 2001) adds to a small but growing body of research addressing this issue, and the findings are cause for both optimism and concern.

Women identified only one of the three dimensions of relationship—prior sex—as a risk factor. Although previous research suggests that the nature of the relationship between dating partners is a risk factor, other studies generally have not separated and independently manipulated relationship type, length, and prior sex. For example, Cook (1995) included the item "They have dated a long time" and found it to be associated with perceived risk. This item combines type and length of relationship, and it may have been assumed by an unknown number of respondents that long dating relationships involve sex. In the present study, when prior sex was independently varied, the type and length of relationship did not affect perceptions of risk of sexual assault. On 0–100% scales of the risk of the man's attempting and successfully completing a sexual assault, ratings rose less than 4% when the couple was described as having had prior sex. Although statistically significant, these increases are too small to be terribly compelling. The objective risk associated with prior sex has not been sufficiently established through empirical research to determine the accuracy of the perceived risk levels observed here.

Women indicated that they believed men who consumed alcohol were more likely to continue their attempts than their sober counterparts. Prior research strongly suggests that they are correct, with a large proportion of men who commit sexual aggression found to have consumed alcohol (e.g., Ginn et al., 1998; Koss, 1988; Schwartz and Pitts, 1995; Testa and Dermen, 1999). Women did not consider it more likely that drinking men would succeed in their coercive attempts. The accuracy of this perception is unclear. Given the evidence that alcohol serves to sexually disinhibit men (e.g., Barbaree et al., 1983; Bernat et al., 1998) and to produce elevated expectations of engaging in sex (e.g., Rauch and Bryant, 2000; Testa and Dermen, 1999), one can reasonably assume that mildly or moderately inebriated men would be more persistent and thus more likely to succeed in their attempts. However, there is little evidence directly assessing whether intoxicated men are more likely than sober men to succeed in their sexually aggressive attempts, once they initiate them.

The perceived likelihood that the man would continue his attempts was not associated with the woman's drinking, and there are reasons to believe that this perception might be incorrect. Research finds that women who drink alcohol are considered by men to be more sexually available (e.g., Aramburu and Leigh,

1991; George et al., 1988, 1997), and it follows that this expectation might encourage men to misinterpret or disbelieve the woman's signals of nonconsent and to continue their advances.

The man's succeeding in his attempts was considered more likely when the woman was described as drinking. This squares with the previously mentioned victimization research, which shows that a large proportion of victims of date rape were drinking. There is considerable evidence that alcohol places women at risk by impairing their ability to detect cues, suppressing their inhibitions, and reducing their physical and cognitive ability to resist once they are threatened (e.g., Abbey et al., 1996; Cleveland et al., 1999; Murphy et al., 1998; Ullman et al., 1999).

When the woman in the vignettes was described as physically resisting, the perceived likelihood that the man would continue his attempts and succeed declined. Again, these appear to be accurate perceptions, given the evidence that more vigorous physical resistance results in higher rates of rape avoidance (e.g., Ullman, 1997; Zoucha-Jensen and Coyne, 1995). The form of the woman's verbal resistance was not associated with either perceived risk measure. This represents inaccurate perception. Many studies have found that women who offer relatively passive forms of verbal resistance, such as pleading or attempting to reason with the offender, are less successful in resisting their assailant than those who engage in more assertive or aggressive verbal resistance, such as screaming or yelling for help (e.g., Quinsey and Upfold, 1985; Ullman, 1997; Ullman and Knight, 1992).

The type of coercion the hypothetical men used significantly affected both risk ratings. Threatening to hurt the woman and slapping her were both considered more likely than holding the woman down and continuing. These perceptions are probably inaccurate: Several studies find that it is more common for male dating partners to hold women down or use verbal coercion than to hit them or threaten physical harm (e.g., Koss, 1988; Muehlenhard and Linton, 1987; Tyler et al., 1998).

Location was expected to affect the perceived likelihood that the man would continue and succeed in his attempts, with ratings being higher when the event occurred at his residence, lower when it occurred at hers, and lowest when it occurred at a party. However, women rated the risk associated with all of the locations nearly identically. This is cause for concern, since the evidence is clear that risk varies across locations (e.g., Koss, 1988; Ullman et al., 1999).

For several reasons, consensual foreplay was also expected to affect risk ratings. Research finds that women's voluntary engagement in sexual foreplay is often considered to imply consent for intercourse (e.g., Muehlenhard et al., 1985; Warshaw, 1988). It has also been argued that there is widespread social acceptance of the idea that men have little ability to stop themselves from pursuing intercourse once they are sexually aroused, and the women responsible for their arousal are expected to provide sex (e.g., Smith, 1999; Warshaw, 1988). If men's use of force is considered more understandable when women consent to foreplay, and if foreplay is seen as a form of implied consent for intercourse, it would be expected that in this study men would be considered more likely to continue their attempts to have sex and to succeed when the vignettes described the hypothetical couple as engaging in foreplay. The results were contrary to these expectations, with foreplay having no significant impact on risk judgments. This finding is another cause for concern. If men see women's consent to fore-play as indicating their consent for intercourse, it is less likely that they will take seriously women's resistance to their attempts at intercourse.

SUGGESTIONS FOR FUTURE RESEARCH

An obvious next step in this line of research is replicating the study described in this chapter using random samples of students across different schools, rather than a convenience sample from a single university. In addition, a greater range of individual traits could be examined to develop a more complete understand-ing of risk perception. For example, Wilson et al. (1999) compared the time it took for women who had and had not been repeatedly sexually victimized to per-ceive that a videotaped dating scenario was evolving into a sexual assault. They concluded that PTSD-related symptoms increased sensitivity to risk cues. A potentially fruitful extension of the present study and Wilson et al.'s would be to assess respondents' sexual assault history and symptoms of trauma from such vic-timization and examine how they affect the perception of risk in factorial survey vignettes. This would build on Wilson et al.'s study by allowing analysis of how separate situational risk factors (and combinations of elements) are perceived by people with different sexual assault histories, and would build on the present study by adding personal victimization to the risk judgment model.

It would also be beneficial to more thoroughly examine several of the dimensions of dating scenarios addressed in the present study. For example, given the importance of location as a risk factor, a factorial survey should be con-ducted that examines several dimensions of location rather than the single vari-able used in the current survey. Although the presence of other people is implied in some of the dimensions manipulated in the present study (e.g., a party), it was not explicitly stated and manipulated, so its impact on risk judgments cannot be estimated. Given that women can be drawn further into positions of vulnerability if they are depending on their date for transportation home, women's access to independent transportation could also be examined as a risk factor related to location.

There are many other aspects of how people respond to sexually aggressive dating situations that would benefit from systematic examination. For example, under what conditions do women continue resisting? What conditions alter judgments of the likelihood that female victims will contact the police and, if so, whether the offender would be arrested and legally sanctioned?

In addition, a better understanding of communication in sexual situations is needed, since miscommunication is so frequently cited as a cause of date rapes (e.g., Abbey, 1991; Koss et al., 1987; Shotland and Hunter, 1995). Factorial surveys would be an effective means of examining the extent that men and women agree on the level of desire or consent to have sex (and how this desire is communicated and perceived) under a variety of conditions.

IMPLICATIONS FOR PREVENTION

The idea that rape prevention can be advanced by educating women about risk factors is not new. For years, many prevention programs have focused on raising women's awareness of risk in dating situations (Gray et al., 1990; Lonsway, 1996; Schultz et al., 2000). What the present study provides is information that can help to more clearly target the kinds of risk factors that should be emphasized in preventive education programs, since, apparently, certain risk factors are not readily perceived as such. For example, the women in the present study correctly perceived that a man who consumed alcohol was more likely to continue his sexual advances in spite of his date's resistance and that he was more likely to succeed in his attempts if the woman was inebriated. On the other hand, they completely ignored location as a very important risk factor. It is important to continue raising awareness about *all* known risk factors, but the present results suggest that educational efforts should place more emphasis on helping women to recognize risk factors to which they may not ordinarily respond.

References

Abbey, A. (1991) Misperception as an antecedent of acquaintance rape: A consequence of ambiguity in communication between men and women. In A. Parrot and L. Bechhafer (Eds.), *Acquaintance Rape: The Hidden Crime.* New York: Wiley.

Abbey, A., Ross, L. T., McDuffie, D., and McAuslan, P. (1996). Alcohol and dating risk factors for sexual assault among college women. *Psychology of Women Quarterly*, 20, 147–169.

Alder, C. (1985). An exploration of self-reported sexually aggressive behavior. *Crime and Delinquency*, 31, 306–331.

Applegate, B. K., Turner, M. G., Sanborn, Jr., J. B., Latessa, E. J., and Moon, M. M. (2000). Individualization, criminalization, or problem resolution: A factorial survey of juvenile court judges' decisions to incarcerate felony youths. *Justice Quarterly*, 17, 309–331.

Aramburu, B., and Leigh, B. C. (1991). For better or worse: Attributions about drunken aggression toward male and female victims. *Violence and Victims*, 6, 31–41.

Barbaree, H. E., Marshall, W. L., Yates, E., and Lightfoot, L. O. (1983). Alcohol intoxication and deviant sexual arousal in male social drinkers. *Behavioral Research and Therapy*, 21, 365–373.

Bernat, J. A., Calhoun, K. S., and Stolp, S. (1998). Sexually aggressive men's responses to a date rape analogue: Alcohol as a disinhibiting cue. *Journal of Sex Research*, 35, 341–348.

Breitenbacher, K. H. (1999). The association between the perception of threat in a dating situation and sexual victimization. *Violence and Victims*, 14, 135–146.

Brener, N. D., McMahon, P. M., Warren, C. W., and Douglas, K. A. (1999). Forced sexual intercourse and associated health-risk behaviors among female college students in the United States. *Journal of Consulting and Clinical Psychology, 67,* 252–259.

Bryk, A., Raudenbush, S., and Congdon, R. (1996). *HLM: Hierarchical Linear and Nonlinear Modeling with the HLM/2L and HLM/3L Programs.* Chicago: Scientific Software International.

Burt, M. R. (1980). Cultural myths and support for rape. *Journal of Personality and Social Psychology, 38,* 217–230.

Cleveland, H. H., Koss, M. P., and Lyons, J. (1999). Rape tactics from the survivors' perspective: Contextual dependence and within-event independence. *Journal of Interpersonal Violence, 14,* 532–547.

Coker, A. L., Walls, L. G., and Johnson, J. E. (1998). Risk factors for traumatic physical injury during sexual assaults for male and female victims. *Journal of Interpersonal Violence, 13,* 605–620.

Cook, S. L. (1995). Acceptance and expectation of sexual aggression in college students. *Psychology of Women Quarterly, 19,* 181–194.

Cue, K.L, George, W. H., and Norris, J. (1996). Women's appraisal of sexual assault risk in dating situations. *Psychology of Women Quarterly, 20,* 487–504.

Davidson, J., Hughes, D., George, L., and Blazer, D. (1996). The association of sexual assault and attempted suicide within the community. *Archives of General Psychiatry, 53,* 550–555.

Ellis, A., and Brancale, R. (1956). *The Psychology of Sex Offenders.* Springfield, IL: Thomas.

Estrich, S. (1987). *Real Rape: How the Legal System Victimizes Women Who Say No.* Cambridge, MA: Harvard University Press.

Ferraro, K. F. (1996). Women's fear of victimization: Shadow of sexual assault? *Social Forces, 75,* 667–690.

Gebhard, P. H., Gagnon, J. H., Pomeroy, W. B., and Christenson, C. V. (1965). *Sex Offenders: An Analysis of Types.* New York: Harper and Row.

George, W. H., Gournic, S. J., and McAfee, M. P. (1988). Perceptions of post-drinking female sexuality: Effects of gender, beverage choice, and drink payment. *Journal of Applied Social Psychology, 18,* 1295–1317.

George, W. H., Lehman, G. L., Cue, K. L., Martinez, L. J., Lopez, P. A., and Norris, J. (1997). Post-drinking sexual inferences: Evidence for linear rather than curvilinear dosage effects. *Journal of Applied Social Psychology, 27,* 629–648.

Ginn, S. R., Walker, K., Poulson, R. L., Singletary, S. K., Cyrus, V. K., and Picarelli, J. A. (1998). Coercive sexual behavior and the influence of alcohol consumption and religiosity among college students in the Bible Belt. *Journal of Social Behavior and Personality, 13,* 151–165.

Gray, M. D., Lesser, D., Quinn, E., and Bounds, C. (1990). The effectiveness of personalizing acquaintance rape prevention: Programs on perceptions of vulnerability and on reducing risk-taking behavior. *Journal of College Student Development, 31,* 217–220.

Greenfield, L. A., and Snell, T. L. (1999). *Women Offenders.* Washington, DC: U.S. Department of Justice, Bureau of Justice Statistics.

Jacoby, J. E., and Cullen, F. T. (1999). The structure of punishment norms: Applying the Rossi-Berk model. *The Journal of Criminal Law and Criminology, 89,* 245–312.

Johnson, I. M., and Sigler, R. T. (2000). Forced sexual intercourse among intimates. *Journal of Family Violence, 15,* 95–108.

Katz, B. L. (1991). The psychological impact of stranger versus nonstranger rape on victims' recovery. In A. Parrot and L. Bechhofer (Eds.), *Acquaintance Rape: The Hidden Crime* (pp. 251–269). New York: Wiley.

Kilpatrick, D. G., Best, C. L., Veronen, L. J., Amick, A. E., Villeponteaux, L. A., and Ruff, G. A. (1985). Mental health correlates of criminal victimization: A random community survey. *Journal of Counseling and Clinical Psychology,* 53, 866–873.

Koss, M. P. (1988). Hidden rape: Sexual aggression and victimization in a national sample of students in higher education. In A. B. Burgess (Ed.), *Rape and Sexual Assault II* (pp. 3–25). New York: Garland.

Koss, M. P., Dinero, T. E., Seibel, C. A., and Cox, S. L. (1988). Stranger and acquaintance rape: Are there differences in the victim's experience? *Psychology of Women Quarterly,* 12, 1–24.

Koss, M. P., Gidycz, C. A., and Wisniewski, N. (1987). The scope of rape: Incidence and prevalence of sexual aggression and victimization in a national sample of higher education students. *Journal of Consulting and Clinical Psychology,* 55, 162–170.

Kroner, D. G., and Mills, J. F. (1998). The structure of antisocial attitudes among violent and sexual offenders. *International Journal of Offender Therapy and Comparative Criminology,* 42, 246–257.

Lonsway, K. A. (1996). Preventing acquaintance rape through education: What do we know? *Psychology of Women Quarterly,* 20, 229–265.

Mezey, G. C., and King, M. B. (1992). *Male Victims of Sexual Assault.* Oxford: Oxford University Press.

Muehlenhard, C. L., Friedman, D. E., and Thomas, C. M. (1985). Is date rape justifiable? The effects of dating activities, who initiated, who paid, and men's attitudes toward women. *Psychology of Women Quarterly,* 9, 297–310.

Muehlenhard, C. L., and Linton, M. A. (1987). Date rape and sexual aggression in dating situations: Incidence and risk factors. *Journal of Counseling Psychology,* 34, 186–196.

Murdoch, M., and Nichol, K. (1995). Women veterans' experiences with domestic violence and with sexual harassment while they were in the military. *Archives of Family Medicine,* 4, 411–418.

Murphy, S. T., Monahan, J. L., and Miller, L. C. (1998). Inference under the influence: The impact of alcohol and inhibition conflict on women's sexual decision making. *Personality and Social Psychology Bulletin,* 24, 517–528.

Norris, J., Nurius, P. S., and Dimeff, L. A. (1996). Through her eyes: Factors affecting women's perceptions of and resistance to acquaintance sexual aggression threat. *Psychology of Women Quarterly,* 20, 123–145.

Norris, J., Nurius, P. S., and Graham, T. L. (1999). When a date changes from fun to dangerous: Factors affecting women's ability to distinguish. *Violence Against Women,* 5, 230–250.

Oliver, L. L., Nagayama Hall, G. C., and Neuhaus, S. M. (1993). A comparison of the personality and background characteristics of adolescent sex offenders and other adolescent offenders. *Criminal Justice and Behavior,* 20, 359–370.

Petrocelli, W., and Repa, B. (1992). *Sexual Harassment on the Job.* Berkeley, CA: Nolo Press.

Quinsey, V. L., and Upfold, D. (1985). Rape completion and victim injury as a function of female resistance strategy. *Canadian Journal of Behavioral Science,* 17, 40–50.

Rauch, S. A., and Bryant, J. B. (2000). Gender and context differences in alcohol expectancies. *Journal of Social Psychology,* 140, 240–253.

Richman, J., Flaherty, J., Rospenda, K., and Christensen, M. (1992). Mental health consequences and correlates of reported medical student abuse. *Journal of the American Medical Association,* 267, 692–694.

Rossi, P. H., and Anderson, A. B. (1982). The factorial survey approach: An introduction. In P. H. Rossi and S. Nock (Eds.). *Measuring Social Judgements: The Factorial Survey Approach.* Beverly Hills, CA: Sage.

Schultz, S. K., Scherman, A., and Marshall, L. J. (2000). Evaluation of university-based date-rape prevention program: Effects on attitudes and behavior related to rape. *Journal of College Student Development,* 41, 193–201.

Schwartz, M. D., and Pitts, V. L. (1995). Exploring a feminist routine activities approach to sexual assault. *Justice Quarterly,* 12, 9–31.

Shively, M. (2001). Male self-control and sexual aggression. *Deviant Behavior,* 22, 295–321.

Shotland, R. L., and Hunter, B. A. (1995). Women's token resistance and compliant sexual behaviors are related to uncertain sexual intentions and rape. *Personality and Social Psychology Bulletin,* 21, 226–236.

Silverman, D. C., Kalick, S. M., Bowie, S. I., and Edbril, S. D. (1988). Blitz rape and confidence rape: A typology applied to 1000 consecutive cases. *American Journal of Psychiatry,* 145, 1438–1441.

Smith, P. (1999). Social revolution and the persistence of rape. In Keith Burgess–Jackson (Ed.), *A Most Detestable Crime: New Philosophical Essays on Rape.* New York: Oxford University Press.

Sorenson, S. B., Stein, J. A., Siegel, J. M., Golding, J. M., and Burnam, M. A. (1987). The prevalence of adult sexual assault: The Los Angeles Epidemiological Catchment Area Project. *American Journal of Epidemiology,* 126, 1154–1164.

Spaccarelli, S., Bowden, B., Coatsworth, J. D., and Kim, S. (1997). Psychosocial correlates of male sexual aggression in a chronic delinquent sample. *Criminal Justice and Behavior,* 24, 71–95.

Spitzberg, B. H. (1999). An analysis of empirical estimates of sexual aggression victimization and perpetration. *Violence and Victims,* 14, 241–260.

Stermac, L., DuMont, J., and Dunn, S. (1998). Violence in known-assailant sexual assaults. *Journal of Interpersonal Violence,* 13, 398–412.

Testa, M., and Dermen, K. H. (1999). The differential correlates of sexual coercion and rape. *Journal of Interpersonal Violence,* 14, 548–561.

Tjaden, P., and Thoennes, N. (1998). *Prevalence, incidence, and consequences of violence against women: Findings from the National Violence Against Women Survey.* National Institute of Justice and Centers for Disease Control and Prevention: Research in Brief.

Tyler, K. A., Hoyt, D. R., and Whitbeck, L. B. (1998). Coercive sexual strategies. *Violence and Victims,* 13, 47–61.

Ullman, S. E. (1997). Review and critique of empirical studies of rape avoidance. *Criminal Justice and Behavior,* 24, 177–204.

Ullman, S. E., Karabatos, G., and Koss, M. P. (1999). Alcohol and sexual assault in a national sample of college women. *Journal of Interpersonal Violence,* 14, 603–625.

Ullman, S. E., and Knight, R. A. (1992). Fighting back: Women's resistance to rape. *Journal of Interpersonal Violence,* 7, 31–43.

———. (1995). Women's resistance strategies to different rapist types. *Criminal Justice and Behavior,* 22, 263–283.

Vannatta, R. A. (1996). Risk factors related to suicidal behavior among male and female adolescents. *Journal of Youth and Adolescence,* 25, 149–160.

Vogel, R. E., and Himelein, M. J. (1995). Risk factors and sexual victimization: An analysis of risk factors among precollege women. *Journal of Criminal Justice*, 23, 153–162.

Waldner-Haugrud, L. K., and Magruder, B. (1995). Victimization in dating relationships: Gender differences in coercion techniques and outcomes. *Violence and Victims*, 10, 203–215.

Warshaw, R. (1988). *I Never Called It Rape: The Ms. Report on Recognizing, Fighting, and Surviving Date and Acquaintance Rape.* New York: Harper and Row.

Wilson, A. E., Calhoun, K. S., and Bernat, J. A. (1999). Risk recognition and trauma-related symptoms among sexually revictimized women. *Journal of Consulting and Clinical Psychology*, 67, 705–710.

Wolfe, J. E,. Sharkansky, J., Read, J. P., Dawson, R., Martin, J. A., and Ouimette, P. C. (1998). Sexual harassment and assault as predictors of PTSD symptomatology among U.S. female Persian Gulf War military personnel. *Journal of Interpersonal Violence*, 13, 40–57.

Zoucha-Jensen, J. M., and Coyne, A. (1995). The effects of resistance strategies on rape. *American Journal of Public Health*, 83, 1633–1634.

CHAPTER 3

In Harm's Way
The Client in Professional Sexual Misconduct

Jennifer Eastman

Introduction

In the last decade, there have been numerous widely publicized incidents of professional sexual misconduct. In 1990, Father Bruce Ritter, noted director and founder of the Covenant House charity in New York, was charged with sexual misconduct toward young boys in his care (Schoener, 1995). In 1992, a respected female Harvard psychiatrist was accused of sexually abusing a male medical student who later committed suicide (Chafetz and Chafetz, 1994; McNamara, 1994). In 1995, the story of a male gym teacher accused of molesting many of his female students made headlines. In the summer of that same year, Senator Robert Packwood faced congressional hearings concerning allegations that he had abused at least 19 female associates. And in the winter of 1999, Presiden Clinton was impeached on charges of perjury in testifying about his sexual relationship with a White House intern, Monica Lewinsky. Later that year in Arkansas, he faced disbarment for misconduct when he was governor of that state in a sexual harassment case brought by Paula Jones.

All of these relationships raise questions. Questions about power, about trust, about the very nature of the relationship. When these relationships occur, we can ask, Is it exploitation of one person by another that the very designation of professional sexual misconduct suggests, or rather consensual sex? Is the client in the professional relationship in which sex occurs safe or in harm's way?

Sexual relationships between the professional and the client occur in many professions: psychiatry, law, the clergy, education, and, as in the cases of Senator Packwood and President Clinton, politics. The statistics are surprisingly uniform throughout the professions for the frequency of sexual misconduct. For example, up to 12% of psychiatrists have engaged in such conduct (Gartrell, Milliken, Goodson, Thiemann, and Lo, 1995). Roughly 12% of clergy report that they have had sexual intercourse with a parishioner (Fortune, 1995). In a study of 500 psychology educators, an average of 13% engaged in sex with their students (Pope, 1989). In this chapter my focus is on the nature of sexual relationships between professional and client in the field of psychiatry. After giving a brief history of doctor–patient sexual relations, I present a detailed description of the first successful suit brought against a psychiatrist who engaged in sexual relations with a female patient. This happened 20 years ago. I then analyze the nature of the therapeutic relationship, and why it may be particularly susceptible to such behavior, and discuss the advantages and disadvantages of the various remedies available to the patient who feels victimized. A relatively new remedy is the criminalization of the sexual behavior. Discussion of this remedy, now operational in 15 states, brings us back in the end to a further exploration of the nature of the therapeutic relationship.

History of Doctor–Patient Sexual Relationships

Prohibition of sexual relationships between doctor and patient extends back to the Hippocratic oath, formulated in the fourth century B.C., which reads in part as follows:

> Whatever houses I may visit, I will come for the benefit of the sick, remaining free of all intentional injustice, of all mischief and, in particular, of sexual relations with both female and male persons, be they free or slave. (Freeman and Roy, 1976, frontispiece)

Later authorities prohibited a sexual relationship between doctor and patient and incorporated this charge in the oath. In the nineteenth century when Sigmund Freud discovered the possibilities of psychoanalytic treatment, he readily acknowledged that a wide range of feelings, including sexual tension or feelings between doctor and patient, occurred in the treatment setting. Freud insisted that these feelings were not to be acted on, but after the further development of psychoanalysis, there were several known instances of sexual intimacy between therapist and patient; for example, Sabrina Spielrein and Carl Jung in the early part of the twentieth century (Baur, 1996), and Karen Horney and a young male patient in the late 1940s and early 1950s (Schoener, 1995). In the 1960s, during an era of sexual experimentation in the general population, sexual relations between therapist and client were often accepted and regarded as therapeutic. Therefore, over time, these relations have been both proscribed and prescripted.

The Roy–Hartogs Case

A first attempt to limit if not punish such behavior occurred in the 1970s. In a widely publicized case in New York, Julie Roy charged a noted doctor, Renatus Hartogs, with sexual exploitation (*Roy v. Hartogs*, 1976). Roy was a secretary at *Esquire* and Hartogs, an eminent psychiatrist, was a member of several psychiatric associations and the author of several books and a column for *Cosmopolitan*. Roy's case contained many features common to cases where sexual misconduct is claimed.

Roy's personal history was depressing. She grew up in the Midwest, the product of a loveless marriage. Her parents were divorced when she was three. She was the youngest of four children, three girls and a boy. Because the family moved often, Roy attended at least 14 schools before receiving her high school diploma. She always did poorly in classes and had few friends. Later, looking back, she remembered that she was always an obedient and submissive child doing what her mother wished. She had fewer memories of her father, although she did recall that once he had kissed her on the lips when she was 12, which made her feel peculiar. When she was 24, her older brother, to whom she was close, committed suicide. Throughout her childhood, youth, and early adulthood, she later recalled, she had always been depressed (Freeman and Roy, 1976).

When Roy moved to New York City, her personal conflicts became so troublesome that she decided to consult a psychiatrist. She moved to the city after she married in 1961 and began work as a secretary in the advertising department of *Esquire* magazine. She was divorced in 1965. After the divorce, she entered into a lesbian relationship. When this relationship ended, she became extremely depressed, more so than usual and her only female friend encouraged her to seek psychiatric help. It was then, in March 1969, when Roy was 30 years old, that she met Dr. Renatus Hartogs. On her first visit, she met with Hartogs for 15 minutes. They agreed at that time to meet three times a week in the future. Roy told Hartogs that she could afford to pay $10 a visit (Freeman and Roy, 1976).

Shortly after the two began to meet, Hartogs suggested that they engage in different forms of sexual activity. He first suggested that they have a bathtub party. Roy refused. Several sessions later, he suggested that they have sex, stating, "It will cure you of being a lesbian; your trouble is that you are afraid of men" (Freeman and Roy, 1976, p. 51). By April 1969, Hartogs and Roy were hugging and kissing. By May, they were lying together unclothed on his couch. All the while, Hartogs encouraged Roy to have sex with him. Although she was frightened and confused by these demands, by August 1969, Roy decided to say yes. During a 10-minute session at his office, the two engaged in sexual intercourse for the first time. Thereafter, Hartogs and Roy generally had sex during the 10- to 15-minute scheduled appointments in his office (Freeman and Roy, 1976).

Hartogs moved to a new apartment in 1970 and sometimes invited Roy to stay overnight. It was at this time that problems emerged. During one overnight visit, Roy discovered that Hartogs was sleeping with other women. She then realized that she was not the only woman in his life. Then Hartogs forgot to acknowledge her birthday. This neglect made Roy decide that she no longer wanted to see him. In making the decision, she realized that "she was as depressed as ever and that she hadn't changed at all" (Freeman and Roy, 1976, p. 94). She was also aware that when she began to make demands on Hartogs he rejected her. It took Roy several weeks after reaching the decision to act on it, but eventually, she made her feelings known to the doctor and left (Freeman and Roy, 1976).

After Roy stopped seeing Hartogs, she consulted other professionals and told them her story. As she retold and relived her relationship with Hartogs with other psychiatrists, she became so disturbed that she had to be hospitalized twice. She had never been hospitalized before. In addition to consulting other doctors, she returned to the lawyer who had helped her obtain her earlier divorce. She told him what had happened with Hartogs, and he agreed to file a malpractice suit against the doctor on the grounds that he had used sex with her as therapy. The attorney knew that he was treading on new ground legally, since this suit against Hartogs was the first of its kind (Freeman and Roy, 1976).

At trial, Roy presented her case first. Hartogs was absent during the presentation. When his turn came to explain his actions, he appeared in court and through his attorney presented several defenses. First, he denied that he had ever had sexual relations with Roy. Second, he testified that because of a physical problem, he had been incapable of having sexual intercourse during the time when Roy was in treatment with him. Third, and most important, he characterized Roy as delusional. It made no difference to him that, as cross-examination of Roy had revealed, she had engaged in several sexual relationships with both men and women while she was in treatment with him, thereby suggesting, among other things, that she was sexually promiscuous (Freeman and Roy, 1976). Instead, he emphasized her psychiatric problems, insisting that Roy was a schizophrenic, paranoid type with catatonic features. He told how throughout their work together, Roy had hated him and that her belief that she had had sexual intercourse with him was merely a part of her sickness. While other psychiatrists with whom Roy consulted agreed with the diagnosis, none believed that the sexual relationship with Hartogs was a delusion and a product of her sickness. All of them believed that the sexual relationship had in fact occurred (Freeman and Roy, 1976).

Several witnesses came forward to rebut Hartogs's testimony. Among them were former patients of Hartogs's, who stated that during their treatment with him, they had engaged in sexual relations at his request. Hartogs tried to dismiss these witnesses by claiming that they also were mentally ill and delusional. Other witnesses claimed that there were treatments available for Hartogs's alleged physical problems, which he claimed rendered him sexually impotent during the time he treated Roy. These rebuttal witnesses were apparently persuasive—the jury returned a verdict in Roy's favor (Freeman and Roy, 1976).

With this trial, a pattern of accusation and defense between doctor and patient was established. The patient, if a woman, would claim that at the doctor's suggestion and in the guise of treatment, she would engage in sexual relations with the doctor. The doctor would deny such behavior and suggest that it was a fabrication of the patient, a product of mental disease and a delusional mind (Noel and Watterson, 1992).

The Nature of the Therapeutic Relationship

Although every human relationship contains a sexual quality, many would say that the psychiatrist–patient dyad seems particularly susceptible to the possibility that this sexuality will be acted on. This is so despite the fact that most practitioners, starting with Freud, agree that sexual intimacies with a patient are unethical and that the guidelines for the American Psychological Association prohibit such behavior.

Several factors explain the susceptibility. First, both the therapist and the patient may bring to the relationship several vulnerabilities that encourage the sexual activity. The patient may be triply vulnerable. If the patient is a woman (and most are in these relationships), she may be repeating earlier sexual or psychological abuses of her childhood in the context of the current relationship with the therapist. This feature of the relationship is known as the transference (Friedman and Boumil, 1995). Many argue that these feelings from the past brought into the present are so powerful that they obscure the actual feelings the patient may have toward the therapist and render impossible true consent to a sexualization of the relationship. In addition, she may have suffered profound loneliness and psychological abandonment as a child and, in a form of role reversal, may have assumed the role of healer for her parents and siblings. She may bring this role reversal into the therapeutic relationship and begin to take care of the therapist. Finally, she may be assuming the cultural norm that a woman's role is as sexual partner to a more powerful male—if not so in actuality, than perceived to be (Hawkins, Ivera, Barnard, and Herkev, 1994). As for the therapist, if male, he may be suffering from what one commentator has called "lovesickness."

This "illness" includes such characteristics as emotional dependence on the patient and a need to share his life with her, a need to idealize qualities about the patient that have no basis in reality, physical attraction to the patient that seeks an outlet, or a sense of incompleteness and an altered state of consciousness in the patient's presence (Twemlow and Gabbard, 1989). At the root of such lovesickness is a form of narcissism reflecting the therapist's need to be loved and idealized.

In the Roy–Hartogs case, we can see several of these factors at work. Roy had suffered psychological abandonment and loneliness as a child. She was keenly aware that as she related to Hartogs, he reminded her of her father and that this was a kind of repetition of the unsatisfying and slightly disturbing relationship she had first experienced in her family. For his part, Hartogs behaved in a narcissistic manner throughout the treatment with Roy. He treated her as an object to satisfy his own needs, insisting on sex right from the start.

Another feature peculiar to the therapeutic relationship is the context in which it occurs. The therapist and the patient spend many hours alone with each other in a closed room, discussing the most intimate details of the patient's private life. Quite often in cases in which a sexual relationship develops, the therapist has revealed aspects of his own private life. Because the relationship is isolated, the two individuals develop heightened feelings for each other on which the outside world has little effect. In this respect, the relationship is unique and unlike other relationships, which are generally created and maintained in a web of interrelated interactions with others. The fact that the activity is generally proscribed makes it even more enticing. As the lines between having feelings and acting on them, and between the professional and the private, become blurred, there are no outside forces or people to intervene and prevent the sexual activity from occurring (Hawkins, Ivera, Barnard, and Herkev, 1994).

Who is more vulnerable in this relationship? Most would say that it is the patient. Certainly, the Roy–Hartogs case suggests this. A vulnerable woman under the influence of a vulnerable (in other ways) yet apparently powerful person in the community. In her article "Patient–Therapist Sex: Criminalization and Its Discontents," Patricia Illingworth (1995) suggests a different paradigm of the therapeutic relationship. Instead of a particularly vulnerable patient, she posits one with an "enhanced ability to make decisions, because he or she may be more aware of his or her own weaknesses and unconscious motivations than those who have not participated in therapy" (p. 398). Furthermore, instead of being submissive and dependent, the patient may be more autonomous than others. Illingworth states that to assume the patient always seeks therapy because of impaired abilities is to fall prey to prejudices about patients in therapy.

Illingworth (1995) goes on to suggest that the very nature of the therapeutic relationship is often misperceived. She explains that the feature that was deemed most troubling about the Roy–Hartogs relationship was that it was a fiduciary relationship gone bad. In that case, a fiduciary relationship was defined as one that arises "whenever confidence is reposed on one side and domination and influence result on the other" (p. 403). Power resides, then, with the therapist, and dependence, with the patient. Illingworth claims that the kind of psychotherapy practiced today is therapy informed by the value of individual autonomy. In insight-oriented psychotherapy or psychoanalysis, the patient does not delegate power to the therapist, and the therapist does not abuse whatever power he or she may have by telling the patients what to do. Illingworth believes that the trend in relationships between therapist and patient is toward an alliance in which the two partners work together as equals. She believes that this new relationship does not fit into the paternalistic mode that characterized the fiduciary relationship shared by Roy and Hartogs and believes that the latter model rests on a "fictionalized and troubling version of psychotherapy" (p. 408).

Given this model of equal partners in a therapeutic dyad, Illingworth believes that the patient is free to consent or to withhold consent to a sexual relationship. She believes, for example, that the transference issues that others deem an impediment to free consent are no more frequent in psychotherapy than in other relationships. Illingworth does not condone sex between therapist and patient and would place major responsibility on the therapist should sexual contact occur. Here she resembles other commentators in believing, for example, that the therapist is under a duty to refrain from sex with patients because of a need for objectivity and impartiality (Illingworth, 1995). But she differs in her conclusions about what happens when the therapist breaches this duty and suggests that sexual relations with the patient take place. Because in her paradigm, the patient is not very vulnerable or hobbled by transference issues, Illingworth believes that the patient is free to enter into such a relationship even though it may cause harm. Here, one must imagine that Illingworth refers to the normal pain that a person risks in entering into any relationship.

One problem with this paradigm is that the harm to which the Illingworth patient consents is potentially quite extreme. In many cases, as a result of the sexualized therapeutic relationship, the patient may suffer from a form of post-traumatic stress disorder that might include severe depression, anxiety, loss of self-esteem, and the ability to trust others. The patient might find it difficult to enage in intimate relationships, or may experience a decline in his or her interest in sexual interaction, or hypersexuality, and increased vulnerability with inadequate coping skills to handle these side effects. (Pope, 1989b). The patient may experience a wide array of feelings. If the patient is a woman, she may feel guilt, remorse, helplessness, rage, anger, fear, hopelessness, grief, loss, or shame. She may have strong desires to seek revenge or may be at an increased risk for suicide (Pope, 1989b). In Roy's case, she experienced this panoply of emotions and even became so distraught that after she had left Hartogs, she had to be hospitalized twice, confinement she had never required before. Most, then, would say that sexual activity within the therapeutic relationship exacerbates whatever problems the patient may have had before entering therapy and often creates a desperate need for help. Sometimes, it can take years before the patient can recover a sense of balance.

Remedies

Given the amount of harm that results from these relationships, it is natural that the patient will feel victimized and seek some form of redress. All of the remedies, both civil and criminal, hold out some promise of redress to the victim. All of them are also flawed.

The victim in such a relationship can seek out an administrative solution initially. She or he can complain to the local licensing board with the hope that the state will revoke the practitioner's license. The complaint remains private, which is advantageous to the victim. In some states, however, the board does not exert control over licensing and thus the practitioner is left free to practice his or her profession (King, 1995).

A second alternative remedy for the victim of a sexualized therapeutic relationship is to bring a civil lawsuit against the therapist, alleging tort theories such as malpractice or infliction of emotional distress. If victorious, the injured patient may regain the sense of self and self-respect lost during the relationship. However, the patient may pay a high price for the victory because in gaining it, she or he may have to disclose private emotional and mental states to the public. During a civil trial, the patient waives the right to confidentiality and privilege that attaches to the therapeutic relationship (Gabbard and Pope, 1989). The therapist therefore may discount the patient's complaint and use as evidence against the victim material from the therapy. Such material can include anything the patient may have said in therapy or any professional opinions the therapist has formed throughout the therapy. These assertions in defense of the therapist may become part of a public record or of newspaper accounts. "In this manner, the most private aspects of the patient's life may become public" (Gabbard and Pope, 1989, pp. 121–122). In the Roy–Hartogs case, Roy's private life became public as Hartogs claimed that she was mentally ill and delusional about the alleged sexual relations.

A third and more recent alternative is to seek redress in the criminal justice system. As early as 1976, Masters and Johnson, authors of the book *Human Sexual Inadequacy,* suggested that civil remedies to redress the harm done when a therapist and patient engage in sexual relations were not sufficient. They believed that such relations should be made a criminal offense (Jorgenson, Randles, and Strasburger, 1991). As more cases of such relations surfaced and statistics began to reveal how frequent this behavior was, several states began to pass legislation criminalizing the conduct. In 1983 Wisconsin became the first state to make therapeutic sexual misconduct a criminal offense (Kane, 1995). Since then, 14 other states have made the conduct criminal: Arizona, California, Colorado, Connecticut, Florida, Georgia, Iowa, Maine, Minnesota, New Mexico, New Hampshire, North Dakota, South Dakota, and Texas. Several other states, such as Massachusetts, have spent many years arguing about the merits of criminalizing such conduct. In the states that have criminalized the conduct, the proscribed behavior has included sexual interaction between psychotherapists, counselors, clergy, or other professionals and their patients and clients. Most of the statutes specify that the victim's consent to the act is no defense, because it is the therapist's duty and obligation as mandated by the psychiatric guidelines to avoid sexual involvement with a patient regardless of the patient's behavior. Several of the statutes contain victim shield provisions that provide that the client's sexual history will not be admitted into evidence. Such provisions prevent in part any defensive attempt to place the victim on trial, as in rape cases (Estrich, 1987).

There are several advantages and disadvantages to the criminalization of sexual activity between therapist and patient. The major advantage for the patient is that she or he will be empowered by the fact that the therapist is publicly punished. The patient will know that the therapist cannot harm other patients, and the public safety will therefore be enhanced (Strasburger, Jorgenson, and Randles, 1991).

There are several disadvantages, however. First, the criminal case will be in the hands of the public prosecutor, with the result that the patient/victim may lose control of the case and how she or he wishes it to be handled. Second, the criminal case may affect any civil case the victim desires to bring. The criminal case, which in all probability will precede the civil case, will determine the outcome of the latter. If the victim loses the criminal case, her or his chances for success in a civil suit are minimal. Third, and again as in a civil suit, the victim's privacy may be invaded, and instead of feeling empowered by the laws, she or he may feel demeaned, attacked, and revictimized (Glasgow, 1992). The advantage to the therapist under the criminal statutes is complete vindication if found innocent; the disadvantage of the criminal statutes is that they sweep with a broad brush. They do not take into account whether the therapist is a habitual abuser who requires public censure and punishment or one who has strayed only once and simply needs some rehabilitation (Friedman and Boumil, 1995).

The laws are too new to provide clear-cut evidence of these advantages and disadvantages. Thus far, the statutes have remained underutilized for several reasons. In Wisconsin from 1983 until December 1993, only 30 cases were brought in which a professional was convicted of a criminal offense. Twenty-one of them were prosecuted under the statute prohibiting sexual assault; only nine were charged with violating that part of the statute that prohibits sexual exploitation. In some cases, the charge was the result of a plea bargain, but in other cases, the prosecutor felt more certain of a conviction if prosecuting for sexual assault. Overall, criminalization of the sexual activity in Wisconsin reveals that victims fear they will be revictimized by the system. They are reluctant to come forward even with a criminal complaint. A survey of 72 district attorneys concluded:

> The statute has not reduced it (sexual misconduct) because laws cannot stop victims from declining to report such abuse because of embarass-ment, fear of retaliation by the therapist/clergy member, fear of ostracism by their religious group, or fear of not being believed. Criminalization could, in some cases, actually hinder some victims from reporting because they don't want to cause trouble for the therapist or clergy member. (Kane, 1995, p. 321)

In Colorado, the statute criminalizing therapeutic sexual misconduct has similarly been underutilized. The statute, effective since 1988, has been invoked only 20 times. In several cases, the dispositions remain unknown at this time. Records from district attorneys' offices since 1988 indicate most of the out-comes: Two cases were turned down outright; three or four cases resulted in a later dismissal; two cases received deferred judgments, which meant that the charges would be dropped if there were no further violations; two therapists received probation; three therapists received jail sentences; one therapist was found not guilty; and five other cases were recently filed and are still in process (Roberts-Henry, 1995). Attitudes of the prosecuting attorneys seem to be responsible for the limited number of cases. Some remain unfamiliar with the law and so are reluctant to use it, and others are unwilling to believe the victim's story in what they perceive will be a contest between the patient's word and the therapist's word (Roberts-Henry, 1995).

The prosecuting attorney is not the only party who may not believe the vic-tim of sexual relations in the therapeutic context. Sometimes other attorneys and fellow psychiatrists to whom the victim turns are no more knowledgeable or sympathetic than the prosecutor. It must be remembered that the victim is already suffering from guilt, depression, confusion, ambivalence, and a deep inability to trust when she or he turns to someone for help (Pope, 1989b). These feelings make it difficult to establish meaningful contact with a new professional. And yet, the new professional, whether another psychiatrist or attorney, may mis-perceive the situation for numerous reasons: ignorance that therapist–patient sex is wrong and has been prohibited by mental health organizations; narrow precon-ceptions about the occurrence of therapist–patient sex; the bizarreness of the episode; the apparent normal, or abnormal, functioning of the patient; the fact that the patient is so angry that her or his personal style is offensive to the new professional; sympathy for a fellow professional; bias stemming from beliefs that sexual activity between professional and client cannot be so harmful; or last, and not infrequent, the belief that the activity was the result of the mental problems for which the patient sought help to begin with (Pope, 1989b). All of these atti-tudes can further demoralize an already distressed client.

Thus, we have the victim reluctant to come forward and, if she or he does finally do so, facing skeptical professionals who do not comprehend the nature of the complaint. We have criminalization of behavior that is not uniformly considered a crime. The only other crime that seems to raise similar questions and that prosecutors are reluctant to prosecute is acquaintance rape. The two crimes, professional sexual misconduct and acquaintance rape, share certain features. First, the relationship is private (in the case of therapy, conducted in private though apparently professional in nature) and not the business of the public. Second, the cases are deemed less serious and the defendants less blameworthy, and the patient may also be blameworthy in some respect. Third, and most important, because the relationship is personal, it is seen as less terrifying and therefore deserving of less punishment (Estrich, 1987). In the case of therapeutic sexual misconduct, I argue that the very combination of the personal and the professional, the past and the present feelings and remembrances, in the relationship tends to make it more, not less, terrifying. Overall, prosecutors and others seem not to understand the complexities of the relationship with which they are dealing. For this reason prosecutors have tended to stay away from enforcing the new laws. Thus whether or not these laws are an effective means of redressing a harm remains an open question. It remains open, I suggest, because of this very lack of clarity concerning the nature of the therapeutic relationship.

Conclusion: The Nature of the Therapeutic Relationship Redux

Let's return to the two models of the therapeutic relationship discussed earlier. In one, the patient, vulnerable, weak, and troubled, gives her- or himself over in trust to a vulnerable though still powerful, more secure advisor. In this model, if sex enters the relationship, it is usually seen as exploitation of the client by the professional. In the second model, the patient, aware of her- or himself and autonomous, enters into a relationship with an equally astute caregiver and they work together as partners. If sex enters this relationship, the client knowingly consents to the ramifications even if harm should come. This is deemed consensual sex between two fully autonomous human beings. In such a paradigm, the "mis" in professional sexual "misconduct" is amiss.

Which model is more accurate? Earlier I discussed the 1970s case between Roy and Hartogs. Let me now refer to a more recent case. In this case the patient, Paul Lozano, was a Harvard Medical School student who sought the help of Dr. Margaret Bean Bayog, a psychiatrist associated with Harvard. Lozano remained in treatment with Bean Bayog for several years and then, when she insisted, stopped seeing her. Lozano later committed suicide. In 1992, Lozano's family accused Bean Bayog of having seduced him and, as a result, having driven him to his death. Bean Bayog denied any wrongdoing and indicated that her treatment of Lozano, a kind of regression therapy in which she attempted to play the role of his mother, was, if not quite orthodox according to established therapeutic standards, nonetheless geared toward the reality of Lozano as a quite disturbed patient. Bean Bayog insisted that it was Lozano who had tried to sexualize their relationship and that her own notes, filled with her own sexual fantasies, were merely part of this treatment. We see here the same pattern as in the Roy–Hartogs case: charges by the patient or, in this instance, the patient's family, of a sexualization, if not actual sex activity, in a therapeutic relationship, and denial of these charges by the therapist. The parties settled before going to trial. Bean Bayog gave up her medical license and her appointment at Harvard. Otherwise, she continued to see patients (fewer in number than before) and get on with her life (Chafetz and Chafetz, 1994; McNamara, 1994). Lozano forfeited his life. Perhaps his fate stemmed in part from the fact that he was male.

> There are a number of barriers that keep boys and men from reporting a sexual abuse history. Primary is the socialization of boys and men toward stereotypical masculine roles. Society and its institutions train males to be strong and to deny hurt or significant emotional distress. Competition leads to a "go it alone" way of dealing with others and their feelings—a need to feel invulnerable and always in control or the aggressor rather than admitting being the victim or loser. Finally, these strong socialization features lead to shame about admitting being a victim, or even a psychological repression and denial of that position. Literally, boys cannot see themselves as being a victim, especially of sexual abuse. (Bera, 1995, p. 95)

Perhaps it stemmed from other reasons. We shall never know. But it strikes me that Paul Lozano and Julie Roy shared a certain level of disturbance that left them open to exploitation by their more powerful caretakers. Neither Paul nor Julie represents the kind of patient to which Illingworth refers in her model, one who is seeking insight-oriented psychotherapy or psychoanalysis. They were both of the more vulnerable type, more in need of a relationship in which they could invest their trust than a relationship in which they could work together as a partner with the therapist. Given these two examples of what can happen when sex enters the therapeutic relationship, it is clear that Illingworth's model of the autonomous patient and therapist working together as partners and perhaps entering into consensual sex applies only to certain therapists and patients and certain kinds of therapies. In fact, it borders on the ideal. If all patients and therapists behaved as Illingworth suggests they should, no laws would be necessary to proscribe behavior between them.

But one of the functions of the law is to protect people from others, to protect the weak from the strong, the exploited from the exploiter, the victim from the victimizer. In most of the literature on the subject of sexual relations in the therapeutic relationship, the patient is perceived to be the victim. Illingworth's view that the patient is an autonomous adult who can consent freely to this type of behavior seems weakest when she states that the patient can consent to whatever harm may arise from the interaction. I don't think anyone, autonomous or vulnerable, would knowingly consent to the harms that resulted in the Roy and Lozano cases—hospitalizations and suicide—or the harms that are known to have occurred to others. Therefore, the burden of assuming responsibility for the nature of the relationship and any potential sexual misconduct must be assumed by the therapist or other professional. Therapists and other professionals may be personally vulnerable, but they are under a professional duty to refrain from causing harm. This responsibility has belonged to the professional since the time of Hippocrates in the fourth century B.C. In the absence of therapeutic vigilance and/or knowledge of this professional duty and responsibility, I believe that more, not fewer, laws are needed to protect the victims. Professional sexual misconduct is not a misnomer. There is nothing amiss about the "mis" in "misconduct." Professional sexual misconduct is what it purports to be. In the legal system, the more severe the injury, the more severe the legal penalty. Clients in professional sexual misconduct cases are in harm's way. The appropriate remedy is to bring to bear the full weight of the laws, including criminal sanctions, against the malefactor.

References

Baur, S. (1996). A brief history of sexual intimacy in psychotherapy. In K. H. Ragsdale (Ed.), *Boundary Wars: Intimacy and Distance in Healing Relationships* (pp. 1–28). Cleveland, OH: The Pilgrim Press.

Bera, W. H. (1995). Betrayal: Clergy sexual abuse and male survivors. In J. C. Gonsiorek (Ed.), *Breach of Trust: Sexual Exploitation by Health Care Professionals and Clergy* (pp. 91–112). Thousand Oaks, CA: Sage.

Chafetz, G. S., and Chafetz, M. E. (1994). *Obsession: The Bizarre Relationship between a Prominent Harvard Psychiatrist and Her Suicidal Patient.* New York: Crown.

Estrich, S. (1987). *Real Rape.* Cambridge, MA: Harvard University Press.

Fortune, M. M. (1995). Is nothing sacred? When sex invades the pastoral relationship. In J. C. Gonsiorek (Ed.), *Breach of Trust: Sexual Exploitation by Health Care Professionals and Clergy* (pp. 29–41). Thousand Oaks, CA: Sage.

Freeman, L., and Roy, J. (1976) *Betrayal.* New York: Stein and Day.

Friedman, J., and Boumil, M. M. (1995). *Betrayal of Trust: Sex and Power in Professional Relationships.* Westport, CT: Praeger.

Gabbard, G. O., and Pope, K. S. (1989). Sexual intimacies after termination: Clinical, ethical and legal aspects. In G. O. Gabbard (Ed.), *Sexual Exploitation in Professional Relationships* (pp. 115–129). Washington DC: American Psychiatric Press.

Gartrell, N. K., Milliken, N., Goodson W. H., Thiemann,S., and Lo, B. (1995). Physician–patient sexual contact: Prevalence and problems. In J. C. Gonsiorek (Ed.), *Breach of Trust: Sexual Exploitation by Health Care Professionals and Clergy* (pp. 18–29). Thousand Oaks, CA: Sage.

Glasgow, J. B. (1992). Sexual misconduct by psychotherapists: Legal options available to victims and a proposal for change in criminal legislation. *Boston College Law Review, 33,* 645.

Hawkins, G. C., Ivera, M., Barnard, G. W., and Herkev, J. (1994). Patient–therapist sexual involvement: A review of clinical and research data. *Bulletin of American Academy of Psychiatry and the Law, 22* (1): 109–127.

Illingworth, P. M. L. (1995). Patient–therapist sex: Criminalization and its discontents. *Journal of Contemporary Health Law and Policy, 11,* 389–416.

Jorgenson, L., Randles, R., and Strasburger, L. (1991). The furor over psychotherapist–patient sexual contact: New solutions to an old problem. *William and Mary Law Review, 32,* 645–732.

Kane, A. W. (1995). The effects of criminalization of sexual misconduct by therapists: Report of a survey in Wisconsin. In J. C. Gonsiorek (Ed.), *Breach of Trust: Sexual Exploitation by Health Care Professionals and Clergy* (pp. 317–338). Thousand Oaks, CA: Sage.

King, D. (1995, January 15). Law closes psychiatrists' loophole. *Boston Globe,* p. 1.

McNamara, E. (1994). *Breakdown, Sex, Suicide and the Harvard Psychiatrist.* New York: Pocket Books.

Noel, B., and Watterson, K. (1992). *You Must Be Dreaming.* New York: Fawcett Crest.

Pope, K. S. (1989). Teacher–student sexual intimacy. In G. O. Gabbard (Ed.), *Sexual Exploitation in Professional Relationships* (pp. 163–177). Washington, DC: American Psychiatric Press.

———. (1989b). Therapist-patient sex syndrome: A guide for attorneys and subsequent therapists to assessing damages. In G. O. Gabbard (Ed.) *Sexual Exploitation in Professional Relationships* (pp. 39–57). Washington, DC: American Psychiatric Press.

Pope, K. S., and Bouhoutsos, J. C. (1986). *Sexual Intimacy Between Therapists and Patients.* Westport, CT: Praeger.

Roberts-Henry, M. (1995). Criminalization of sexual misconduct in Colorado: An overview and opinion. In J. C. Gonsiorek (Ed.), *Breach of Trust: Sexual Exploitation by Health Care Professionals and Clergy* (pp. 338–348). Thousand Oaks, CA: Sage.

Schoener, G. R. (1995). Historical overview. In J. C. Gonsiorek (Ed.), *Breach of Trust: Sexual Exploitation by Health Care Professionals and Clergy* (pp. 3–18). Thousand Oaks, CA: Sage.

Strasburger, L., Jorgenson, L., and Randles, R. (1991). Criminalization of psychotherapist–patient sex. *American Journal of Psychiatry, I* 48, 859–863.

Twemlow, S. W., and Gabbard, G. O. (1989). The lovesick therapist. In G. O. Gabbard (Ed.), *Sexual Exploitation in Professional Relationships* (pp. 71–89). Washington DC: American Psychiatric Press.

CHAPTER 4

The Media's Influence on Behavior and Violence
Is Society the Victim of the Media?

Judith M. Sgarzi

Introduction

No one can deny the influence that television and the electronic media have had on children in contemporary American society. Many researchers argue that in fact television no longer *reflects* culture, but rather is the central cultural arm of American society. It is an agency that enculturates the viewer to its point of view (Heath and Gilbert, 1996, p. 378).

Newspapers and the print media are no less important in their impact and are also part of the electronic media's web. "In spite of the differences, newspapers show many of the same patterns as television programming. Sex and violence are staples in the newspapers as well" (Heath and Gilbert, 1996, p. 380).

Headlines and news media coverage are presenting stories of more and more violent behaviors, often committed by children of younger and younger ages. Most recently, two boys, ages 7 and 8, were charged with murdering an 11-year-old girl in Chicago. The offenders were reported to be the youngest on record for this type of crime. We were told that the boys killed the young girl so they could have her new bicycle. The crime was similar to one committed by two British youngsters who kidnapped a two-year-old from a shopping mall and stoned him to death with rocks.

Also, a series of recent school killings has left parents and children questioning the safety of the schools, once considered a safe haven for children. Just before the sentencing of two recent child killers, from Jonesboro, Arkansas, one of the boys, 14-year-old Mitchell Johnson, stated, "I didn't mean to do it. I thought we were going to shoot over their heads" (Lieb, 1998, p. A1). The younger boy, Andrew Golden, already an award-winning marksman at age 12, had no apology and nothing to say.

I suggest that a major influence on the growth of violent behavior occurs in the prime of a child's emotional developmental life.

As our children grow and develop attitudes and beliefs about the world and how it works, they are plugged into the electronic media from morning to night. The pictures, images, and sounds they hear are being imprinted practically from birth. If we, as concerned citizens, do not begin to address the presentations of violence, senseless killing, and merged sex and violence in the electronic media, we become at risk for even greater proliferation of such images and the loss of more and younger children to their influence.

This chapter addresses the electronic media's popularization of violent behavior in our society. Treatments of this topic, both in the news and in popular entertainment areas, have often been irresponsible, inaccurate, and highly sensationalized.

Movies, television, evening news programs, and the print media are filled nightly with images of women as victims, as prey, and as targets of stalkings, anger, hatred, or revenge. These depictions are often linked to sex and violence. Society is saturated with such images, which are portrayed as normal behaviors, suggesting to viewers that they may be acceptable. These illustrations of violent behaviors, including stalking, are sensationalized. Violence and sex frequently are merged, obscuring the fact that they are mutually exclusive behaviors that are inappropriately bound together.

Mugford and O'Malley (1991) found that "leisure is increasingly commodified and, therefore, subject to what Simmel (1950) called neurasthenia: that is each new thrill eventually pales, requiring, therefore, bigger and bigger thrills to excite the faded palate" (p. 11).

The point made by Mugford and O'Malley (1991) is that "in American society today, where image management has become a lucrative business and a matter-of-fact necessity in commerce, industry, politics and personal relationships, style has ripened into an intrinsic form of information" (p. 11). Enter the electronic media with its image projections. In countless aspects of life, the powers of appearance have come to overshadow or shape the way we comprehend matters of substance (p. 14). No other force goes beyond the electronic media's reach in sending us those images by which we check to see what reality is.

In the visions from the electronic media, there are "two key aspects—the monopolization of physical violence, and lengthening of the chains of socialization of and dependence" (Elias, 1982, p. 31, cited in Mugford and O'Malley, 1991, p. 10).

We plug into our mass media to find out who we are and what we are to do. We don't think, and we use images of violence to enliven the alienation we feel within ourselves. We tune in and turn on to the media, to be at peace again with its images, to stimulate our emotional responses, to tell us we can feel, we are alive, and, in some cases, we aren't that bad.

There is a conflict between those who defend the media and those who suggest the media create violence in our society. Some media defenders argue that the media either have no effect or in fact have a cathartic effect, allowing viewers an outlet for their aggression. The evidence in support of this idea is that most people don't commit violent crime after viewing thousands of media images depicting these crimes (Bender and Leone, 1988). When these proponents of the media do admit to even a slight chance of media effect, they blame the public for overwatching (Bender and Leone, 1988). Their position is, if people get in trouble with the media, it is because they watch too much television and too many movies. We, in essence, make victims of ourselves.

The contrasting view, held by many political scientists, educators, and criminologists and much of the general public, is that the media do have influence and, in fact, provide our cultural training ground. We learn from the media what our role expectations are in society. Often these role messages are confusing, inaccurate, and distorted. Often they are not counterbalanced with an opposing point of view.

Edgework—the abandonment of calculative rationality in the pursuit of excitement—is the new philosophy of our electronic media productions (Mugford and O'Malley, 1991). Further, edgework is believed to be the seduction at work in the electronic media that causes many to pursue the edgework of excitement through images of violence, sexuality, and gore.

Those who doubt the force with which the electronic media have not only enculturated our society, but become it, need only go to Capitol Hill, where movie stars now represent the mainstream American and are called on with their celebrity expertise to give testimony on everything from the environment and AIDS to abortion rights.

Frequently, when celebrities come out on issues, not only do they get extensive press coverage but their statements receive unmerited attention and respect from members of Congress and others. Often, far more respect is given to celebrities than to educators, parents, and scientists. We need to ask some very poignant questions when our causes are led by celebrity champions. Do these champions truly represent our values and our lifestyles, or are the electronic media promoting their own versions of culture at our expense, thus victimizing their captive audience?

Attitudes That Pervade Our Culture

If a girl is seductively dressed, she has lost the right to say no. If a girl says no, she really means yes. Where do people get these attitudes from? Images promoted by the media give women double messages: Be sexy, be alluring, be free—and don't complain if people think you're asking for it. Often female victims accept the blame for their own victimization, making statements such as "I shouldn't have been there," or "I shouldn't have worn this outfit," or "I shouldn't have expected him not to want more than a kiss." Generations of women are told that they should act like sexual objects, play like sexual objects, but if someone crosses the line, it's the woman's behavior that caused the action (Jhally, 1990). The electronic media, particularly video and film, foster this point of view.

The cultural messages do not reflect mainstream values—they aren't even close! What they reflect are the messages presented by soap opera television and the electronic media (particularly MTV). Children today are not shielded from knowledge of anything. They see group sex, masturbation, issues of abortion, sadomasochism, and fetishism at younger and younger ages. A recent documentary film on modern cult behaviors, specific to satanism, states that almost all elementary school children know, for example, that the sign of the devil is 666 (Passport Magazine Productions, 1988). Where do these images come from? Many children state that they see them on television, or in videos or movies.

Research by McCormack (1987) on the presentation of machismo in the media suggests there are two lines of study. One condones pornography as an innocent pleasure without serious social consequences, and the other condemns media violence as leading to senseless brutal acts; however, they are unified when the variable machismo is addressed. Machismo refers to an attitude of male pride and sexual virility, a form of narcissism that condones sexual use and abuse of women and, in the extreme, views violence as a dimension of sexual gratification or instrument of sexual goals.

Cultural Messages: What Are We Learning?

The cultivation hypothesis (Gerbner and Gross, 1976) provides the backdrop for much of the work on television's effect on fear of crime. Gerbner and Gross suggest that "television is the central cultural arm of American society. It is an agency of the established order and as such serves primarily to extend and maintain rather than to alter, threaten, or weaken conventional conceptions, beliefs, and behaviors . . . Its function is, in a word, enculturation" (p. 175). In regard to fear of crime, Gerbner and Gross suggest that the fear and heightened perceived risk that television may enculture leads to "increased acquiesence to and dependence upon established authority" (p.194). (Heath and Gilbert, 1996, p. 1)

Leonard Eron of the University of Illinois followed 800 children who were in third grade in 1960 until they were 30 years old. He found that the amount of television violence that the children watched at age 8 was the best indicator of their behavior at age 19 (Faivelson, 1987, p. 24).

Movies no longer fade to black to give us a sense of time or points at which we can reflect and consider what we have seen. Rather, "movies are marketed to aim directly to the lowest levels of the mass media, [that is] your brain seeking a reaction that is not only positive, but unconscious and immediate" (Miller, 1990, p. 50). When our primary emotions and drives are focused, we will pay attention.

Video, MTV, and movie presentations focus on our emotions. They use music to override their visual effect. If we listen closely and watch MTV often, we realize the music does *not* fit the action or visual presentation. "Movies more and more supply us with images that are paradoxically non-visual, because the music tries to force us to shut our eyes, stun our minds and jolt our visceral gut level reactors" (Miller, 1990, p. 50). Special effects are routinely used to portray the annihilation of a person—and it is seen as good! "The wipe-out might be violent, as at the end of *Raiders of the Lost Ark* when Nazis are melted down or shriveled up by the wrathful ark as light, or as in the horror movies where, say, Jason burns, zaps and mangles several teens, until some teen burns or zaps or mangles Jason" (p. 50). We become emotional hostages to the electronic media's devices, and therefore their victims. Often it is difficult to find the line between hero and villain. The movie *Batman*, for example, leaves many wondering about Batman and his motivation and use of violence. In *Terminator*, the title character's name alone tells us what his mission in life is. In the film *Cobra*, it is difficult to tell the difference between the hero and the psychopaths he chases (Miller, 1990). *Silence of the Lambs* depicts the psychopath as the hero. The last line of the film is a comic statement about Hannibal Lecter's having a friend over for dinner. (We all realize this means eating the friend for dinner, but the audience is brought to laughter, rather than horror.) (Medved, 1992, p. 163)

What Are We Learning from the Media?

In a recent article in *Time* titled, "Kids Who Kill," we see that time and time again children state that they don't have any idea at all why they shot their best friend. They respond, "[I] just did." Researchers are finding that conscience doesn't matter. If it does come forth, it will do so after—not before—a kind of "aw, shucks" attitude (Witkin et al., 1991, p. 31).

As many researchers have noted, modeling is a major concern. What gets modeled? What gets internalized? And who's helping children make the distinction between approved and unapproved aggression? The film *The Burning Bed*, which depicts the reality of family violence and the difficulty of escaping a former partner's wrath, even when the marriage is dissolved, shows what may be learned is that the act of murder is the only, final solution. Killing a love partner seems often like the most reasonable solution to a bad relationship.

Researchers have suggested that the effect of pleasant arousal followed by violence desensitizes viewers toward violence. It not only makes violence more acceptable and exciting, but also, one could argue, more pleasing (Donnerstein et al., 1987, cited by Wilson, 1991).

When images merge sexuality with violence, we must ask what the long-term desensitizing effects might be. Do sexuality and violence merge in the minds of those who are presented a constant barrage of these images? Images of violence and sexuality become blurred as one scene flows into another. Victims may start out saying no, but end up in sexual scenes that appear more like rape than like mutual consent between two loving partners.

A good example of the merging of violence and sex is the opening scene of the movie *Basic Instinct.* In it the victim is tied to the bed post in what is first presented as consenting sexual play between two partners. Suddenly, sex turns to violence when the male victim, who is tied, is stabbed to death while in the process of climaxing with his female partner. What messages are sent from such depictions of the merging of sex and violence? Are we to view this as the ultimate sexual climax?

In his ground-breaking book *Lovemaps,* Money (1986) presents case studies demonstrating that violent sexual movies provided some of our most serious violent offenders with the specific erotic fantasies they needed to develop their particular sadistic violent profile and later used on their victims.

Frasier (1974) notes that violence is the perfect grist for entertainment. He says the functions of violence are numerous. "Violence as a release, as self-affirmation, or self-defense or self-discovery or self-destruction; violence as a flight from reality, violence as the truest sanity in a particular situation, and so on" (p. 9). Violence is the edgework philosophy of living on the edge, from thrill to thrill (Lyng, 1990).

The Willing Victim (She Likes It)

What about the victims in the electronic media? How are they portrayed?

Wilson (1991) states that the media tell us "we have an appetite for violence. We need it, crave it, thirst for it, and have built a high tolerance for mayhem and viciousness, as long as the players follow the rules" (p. 145).

Many authors have written about the media's portrayals of the willing victim. This is one of the most compelling and disturbing types of violence. A scene may start out as a rape or other act of sexual violence and then suddenly show us that the female victim has had a change of heart. This tells viewers, "Don't worry if she first resists and says no, just be forceful and eventually she'll want it, like they all do" (Wilson, 1991, p. 136). In his film *Dreamworlds,* which examines MTV images of women, Jhally clearly shows that women are depicted as wanting sex, pining for sex, needing sex, and, when they say no, really meaning yes.

After repeated exposure to proliferating scenes of graphic sex and violence in the media, some viewers gradually come to think of sex and violence as belonging together. To clearly and emphatically understand and digest media presentations, we need to distinguish between extremist and mainstream behavior. Many seem to have lost the ability to draw the line between acceptable and unacceptable behaviors.

If society accepts the extremes of media presentations as the norm, these presentations gradually become part of the collective consciousness, where they are difficult to erase. Eventually, extreme violence is viewed as the norm, rather than the exception.

Cultural Norms: Violence Run Amok

How far has the media gone? In 1991, public television station KQED petitioned the court for permission to televise public executions, arguing that this was covered as a First Amendment right and part of the people's "right to know." The petition was denied by the California Supreme Court (Angelo and Hollis, 1991). One can only imagine young children and teens videotaping these executions for later replay.

In *Television vs. America,* Medved (1992) reminds us that "the Academy of Motion Picture Arts and Sciences has given every one of its most prestigious awards to *Silence of the Lambs*" (p. 164). One of the best examples of how far the media will go to present the gore that it says the audience craves is shown in *Silence of the Lambs.* In the film, the audience is brought to an autopsy and presented with the dead victim's bloated, naked body, a green and black and blue corpse with its skin peeled away in various places by an unknown assailant. Viewers not only attend the autopsy, but also participate in the slow, methodical autopsy procedure itself. We need to question the need for this procedure to be part of our general media entertainment menu.

Medved (1992) further states, "This penchant for praising the most startling and disturbing forms of entertainment now pervades the entire entertainment industry. It is increasingly obvious that the tendency involved is more than acceptance of ugliness as one aspect of our reality; it amounts to its glorification as the highest aesthetic ideal" (p. 163). As researchers, educators, doctors, and practitioners we need to examine why our society appears to need to view these types of events as the norm, not the extreme.

Critic Stephen Farber's denouncement of *Silence of the Lambs* was forgotten amid the awards and accolades the film received. So numerous were the awards that it was impossible to view the film as the perverted and twisted slice of life that it portrayed. Medved (1992) asserts that the kudos this film received were not in spite of its ugliness and gore, but because of it (pp. 162, 243).

Medved (1992) states that the compulsion to shock audiences has reached its zenith in the past five years and outlines numerous plots in recent movies that feature cannibalism as a prominent part of the story line. Examples of this new craze in filmdom appear in many recent releases, including *Cape Fear, Fried Green Tomatoes, The Cook, The Thief, His Wife and Her Lover, Out Cold, Auntie Lee's Meat Pies, Lucky Stiff, Consuming Passions, Society, Eat the Rich, The People Under the Stairs,* and *Alive,* to name just a few. Filmmakers seem to feel a need to offend in this manner (Medved, p. 245).

"Some film makers," Medved (1992) reports, "are now using a combination of incest and cannibalism to attract viewers. We are exposed to this new slant in the films, 'Voyager' and 'Sleepwalkers.' The glorification of ugliness appears to know no bounds" (p. 251).

Farber, the former film critic for *California Magazine,* states that "it has become chic to praise a movie for being nihilistic, macabre, unsentimental," and that the greatest movies were the cold-blooded dissection of human venality and depravity (Medved, 1992, p. 162).

Psychologists view cannibalism as the ultimate rage, and the mass media want us to give the idea credibility in our culture. In response to charges that it promotes violence through constant portrayal, the movie industry speaks with a forked tongue, saying,

1. "No one is seriously damaged by the fleeting images or subtle themes in a movie," and
2. Their "product is more disturbing, violent, and sexually explicit than ever before because they are responding in an honest and artistic way to powerful trends in our society" (Medved, 1992, p. 358).

Could it be true that cannibalism is rampant in the United States? Where are these people, and why haven't we been informed about this pervasive societal problem?

Medved (1992) also reports that in the scientific literature there is mounting evidence of a connection between a violent media and aggressive or antisocial behavior. Among studies completed are "The Surgeon General of the United States Report" and a five-year study by the American Psychological Association that provide conclusive evidence of a correlation between viewing televised violence and having aggressive attitudes, values, and behavior patterns, particularly in children (Medved, 1992, p. 365).

Jennings Bryant of the University of Alabama warns of the "stalagmite effects," whereby "cognitive deposits build up almost imperceptibly from the drip-drip-drip of television's electronic limewater." He warns that the cumulative effects of exposure are potent, and particularly so in adolescents (Medved, 1992, p. 365).

Other researchers warn that violent messages are targeted to the very young and are prominently featured in children's programming. Children, however, are not the only ones who are affected by the violent viewing. Radecchi asserts that adults who watch TV are more likely to purchase handguns and support military solutions to world problems, as well as overestimate the amount of real violence in the world (Medved, 1992).

The influence of the electronic media is inescapable. Because the media permeate the fabric of our society, we are all vulnerable to the message. We cannot bury our heads in the sand, because the evidence comes at us from all directions in the form of the behavior of those with whom we must interact in our everyday lives. A 1989 article in *Time* notes that kids are fed a steady diet of glorified violence and that "television cartoons feature dehumanized, machine-like characters such as 'Transformers' and 'Gobots' engaged in destructive acts. But viewers see no consequences, as victims never bleed and never suffer. By 16 years of age the typical child has seen an estimated 200,000 acts of violence, including 33,000 murders" (Toufexis, 1989, p. 168).

From rock music lyrics (by groups such as Guns N' Roses) to comic books to slasher films—with their graphic erotic scenes of female mutilation, rape, or murder—children are repeatedly given the message that this is what behavior is all about. This is what they are supposed to do. Toufexis (1989) states, "They simply become conformists, not deviants" (p. 168). This is the cultural message children learn.

The Serial Killer Phenomenon: The Media's Sensationalization of Serial Killers

Media images of violence have crossed into the ultra-extremes, and these images have become the training films of our culture. In effect, the electronic media now present the how-tos of the most violent acting-out behaviors as a smorgasbord from which we can pick and choose and adopt our personal favorites.

Many authors, including Wilson, Jenkins, Leyton, Fox, and MacDonald, have written on the increasing popularity of the multiple murderer. The news media have made serial killers one of the most popular topics for crime reporting. We are riveted to news coverage of the mass killer and serial killer. Many of our most popular cinema and TV films now represent serial killers as folk heroes. HBO even does documentary films such as *Murder: No Apparent Motive*, which rivets viewers in their chairs in fear. This film, one could argue, could also be a how-to for serial killers.

Wilson (1991) maintains that it is not uncommon for one sensational killing to get six months of cliff-hanging media reporting, with the prospects of updates. The presentation of true crime by the media is very important. "The challenge," Wilson tells us, "lies in orchestrating the presentation of the case with exclusive interviews, story revelations, to outclass the competition (other media vying for the same viewer's attention)" (p. 186).

Because we all get news and information from the electronic media and most of our crime coverage comes on the nightly local channel, Wilson (1991) and others have suggested that the mass media grant disproportionate amounts of time and space to murders. We tune in nightly to get a sense of where we are in the world and how our immediate neighbors are doing. White (1988) says, "We want to know it's happening someplace else, so we can feel safer" (p. 106).

On January 27, 1994, a full-page advertisement appeared in the *Washington Post* urging the entertainment industry to take voluntary steps to reign in television violence before Congress does it for them. At that time polls showed that violence was our nation's number one concern, even before the economy. In 1998, violence was holding at the number two position. Violence is now a public health issue. Janet Reno, attorney general in the Clinton administration, warned the media industry to change or be prepared for some type of legislation to force change.

A 1992 study by *TV Guide* concluded that "violence is a pervasive major feature of contemporary television programming and is coming from more sources and in greater volume than ever before" (Hickey, 1992, pp. 10–12). A major longitudinal study done by ERON concluded that television violence affects youngsters of all ages, of both genders, at all socio-economic levels, and at all levels of intelligence (cited by Hickey, 1992, p. 11).

Cultural Lessons

What are we learning? What are some of the victim outcomes?

The media often play directly to the stereotypical abuser by showing images of men with total control over their victims or with the need for total control. Any sign of independence by the victim is seen as unbearable rejection. Men are portrayed in the media as dominating women in whatever way works best. Herman's (1989) profile of a stalker suggests that stalkers and abusers use the following types of behaviors: dominance by isolation, enforced dependency, jealous surveillance, threats, verbal abuse, meticulous enforcement of petty rules, and even physical exhaustion (pp. 4–6).

In his 1990 film, *Dreamworlds*, Jhally states that all of these behaviors are part of the depictions of women, by both male and female video stars, on MTV. These presentations of violence and sexuality are viewed through subtle images, catering particularly to adolescent male viewers as a way of capturing their adolescent sexual fantasies and excitement. The media images show penetrating messages that excite the viewer and the audience. Male sexuality is visual, and this information is not lost on advertisers, who market to a generation of children who by and large are their principal viewing audience.

Articles abound on erotomania and the stalking of media personalities. Referring to a syndrome that has also been named "pathological love," Persaud (1990) describes erotomaniacs as people who bring their disturbed view of pathological love into the open, often by stalking their victims and living in their own world of fantasy (p. 148). Cosgrove (1990) states that star-stalking—obsessively pursuing the rich and famous—"is one of the more sinister by-products of the media age" (p. 31).

The definition of stalking behaviors varies. According to California state law, "a stalker is anyone who willfully, meticulously and repeatedly follows or harasses another person, who makes a credible threat with the intent to place that person in reasonable fear of death or great bodily injury" (Kolarik, 1991, p. 35).

The literature shows that erotomania, or pathological love, is more often perpetrated by males than by females. Persaud (1990) suggests that this may relate to gender differences in violent behaviors in general and that it is not surprising that men may be more predisposed to stalking, because they are more prone to aggression and acting upon their aggression in violent ways.

Considering that nearly 90% of all women murdered were initially stalked by their perpetrators, one needs little more evidence of the growing problem of stalking behavior. Stalkers live in a fantasy world that they cannot distinguish from reality. This is not unlike the world presented to them by the mass media, which often blurs the line between reality and fantasy.

The profile of the stalker is complex; in fact we are told that no single profile exists:

> Typically the stalkers are young men between the ages of 20 and 34. They are generally unable to form relationships and resort to fantasized intimacy as a means of legitimizing themselves. Stalkers also have an intense interest in the media, they have demonstrated a history of unsuccessful efforts to establish their identity, and they have a strong desire for attention and recognition. Most stalkers do not harbor any animosity towards their victims until they perceive that their unrequited love has been spurned. At this point stalkers turn violent. (National Rifle Association, 1992, p. 96)

The acceptance of violence as normal behavior needs to be challenged. By producing prolific images that suggest stalking is an option for troubled relationships and a way of dealing with issues of control, the media further legitimize this behavior. Galtung (1990) suggests that cultural violence is defined as "aspects of culture which are the symbolic spheres of our existence" (p. 292). We see these symbolic aspects in religion, ideology, language, art, empirical science, and formal science, and often these symbols are used to legitimize direct or structural violence. Galtung states, "We make violence look right and feel right" (p. 292). We legitimize it, therefore normalizing it. Because we cloud violence, we often are not clear who the bad guy is and who the good guy is.

If our cultural lessons continue to be viewed through the distorted lens of an electronic media that presents us with an overabundance of violent images that constantly reinforce deep-seated attitudes of male dominance and power over others (women in particular), then our society will continue to allow stalking and other violent behaviors to increase. As researchers have suggested, we must clear our vision and remove the opaque lens through which we view society's images (Galtung, 1990, p. 294).

Conclusions and Implications

Some analysts suggest that the question is no longer, What's wrong with our public schools? or Which television shows are okay? but rather, What has happened to the entire social, moral, and developmental fabric of our children's lives? The electronic media, especially television, has introduced radical changes in our lives. The current generation of children needs help now, and the electronic media's influence must be debated at every level within our communities.

We need to understand how complex the issue of violence has become and that it is now interwoven in the fabric of our lives. In one of the most prestigious journals published by the American Medical Association, in a June 1992 special edition, one will find 69 articles relating to violence in our society. Can this leave any doubt as to the seriousness of this problem?

The *Journal of the American Medical Association* has not forgotten about the media's impact on violence. In an article in their special communication section titled, "Television and Violence: The Scale of the Problem. Where to Go from Here," Centerwall (1992) states, "The effect of television violence on children and youth first alerted the medical community to the deforming effects the viewing of television violence has on normal child development. Neonates are born with the instinctive capacity and desire to imitate; they *do not have* an instinct for knowing whether a behavior should be imitated. They will imitate anything, including a behavior that is destructive and anti-social" (p. 3059).

Studies show that infants as young as 14 months old demonstrate the ability to observe and incorporate behaviors seen on television (Centerwall, 1992). By 1990, the average American child age 2–5 was watching over 27 hours of television per week, a number that continues to grow. Serious violence is most likely to erupt at moments of severe stress, and it is precisely at such moments that adolescents and adults tend to revert to their earliest, most visceral sense of what violence is. The learning occurs early in a child's development.

Centerwall (1992) concluded that exposure to television is also a major causal factor behind a large proportion, perhaps even one half, of rapes, assaults, and other forms of interpersonal violence in the United States.

Kochanska (1993) summarizes the orgins of moral development from this point of view:

> The foundations of the moral self derive from repeated early interactions with consistently available—not threatening, as suggested by early psychoanalysis—caregivers. During the continual early affective exchanges, a young child develops a sense of connectedness and the ability to read others' emotions and to react with distress, empathy and a prosocial activity to others' distress . . . Development of a moral conscience is also central to moral development. (p. 325)

Children, however, are bombarded with confusing messages along with images of immoral behaviors that don't result in any punishment or negative effects for the perpetrators. Faced with such ambiguity, children are not able without the assistance of a parent or other adult to understand right from wrong.

Children learn their morality from parents, and the emotional signals that parents give off function as inhibitors of forbidden acts (Kochanska, 1993, p. 325). When true emotion and meaning are stripped away from the contexts of violence and sexuality, as they are in the mass media images that our children are continually bombarded with, children cannot internalize moral judgments of right or wrong, or develop a moral conscience. Therefore everything looks okay to them. The entertainment industry would like us to believe that what they present is in some way neutral and therefore okay for even children to see.

Travers et al. (1993) suggest that to assist children in becoming moral citizens, education is needed that imparts

- A sense of self-respect that emerges from positive behavior toward others;
- Skill in social perspective-taking, that is, asking how others think and feel;
- Moral reasoning about the right thing to do;
- Moral values such as kindness, courtesy, trustworthiness, and responsibility;
- The social skills and habits of cooperation;
- An openness to the suggestions of adults (p. 113).

From this list one can easily see that all mass media viewers, and children in particular, are not often presented situations that give quality examples in which viewers can learn and experience examples of moral dilemmas from which clear understanding of right and wrong can be discerned.

Consequently we have a generation of children raised on credos like "Do your own thing," "If it feels good, do it," and so on.

In his article "Kids Are Killing, Dying, Bleeding," Henkoff (1992) states that juvenile arrests for aggravated assault and forcible rape are rising dramatically. Further, he states that kids are killing each other with no remorse at all. Can we wonder why they haven't learned remorse, when the electronic media flood us with messages that consistently tell us that violence is the way to solve our problems?

In the movies and on television, many characters either carry a weapon or become a victim, and no one should lose a fight! It is also clear that revenge is always the appropriate way to even the score with an opponent. Children state they need a weapon in order to protect themselves. Consider the following statistics gathered by Feder (1990) about kids and television viewing:

- By the time a child reaches college age, she or he will have viewed 200,000 commercials and 100,000 hours of violent programming.

- A typical 16-year-old has seen 250,000 violent acts, including 33,000 dramatized murders and tens of thousands of simulated rapes, assaults, and shootings.
- Much of the violence viewed is glorified and perpetuated by heroes, in what are presented as just causes.
- The subliminal message is that violence is heroic; guns, knives, and fists are appropriate problem-solving tools.
- The American Family Association found that 77% of all allusions to sex on network television were about sex that was outside of marriage.

In addition to watching television, 85% of U.S. teens listen to at least two hours of rock music each day, and perhaps many listen to a great deal more (Briggs, 1988). This means that during her or his teenage years every child will hear 75,000 songs with lyrics like

Slide down to my knees, taste my sword. (Motley Crue, "Tonight We Need a Lover")

Cause when I go through her, it's just like a hot knife through butter. (KISS in their song, "Fits like a Glove")

My sister never made love to anyone else but me; incest is everything it is said to be. (Prince, in his solid gold hit, "Sister")

Songs about sex, incest, murder, devil worship, necrophilia, sadomasochism, cannibalism, and torture leave nothing to the imagination, and each group seems to try to outdo the others in its assault on society's basic values of right and wrong.

Many children spend more time with the electronic media than they do with their parents. It is from the media that they learn about family life and family values and what our society is all about. One might even argue that many kids' primary relationship is with the television, which is introduced from the very earliest moments of their childhoods as the background display of culture.

Television and the electronic media have been likened to narcotics pushed by the cultural elite—the Hollywood–New York crowd of writers, artists, producers, and stars whose sense of values may not reflect what we want our children to view (Plangens, 1991).

In fact, this upper echelon of media moguls, we are told, numbers about 100 people. These 100 or so individuals make our viewing decisions for us, and they will continue to do so as long as we mindlessly accept the fare they produce. These "technocrats . . . tend to mistrust the judgment of ordinary people, and . . . there is a growing commitment to what some observers call 'lifestyle liberalism.' At the core of this view is personal autonomy and self-creation" (Woodward, 1992, p. 55).

We are in a culture war. "There are whole libraries of scholarly books and essays attesting to the fact that a culture war is going on in American society. Education, the arts, religion, law, politics, and the entertainment media are its most visible battleground" (Woodward, 1992, p. 55). We need to be more aggressive and speak out about what is good TV, especially for kids. To change the media, we need to become part of the process, not the victimized viewers of the process.

IMPLICATIONS

How can we change our status as victims? Oskamp suggests that we need to ask some hard questions:

1. Can the electronic media change?
2. Can the electronic media present prosocial values? What does this term mean? Who will it define?
3. Or must the change come from viewers' uses and reactions to the electronic media presentations?

Is it possible to make the media responsible? Centerwall (1992) asks rhetorically, "Is it true that the television industry operates under a higher standard of morality?" Apparently not. "Even before the National Commission on the Causes and Prevention of Violence published its recommendations for the television industry, the four major networks stated that . . . there would be no substantive changes in programming content" (p. 3061).

The American Academy of Pediatrics recommends that pediatricians advise parents to limit their children's television viewing to one to two hours per day. Centerwall (1992) suggests that children's exposure to television and television violence be made part of the public health agenda, along with safety seats, bicycle helmets, immunizations, and good nutrition. New program labeling for parents is a good start, but is still confusing to many.

Koop and Lundberg (1992) state: "We believe violence in America to be a public health emergency, largely unresponsive to methods thus far used in its control" (p. 3076). They suggest a three-pronged approach that persons in authority can adopt:

1. Support additional research on the causes, prevention, and cure of violence.
2. Stimulate the education of all Americans about what is known and what can now be done to address this emergency.
3. Demand legislation intended to reverse the upward trend of firearm injuries and deaths—the most serious and out-of-control result of violence (p. 3076).

There is no one formula for solving the problem of violence and its portrayals in our society—only multifaceted approaches will serve. Violence, society, and social problems are all ultimately intertwined.

Articles in *Fortune* (1992) and *TV Guide* (1992) suggest some ways that we as a society can deal with the violence problem:

1. Help parents to be parents.
2. Teach children how to manage anger.
3. Keep guns away from kids.
4. Watch TV with our children.
5. Discuss violence with our children.
6. Explain that violence is faked for entertainment and is not real.
7. Encourage children to watch programs with characters who cooperate with, help, and care for each other.
8. Make television part of the public health agenda (like smoking and drunk driving) and publicize this through vigorous public information campaigns.
9. Establish courses in critical-viewing skills as a regular aspect of high school curricula.
10. Support the resolution of the American Psychological Association urging broadcasters and cable industries to "take a responsible attitude in reducing direct imitable violence in live action children's shows and violent incidents in cartoons" (Henkoff, 1992; Hickey, 1992, p. 23).

There are many other suggestions stated by the authors and publishers of the research, but we need to be mindful that violence against children undermines the very foundation of our culture. Beyond controlling guns, we need to reassert the principles of parental and community responsibility (Henkoff, 1992). Television may be the most important catalyst to moving our society to a common sense of values—it is in most homes, and is on several hours a day. The electronic media need to be responsible about the depiction of violence and the reality of its outcomes. Films, television, and other media rarely show the real outcomes of violence. After a violent act, we seldom see people in pain, recovering from injuries or coping with permanent disabilities. It may be because real pain and loss are not salable commodities, unlike the sanitized violence and sex offered by the entertainment industry. In this mainstream view of sex and violence, anything goes—with no bad outcomes or messy consequences for even the most reckless behavior. The message is: Just do it!

MONEY TALKS

The electronic media are fed by money, pure and simple. Advertisers can pay up to $1 million for spot commercials with large audiences. We all need to choose our products wisely, because money talks for us through the electronic media.

As parents, when we see television shows with content that is not appropriate for young viewers, we need to become responsible and write to the CEOs of these companies to complain and boycott their advertisers' products. Major sponsors often market their products with references to teens who cheat in school, drink, curse, and smoke; anti-Semitic and racial stereotypes; sexualized images of children; and so on. The violence problem pervades our culture. It is not possible to remove ourselves from the influence of the electronic media; hence, we need to become part of the solution to the problem. The media need to be held accountable for their effect on society.

As criminal justice students and professionals committed to our own fields of expertise, we need to continue our vigilance, particularly as it relates to influences in society that are assaulting us daily. We must challenge the mass media moguls and pressure policymakers to place the burden of responsible behavior squarely in their hands.

Violence is a number one concern—a priority for future generations—our children. There are no clear-cut answers. Our society must link together to face this critical dilemma. We cannot ignore this problem in the hope that it will go away on its own, through the magic of television or any other media presentation.

Accountability for everyone and action against the problem are necessary if we are to turn back the tide of violence lapping at our doors. Every citizen has an obligation to help create a society in which people are not threatened by an entertainment culture that accepts violence as a way of life.

FURTHER RESEARCH

Developmental psychologists have long known the crucial role that a child's social–emotional development plays in his or her conscious development and ability to use reflective moral thought. Spending hours in front of the television interferes with this process. Children may consider television the critical role model in their lives, rather than family and the values it represents.

Further research must be done, and done now. We need to declare war on the media's presentation and packaging of violence to our society. Nothing short of waging our own media blitz will stop this wave from continuing to wash over all of us. Shall we wait to get the definitive answers to causality, or can we assume intellectually that something is being presented to our youth and society at large that can no longer be tolerated?

References

America's best kept secret. A look at modern Satanism. (1988). *Passport Productions Magazine.*

Angelo, B., and Hollis, R. (1991). The ultimate horror show. *Time,* 59.

Bender, D., and Leone, B. (1988). The mass media. In *Opposing Viewpoints.* San Diego, CA: Greenhaven.

Briggs, D. (1988, November/December). Many turned off by message of the new "religion"—TV. *AFA Journal.*

Centerwall, B. S. (1992, June 10). Television and violence. *Journal of the American Medical Association, 267,* 3059–3063.

Cosgrove, S. (1990, July 27). Erotomania (star stalking). *New Statesman and Society, 3,* 31–32.

Faivelson, S. (1987, October 1). Verdict on T.V. violence. *Woman's Day,* 24.

Feder, D. (1990, November/ December). Congress believes capitalism—not smut—corrupts kids. *AFA Journal,* 5.

Frasier, J. (1974). *Violence in the Arts.* London: Cambridge University Press.

Galtung, J. (1990). Cultural violence. *Journal of Peace Research, 27, 3,* 291–305.

Heath, L., and Gilbert, K. (1996, February). Mass media and fear of crime. *Public Opinion on Justice in Criminal Justice System* (special issue), 39(4): 378–386.

Henkoff, R. (1992). Kids are killing, dying, bleeding. *Fortune,* 62–70.

Herman, J. L. (1989, April). Insights. *Harvard Medical School Mental Health Letter, 5,* 4–6.

Hickey, N. (1992, August 22). How much violence? *TV Guide,* 11–23.

Jhally, S. (1990). *Dream Worlds: Desire/sex/power in rock video.* Amherst: University of Massachusetts Foundation for Media Education.

Kochanska, G. (1993). Toward a synthesis of parental socialization and child temperament in early development of conscience. *Child Development, 64,* 325–347.

Kolarik, G. (1991, November). Stalking laws proliferate. *ABA Journal,* 35–36.

Koop, E. C., and Lundberg, G. D. (1992). Violence in America: A public health emergency. *Journal of the American Medical Association,* 3075–3076.

Lieb, D. A. (1998, August 12). 2 Arkansas schoolboy killers are sentenced. *Boston Globe,* p. A1.

Lyng, S. (1990, January). Edgework: A social psychological analysis of voluntary risk taking. *American Journal of Sociology, 95.*

McCormack, T. (1987). Machismo in media research: A cultural review of research on violence and pornography. *Mass Communication Review Yearbook.* Newbury Park, CA: Sage.

Medved, M. (1992). *Hollywood vs. America: Popular Culture and the War on Traditional Values.* New York: HarperCollins.

Miller, M. C. (1990, April). Hollywood the Ad. *Atlantic Monthly,* 41–54.

Money, J. (1986). *Lovemaps: Clinical Concepts of Sexual/Erotic Health and Pathology and Gender Transposition in Childhood, Adolescence and Maturity.* New York: Irving.

Mugford, S., and O'Malley, P. (1991, November). Crime, excitement and modernity. *American Society of Criminology.*

National Rifle Association. (1992). *Crime Strike Report.* Fairfax, VA: National Rifle Association.

Persaud, R. D. (1990, March). Erotomania (pathological love). *Contemporary Review,* 256(148): 5.

Plangens, P. et al. (1991, April 1). *Newsweek,* 46–52.

Toufexis, A. (1989, June 12). Our violent kids. *Time,* 52–55.

Travers, J. F., Elliot, S. N., and Kratochurll, T. R. (1993). *Educational Psychology: Effective Teaching, Effective Learning.* Madison, WI: Brown and Benchmark.

White, J. (1988, November/December). Children will mimic the things they see and hear. *American Family Association Journal.*

Wilson, W. (1991). *Good Murders and Bad Murders: A Consumers' Guide in the Age of Information.* New York: University Press of America.

Witkin, G. et al. (1991, April 8). Kids who kill. *US News and World Report,* 26–32.

Woodward, K. L. (1992, July 20). Ideas: The elite and how to avoid it. *Newsweek,* 55.

PART II

VICTIMS OF POLITICAL OR IDENTITY STATUS

CHAPTER 5

Major Problems Facing Victims of Child Abuse

Patricia Smith and Judith M. Sgarzi

Introduction

Children represent the innocence within a society, and the victimization of a child through physical, mental, or sexual abuse is shattering. Andrews found that "society [was] unable to cope psychologically with stories of burning and beating; we assured ourselves that these things don't happen very often, and if they did happen, we told ourselves, obviously the abuser was taken care of in the criminal justice system" (Andrews, 1998, p. 314).

The impact of abuse on the child can be unknown for years or even decades. Children inherently trust, and in cases of abuse involving extremely young children, the victims may be completely unaware that they are victims until they become old enough to recognize within themselves that the behavior they have been experiencing is not appropriate.

In this chapter we discuss the more serious forms of child abuse and their implications, although we are in no way suggesting that maltreatment such as emotional abuse and neglect are any less serious to the developmental outcomes that one can expect as the child grows into adulthood.

Probably one of the most striking cases of child abuse is that of David Rothenberg. David was set afire by his father in 1983.

> One rainy evening in 1983, while six-year-old David Rothenberg slept in a motel room near Disneyland, his father, Charles, doused the room with

kerosene and set it ablaze. David was burnt over 90% of his body. [H]is face terribly disfigured, he became a symbol of child abuse at its most extreme. (A young boy's trial by fire, 1994, p. 170)

Although David's father did not sexually abuse him, this case is a prime example of the types of hideous behaviors that some parents inflict on their children.

The worst offense a parent can inflict on a child, however, is taking away the child's innocence through incest, that is, sexual activities between individuals who are closely related by kinship (Nelson and Meller, 1994). In an incestuous relationship, children may be inadequately protected against abuse of power while being denied healthy sexual development and normal familial affection (Nelson and Meller, 1994). When parents or family members disregard the incest taboo in our society, they damage the child for life.

Children of sexual abuse by a parent or close relative suffer what is called "toxic shame" (Zupancic and Kreidler, 1999). Shame develops during the stage in which Erickson says a child should be working through the critical task of "autonomy versus shame and doubt" (Zupancic et al. 1999). If a child is being sexually abused, Zupanic et al. suggest, the child will not become autonomous but rather will define her- or himself as defective.

> Pathological shame is presented as debilitating and restrictive in the expression of appropriate feelings. Each shaming experience is an assault on a person's sense of self-worth. Toxic shame, which is always an outcome in child abuse whether sexual or emotional, is reinforced by continuous negative interactions with the perpetrators of the abuse. Toxic shame is like a sickness within itself, a sickness of the soul. (Zupancic and Kreidler, 1999, p. 29)

A common thread running through cases involving the sexual abuse of children still too young to be completely aware of their sexuality are the statements that they felt "funny" about being touched, but were unable to formulate that this behavior was in fact bad. In this we see one of the major problems facing the victims of child abuse at a very early stage in their development: their inability to understand that they have been abused.

Because of their inexperience, children may undergo excruciating physical pain and mental abuse or suffer sexual assault and still feel love and attachment to the abuser. Money (1986) states that this is how a child's "love map" gets vandalized, changing the direction of a child's normal sexual development for life.

> A love map is not present at birth. It develops in the first few years of life. A love map is a template in the brain on which every person's under-

standing of sexuality is written. For most, it will be differentiated as heterosexual without complexities; if, however, deprivation, neglect or assault enters into the formation of a love map, pathology will develop. (Money, p. xvi)❜

Children need to be reassured and desire attention and approval from adults. This desire allows them to accept negative or even violent attention from those in authority over them. A victim of child abuse is often unable to discern between positive loving treatment and an environment that is abusive and assaultive, especially if the environment is the only one they know.

Children also face the problem of feeling unable to tell someone of abuse they have suffered at the hand of another. Although children may be taught by their parents from the moment they are able to talk to tell someone if they feel uncomfortable with the treatment they receive from someone else, children may still not feel empowered enough to take that step on their own. They may feel they will not be believed. Even children who are older, pre-teens or teenagers, may think that adults will not believe that they are suffering abuse. In many cases, it takes an initial media blitz on one child sexual-assault case to bring other victims forward.

It is also extremely common for abusers to threaten children with even more punishment if they tell. For example, children may be told that they will be placed in a closet or basement for a long time, denied food and water, if the abuser suspects they have attempted to tell someone about the abuse. Children may be told that their family will be harmed or that they will be disowned by their parents for allowing someone to touch them. Fear can be extremely destructive, and children who do not understand that they can fight back against abuse can be completely at the mercy of the abuser. Control and fear are the two main tools of an abuser, and, if manipulated properly, they can provide an abuser with everything they need to control a child and keep them their victims.

Money (1986) talks about the catch-22 dilemma: ❛Vandalism of the child's love map in the vulnerable developmental years may be synonymous with impairment of positive growth secondary to deprivation and neglect. A child is entrapped—if they disclose the abuse they lose and if they don't tell they lose❜ (p. 18). Children who are not able to tell of their abuse or do not remember it (as often happens) may keep more secrets as they grow, and, as Zupancic and Kriedler (1999) suggest, shame continues to rule their lives, inhibiting their emotional, spiritual, and psychological developmental for years to come, often into adulthood.

Society's apathy also is an imposing problem facing victims of child abuse. There is a tendency to look the other way when something that may border on abuse is noticed. We are hesitant to become involved with the workings of another family. Even individuals who are listed as mandated reporters of suspected child abuse, such as teachers and police officers, may not recognize signs of abuse until they become physically apparent. Even then, if the abuse is occurring in the home, a parent may explain away outward signs of abuse by saing that the child is overly clumsy. All too often, abuse is finally "diagnosed" by the child's pediatrician or an emergency room doctor.

In the case of sexual or psychological abuse, signs may not physically manifest themselves as readily. A child may begin to act out or be violent, or may become introverted and noncommunicative.

Children who are sexually abused may begin to express themselves in sexual terms through excessive masturbation or by inappropriate touching of others.

A final thought regarding problems facing the victims of child abuse is that, according to the U.S. Department of Health and Human Services, "parents continue to be the main perpetuators of child maltreatment. More than 80 percent of all victims were maltreated by one or both parents. The most common pattern of maltreatment (45 percent) was a child victimized by a female parent with no other perpetrators. Victims of physical and sexual abuse, compared to victims of neglect and medical neglect, were more likely to be maltreated by a male parent acting alone" (p. 1). A parent who is abusing his or her child is almost the perfect abuser. They have almost constant contact with the child and may be the only individual able to access medical attention for them. If they live in a large metropolitan area, parents may be able to bring a child to several different health care providers or emergency rooms, avoiding suspicion. Without background evidence or cause to investigate an alternative reason for an injury, it is not uncommon for an emergency room to process children and release them back to the custody of their abusive parent or guardian.

Description of Victims

Recognizing a victim of abuse can be much more difficult than one might assume. When a case of abuse becomes public, it's easy for people to say, "How could anyone let that happen?" In reality, a victim of abuse can be very well known and active in a community and still not be recognized as a victim.

Victims of child abuse run the gamut of socioeconomic backgrounds. Social status and money do not offer a shield from abuse. Children can be victims of assault from a parent, acquaintance, or stranger no matter how well cared for they appear to be. Some might assume that children who come from economically depressed households or households of nontraditional nuclear families (i.e., single-parent families) would be the prime candidates for abuse;

however, children from even the most traditional backgrounds are common victims of abuse.

A child is commonly defined as an individual under the age of 17, and child abuse and neglect affect children of all ages.

> Among children confirmed as victims by child protective services agencies in 1997, more than half were 7 years of age or younger, with about 26 percent younger than 4 years old. About 27 percent of victims were children ages 8 to 12; another 23 percent were youth ages 13 to 18. Case-level data from 16 states suggest that the majority of victims of neglect and medical neglect were younger than 8 years old, while the majority of victims of other types of maltreatment were age 8 or younger. (Administration for Children and Families, 2000, p. 1)

Nor does the sex of a child provide a shield from abuse. Both boys and girls experience child maltreatment. "In 1997, about 52 percent of victims were female and 48 percent were male" (Administration for Children and Families, 2000, p. 1). "A survey of high school adolescents showed that 17 percent of girls were physically abused and 12 percent were sexually abused, while 12 percent of boys were physically abused and five percent were sexually abused" (Commonwealth Fund, 1999, p. 1).

History of Child Abuse

Child sexual abuse is not a new phenomenon. DeMause (1975) notes, "During ancient times boy brothels flourished in Rome and virtually every city in Greece. Greek mythology is filled with incestuous themes. Infants were castrated in their cradles for later use as eunuchs in brothels" (p. 86). Children have been sold for slavery, and in many cultures young girls are bought after their birth by the families of young boys so they can be married when they reach a suitable age. A more recent "discovery" is the castration of baby girls in an attempt to deny them sexual pleasure in adulthood and thus ensure that they would be loyal to their future husbands.

There is also a history of infanticide in some cultures if a newborn is not the desired sex. There are well-known historical accounts of children being sacrificed during religious ceremonies or being subject to horrific assaults for the entertainment of adults. During the industrial revolution, children of all ages were forced to work in extremely dangerous conditions for long hours. Child labor still exists today in many Third World countries. In some societies incest is not viewed as a crime, as it is in the United States, and in fact is expected behavior (Fox, 1980).

Unfortunately, neglect, maltreatment, and abuse of children have been ele-mental in all societies at some point.

Specific Consequences of Child Abuse

The results of child abuse are most notable when discussing physical abuse. There are virtually limitless ways of injuring a child. Their size and strength limitations allow for injuries that would not be commonly found on an adult victim of a physical assault. "It is generally accepted that hands and fists are the most common 'weapons' used during child abuse. If actual weapons or objects are used, they often are common household instruments. The overall size and shape of the injury pattern left on the child's body may indicate the actual object used" (Shepard et al., 1995, p. 8). Most of us remember being scolded by our parents and even being disciplined through some form of corpo-ral punishment; however, the physical assault inflicted in a case of abuse is much more damaging than the stinging and reddening of the skin that can come from a quick slap against the buttocks. A child may suffer deep contusions and lacera-tions from being struck repeatedly by a belt or an electrical cord. A child will also suffer soft tissue injuries from being assaulted with a hard object such as a paddle.

Devastating injuries can result when a child is thrown against an object or picked up and struck against a solid surface. Many people forget that a child, compared to a full-size adult, can weigh relatively little and present little resist-ance to being hurled across a room. A subdural hematoma, the collection of blood in the outer covering of the brain, is a very possible result if a child is assaulted in this manner and there is a strike to the head.

However, there may not be outward signs of physical trauma when a head injury of this kind is inflicted on a child.

More than 50 percent of children with subdural hematomas have no associated skull fracture, bruising, or swelling over the site of the injury. These cases often are caused by the whiplash shaken infant syndrome or, more commonly, the shaken baby syndrome. The shaken baby syndrome was first documented by Dr. John Caffey in 1974 and was described as "the vigorous manual shaking of infants by the extremities or shoulders with whiplash-induced intracranial bleeding, but with no external signs of head trauma." Infants are especially susceptible to this type of injury during the first 24 months of life because of these developmental charac-teristics: a soft flexible skull due to open sutures; a soft pliable brain, allowing excessive stretching of the brain and blood vessels; [and] a larger, heavier head with weaker neck muscles. The two-phase cycle of acceleration and deceleration causes a flexing of the head during which the chin strikes the chest, followed by the extension of the head back into the spine. Case history and research support the fact that infants usually are subjected to numerous shaking episodes prior to the discovery of an injury. The shaking could take place over a period of days, weeks or even months. (Shepard et al., 1995, p. 26)

Infants are not the only potential victims of shaken baby syndrome. A much older child can also be injured severely by violent shaking, and if the child does not weigh more than 50 pounds it may be easy for an adult to inflict severe physical harm, even with the reality that a great deal of force must be applied.

In addition to blunt force trauma and trauma caused by shaking, there are other obvious forms of physical abuse. Children may have their leg or arm twisted until a break occurs, or they may suffer dislocations if their joints are violently twisted or pulled. They may also be burned—commonly by having a burning cigarette placed against their skin. Another form of burning is immersing a child or a body part in scalding water long enough to produce third-degree burns and, in the most gruesome cases, permanent removal of skin down to muscle or bone. Objects such as curling irons or hot vehicle exhaust pipes may also be used to burn a child.

The obvious results of such physical abuse range from scars to internal injuries to organs and bones that produce lifelong disabilities. In the most devastating cases, in which a child survives abuse involving some form of head trauma, she or he may be permanently brain damaged and require constant long-term care.

The effects of sexual abuse of a child are not always as obvious as those left by physical maltreatment. A child may show emotional withdrawal or separation from family and friends. As mentioned earlier, the child may begin to express knowledge of sex and sexual language and activities that are not age appropriate for the child. The child could also begin to act out and look for additional attention or affection. Actual visible signs of sexual abuse are most likely to be evident on a child's genitalia. Sexually transmitted diseases can produce physical signs of sexual abuse and, unfortunately, if left unrecognized and treated, could cause later sexual dysfunction or even sterility.

In truth, the effects of sexual abuse or exploitation may not be felt for years after the initial assaults. The psychological effects can be far-reaching, manifesting later as sexual difficulties when relating to a partner, sexual exploitation of oneself in an effort to feel emotional gratification, or even the transference of sexual desire onto a child. In this way, children sexually assaulted by an adult can themselves become abusers of children later in life. A child may also suffer emotionally through the realization that she or he has been betrayed by the adult who forced the sexual contact.

Christopher Reardon, a 27-year-old youth worker from Middleton, Massachusetts, was indicted in 2000 on more than 100 criminal counts of child sexual assault on 29 pre-teen boys in Essex County. After the charges were publicized, many of his victims expressed fear, embarrassment, betrayal, and even continued caring for Reardon. Several statements made by the victims, quoted in the September 7, 2000, issue of the *Boston Herald* newspaper, show the range of emotions that sexually exploited children feel toward their exploiter:

> I think he's just a big jerk now.
> I feel sort of stupid.
> I'm worried my mom won't give me trust.
> I'm scared that he would get out and hurt me.
> Me and my brothers and [name deleted] were going to talk to him in jail, but they wouldn't let us in. We sent cards. He's still my friend, but I don't respect him as much any more. I kind of knew there were other kids, but I didn't know there was so much. I was surprised that he might have touched other boys, but knew he had the chance. (Farmer, 2000, pp. 1 and 14)

The emotional toll on a juvenile who has been a victim of neglect or maltreatment can never truly be measured. It is not uncommon for these children to grow up to become chemically dependent, have numerous legal problems associated with illegal behavior, become involved in abusive adult relationships, or, in some cases, be so emotionally tormented that they inflict pain on themselves or even commit suicide. What keeps a child from falling into one of these emotional traps greatly depends on the resources and help given the child after the abuse.

A final consequence of abuse that is often overlooked is the effect it can have on a community. The entire town of Middleton was devastated by the allegations and subsequent indictments against Christopher Reardon. Parents found out that their children had been victims and, with that, felt victimized also. The community felt a combination of shock and anger, and the underlying pillars of trust were rocked. In this case, "How could it happen?" becomes the operative question, and members of the community have to look inward to determine if there could have been any way to prevent a case of abuse. Even with the knowledge that the abuse was very well hidden and difficult to detect, the feelings of guilt can linger for a very long time.

Support for Victims

There are many different outlets for victims and their families. One of the first resources that maltreated children come in contact with is their state's department of child or youth services, which oversees the care and well-being of children living in their respective state. The U.S. Department of Health and Human Services works in tandem with these state agencies to look after the welfare of youths. A child who is suspected of being a victim of abuse may be reported to youth services, or what's commonly called "child welfare," by a mandated reporter. In the state of Massachusetts, a mandated reporter, such as a police officer or physician, files a verbal complaint with the department immediately upon discovering the maltreatment and within 48 hours follows up with a written report outlining the incident and the child's condition. This report, titled 51A, is reviewed by a Department of Youth Services (DYS) social worker and a check of the child is performed. If the child is found to be endangered and suffering maltreatment, DYS will take the child into its custody. A child may be placed in a youth home or with a foster family, and she or he will be evaluated and provided with physical and psychological care.

In addition to state and local government agencies, there are many other organizations that assist victims of neglect and exploitation. With an "estimated 984,000 children victims of maltreatment nationwide and forty-three states reporting 440,994 victims of neglect; 197,577 victims of physical abuse; 98,339 victims of sexual abuse; and 49,338 victims of psychological abuse or neglect" (U.S. Department of Health and Human Services, Children's Bureau, 1999, p. 1), these organizations have an enormous amount of ground to cover. These additional resources working in tandem with government agencies are extremely important to the assistance of abuse victims.

One of the most recognized of these organizations is the National Center for Missing and Exploited Children (NCMEC), which acts as the nation's resource center for ensuring children's safety throughout the United States and is the primary workhorse for locating and recovering missing children. The organization also provides the public with information on how to prevent child abduction, molestation, and sexual exploitation. The NCMEC was created in 1984 under a Congressional mandate and is a private, nonprofit organization that works in tandem with not only the U.S. Department of Justice's Office of Juvenile Justice and Delinquency Prevention, but also with federal and local law enforcement agencies, social services, and the judicial system to educate the public and end the exploitation of children.

There are many other nonprofit organizations that also work to ensure the safety and comfort of abused children. The National Clearinghouse on Child Abuse and Neglect, the National Resource Center on Child Abuse and Neglect, and the National Resource Center on Child Sexual Abuse all provide information and collect statistics regarding child maltreatment and exploitation. The National Child Abuse Hotline provides help to victims of abuse and abusers who call regarding their behavior, and serves as a reporting location for people who believe a child is being sexually abused. The National Organization for Victim Assistance, located in Washington, DC, provides a hotline for information and crisis counseling. There are also organizations for specific victim identities, such as the National Organization on Male Sexual Victimization, based in Tucson, Arizona, which provides support for males who have been victims of sexual assault and abuse. All of these support agencies and organizations provide invaluable resources to survivors of abuse and those who care for young victims, and are also incredibly important to the reestablishment of victims' self-esteem and confidence.

Conclusions and Future Directions

With the establishment of April as Child Abuse and Prevention Month, the federal government is making an attempt to bring more attention to the victims of child abuse. Local law enforcement communities as well as child protective services and local governments have found that making greater attempts to work together is highly beneficial to the identification and assistance of victims. Education and understanding in respect to child abuse are key elements for early detection and proper reaction when a case of maltreatment or neglect comes to light.

Breaking the cycle of abuse is key to reducing abuse. Education and support services for high-risk parents, such as those who are younger and may be suffering from outside stressors such as lack of financial security, adequate housing, or substance abuse problems, can do much to curb the cycle. Family counseling and parenting classes in tandem with vigilant oversight by state and local child welfare services can do much to establish proper parenting techniques and steer families away from abusive situations.

Educating children through school-based programs that teach them to understand that they have the right to reject unwanted attention from an adult is also extremely important. These programs also help children recognize if they are suffering abuse or neglect and realize that this situation is not appropriate or normal. Many children feel they are unable to ask for help from adults in their community, such as teachers and police officers. However, with the right information and encouragement, they can be helped to feel more comfortable expressing feelings and telling someone that they are being abused.

By compiling statistics and providing public services, nonprofit organizations and the government agencies under the Department of Justice and Department of Health and Human Services make information and counseling readily available to the public. They also raise the public's consciousness about abuse in general and what a child victim of abuse experiences and needs to overcome the situation. These agencies also assist researchers who wish to study the effects of abuse and the main causes of neglect and maltreatment. The most important impact of these organizations is to assist victims and thereby end the cycle that was started when the child was originally abused or neglected.

Enacting federal and state laws that are meant to protect children from exploitation is also extremely important. The Child Protection Act of 1984 was established in an effort to bar individuals from receiving child pornography through the mail. Laws such as this help curb the accessibility of sexually explicit depictions of children in the United States and make it possible for the government to bring charges against individuals who exploit and abuse children in this manner.

It would be wonderful to have a society where no child has to suffer physical, mental, or sexual abuse or goes unloved, neglected, or malnourished. How far we may have to evolve to achieve this goal is a complete unknown at this point, but with each progressive step toward ending that cycle of abuse for one child, we get one step closer. Caring, education, and, most important, willingness to act on behalf of a child are essential to making an abuse-free world a reality.

References

Administration for Children and Families. (2000). The Scope and Problem of Child Maltreatment. Available at: http://www.act.dhhs.gov/programs/cb/ncanprob/htm.

Andrews, A. B. (1988, May). The Psychologically Battered Child. *Social Casework: The Journal of Contemporary Social Work*, 69(5): 314.

Commonwealth Fund. (1999). *Improving the Health of Adolescent Girls: Policy Report of the Commonwealth Fund Commission on Women's Health.* New York: Commonwealth Fund.

DeMause, L. (1975, April). Our forebears made childhood a nightmare. *Psychology Today*, pp. 85–88.

Farmer, T. (2000, September 7). Kids detail alleged abuse by Middleton youth worker. *Boston Herald*, pp. 1, 14.

Fox, R. (1980). *The Red Lamp of Incest.* New York: E. P. Dutton.

Money, J. (1993). *"LoveMaps": Clinical Concepts of Sexual/Erotic Health and Pathology, Paraphilia, and Gender Transposition in Childhood, Adolescence, and Maturity.* New York: Irving.

National Center for Victims of Crime. (1999). Statistics: Child Abuse and Child Sexual Abuse. Available at: http.www.nvc.org/stats/ca_csa.htm.

Nelson, J. A., and Meller, J. (1984). Incest taboo and sexual abuse. In J. J. Krivacska and J. Money (Eds.), *The Handbook of Forensic Sexology Biomedical and Criminological Perspectives* (pp. 80–104). New York: Prometheus Books.

Shepard, (1995). *Child Abuse and Exploitation, Investigative Techniques* (2nd ed.).Washington, DC: U.S. Department of Justice.

U.S. Department of Health and Human Services. (1999). Children's Bureau. Available at: http://www.nvc.org/stats/ca–csa.htm.

———— (2000). HHS Reports New Child Abuse and Neglect Statistics. Available at: http://www.act.dhhs.gov/nws/april00.htm.

A young boy's trial by fire. (1994, March 7). *People Weekly,* 41(9): 170.

Zupancic, M. K., and Kreidler, M. C. (1999, April–June). Shame and the fear of feeling: Child abuse victims. *Perspectives in Psychiatric Care,* 35(2): 29.

CHAPTER 6

The Role of Victimization in the Criminal Offending of Female Youth Gangs

Dana M. Nurge and Michael Shively

Introduction

One of the more consistent findings in the research on female offending is the link between criminal offense and crime victimization. Studies of incarcerated girls and women have repeatedly found high levels of victimization, and these experiences are believed to play an important role in female involvement in crime and delinquency. In this chapter, we discuss the prevalence of violent victimization among juvenile and adult female offender populations, and we review the literature examining the links between victimization and offending. Using findings from a qualitative study of urban female gang members, we further explore the ways in which personal victimization can lead to criminal offending.

The Nature and Extent of Female Offending

Nearly all sources of evidence suggest that women commit most kinds of crimes at a far lower rate than men do (e.g., Bureau of Justice Statistics, 1999). For example, arrests of females accounted for just 22% of all arrests in 1998, and women comprise only about 6% of all state and federal prisoners in the United States (Bureau of Justice Statistics, 1999). However, given the high crime rate in this country, crime committed by females still represents a substantial problem. In 1998, there were 3.2 million arrests of women, and 950,000 women were under the supervision of federal, state, and local correctional agencies (Bureau of Justice Statistics, 1999).

Most female offenders are arrested and incarcerated for nonviolent offenses. Of all arrests of females in 1998, only 17% were for violent offenses such as robbery and aggravated assault (Bureau of Justice Statistics, 1999). The crimes for which women were most often incarcerated in state prisons in 1999 were drug offenses (34%), such as possession and sale of illegal drugs; property offenses (26%), such as burglary and larceny; and public order and other offenses (11%), such as driving under the influence of drugs or alcohol and violating court orders (Bureau of Justice Statistics, 2000). Only 29% of women were in state prisons for violent offenses such as murder, robbery, rape, and assault. In contrast, nearly half (49%) of males were in state prisons for violent offenses, and lower proportions were incarcerated for property crimes (21%), drug offenses (20%), or public order and other offenses (10%) (Bureau of Justice Statistics, 2000).

Rates of Victimization among Female Offenders

Estimates of the prevalence of violent victimization of females vary a great deal, depending on the populations studied and how the information is gathered. However, the weight of the evidence clearly suggests that victimization rates are higher among female offenders than they are among those in the general population. Studies of incarcerated women consistently find that high proportions of the women have been abused. Comparison of surveys of female offenders and female nonoffenders suggests that the rates of sexual and physical abuse may be about twice as high among offenders. For example, in the general population, studies find that about 8–15% of women have been the victim of rape (Bureau of Justice Statistics, 1997; Spitzberg, 1999; Tjaden and Thoennes, 2000), and 10–20% have been physically or sexually abused as children (e.g., Duncan, 2000; Gorey and Leslie, 1997). However, among females known to have committed crimes, the proportion of sexual abuse and assault victims is much higher. Harlow (1999) found that over 50% of women in state and federal prisons or on probation had been abused as adults by an intimate partner. Owen and Bloom (1995) found that about 30% of incarcerated women had been physically or sexually abused as children, 32% had been sexually assaulted, and 59% were physically abused as adults.

Silbert and Pines (1981) studied 200 former prostitutes and found that 60% had been sexually abused before the age of 16. This finding is supported by more recent research. For example, in a study of over 2,700 women in the United

States, Mexico, and Puerto Rico, Klein and Chao (1995) found that childhood sexual abuse was associated with adulthood prostitution. Using national youth surveys that gather information on self-reported crime and individual characteristics, Katz (2000) found that girls who were either sexually or physically abused were significantly more likely to engage in delinquent offending at an earlier age than were girls who were not victimized in this way.

In a series of studies, Widom (1989a, 1989b, 1989c) compared acts of crime and delinquency committed by abused and neglected youth with those of a control group with no known history of maltreatment. The rate of crime and delinquency among the abused and neglected youth was about 50% greater than for the control group. Typically, abused and neglected youth began their delinquency earlier and committed more offenses than the other youth.

General Consequences of Victimization

In addition to the obvious physical impact that violent crime can have on victims, there are serious emotional, psychological, and social consequences. Some of the more common and sometimes more severe and debilitating effects of traumatic experiences have been identified as clinically diagnosed syndromes and disorders. For example, a set of symptoms associated with serious victimization and other types of trauma is referred to as post-traumatic stress disorder (PTSD). According to the National Institute of Mental Health (NIMH, 2001), PTSD is an extremely debilitating condition that can occur after any terrifying event in which the victim feared or received serious physical harm. Among the symptoms of PTSD are flashback episodes in which people have vivid memories or nightmares about the traumatic experience. Such episodes often occur when victims are exposed to something reminiscent of the event, such as an anniversary or a location similar to where they were traumatized. People with PTSD also often experience sleep disorders, debilitating fear, anxiety, irritability, anger, and depression. Emotional numbness, problems in interpersonal relationships, and feelings of guilt about the incident are also common (NIMH, 2001; Dutton, 1995).

It is important to note that there are post-trauma reactions other than PTSD, such as acute stress disorder, dissociative amnesia, and major depressive disorder (Dutton, 1995), and that PTSD is just one of many identifiable disorders that can result from victimization. Researchers and psychologists involved in studying and responding to violence against women have coined the term "battered women syndrome" (BWS) to refer to the social and emotional consequences of domestic abuse. Initially proposed by Lenore Walker in the 1970s, BWS at first focused on learned helplessness. "Learned helplessness" refers to victims' inability to protect themselves when exposed to frequent abuse over an extended period of time. They appear defeated and lose the will to even try to avoid or resist abuse. The BWS model has since come to be defined as a form of PTSD (e.g., Walker, 1991). As one might expect, BWS is distinguished by a set of symptoms similar to that of PTSD, such as depression, anxiety, social withdrawal, irritability, and sleep disturbances.

Whether it is conceived of as PTSD or BWS, it is clear that violent crime has severe consequences for women. One indicator that clearly underscores the seriousness of the negative impact of violent victimization is the increased rate of victims' serious consideration of, or attempts to commit, suicide. For example, rape victims have been found to attempt or seriously consider suicide more than three times as often as victims of other types of violent crime and nonvictims (e.g., Kilpatrick et al., 1985; Vannatta, 1996).

How Does Abuse Lead to Crime among Females?

Although there is consensus among researchers that victimization is associated with subsequent criminal behavior, there are many different theories as to how the association comes about (see Cicchetti and Carlson, 1989, and the review by Smith and Thornberry, 1995). It has been suggested that victimization disrupts normal developmental processes in children and adolescents, and that improper or incomplete social and psychological development can lead to various kinds of behavior problems, including delinquency. Others have argued that although the majority of abused and neglected youth are resilient and appear to overcome the effects of their maltreatment (Rutter, 1987; Zingraff et al., 1993), some develop methods of coping that may help them to endure their treatment but are not appropriate for normal social interactions. Abuse may also lead children to develop negative attitudes toward themselves and others, which can generate patterns of behavior that are delinquent or lead to delinquency. In addition, abused youth may become more aggressive, leading to rejection by their mainstream peers and acceptance into delinquent and deviant peer groups. Association with delinquent peers is likely to increase the likelihood of crime and delinquency (e.g., Mueller and Silverman, 1989; Osgood et al., 1996; Reiss and Farrington, 1991).

Running Away from Home, Street Life, and the Cycle of Violence

There are many ways in which victimization can contribute to offending. The study described in this chapter focused on the connections between abuse, immersion in street life, and crime. By "immersion in street life" we mean the lifestyles of youth who have run away from home or are otherwise homeless, or those who are heavily involved in gangs and delinquent peer groups and are relatively detached from school, work, and their families.

Many studies in the past 20 years have shown that runaways and homeless street youth are drawn from abusive households (e.g., Baron, 1999; Hagan and McCarthy, 1992; Office of Juvenile Justice and Delinquency Prevention, 1990). For example, Silbert and Pines (1981) found that the sexual abuse of girls before the age of 16 almost always was followed by their running away from home. There are many other reasons for running away from home, but sexual abuse is often the most important. Once girls have left home, cycles of events and sets of circumstances make them highly vulnerable to engaging in various types of crime. The influence of running away from home on crime can be *direct, indirect,* or both (Kaufman and Widom, 1999).

Running away can have a direct influence on crime by providing powerful motivations, such as an urgent need for money. For example, many girls younger than 16 have little or no work experience and limited marketable job skills, and being on their own brings an immediate need for food and shelter. They need money to meet their basic needs, and they need it fast. For a displaced youth, prostitution, drug dealing, shoplifting, and petty theft may be the most readily available avenues for generating income or acquiring food. For example, when asked why they started prostituting, 9 out of 10 prostitutes in one study said they needed money and were hungry (Silbert and Pines, 1981), and almost all felt they had no other options available to them.

In addition to direct influences, running away from home and living the street life can influence crime indirectly through the process of "revictimization." That is, many girls and young women run away from home to escape physical or sexual victimization, and doing so usually places them at high risk of subsequent victimization. Until they obtain enough money to provide their own housing, they are usually destined to live on the streets, in shelters, or with whoever will take them in. The acute physical exposure of homelessness (living in parks and on the streets, and occasionally in shelters) obviously leaves young women vulnerable to robbery and physical and sexual assault. Unfortunately, many individuals who provide food and a place to live for runaway girls often do so for reasons besides altruism. Runaways are quite vulnerable to being exploited by older or more experienced individuals who may offer them help with the unstated expectation of being paid back through prostitution, shoplifting, or drug sales.

This second round of victimization can lead to a variety of negative psychological consequences associated with PTSD and BWS, particularly depression and anxiety. To cope with depression and other symptoms of victimization and the bleakness and stress of street life, many girls and women abuse drugs. For example, studies of criminal offenders find that whereas men use drugs primarily for pleasure, women more often do so as a self-medication for depression and to help them endure the stress and danger of the streets (e.g., Inciardi et al., 1993).

Those who become addicted to drugs then have an increased need for money (e.g., satisfying a cocaine addiction can cost several hundred dollars per day) and decreased ability to generate it through legitimate employment. (Few legitimate jobs for teenagers yield high incomes, and addicts often have trouble maintaining good jobs.) Thus, the cycle continues in which victimization leads to street life, street life leads to revictimization, and victimization leads to crime.

Research on Female Gang/Clique Members

Consistent with studies of female offenders, research on female gangs has revealed a high rate of victimization experiences among members. For example, in Joe and Chesney-Lind's (1995) study of female gang members in Hawaii, 62% of the girls reported having previously experienced sexual abuse or assault, and 75% reported physical abuse. In Joan Moore's (1991) research on Mexican American gang youth in Los Angeles, 29% of female gang members reported experiencing incest (she believed this to be an underestimate among this sample). Overall, most of the studies about female gangs reveal a high prevalence of victimization experiences, family problems, and running away behavior among the girls who joined. Research findings suggest that personal victimization experiences are a factor in a girl's decision to join a gang, and that once she belongs to a gang, she is likely to experience additional victimization (at the hands of male gang members or through gang-related violence) (see Miller, 1998; Moore, 1991). In this section we report findings from a study of female gang membership in Boston (Nurge, 1999, 2000) to examine the prevalence of victimization, its role in girls' decisions to join a gang, and the link between members' victimization and subsequent offending experiences.

Between 1997 and 2000, two-hour semistructured interviews were conducted with a community sample of young females (ages 13–24) who considered themselves members of either a gang or a clique in Boston (Nurge, 1999, 2000). With the assistance of local youth outreach workers (most of whom were former gang members or currently worked closely with gang-involved youth), a targeted snowball sample of young women from various gangs across the city was eventually drawn (Watters and Biernacki, 1989). The final sample included 58 females (30 gang members and 28 clique members) of 25 different groups. The average age of the current gang/clique females interviewed was 16; 60% of the young women were African American, 32% were Latina, and 8% were of mixed racial/ethnic heritage.

Gangs and cliques fulfilled similar functions for their members (providing protection, sisterhood, and opportunities to achieve status), and the females who joined each type of group appeared similar in terms of their age, socioeconomic status, family backgrounds, neighborhoods, and school experiences. Despite the similarities between the clique and gang members, the two types of groups were notably different. Whereas cliques were typically small groups of friends (averaging about five members) who displayed minimal or no organization, most gangs were larger and more structured (although usually rather loosely) and had a leader and rules (formal or informal), initiation requirements, and stronger loyalty expectations. Gangs were also involved in more serious crimes than cliques (and committed crime more frequently), but the prevalence of clique and gang members' arrests was roughly equivalent.

About 50% of the clique and gang members had been arrested at least once. However, the majority of the clique members' arrests (91%) were for fighting, whereas gang members' arrests were more varied and included shoplifting, assault and battery, armed robbery, disorderly conduct, drug sales, and attempted murder. Overall, however, there was great variation in the extent to which gangs (collectively) and gang members (individually) engaged in crime/delinquency. Some gangs/cliques regularly sold drugs, engaged in ongoing fights with other gangs, or engaged in other types of crime (e.g., one coed gang specialized in car theft; another frequently shoplifted/boosted), while others were seldom involved in any type of delinquent/criminal activity. However, almost all of the gang/clique members were frequently involved in fights (both alone and with their group), and these altercations usually took place without the use of weapons.

COMMON PATHWAYS FROM VICTIMIZATION TO GANG MEMBERSHIP

Consistent with prior research on female offending and gang membership, many of the females in this sample came from troubled home environments (Acoca, 1999; Chesney-Lind and Shelden, 1998; Moore, 1991). About 50% of the gang and clique members had run away from home in the year prior to being interviewed, and several of the older females had permanently left home at a young age. Twenty-six percent of the sample had lived with other relatives or in foster care, for at least some period of time, and about 10% bounced back and forth between various arrangements.

Although the reasons for leaving home varied, physical or sexual abuse was a primary cause. Approximately one third of all clique and gang members interviewed (32% of current and former gang members and 36% of clique members) admitted they had experienced sexual or physical abuse at the hands of a family member or boyfriend. One girl who joined a gang soon after leaving home emphasized her need to get out of the household:

> If I didn't get outta my house when I did I don't know what would've happened. I was gettin to the point where I was like fantasizing about hurting him [a family member who sexually abused her] . . . Ya know, like what it would be like to slice him up, make him feel that kinda pain . . . I'm glad I left when I did though.

Once out of their household, girls who ran away (and intended to stay away) were in the streets and confronting a host of new challenges related to where and how to live on their own. For many of them, a gang was an attractive option for meeting their immediate need for food and shelter. A gang could offer both economic opportunities, and the social support of members. Zena, a 16-year-old mother of two, was kicked out of her parents' household and did not want to live with her physically abusive boyfriend (her children's father) and therefore opted to join and reside with a coed gang that specialized in car theft. She explained her decision to join this gang, and engage in delinquency/crime with them, in terms of survival:

> That was the way for me to survive and see my kids. Even though it was the wrong way, it was the only way I could've done it . . . They were doing their own little thing—kinda stealing here and there and ya know, I started doing the same thing cuz it was hard for me to get things for my kids, ya know.

Jade, another member, joined and lived with a female gang shortly after leaving home at age 14. She described the sexual victimization that she and a sister had experienced in their household, and why she needed to escape that environment:

> I never felt safe in my house . . . things happened to me there, with family . . . that's why I left. My mother used to always cry, wish I was home. And I was like, if you wish I was home, you get the person that I want out of the house. I don't like being in my house . . . I got abused by both of my brothers, my cousin, and two uncles. That's why I never liked staying there. It was going on for 10 years, since I was 5 til 14. My mother didn't know 'cuz I was scared of telling her 'cuz they used to threaten me saying that if you tell anybody, I'm gonna say you asked for it. So I thought my father—he was very strict—would beat me . . . I used to think it was all my fault . . . I was used.

Mary's gang membership began in a similar manner. After she had been raped and her mother placed the blame for this on her, Mary left home and became involved in two different gangs. In addition to being raped, Mary had been molested by a male cousin during childhood. She explained why gangs were an attractive option for her:

> I was in the streets . . . I had a lot of problems with my family . . . A lot of things happened to me. When I was twelve I went into the gang, and before that I was also raped [by an ex-boyfriend] . . . I told my mother it happened

and she knew cuz I was bleeding and everything—she used to tell me it was my fault. I was hating her for that and I didn't want to be home.

VICTIMS AS OFFENDERS

> Sometimes it just feels so good to kick the shit out of someone . . . I can't really explain it. It just makes you feel so . . . powerful. (Kendra, an affiliate gang member)[1]

Much empirical evidence demonstrates that girls (and boys) who are affiliated with gangs are more involved in delinquency, violence, and drug use than are their peers who are not in gangs (Bjerregaard and Smith, 1993; Esbensen and Huizinga, 1993). Longitudinal and cross-sectional studies comparing gang youth and those not in gangs consistently find that the prevalence of offending is significantly higher among female gang members than among females unaffiliated with gangs and that gang members tend to commit more serious offenses than do their nongang counterparts (Deschenes and Esbensen, 1999; Bjerregaard and Smith, 1993). Although not all of the female gangs or gang members in the Boston sample were highly involved in delinquency/crime, gang membership did appear to increase girls' likelihood of becoming involved in such activities.

Analysis of gang/clique females' descriptions of the violent acts they engaged in and their background characteristics revealed a link between their personal offending and victimization experiences. The connection was not a direct one, whereby females engaged in violent crime only to avoid or confront imminent personal victimization. Instead, the females who engaged in the most violent crimes (and did so the most frequently), and spoke with great enthusiasm about the feelings of power and control they experienced in doing so, were the same females who had suffered the most extensive sexual (and, less often, physical) abuse during their childhood. Although their violent acts were not an immediate or direct response to their victimization, the excitement they expressed with regard to feeling in control and being in charge of a violent situation makes sense in light of their experiences as victims.

There were several females for whom this pattern emerged. Although not all of the girls who reported being sexually (or physically) abused engaged in violent acts, or discussed the rush and pleasure of doing so, this connection was evident in many cases. Jade's and Mary's personal victimization experiences were highlighted in the previous section, and their experiences as perpetrators of violence (within the context of their gangs) are presented here. Their case studies illustrate the sense of power and control that some females described feeling when committing acts of violence, and why such emotions may have been more important and fulfilling for them than others.

Jade's gang regularly engaged in robberies to get money to pay rent and spend on recreational purposes (partying, shopping, etc.).

Q: Who would you rob?

Jade: *We'll rob . . . all we do is just look at the person. If you're walking down the street and you see us just chilling, a whole bunch of girls in baggy pants, you know, dressed like a gang, you know, have their scarf on or whatever. And we see you walking fast, she's easy to run on, just like that. We go up behind you, we have on black jeans . . . we usually rob you at night. We have on black sneakers, black jeans,we always have double clothes on in case 5–0, they try to identify us, we take off our hoodies, jeans, switch sneakers or whatever and, you know, walk right by the person. They can't say it's us.*

Q: Did you do it in your neighborhood, or did you go to other places?

Jade: *We'd go to other places, we go to Jackson Park . . . we go to Horace Ave. Wherever we wanted to go. Wherever we think it was simple to rob somebody.*

Q: Would you usually use a gun?

Jade: *We use a gun, we use a knife, whatever we had to.*

Q: And what would you take?

Jade: *Take all their money. 'Run your loot. You don't run your loot, we're taking you to a corner.' We don't want to hurt you . . . us girls. I don't know about the guys cause we never went to rob with the guys but us girls, we don't want to hurt you, we don't want to shoot you. If you don't run your loot, we're gonna beat your ass. We ain't gonna shoot you, we're just gonna beat you . . . They usually gave us the money . . . We picked people who woulda had some cash . . . We just take their rings, we take their chains, we take their beeper, take their money or whatever. Stuff we needed. Some people we had to jump them, put them in a corner and jump them to give us the money. Not all the time.*

Jade's additional descriptions of her involvement in robberies, drive-bys, and other shootings—and her facial expressions and body language when discussing them—conveyed the sense of empowerment she experienced through these violent acts. "My nickname was 'Loco' cuz I didn't give a °°°° at that time . . . I just did whatever I wanted to . . . it felt good." Although her victimization experiences may not have directly caused her subsequent criminality, the link between them was apparent. After nine years of sexual abuse and utter powerlessness, her gang involvement provided her with opportunities to dominate and control others (and receive respect and status for doing so), and it felt good. She felt loved, in control, and capable. She explained how much the gang meant to her:

> Being in a gang for me was like, they was my family. Cause my family was never there for me. They [the gang] were the ones feeding me. They were the ones giving me what I needed to survive out there or whatever. Cause I still . . . I'm not close with my real blood. I'm having problems with my blood and the people out on the streets care more about me than they do. And no matter what, they still gonna be there for me even if we get into [a] beef or whatever. I'll never put my hands on them cause they were there for me when I really needed somebody.

Mary's gang involvement had many parallels to Jade's. From about age 12 to age 18, Mary was a member of two different female gangs (at the same time), although she was incarcerated on an attempted murder conviction for at least two of those years. One of her gangs was an all-female group of cousins who had their own drug sales business, and the other was a highly organized female affiliate group whose members participated in myriad crimes, the vast majority of which did not involve their male counterparts. Mary explained that she was given the designated role of "shooter" in the latter group, beginning at age 13, while other girls had different roles (e.g., "shoplifter").

> The whole time I was with them [3½ years], I only shot like three people, cause after that I went to jail for two years so I couldn't do anything . . . But in jail I stabbed people.

Like Jade's gang, Mary's group ran its own drug sales business and participated in violent crimes, including robberies and elaborately planned shootings, which were typically staged as sniper attacks from roofs. Mary explained that almost all of the 15 females had a gun on them at all times, and these were immediately disposed of after use.

Before being admitted into this gang, Mary and the other prospective members had to undergo a three-month initiation period, during which they were required to commit a variety of crimes (gang males were not involved in any of these decisions or events):

> We used to snatch old ladies' pocketbooks; we used to sometimes beat other people that we didn't like—we had to just go rush them, hit them with bats, hit them with whatever we wanted to hit them with; I had to break into people's houses, take things, come back out . . . I had to try to take cars—start it up and steal the car, and then I would go around and

pick them up . . . Other things like "you need to go up there and hit somebody and then we'll join you." I'm like "ok," so they gave me a bat . . . It was a lot. I had to do a lot of things.

Q: Did you have any second thoughts when you had to do all this stuff?

Mary: No, back in the day, I loved *doing it. I loved actually doing everything that I was supposed to be doing. My mind was just like . . . it was a good thing for me . . . It's like I wanted to be there . . . I was like mad at everybody and I was like if I get into this I can do whatever I want and hurt all the people that need to be getting hurt. That's how I was feeling.*

The sense of power and fulfillment that Mary and Jade (and some of the other females interviewed) felt through participating in violent crimes appeared to be at least partially linked to their extensive victimization experiences. Both of these young women had been sexually assaulted (more than once and by more than one person) during their childhoods, had left home seeking to escape their abusive situations, and had found support (both emotional and economic) and refuge in gangs. Eventually they became involved in—and derived a sense of empowerment and satisfaction from—violent criminal acts, including robberies and shootings. Aside from the opportunities (otherwise unknown to them) to feel strong and dominant, the gang provided ongoing diversions and excitement that helped to keep their minds off their previous traumatic experiences.

COPING WITH VICTIMIZATION THROUGH THE SUPPORT OF GANG PEERS

In addition to serving as a refuge and providing opportunities for girls to feel empowered (sometimes through participation in violence), some of the groups served a therapeutic function, allowing the young women to share their personal experiences of abuse/neglect with empathetic others. Most of the females who discussed their victimization with interviewers for the study noted that other girls in their groups had experienced similar problems. For example, Zanda did not admit being victimized herself, but many of her fellow clique members had been, and she considered this a primary reason why girls joined such groups:

Half the girls in my clique were abused by somebody . . . we all talk about it together. It's sad sometimes but after we talk about it we're able to laugh and say that it's in the past and behind us.

Zanda further noted that about half of the girls in her clique of 20 had been institutionalized at one time or another for depression, suicide attempts, or other mental health problems.

Yeah we all talk about it together and they don't be ashamed to talk about it. They just come straight forward and be like "Well, when I was little . . . that's why I was in such and such a place [be]cause my father, he used to touch me and stuff and I didn't tell my mother, so I just tried to kill myself and they took me from my mother and I told them why" and so I was like "Oh that's real sad" and then we all just sit there quietly for a minute and [the girl] will be like "What? Come on—I can laugh at it today." And I'll just sit there like "I don't think that's something to laugh about," and then we'll all just start laughing.

An obvious important function of this clique (and certainly many of the other cliques and gangs) was to provide a supportive context in which girls could share their painful experiences. Although these young women probably could have benefited from professional counseling and therapy (which the vast majority did not receive), they received support, advice, and empathy from peers who had experienced similar problems. Mary and some of the other victims of sexual abuse noted the flashbacks they experienced and the ongoing difficulties of coping with prior sexual abuse.[2] Comprising 15 female cousins (many of whom had suffered sexual victimization at the hands of family members), her other gang shared and dealt with traumatic past experiences together:

Yeah we talked about this stuff together. I mean we really wanted to get back at them [their victimizers] but we left it alone. One of my cousins got molested, another one got raped, I got raped and I also got molested . . . it was a boy cousin. The other ones had other problems but it wasn't like that . . . But I mean we just got back at our family but it wasn't hurting the people that did what they did to us . . . We used to just like say how we felt and what we would have liked to done. We used to have like a punching bag so when we started feeling really, really angry we would just punch and kick that—just act like that was that person.

Conclusion

Although not all sexually or physically abused girls become involved in delinquency/crime, evidence from a variety of studies shows that female offenders have higher victimization rates than does the general population of women and girls. How and why some victimized females are more or less likely than others to become criminally involved will continue to be examined through future research, but findings from this study of female gang members in Boston illustrate some of the common pathways between childhood sexual/physical victimization experiences and subsequent offending.

This research suggests that there was, in fact, a link between some of the young women's victimization experiences, their involvement in gangs, and their violent offending. A pattern emerged whereby girls who had suffered the most extensive abuse typically: (a) joined (and often lived with) a gang to get away from their abusive situation and/or enjoy the comfort, support, and familial benefits of the group; (b) were exposed to, and became involved in, violent criminal behavior through their group membership; and (c) found such behavior rewarding and empowering, as it allowed them to exert control and reap other benefits (monetary gains, status, and so forth). While certainly not the sole explanation, girls' victimization experiences appear to contribute to their gang involvement and criminality.

Endnotes

[1]An affiliate gang is essentially a female subgroup of a male gang. Affiliate groups sometimes have separate female leadership and engage in some of their own activities, but for the most part, research has found, female affiliate groups are subordinate to the male gang to which they are connected.

[2]Although not clinically diagnosed as such, it is likely that they, and some of the other young women interviewed had been suffering from PTSD.

References

Acoca, L. (1999). Investing in girls: A 21st century strategy. In *Juvenile Justice* (Vol. VI). Washington, DC: Office of Juvenile Justice and Delinquency Prevention.

Baron, S. W. (1999). Street youths and substance abuse: The role of background, street lifestyle, and economic factors. *Youth and Society,* 31, 3–26.

Bjerregaard, B., and Smith, C. (1993). Gender differences in gang participation, delinquency, and substance use. *Journal of Quantitative Criminology,* 9, 329–355.

Bureau of Justice Statistics. (1997). *Sex Differences in Violent Victimization.* Washington, DC: U.S. Department of Justice.

———. (1999). *Women Offenders.* Washington, DC: U.S. Department of Justice.

———. (2000). *Prisoners in 1999.* Washington, DC: U.S. Department of Justice.

Chesney-Lind, M., and Shelden, R. G. (1998). *Girls, Delinquency and Juvenile Justice.* Pacific Grove, CA: Brooks/Cole.

Cicchetti, D., and Carlson, V. (Eds). (1989). *Child Maltreatment: Theory and Research on the Causes and Consequences of Child Abuse and Neglect.* New York: Cambridge University Press.

Deschenes, E. P., and Esbensen, F. (1999). Violence among girls: Does gang membership make a difference? In M. Chesney-Lind and J. M. Hagedorn (Eds.), *Female Gangs in America: Essays on Girls, Gangs, and Gender* (pp. 277–294). Chicago: Lake View Press.

Duncan, R. D. (2000). Childhood maltreatment and college drop-out rates. *Journal of Interpersonal Violence,* 15, 987–995.

Dutton, D. G. (1995). *The Domestic Assault of Women: Psychological and Criminal Justice Perspectives.* Vancouver: University of British Columbia Press.

Esbensen, F., and Huizinga, D. (1993). Gangs, drugs, and delinquency in a survey of urban youth. *Criminology,* 31, 565–587.

Gilfus, M. E. (1992). From victims to survivors to offenders: Women's routes of entry and immersion into street crime. *Women and Criminal Justice*, 4, 63–90.

Gorey, K. M., and Leslie, D. R. (1997). The prevalence of child sexual abuse: Integrative review adjustment for potential response and measurement biases. *Child Abuse and Neglect*, 21, 391–398.

Hagan, J., and McCarthy, B. (1992). Streetlife and delinquency. *British Journal of Sociology*, 42, 533–561.

Harlow, C. W. (1999). *Prior Abuse Reported by Inmates and Probationers*. Washington, DC: U.S. Department of Justice, Bureau of Justice Statistics.

Inciardi, J., Lockwood, D., and Pottieger, A. E. (1993). Women and Crack-Cocaine. Indianapolis, IN: Macmillan.

Joe, K. A., Chesney-Lind, M. (1995). Just every mother's angel: An analysis of gender and ethnic variations in youth gang membership. *Gender & Society*, 9, 408–431.

Katz, R. S. (2000, June). Explaining girls' and womens' crime and desistance in the context of their victimization experiences. *Violence Against Women*, 6, 633–660.

Kaufman, J. G., and Widom, C. S. (1999). Childhood victimization, running away, and delinquency. *Journal of Research in Crime and Delinquency*, 36, 347–370.

Kilpatrick, D. G., Saunders, B. E., Veronen, L. J., Best, C. J., and Von, V. M. (1987). Criminal victimization: Lifetime prevalence, reporting to police, and psychological impact. *Crime and Delinquency*, 33, 479–489.

Klein, H., and Chao, B. S. (1995). Sexual abuse during childhood and adolescence as predictors of HIV-related sexual risk during adulthood among female sexual partners of injection drug users. *Violence Against Women*, 1, 55–76.

Miller, J. (1998). Gender and victimization risk among young women in gangs. *Journal of Research in Crime and Delinquency*, 35, 429–453.

Moore, J. (1991). *Going Down to the Barrio: Homeboys and Homegirls in Change*. Philadelphia: Temple University Press.

Mueller, E., and Silverman, N. (1989). Peer relations in maltreated children. In D. Cicchetti and V. Carlson (Eds.), *Child Maltreatment: Theory and Research on the Causes and Consequences of Child Abuse and Neglect*. New York: Cambridge University Press.

National Institute of Mental Health (NIMH). (2001). Post-Traumatic Stress Disorder: A Real Illness. Publication #00–4675. Available at: www.nimh.nih.gov.

Nurge, D. M. (1999, November). *R-E-S-P-E-C-T—Find Out What It Means To Me: Female Gang Members and the Code of the Street*. Paper presented at the American Society of Criminology Meetings, Toronto.

———. (2000). *The risks and rewards of membership: A qualitative study of the nature, context and gender dynamics of female gangs and cliques in Boston*. Doctoral dissertation, Rutgers University. Ann Arbor: University of Michigan Dissertation Services.

Office of Juvenile Justice and Delinquency Prevention. (1990). *Missing, Abducted, Runaway, and Thrownaway Children in America, First Report: Numbers and Characteristics, National Incidence Studies*. Washington, DC: U.S. Department of Justice.

Osgood, D. W., Wilson, J. K., O'Malley, P. M., Bachman, J. G., and Johnston, L. D. (1996). Routine activities and individual deviant behavior. *American Sociological Review*, 61, 635–655.

Owen, B., and Bloom, B. (1995). Profiling women prisoners: Findings from national surveys and a California sample. *The Prison Journal*, 75, 165–185.

Reiss, A. J., and Farrington, D. P. (1991). Advancing knowledge about co-offending: Results from a prospective longitudinal survey of London males. *Journal of Criminal Law and Criminology, 82,* 360–395.

Rutter, M. (1987). Psychosocial resilience and protective mechanisms. *American Journal of Orthopsychiatry, 57,* 316–331.

Silbert, M. H., and Pines, A. M. (1981). Sexual child abuse as an antecedent to prostitution. *Child Abuse and Neglect, 5,* 407–411.

Smith, C., and Thornberry, T. P. (1995). The relationship between childhood maltreatment and adolescent involvement in delinquency. *Criminology, 33,* 451–481.

Spitzberg, B. H. (1999). An analysis of empirical estimates of sexual aggression victimization and perpetration. *Violence and Victims, 14,* 241–260.

Teplin, L. A., Abram, K. M., and McClelland, G. M. (1996). Prevalence of psychiatric disorders among incarcerated women. II. Convicted felons entering prison. *Archive of General Psychiatry, 53,* 513–519.

Tjaden, P., and Thoennes, N. (2000). *Full Report on the Prevalence, Incidence, and Consequences of Violence against Women: Findings from the National Violence against Women Survey,* NCJ 183781. Washington, DC: National Institute of Justice and Centers for Disease Control and Prevention.

Vannatta, R. A. (1996). Risk factors related to suicidal behavior among male and female adolescents. *Journal of Youth and Adolescence, 25,* 149–160.

Walker, L. E. (1991). Post-traumatic stress disorder in women: Diagnosis and treatment of battered woman syndrome. *Psychotherapy, 28,* 21–28.

Watters, J. K., and Biernacki, P. (1989). Targeted sampling: Options for the study of hidden populations. *Social Problems, 36,* 416–430.

Widom, C. S. (1989a). Child abuse, neglect, and violent criminal behavior. *Criminology, 27,* 251–271.

———. (1989b). The cycle of violence. *Science, 244,* 160–166.

———. (1989c). Does violence beget violence? A critical examination of the literature. *Psychological Bulletin, 106,* 3–38.

Zingraff, M. T., Leiter, J., Myers, K. A., and Johnson, M. C. (1993). Child maltreatment and youthful problem behavior. *Criminology, 31,* 173–202.

CHAPTER 7

Victims of Domestic Violence

Gwen P. DeVasto

Introduction

In this chapter I present legal and working definitions of domestic violence. It is important to understand the legal standards of victim eligibility for restraining-order purposes and to incorporate a professional working definition into practice to ensure effective intervention. Indicators of abuse are reviewed for the purpose of helping readers identify the signs of domestic violence early. I also profile briefly the victims of domestic violence, including the hidden victims often forgotten by society.

I then take an in-depth look at the myths about domestic violence that persist in our society and perpetuate the problem, along with reporting laws and responsibilities. Guidelines for professionals and suggestions for intervention are presented. A realistic step-by-step discussion of the criminal justice response to domestic violence cases and restraining-order procedures is offered to ensure that the reader fully understands the stages of a criminal case and how to obtain an order of protection. I conclude by discussing what remedies can be ordered by the court, along with the implications about how to deal with domestic violence in the future.

Why Does Domestic Violence Exist?

Domestic violence has likely been a problem since time began. Battering is prevalent not because of psychological defects in the abuser or victim, but because this behavior has been deeply rooted in our legal and social traditions. Our legal system derives from Roman and English law, under which wives were considered possessions of their husbands. Under Roman law, a wife was obligated to obey her husband, and he was given the legal right and moral obligation to control and punish her for any "misbehavior." Most of us have heard the phrase "rule of thumb." But few of us know that the origin of this phrase is the English law that gave a man the right to hit his wife with an object no thicker than his thumb. We were a society that accepted wife abuse as part of a male-dominated culture (Massachusetts Coalition of Battered Women's Service Groups, 1992).

Many professionals believe that men are socialized into devaluing women, and women in turn are socialized to accept male dominance (League of Women Voters of Minneapolis, 1990). A presiding justice of the Quincy District Court in Massachusetts attributes the victimization of women to the sexism that has always permeated secular law: "The right of chastisement has worked itself into the norms of the court, the police, the clerks, and our society, denying women their status as legitimate victims and their right to recourse. Until the feminist movement began to have its effect, there existed a gentlemen's agreement within the patriarchal criminal justice system that recognized the right of men to punish their women" (Winsten, 1993, p. 36).

The battered women's movement gained momentum in England when the first refuge for battered women was opened in 1971 by a courageous woman, Erin Pizzey. Three years later, she wrote the first book about domestic violence from the battered woman's perspective: *Scream Quietly or the Neighbors Will Hear.*

In Massachusetts, wife beating was outlawed in 1871 (*Commonwealth v. McAfee,* 1871), yet the first shelter in Massachusetts (Transition House) was not opened until 1976. In most states, the right of men to inflict physical abuse on their wives and children seems to have been tolerated, if not sanctioned, well into the 1970s (Straus, Gelles, and Steinmetz, 1980).

Domestic violence was not acknowledged as a problem worthy of legal attention until 1976, when Pennsylvania established the first state coalition against domestic violence. It was the first state to create a statute providing for orders of protection for victims. The National Coalition Against Domestic Violence became the national voice when it was established in 1978, and it continues to guide the development and vision of hundreds of local programs and coalitions. Now almost every state has a protective-order statute, and all states have coalitions against domestic violence.

Although we now have more than 1,200 shelters for battered women and their children in this country, there are nearly three times as many animal shelters in the United States (Senate Judiciary Hearings, 1990), and in Massachusetts, we turn away five women for every two we house and eight children for every two we shelter (Massachusetts Coalition of Battered Women's Service Groups, 1990).

It's not surprising that the women's movement has had to fight for years to have this issue heard, since women are the primary victims of this crime. In 95% of reported domestic violence cases, the violence was perpetrated by men against women (U.S. Bureau of Justice, 1993). Similarly, among the murder victims killed by an intimate partner, 70% were female, and females experience more than 10 times as many incidents of violence by an intimate than do males (U.S. Department of Justice, 1994).

We must acknowledge, however, that violence also happens in gay and lesbian relationships and, in a small number of cases, is enacted by women against men. It is imperative that our society view violence against any individual, particularly within an intimate relationship, as unacceptable and that the laws we establish to protect victims from abuse are gender neutral. Specialized services are necessary for the distinctive needs of victims in same-sex battering relationships, male victims of female abusers, as well as a host of other underserved populations. These include victims with language barriers, the disabled, elders, teens, those with substance abuse problems or the mentally ill, and the many immigrants or groups of victims with needs specific to their cultural beliefs. Learning more about these populations is crucial for any professional working with victims of violence.

Historically, statistics were never kept for domestic murders, domestic police responses, or domestic criminal cases, because as a society we never saw violence within a relationship or within the home as a real problem needing public attention. In the last decade, as a nation we have become more concerned with this issue, have begun "naming" it, defining it, and keeping records to document the magnitude of the problem.

The Prevalence of Domestic Violence

Abuse by husbands or boyfriends is the single largest cause of physical injury to women in the United States, causing more injury than burglary, muggings, or all physical crimes combined (Commonwealth Fund, 1993).

¶Studies have shown that one-third to one-half of all American women will be in a violent relationship within their lifetime⌡ Controlling and abusive relationships are not limited to adults. Surveys show that abuse in teenage dating relationships is prevalent: about one in three females will experience violence at the hands of their boyfriends before they reach adulthood (Levy, 1990). When I speak to a group of high school girls or to women, I ask all attendees to look to the person on their left and then to the person on their right, and I point out that statistically, one of these women will experience an abusive relationship at some time during her lifetime.

A woman is beaten by her husband every nine seconds in this country. Almost four million women report being beaten in one year (National Resource Center on Domestic Violence, 1996). Annually one and a half million older adults are physically abused by the people closest to them (American Medical Association, 1996).

The number of children each year who witness their mothers being physically battered ranges in the millions. A nationally known sociologist estimates that 10 million children in the United States are at risk of exposure to woman abuse each year (Straus, 1991). Although adults may try to hide battering in the home, children will nonetheless witness or otherwise be aware of virtually all battering episodes (Hilton, 1992). The affects on the children will be lifelong.

The FBI estimates that domestic violence is underreported by more than 10 to 1 (Buel, 1990). Although we could speculate on the many reasons for underreporting, a primary reason for battered women is the fear of retaliation. Almost six times as many women victimized by intimates as those victimized by strangers said that they did not report their violent victimization to police because they feared reprisal from the offender (U.S. Bureau of Justice, 1993). Silence perpetuates the problem of domestic violence, yet many individuals who are berated, humiliated, controlled, and assaulted go uncounted in the sea of statistics.

This is clearly a trauma that every day affects millions of people across our nation, yet it is ignored by many and allowed to breed generation after generation. Although laws against this behavior are now in place across most of our nation and much attention has been given to this issue through the media (television news, movies, talk shows, documentaries, fundraisers, public service announcements, talk radio, music), statistics tell us that this problem is not going away. In 1990, Massachusetts found that a battered woman was murdered by her husband or boyfriend every 22 days; by 1993, one battered woman was killed every 12 days; and during the first 3 months of 1995, a battered woman was murdered every 4 days (Buel, 1990). Much more needs to be done to curtail this social atrocity.

My personal experience has been that even when victims find themselves in court as witnesses as a result of the arrest of their partners, they often describe the incident as "not really abuse" or "the first time this ever happened" during their plea to dismiss the charges. After developing a trusting relationship with domestic violence advocates or counselors and learning about the dynamics of abuse, many will gradually disclose the years of abuse and come to realize the benefits of court intervention. This suggests that any statistics of reported abuse are realistically much higher; it emphasizes just how important it is to evaluate the initial reporting of the history of violence; and, most important, it points to our need to provide outreach intervention and education in our communities to increase reporting.

In a report issued by the U.S. Bureau of Statistics (1991), separated or divorced women were 14 times more likely than married women to report having been a victim of violence by a spouse or ex-spouse; they reported 75% of the spousal violence (Harlow, 1991). In my experience, women often don't report the abuse until all efforts are exhausted, as they have given the abuser every possible chance to change, and have concluded that separation or termination of the relationship is the only solution. In some cases, even after the victim chooses to leave, the threats and abuse escalate to the point that she finally reports the abuse in an effort to stop it.

I have found that most women victims of domestic violence are very reluctant to report the abuse because they still have feelings for the perpetrator and don't want to do anything that seems retaliatory. Women are brought up to be nurturers in our society, particularly in relationships where they take on the role of keeping their partner happy. Every day, victims are saying to domestic violence advocates that they want the abuse to stop, but they don't want the relationship to stop. Unfortunately, in many cases, after exhausting all efforts to live an abuse-free life, victims find that the only option left is to terminate the relationship and, in some cases, go into hiding.

Some batterers continue to pursue their partners even when ordered not to by the court. In these cases and others, I have found, once the relationship is over in the mind of the victim, the risk for more serious abuse is greater. An abuser needs to be in control of his or her partner. Once the abuser senses the partner is pulling away emotionally or physically, he or she rushes to regain control. The abuse often increases in severity and, in some cases, tragically ends with murder.

According to the U.S. Bureau of Statistics, of those who did report the violence, 51% of the victims of intimate violence reported the incident to keep it from happening again, but only 24% reported it to punish the offender (Harlow, 1991).

Similarly, the medical profession has not yet gained the trust of victims: 92% of women who were physically abused by their partners did not discuss these incidents with their physicians; 57% did not discuss the incidents with anyone (Commonwealth Fund, 1993). Although many states have begun to encourage and train medical personnel to inquire about and suggest intervention protocol with suspected domestic abuse patients, one 1992 Midwest study of 394 women found that only 6 women said they had ever been asked about domestic violence by their physician (Hamberger, Saunders, and Hovey, 1992).

This enormous social problem costs society not only in the lives and health of its members, but also financially. Researchers estimate that family violence costs our nation between $5 billion and $10 billion each year (Meyer, 1992).

What Is Domestic Violence?

A LEGAL DEFINITION OF DOMESTIC VIOLENCE

Under *Massachusetts General Laws,* Chapter 209A, the definition of a domestic violence victim, for the purpose of obtaining an order of protection against an abuser, is anyone who has been physically harmed; placed in fear of imminent serious harm, including attempted harm; and/or engaged involuntarily in sexual relations by force, threat, or duress by a present or former family member related by blood or marriage, by a household member, by a parent of the victim's child, or by a partner in substantive dating or engagement relationship. This means that if a person has ever had a relationship with an individual, has lived with that individual, or is related to him or her, and if that individual has attempted to harm or has harmed the person, or has placed this person in fear, the victim is legally eligible for a protective order known as a TRO (temporary restraining order). What can be ordered by the court will be discussed later in the chapter.

Police departments and district attorneys' offices across the country are beginning to define domestic violence criminal cases in an attempt to separate them from other criminal cases for statistical purposes. In some states, domestic violence cases are handed over to specialized prosecutors and advocates for aggressive prosecution. Cases are often tagged as domestic violence cases if the crimes have any violent overtones (e.g., assault and battery, assault and battery with a dangerous weapon, threats, destruction of property) or if intimidating or harassing behaviors are evident (e.g., annoying phone calls, threatening a witness, harassment) and the victim and perpetrator ever had any kind of relationship including husband/wife, boyfriend/girlfriend, same-sex, parent/child, sibling, stepparent/child, grandparent/child.

Prosecution strategies and philosophies have changed drastically over the past several years to the point that many professionals now believe that the burden of prosecution should not be on the victim. The criminal court system, it is believed, should go forward without the testimony of hesitant or frightened victims. The prosecutor should be gathering other kinds of evidence to present at trial.

Police and prosecutors from the model San Diego program told me that prosecution goes forward on 60% of the cases in which the victim is unwilling or too afraid to testify, and they claim to have a 90% conviction rate. The Norfolk County District Attorney's Office in Massachusetts has trained all police departments within its county in evidence gathering and effective report writing to increase the chances of going forward on cases without the victim's testimony.

Police departments are trained to understand that arrest is one of the biggest deterrents to repeat abuse and that victims should not be asked to decide whether an arrest should be made or charges brought forward. Domestic violence is a crime and should be treated as such. We don't ask bank tellers if they would like us to file charges when they are robbed, and we certainly go forward on homicide cases without the victim and without asking the victim's family if they want to go forward. We should treat all domestic violence cases as seriously as we treat cases of nondomestic violence. Perhaps then we will begin to form a society that doesn't minimize the abuse of loved ones.

A WORKING DEFINITION OF DOMESTIC VIOLENCE

When working with the domestic violence victim population, it is extremely important to consider a working definition of domestic violence. This definition should include a range of abusive behavior beyond the obvious physical abuse, because, as one police sergeant stated, "Domestic violence is a process, not an event" (Day, 1994). My suggested definition is "imbalanced power that is maintained by a pattern of coercive tactics of control carried out by actual or threatened physical, sexual, psychological, economic, or verbal abuse, which places an individual with whom there is a past or present intimate relationship, in fear."

When working with a victim population, one must explore the wide range of behaviors that are considered abusive, such as controlling all money; isolating the victim from friends and family; not allowing the victim to work outside the home or demanding unreasonable work hours; threatening to harm the victim's family members, friends, or pets; using the children; humiliating the victim, withholding affection, food, or medication; using intimidation; and exercising entitlement. Unless the various forms of control and abuse are discussed, many victims would never consider themselves victims. The Domestic Violence Intervention Project in Duluth, Minnesota, designed the Power and Control Wheel shown in Appendix 1 to help illustrate some of the ways batterers control their partners. "Domestic abuse is a high-stakes game of control and batterers are expert players" ("Till death do us part," 1994, p. 25). In contrast, readers will see in the Equality Wheel in Appendix 2 what a nonabusive, noncontrolling relationship can look like. It is helpful for victims to review both of these wheels with a domestic violence specialist from the criminal justice system, a shelter, or a social service agency.

Indicators of Abuse

Victims of domestic violence often do not define themselves as "battered" or "abused." Therefore it's crucial to ask specific questions around the behavior instead of asking if they have been abused. It's often helpful to use the Power and Control Wheel, a checklist, or a series of questions when interviewing a suspected victim of domestic violence—see Appendix 3 for the Violent and Controlling Behavior Checklist. Like all the indicator lists provided in this chapter these items are only indicators, not predictors. They are red flags to alert staff to look even more carefully at the situation. Service providers and criminal justice personnel should assess a victim's safety once the violence is disclosed (see the sample Safety Plan in Appendix 5). This should be any professional's number one priority in working with suspected victims of domestic violence.

Although there is no absolute measure for perpetrator lethality, several questions should be asked to determine whether a victim is at greater risk for lethality or serious injury (see Appendix 4 for the Assessment of the Lethality of the Batterer). Extreme jealousy and possessiveness, as demonstrated with statements such as "If I can't have you, no one will," even when the abuser is in another relationship, are an immediate red flag for danger. Stalking or surveillance of the victim is common behavior of a batterer, certainly behavior that needs to be evaluated. Another indicator of dangerousness we use within the court system is whether the physical abuse has escalated over time and has reached the point of physical injury and/or threats to kill.

Although victims of domestic violence may minimize the danger to themselves and their children, it is always useful to ask them for their opinion of the batterer's lethality. If the victim is concerned, we all should be concerned and look into the matter with great caution. If the victim does not express concern, professionals should take other information into consideration in assessing lethality, since the victim may be blind to the true level of danger. Traumatized victims often develop survival skills for daily functioning, one of which is numbing out much of the ongoing abuse and violence.

The following are some behaviors that may indicate that a person is in an abusive relationship:

Victim	Abuser
• mood changes	• extreme jealousy/possessiveness
• isolation from friends/family/ coworkers	• checking up on/stalking behavior
• missed appointments or work	• accusations/harassment
• frequent fleeing from home	• inconsistent public/private behavior
• difficulty making decisions	• insisting on making all decisions
• looking to partner to answer questions	• not allowing partner to be questioned alone
• concern about children's welfare	• threatening to take children away
• changes in dress to cover injuries	• controlling—money, behaviors, work, friendships
• delaying treatment of injuries	• preventing or delaying treatment of injuries
• onset of alcohol or drug use	• alcohol or drug problem
• reporting of abuse/threats by a friend	• trying to convince others of partner's insanity
• withdrawn/crying—denial of problem	• denial and blaming of others
• signs of anxiety, depression, suicidality	• signs of anxiety, depression, suicidality
• any pregnant woman with injury	• inconsistent explanation of events with injury
• protecting abuser	• expressing entitlement with sex

This list is also an excellent assessment tool for professionals working with victims and batterers.

Is Domestic Abuse behind Closed Doors?

Source: Dave Granlund. Used by permission.

Most people have heard it said that "Domestic violence happens behind closed doors." Athough much of the actual abuse does happen behind closed doors, there are many signs and indicators from all family members that we, as professionals or community members, should be picking up on much sooner and are not. Sixty percent of the 100 women interviewed in the Quincy District Court in Massachusetts who came in for a restraining order also reported having suffered 12 or more serious incidents of abuse before seeking the court's assistance (Kramer, 1989). The critical question is, Where were all the professionals, friends, family, and concerned citizens during and after these 12 incidents? And what kind of assistance, if any, was provided?

I believe it is the responsibility of the professional in any setting to look for signs of domestic abuse from victims, perpetrators, and the children living in that environment. The goal should be to provide intervention before serious abuse occurs and injuries result.

Effects of Domestic Violence on Children: A Serious Problem

The effects of living in a violent home are immense. My work with children has shown me that children who witness violence in the home often experience feelings of worthlessness and powerlessness. They also fear for themselves, their siblings, and their parents and have feelings of rage, embarrassment, humiliation, and guilt. Many children feel responsible for the abuse and try to prevent it from recurring, but ultimately learn to accept violence as part of a loving relationship.

The effects of witnessing domestic violence also include acting out, as well as withdrawn or pleasing behaviors. These children may experience anxiety, have a short attention span, or use violence to express themselves in their environment. Most children display some form of developmental delay, problems with school performance, or attendance problems. Physical clues include crying, tantrums, bed-wetting, sleep disturbances, headaches, stomachaches, or eating disorders.

We see many families engage in role reversal, whereby the children or one child takes on the parental role of caring for the other children, preparing meals, or cleaning the home. Although it is rarely successful, this is the child's attempt to prevent further abuse since child care issues, the readiness of meals, and the cleanliness of homes are often the expressed justifications for abuse. Some children are neglected, physically abused, or sexually abused in addition to being emotionally affected by witnessing abuse against another family member. It is important to note, however, that children exposed to the battering of their mothers suffer the same harm and display the same symptoms as children who are actually abused, including the symptoms of post-traumatic stress disorder (Jaffe, Wolfe, and Wilson, 1990; Peled, Jaffe, and Edleson, 1995). Unless this is pointed out to them, many parents are unaware of these devastating affects.

Drawings by children living in violent homes clearly demonstrate how catastrophically they are affected by the violence. I have seen one child draw the family home with bars on it like a prison cell. Another child drew a picture of the house with bombs falling from the sky through the roof over the father's head. In another drawing, a child was drowning. Another child drew a picture of a tornado in his home. A 16-year-old drew a picture of his father fleeing from the home and the teen pointing a rifle at him; the caption over the teen's head said, "Revenge is sweet, I'll count to three." Clearly, children of all ages are affected and are in need of an enormous amount of support and counseling around these expressions of feelings that often were repressed and buried during years of continued experience with the batterer.

Witnessing domestic violence has other peripheral effects: Living in a violent home is the single best predictor of juvenile delinquency and other problems. One Boston study found that children of abused mothers are 6 times more likely to attempt suicide, 74% more likely to commit crimes against the person,

24 times more likely to commit sexual assault crimes, and 50% more likely to abuse drugs or alcohol than are children whose mothers are not battered (Guarino, 1985).

Research indicates that unless steps are taken to protect children from the devastating harm that is often caused by violence against their mothers, far too many children will live out these life lessons in their adult relationships, including those with their own children (Straus, 1990; Jaffe, Wolfe, and Wilson, 1990). If we don't intervene with this cyclical social issue, we will continue to create generation after generation of young people who grow up with multiple problems and the belief that abusive behavior is acceptable.

Myths about Domestic Violence

MYTH 1: CHILDREN ARE RARELY AFFECTED

I have already addressed one myth with the statistics presented at the beginning of this chapter: the myth that children are rarely affected by domestic violence. My experience in the past 20 years has been that *all* children are affected in some way, and most are aware of the violence in the home. Sometimes children are the identified victims of abuse. If a child is assessed as having been abused physically or sexually, it is crucial to also inquire whether the mother of the child is being abused. This may be another way of identifying the ongoing cycle of spouse abuse. The Children's Hospital in Boston began interviewing the mothers of abused children and found that 60% of them had in fact been abused and were in need of services themselves. To help children, we must help parents. After the AWAKE Project was begun at Children's Hospital, once the mothers were offered support and services, only a small percentage of children had to be removed from the home.

MYTH 2: ALCOHOL, DRUGS, THE ECONOMY, OR STRESS CAUSE VIOLENCE

It is commonly believed that there are external causes for domestic violence. These are only excuses; batterers make choices. It is critical to keep in mind that many people have substance abuse problems and most people suffer some form of stress in their lives, yet they do not make the choice to abuse their partners or children.

MYTH 3: VICTIMS PROVOKE THE ABUSE, DESERVE IT, AND ARE RESPONSIBLE FOR MAKING IT STOP

The abuser tells the victim this, and society reinforces it: "She should've kept her mouth shut"; "She pushed him to his limit"; and "With all that she does, she deserves it." An excerpt from a 1992 *Boston Herald* article written by Margery Eagan illustrates this point:

> A 22-year-old woman testified in what seemed like an open and shut case . . . the jury saw gruesome color pictures . . . they showed her face so bloody, you could not make out her features. They showed her legs, her arms, most of her body, in fact, swollen and bruised . . . The jury heard . . . her statement to the emergency room doctor: that her ex-boyfriend hit her. The jury heard testimony from two police officers who did everything right . . . The jury heard all this and could not reach a verdict . . . The young woman was not that illusive perfect victim . . . we demand in cases like these . . . The woman who was beaten admitted that she was drunk at the time of the attack . . . Had he been a stranger on the street, the verdict might have been different. (p. 12)

MYTH 4: THE PERPETRATOR IS "CRAZY" AND THEREFORE NOT RESPONSIBLE FOR HIS ACTIONS

Most batterers are not mentally ill. It's important to differentiate treatment of mental illness with batterer's treatment (now being referred to as intervention). In batterer's intervention, abusers come to realize that they are in control, they chose who, when, and how to abuse. Most batterers come into treatment minimizing, denying, and blaming. In Massachusetts, convicted batterers who are court-ordered into batterer's treatment must attend a certified program with strict standards (Massachusetts Department of Public Health, 1995).

MYTH 5: VIOLENCE HAPPENS ONLY TO POOR PEOPLE FROM CERTAIN SOCIAL, CULTURAL, OR ECONOMIC GROUPS

Those of us who work with the domestic violence population see all walks of life: doctors, lawyers, police, top executives, ministers, social workers, nurses, teachers, blue-collar workers, the unemployed, and everything in between. Perpetrators and victims come from the wealthy and poor side of town with all levels of education. It has been shown that all cultures have the propensity for this social problem. This is happening in every village, town, or city around the world.

Would the general public have been so shocked at the notion that O. J. Simpson was an abuser or a murderer if he were a blue-collar worker living in an ethnic community? I believe that some of Simpson's support came from people who just could not believe that someone of his stature could possibly do such a bad thing. After listening to compelling 911 tapes, many people came to believe that he abused his wife to some degree, but many continued to justify that behavior and then emphatically disbelieved that such a superstar could ever actually kill his wife.

MYTH 6: MOST INSTANCES OF ABUSE ARE ISOLATED INCIDENTS

Physical abuse is part of a continuum of abuse that often starts gradually with actions to undermine the victim's self-esteem and independence, followed by escalating verbal abuse, threats, and physical/sexual assaults. Often the abuse is cyclical in a predictable pattern of increasing tension, an abusive incident, and then a "honeymoon" or "manipulation" phase. If the abuser doesn't express remorse or make promises after an incident, the manipulation to maintain the relationship may be in the form of blaming, denial, or threats. Unfortunately, this cycle usually continues over and over again, with incidents becoming more severe and more frequent over time.

MYTH 7: LEAVING = SAFETY

Just read any newspaper, and you'll see that this is not true. It is my experience, and that of Dr. Angela Browne and the Massachusetts Department of Social Services, that when the victim is leaving is when the most serious injuries occur (Browne, 1993). When a victim leaves, he or she takes control away from a controller. Women are five times more likely to be killed during or after separation from the offender (Massachusetts Department of Social Services, 1995). This may be when an abuser feels he has nothing to lose and chooses to take harmful or even lethal action against the victim and often against the entire family.

Similarly, a restraining order doesn't solve everything; it's only a single step toward an abuse-free life. In one case, an abuser was traced making 274 calls in two days to his ex-girlfriend—after being served with a restraining order informing him that it would be a criminal offense to contact her in any way! Extra safety precautions must be considered when taking out a restraining order. Counseling and safety planning with specially trained professionals are crucial for the victim who is planning to leave the relationship, with or without an order of protection.

MYTH 8: MARRIAGE OR COUPLES COUNSELING IS BEST

This is only true if your goal is putting victims at more risk and giving them the message that the abuse is equally their and the perpetrator's responsibility. Couples work, when violence is present, forces the victim to negotiate when there is already unequal power and fear of retribution. Couples work often includes discussion about provocation or shared responsibility for the problems. In working with victims of violence over many years, I have found that nothing justifies violence except self-defense; and the violence is solely the responsibility of the abuser. If marriage counselors do not have specialized training in dealing with the dynamics of abuse, traditional couples counseling could give unsafe and ineffective messages to participants and, beyond this, put victims at greater risk within their environment. Before research and my experience provided evidence that couples counseling was not appropriate, I in fact had tried couples work with domestic violence cases. In one case, after the very first session, the victim was beaten by her husband in the parking lot for disclosing information about the abuse. It is never safe for a victim to disclose in the presence of the perpetrator.

Batterer's group treatment works best when group members confront one another, provide support for positive efforts, and educate each other about the effects of their abusiveness. Group treatment is a means of monitoring the batterer's behavior for court and for victim safety, and ultimately the group holds the perpetrator accountable for his or her behavior. Educational/support groups for the victim provide education around the dynamics of abuse and affects on children while being supportive in reviewing options available. Although there may be issues in the relationship in addition to the abuse, there is little hope of addressing them until the violent and controlling patterns are acknowledged and eliminated.

MYTH 9: THIS IS A PRIVATE MATTER

Family violence is not a private matter; it's a crime. Yet, many men and women believe it's appropriate for a man to hit his wife under certain circumstances. We're gradually seeing change, but it often takes women's and children's dying to get people's attention. Have you seen the local public service announcement where the couple is lying in bed listening to a woman being beaten? After looking at one another, then at the telephone, they simply turn out the light and do nothing. What does this tell us about domestic violence being our business? Hopefully this public service announcement is making us all think about our role in helping to end this problem. How we respond as a bystander is critical; silence can be deadly.

MYTH 10: APPEARANCES ARE ACCURATE

After an incident, the batterer often appears calm and rational and is very convincing to authorities or family members, while the victim may be anxious, overwhelmed, depressed, and unable to express herself. It's important that we look beyond the picture presented to us before evaluating the situation. The batterer could be your doctor, your dentist, your neighbor, or the wonderful person you're dating; to the public eye, and in the beginning of a relationship, batterers are charming and very attentive. Every woman is at risk of becoming involved with someone capable of abusing her.

THE REAL ISSUE

These and other myths only shift the focus away from the real issue. The real issue is our tolerance for violence in general, but particularly violence against women. I recently attended a domestic violence training symposium in a western state. During the closing panel discussion, one doctor disclosed that before the conference she had not considered domestic violence a crime; in fact, she responded to an out-of-state family member's question about crime in her state by saying they really didn't have much crime, only domestic problems. Men and women in our society must see domestic violence as the crime it is in order to deal with it effectively.

Consider this: There is public outrage when children are abused, and we cringe and say it's disgusting when an elder is abused; but when a woman is abused, often the response is silence or indifference. We ask, "What's wrong with her?", "What did she do to provoke him?", "Why does she stay?," or "What's in her background that makes her get into these predicaments?" We either question the victim's behavior or tell her to try harder to make the relationship work. Why are we as a society still tolerating this behavior, instead of focusing on the crime and the consequences of this crime? When crimes are committed by strangers, we are not so quick to blame the victim; we all seem to agree that the perpetrator is responsible for his or her actions and there should be consequences. We need to start asking different questions: Why do people, particularly men, batter? What should the consequences be? and What can we do to stop it?

Obstacles to Leaving the Relationship

Instead of asking, Why does she stay? we need to ask, What are the obstacles to leaving? There are literally hundreds of obstacles that victims face when they consider leaving an abusive relationship. Our society does not adequately assist abuse victims in their attempts to flee to safety. Resources are limited, and, realistically, law enforcement cannot guarantee protection for many victims. The fear of the unknown is far worse than the daily surviving, as the victims have already learned so well. The following are obstacles to leaving that are most often emphasized by women who come into the court system (I am emphasizing women as victims because the predominant gender of victims whom I have worked with for over 20 years has been female):

Fear

- of greater danger to self, kids, family, friends, and/or abuser: "He'll kill me, others, or himself."
- of losing custody or of the abuser's kidnapping the kids

- that the system won't protect them
- of loneliness, making life changes, the unknown, not being believed
- of being crazy or of people thinking she's crazy

Financial Need

- economic dependence: "How will I support myself and the kids?"
- lack of alternative housing
- lack of job skills
- unenforcement of support orders
- cost of day care

Societal Pressures

- preservation of the family at all costs: "It's my duty; he needs me."
- cultural/religious beliefs: "for better or worse," "till death do us part," "I must obey."
- urging by friends, family, and clergy to reconcile

Social Isolation

- gradual isolation of the victim from family and friends as the abuser repeatedly moves the family or makes it uncomfortable for continued contact: "I have no one else in my life, nowhere to go."
- the threat of deportation when immigration status is dependent on the abuser
- " I don't know anyone in this town [state/country]."

Lack of Knowledge

- lack of knowledge about police role, court options, and services available
- belief that she has no options or that services are impossible to access
- poor response in past from professionals

Children

- belief that the children need a father: "A violent father is better than no father at all."
- staying as a means of keeping the children fed and housed
- fear of loss of custody: "At least I have my children."
- "He's my only option for child care; how could I work?"

Emotional Factors

- history of abuse, the belief that abuse is just part of life
- the feeling she deserves the abuse
- guilt, sense of responsibility: "I can help him; we need each other."

- embarrassment, shame: "I don't want anyone to know."
- substance abuse: "He'll tell . . . I'll lose the kids" or "He needs my help."
- emotional depletion, the feeling she has no control over her life
- ambivalence: "I want the relationship, I just don't want the abuse" or "I love him."

Belief That the Abuser Will Change

- holding onto hope for the future and for change
- "Maybe if I . . . things will get better."
- "He used to be so loving and kind; I'll help him to be that way again."

In individual or group counseling, victims come to understand that the abuse is not their fault and that it escalates regardless of all attempts to stop it. Once they identify with one or more of these obstacles, they are able to consider what needs to be done to change the situation. Change is difficult for everyone. For someone attempting to leave an abusive partner it may mean living a totally different lifestyle, often staying for a time in a shelter or different housing, sending the kids to a new school, being a single parent, having a limited income, and perhaps needing to change jobs or find training opportunities or education to enter the job market—and all this is often done with the batterer in full pursuit, armed with either promises or threats.

Suggestions for Intervention

In work with adult victims of domestic violence, it's essential to explore existing safety issues around the children as well as the identified victim. It is equally essential to know who the mandated reporters of suspected child abuse are and when and how they must report suspected abuse. All children living in an abusive home are at risk of being neglected or abused themselves. For domestic violence advocates, the key to the success of intervention is to not blame the victim when discussing the well-being of her children. To help the children we must help the parents first.

Although there is not a law mandating the reporting of abuse toward all individuals, there are laws to report suspected child abuse, abuse of the elderly, and abuse of disabled persons. An acronym used by the Massachusetts Medical Society (1992) to briefly outline the intervention expected of all medical personnel when they suspect domestic violence is **R-A-D-A-R**. This five-step intervention is appropriate for all professionals and suggests that they take the following actions:

Routinely ask about partner abuse in all intake interviews.
Ask client questions about abuse directly and privately (batterers often prevent their partners from being interviewed alone).

Document *all* findings. Prosecutors can attempt to go forward with criminal cases without the testimony of frightened or intimidated victims if they have other forms of evidence.

Assess victims' safety—what they can do to increase their safety at home, school, and work. Help initiate a safety plan (see Appendix 5: A Safety Plan).

Review options with the victim. She may not be ready to take major steps at that moment, but one of the most important things you can do for a victim of violence is help her understand that assistance is available when she is ready. If you develop rapport by making the person feel listened to and understood without judgment, trust will result. Victims need to trust that their social worker, advocate, or counselor will not judge them but will support them in their efforts to live an abuse-free life.

If domestic violence is suspected but not yet identified, a good initial question is, "At any time has a partner hit, kicked, or otherwise hurt or frightened you?"

If domestic violence has been identified, intervention should include several things. First, always reframe the violent behavior as unacceptable, saying, for example, "No one deserves to be treated that way. It's not your fault." Second, communicate your concerns for the victim's safety and the safety of her children, saying, for example, "I'm afraid someone is going to get hurt" or "I'm afraid for your children." Many victims have low self-esteem from years of verbal and emotional abuse, so they may be more able to take difficult steps for their children than for themselves. Predict that the violence will get worse.

Referrals should be made for appropriate medical treatment, specialized counseling/support services, and restraining-order or court assistance. Advocates/service providers need to create a complete resource manual for their specific geographic area (see Appendix 8: Resources). In all cases, mandated reporters of suspected abuse or neglect must evaluate the need to report the violence, and, most important, we all should offer assistance and support whenever the victim is ready to take any action. The most empowering thing we can do is explore with the victim her options and the consequences of each option, allowing her to make decisions without pressure.

When offering victims of domestic violence more comprehensive information and support, it is useful to work within the scope of the intervention and treatment issues listed in Appendix 6. Depending on each individual's immediate needs, the order may vary but the content is helpful for most victims. Many battered women's shelters and specialized services for victims of domestic violence provide this kind of intervention in a group setting where increased support and decreased isolation are accomplished. However, when the victim is in acute crisis and is in need of more comprehensive individual attention, these issues can be addressed in individual counseling as well.

It is helpful to review an individualized safety plan with a victim. It is also helpful to review the plan again after the immediate crisis has been addressed and questions have been answered. It is difficult to concentrate on the details of safety planning unless the immediate situation has been calmed and the victim feels some degree of control over the circumstances. I recommend the safety plan used in Norfolk County, Massachusetts, and shown in Appendix 5. It can be used as a handout to review with every suspected victim of domestic violence. The more prepared victims are, the safer they will be. Any community can create a similar handout for its jurisdiction by simply inserting its own local resources. In reviewing a safety plan with individuals, discuss a range of options, including places they might go if they need to flee, actions they could take to prevent being found, and legal remedies.

When working with victims who are ambivalent about the relationship or are considering reconciliation, it is also beneficial to review the questionnaire "How Do I Know If the Abuser Is Changing?", shown in Appendix 7. These questions help individuals evaluate their partner's behavior before making important decisions that affect their safety and the safety of their children.

The Criminal Court Process/Advocate Role

If the police respond to a call at a home involving domestic violence, and they have probable cause to believe a crime has taken place, they are mandated (or it is a preferred response in many states) to arrest the abuser and sign a criminal complaint against him. If police are not called at the time of the incident, every victim has the right to come forward to the police or prosecutor's office after the fact to report the crime. (The statute of limitation, or length of time the victim can wait, differs for various crimes.) The advocate's role is to assist a victim throughout this court process and explain the benefits of having the court involved. Criminal charges are often an effective means to get an abuser into court-ordered batterer's treatment/intervention and substance abuse treatment, if applicable. In addition, when batterers are held accountable, they, their victims, and society as a whole get the message that this behavior is not acceptable and carries consequences. This message ultimately serves to offer more protection to the victim.

Some women choose not to report criminal activity or participate in the criminal court proceedings; we should always respect a victim's choice, since she knows best what will keep her most safe. Victims have legitimate reasons for not pursuing criminal action: fear of retaliation, loss of financial support (especially if the abuser is incarcerated), or a decision to continue in the relationship.

Even if the victim is hesitant or unwilling to testify in a criminal case, prosecutors will often pursue the case without the testimony of the victim. It is the belief in the Norfolk County District Attorney's Office in Massachusetts and many other jurisdictions across the country that the burden of prosecution should not be on the victim. After taking victims' safety into consideration and gathering information about the history of violence, prosecutors work closely with advocates and police to decide the best way to go forward on domestic cases. With photographs, detailed police reports outlining the statements and demeanor of victims and witnesses, 911 tapes, hospital records, and other evidence, domestic violence cases can be prosecuted successfully without testimony from the victim.

It is helpful to describe the entire court process to victims considering involvement with a criminal case. Many women have concerns and questions about what will happen to the defendant if they testify and he is found guilty. It's extremely important to explain the reality of the court process and possible outcomes or dispositions. If the defendant has no record or history of violence and the injury was not severe, the reality is that it's unlikely he would be sentenced to jail. One common disposition might be a guilty finding with lengthy probation (one to three years) and specific conditions of probation: attendance at a batterers' intervention program for a minimum of one year, substance abuse testing and treatment, a stay-away order (prohibiting any contact with the victim, and the children in some circumstances), and possible restitution (an order to pay any out-of-pocket expenses the victim incurs as a result of the abuse). Another disposition might be a suspended sentence hanging over the defendant's head: If he doesn't follow the conditions of probation, the sentence is already determined. A third disposition might be a "continued without a finding," in which case guilt is not determined and the case is left open for a period of time. In any case, if the defendant does not comply with the conditions of probation, or he commits new crimes, he will face the judge once again for possible incarceration. These dispositions give the defendant a chance to prove himself and give the victim a chance to make decisions about the relationship and her safety. Of course, some defendants do get sentenced to jail, whereas others are found not guilty or the cases are dismissed for lack of evidence.

THE LIFE OF A CRIMINAL COMPLAINT

There are several steps in the criminal complaint process. (I refer here to Massachusetts law and court procedures; check local laws and court process for other states or countries.) If the abuser is not arrested, the complaint may be brought before a clerk magistrate for a hearing to make the decision to issue the complaint (which means the case continues in the system), not issue the complaint (which means everything ends there), or continue the complaint for a period of time (to see if problems resolve).

If there is an arrest or the clerk issues the complaint, the defendant is arraigned. At the arraignment, the defendant is formally charged with the crime by a clerk in front of a judge. The defendant must be present, or a warrant will be issued for his arrest. The victim does not have to be present. At the arraignment, bail may be argued, a dangerousness hearing may be requested to hold the defendant without bail, or conditions may be placed on the defendant while he awaits trial. A court-appointed attorney is assigned if the defendant cannot afford an attorney. When possible, it's helpful for the prosecutor and/or advocate to speak to the victim as part of gathering a history of the violence and gauging the defendant's level of dangerousness and the victim's fear of him.

The second step in prosecution is the pretrial conference. The conference allows the defendant and his attorney to meet with the prosecutor before trial to assess whether they can come to an agreement without going to trial. The defendant's record, the severity of the crime, whether there is a history of violence, and the victim's feelings should all be taken into consideration before a disposition is agreed upon. Once again, it is not considered appropriate intervention to automatically dismiss all domestic cases where the victim is unwilling to testify. Sometimes the defendant will admit to the charges but the prosecutor and defense attorney go before the judge with divergent recommendations. The judge makes the final decision on dispositions.

If a case goes to trial, the victim is asked to testify as a witness. If she declines, legally there is immunity for her if she is married to the defendant, but it's also a wise policy not to revictimize any victim by putting undue pressure on her to testify. In some cases, once the victim finds support in a battered women's group, she comes to understand how testifying might be in her best interest. In other cases, it's clearly much too dangerous for the victim to testify. The advocate's role is to unconditionally support victims and help them evaluate their ambivalance and fears.

If the victim does participate in the trial as a witness, she will spend time with the prosecutor and advocate going over the facts of the case and the questions that will be asked on the stand. The defendant makes the decision as to whether he wants the facts of the case heard before a judge or a jury. In preparing a witness for trial it is important to stress that she should answer only the question asked, should listen carefully to the question, and should feel comfortable asking that the question be repeated or rephrased if she doesn't understand. If she does not know the answer, she should say so; she should not guess.

The defense attorney will have an opportunity to question the witness on the testimony she gave. This is called cross-examination. The role of the defense attorney is to try and destroy the effect of the victim's testimony. This may be done by intimidating the victim, suggesting that she is confused about her testimony, or destroying her credibility. It is extremely helpful to prepare victims and witnesses for this process. If the prosecutor objects, the victim/witness should not answer until the judge rules: If the objection is sustained, the witness does not have to answer; if the objection is overruled, the witness must answer.

VICTIM RIGHTS

The role of the advocate also includes informing the victim/witnesses of all victim rights. The Massachusetts Victim Bill of Rights (*Massachusetts General Laws,* Chapter 258B) mandates the following rights and protections for victims, family members, and witnesses of crimes. See local state laws for states other than Massachusetts.

- The right to file a victim impact statement detailing the financial, physical, and psychological effects suffered as a result of the crime.
- The right to be notified when expected to appear in court, when there is a delay in the proceedings, and when there are changes in case developments.
- The right to assistance in seeking witness fees or victim compensation.
- The right to receive information on the level of protection available when they are threatened by a defendant.
- The right to be notified of the final disposition of a criminal case.
- The right to be informed by custodial officials whenever an offender is given a temporary, provisional, or final release from custody.
- The right to transportation assistance.
- The right to creditor and employer intercession services.
- The right to expedited return of property.
- The right to assistance in seeking child care and other family support services during criminal proceedings.
- The right to safe waiting areas during a trial or hearing.

THE RESTRAINING ORDER OF PROTECTION

Most states have legislated orders of protection for victims of abuse that offer a range of remedies. In 1978 Massachusetts passed legislation that provides protection from abusive household members, spouses or former spouses, blood relatives, the parent of the victim's child, and partners in significant dating relationships. *Massachusetts General Laws,* Chapter 209A, provides access to court orders including

- a *refrain from abuse* order (the abuser is ordered not to abuse again),
- a *vacate* order (the abuser is to move out immediately),
- a *no contact* order (the abuser is not to contact the victim directly or indirectly),
- a *custody and support* order (the victim may be awarded temporary custody and support until the family and probate court makes more permanent orders), and
- *restitution* (repayment for lost medical expenses or other out-of-pocket expenses resulting from the abuse).

In Massachusetts, the restraining-order law also allows the judge to order that the abuser's license to carry firearms be revoked and any firearms be confiscated by the police.

In Massachusetts a person is eligible for an order of protection under Chapter 209A if the abuser (1) caused or attempted to cause physical harm;

(2) put another in fear of imminent serious physical harm; or (3) caused another to engage involuntarily in sexual relations by force, threat of force, or duress.

These orders can be obtained anytime during court hours at any courthouse within the jurisdiction of the victim's residence or wherever the victim flees to escape the abuse. After court hours or on weekends or holidays, Massachusetts has a *24-hour emergency judicial response* system that allows the local police to access a judge for an order that is in effect until the next court day. The victim would need to go to court for a continuance of that emergency order.

The abuser will be served by the local police with the initial order sought by the victim. The abuser has the right to be heard on the second hearing, scheduled within 10 days of the first order. At that time, the judge may extend the initial order for up to one year. Victims can request an order of protection without filing for divorce, without an attorney, and at *no cost*. Victim advocates are available in most courts to assist in the court process and answer any questions. It is at this time that it's most helpful to offer educational and support groups to victims of domestic violence. An enormous amount of support is needed for victims to follow through with the difficult steps that they must take to live an abuse-free life.

Violation of this civil order of protection is a *criminal offense* punishable by a maximum of two-and-a-half years and/or a $5,000 fine. Under this law, when responding to a domestic call, police are required to use all reasonable means to prevent further abuse; to remain on the scene as long as someone is in physical danger; to take the victim to a safe place (shelter, hospital, or friend); to assist in obtaining medical treatment; to give the victim a card explaining her or his rights; and to arrest the abuser if a restraining order is in effect. If the victim does not have a restraining order, the law specifies that arrest is the preferred response if probable cause is found.

Many states have mandatory arrest laws, since it is commonly believed that arrest is a deterrent to further abuse, giving the message to all parties that this is a crime for which there will be consequences. Again, the emphasis is on holding batterers accountable.

What Can You Do?

FOR THE VICTIM

What can we all do to help combat this enormous social problem? Since the single most important thing an emotionally or physically abused victim needs is an extensive support system, you can support a victim or suspected victim of domestic violence by doing the following:

1. Share her concern: Tell the victim you're afraid for her safety and the safety of her children. Tell her it will get worse.

2. Remain nonjudgmental and supportive. Say things like "It's not your fault," "You're not alone," "Nothing justifies violence," and "I'll be there to help when you're ready."
3. Help the victim become aware of the resources and options available: Locate hotline numbers, shelters, emergency police numbers and court referrals, counseling, housing and welfare resource numbers, medical, and legal assistance.

FOR THE BATTERER

Here are the most important things you can do for a friend or relative who is emotionally or physically abusive:

1. Share your concern, saying, "I'm afraid someone will get hurt" or "Without help, it will get worse."
2. Don't accept the "blame game"—batterers always blame someone or something else. Point out the consequences of this behavior: "It doesn't matter what she said; you can't hit her" or "That's a crime; you could go to jail." Batterers must be held accountable. Emphasize that nothing justifies controlling behavior and violence.
3. Support him in seeking specialized help for abusers: Find out if your state has certified batterers' treatment programs and how to access them.

IN GENERAL

What else can we do? We can model nonviolent behavior in our attitudes, actions, and language. We can be responsible citizens and report crimes of domestic violence. Every one of us can turn our outrage into action. Anyone can donate clothing, food, toys, or money to a local shelter or program for victims of violence. We might participate in a local fundraiser, join a walk or a vigil in support of eradicating domestic violence, or begin a new group effort. Talk about it and let people know it is wrong: "No exceptions."

High school students have begun their own groups—for example, Students Against Violence Everywhere and Students Against Domestic Violence in Weymouth and Quincy, Massachusetts, respectively—or have joined alliances (e.g., the Massachusetts Student Alliance Against Racism and Violence) to make a difference in their generation. As adults, we can support the efforts of our youth and empower them to live without abuse as well.

The corporate world has also begun to look at its role in providing a safe work environment for all employees. They are looking beyond the workplace and into their communities. Polaroid and six other large companies in the country have policies and programs specifically designed to help battered employees

(Lewis, 1994). Polaroid demonstrates concern for this social issue by educating staff to recognize abused workers and understand the devastating effects of domestic violence. They have set policy for company response to this problem; they offer victims an array of services; and, when appropriate, they offer leaves of absence. Polaroid is a leader in taking its violence prevention commitment into the community. The CEO Project encourages local businesses to adopt a local shelter; they provide hundreds of educational trainings on this issue nationally and internationally; and they have produced thousands of manuals about the Quincy Court Model Domestic Violence Program in an effort to share with others some tools for effective intervention and prevention. Other companies need to take on similar initiatives to create more awareness and change.

Different states are being creative in finding ways to address this issue. One state I recently visited shows its commitment by putting violence-prevention bumper stickers on all police and fire vehicles. Another state gives out domestic violence warnings on its marriage licenses. Still another state deputizes shelter workers to assist with 24-hour protective orders. Here in Massachusetts, we have been extremely proactive in domestic violence prevention. One innovative way that many professionals in this field disseminate information to victims is to attach flyers to the inside door of public bathroom stalls. Many battered women do not feel safe stopping for information left out in public view. The November 1994 issue of *Self* magazine lists 60 other ways to try to stop domestic violence.

On a grander scale, we all can chip away at this issue if we learn as much as we can about domestic violence by attending educational seminars and keeping informed about any laws being proposed. Just write or call your local representatives with your feelings or comments in support of legislation that may further the safety of constituents.

The Quincy Court Model Domestic Violence Program: A Model Intervention

In the past two decades, a number of model domestic violence programs have gained national attention, such as those in Duluth, Minnesota; San Diego, California; Quincy, Massachusetts; and Seattle, Washington. When advocates are looking to improve intervention or prevention in any community, it makes sense to contact programs that are in place and have proven to be effective, rather than reinventing the wheel.

Having worked in the model program in Quincy through the Norfolk County District Attorney's Office for 20 years, I can recommend this program as one of the many extraordinary violence-prevention programs in this country.

From the time the state's first Abuse Prevention Law was enacted in 1978, Norfolk County has served as a model of interdisciplinary coordination involving the court, probation, district attorney's office, local government, police, battered women's advocates, area shelters, housing and welfare assistance programs, mental health and alcohol treatment programs, medical facilities, schools, child protection, and other community agencies. It is an integrated system. The Quincy Court Model Domestic Violence Program was chosen by the Domestic Violence Advisory Committee of the National Council of Juvenile and Family Court Judges as one of the 15 best court-based domestic violence programs in the country (Winsten, 1993).

As the domestic violence community education and training coordinator for the Norfolk County District Attorney's Office, I was responsible for providing ongoing in-house domestic violence training for all staff. I also spent a great deal of time training a wide range of professionals from the departments and agencies listed above as well as the community at large. Our office has made the long-term commitment to maintain a well-trained staff and to flood the community with training around this issue to create a community that is less tolerant of violence and more comfortable reporting abuse and accessing available resources.

Along with training and integration of all departments and agencies, key ingredients for effective domestic violence prevention are early intervention and ongoing support; the understanding that domestic violence is a serious crime; prioritization of victim safety as the number one concern for everyone involved; the existence of a user-friendly system for victims; specialized domestic violence staff; consistent consequences for offenders; and a domestic violence policy that is set out and reinforced by the top administrators.

One unique aspect of the program involves early intervention and tracking of cases. Domestic violence counselors from the district attorney's office follow up on all family disturbance calls to the Quincy Police, regardless of police action, even when a neighbor calls about a loud argument. Our philosophy is not to wait for crimes to be committed to offer intervention. Over 1,600 families annually receive follow-up letters offering information, support, and referrals. For many families, this contact may be the first step in recognizing that a problem exists and resources are available. When any physical abuse is alleged or there have been repeat calls to a residence, counselors also attempt to make telephone contact to ensure that the identified victim understands her or his rights and options.

Victims are also identified when they seek protection from the court by way of a restraining order. A separate office for protective orders is staffed by trained clerks who assist applicants with the paperwork. Domestic violence counselors from the district attorney's office conduct daily briefings for applicants to explain the court process; victim rights, including criminal charges; safety planning; and community resources, including an eight-week educational group offered by the district attorney's office. Individual crisis counseling and information about batterer's intervention, children's, substance abuse, and mental health services as well as housing and welfare programs are also made available to the victims and the community at large.

All police departments have been trained by the district attorney's office. They are trained in the dynamics of abuse; the effective response to victims and perpetrators; police responsibility under the law, including mandatory arrest; investigation; and evidence gathering for effective prosecution without the testimony of the victim. The burden of prosecution should not be on the victim. Presentations by survivors of domestic violence are part of the training to help address the feelings police officers have around victims' ambivalence about the perpetrator and reluctance to report abuse and use their legal options.

Prosecutors view victims' safety as a primary concern when arguing for bail, holding the batterer accountable regardless of victim testimony, and seeking stiff dispositions. Specialized prosecutors and criminal court advocates work as a team to decide the best way to go forward on each individual case. Similarly, judges impose strict sanctions and comprehensive orders, including firearms seizure. Also included are long-term batterer's intervention, mandatory abstinence from alcohol and drugs, and random urine testing for offenders.

A further component in Quincy's response system involves working closely with probation, enforcing maximum surveillance of the abuser and supervision of the terms set out by the judge. If batterers fail to comply with any condition of probation, they are immediately surrendered to the court for sentencing. If they fail to show up at court for the surrender, their pictures and a description of their crime are printed in the local newspaper presenting them as "wanted" probation absconders. Enlightened citizens call in sightings of these individuals, with the result that over 85% are picked up by the police or turn themselves in. The chief probation officer outlines why wife beaters are the most significant supervision challenge: "Batterers share traits of high risk offenders: they don't believe what they do is criminal; they blame the victims; they have substance abuse problems; they have easy access to the victim; many times they are tied to their victims by kids and visitation rights; and they are very resistant to court orders" (Winsten, 1993, p. 36).

Evaluation: An Ongoing Process

We have found that the most effective way of evaluating existing program efforts is by simply asking the victims: Develop a brief survey for victims to fill out anonymously about how helpful each service provider or department was and ask what would have been even more helpful. We found in our survey that 97% of the victims who were briefed when they applied for a restraining order thought that the briefing answered all of their questions. Ninety-five percent reported that they felt prepared for the court process, and another 93% thought the briefing provided useful information and referrals. Dozens of survey respondents expressed gratitude for the tremendous understanding and support that the staff provided. Here are some of the comments made by responders:

> I've got restraining orders before, but briefings and their support make me able to come back when he violated the order.
>
> The briefings and support group helped me so much. I am a stronger person, have learned so much about myself.
>
> The briefings eased the fear . . . I didn't understand the process. The briefings supported me, I didn't feel like I was by myself.
>
> I had no idea what was going to happen. She explained step by step. It was very helpful.
>
> I thought you guys did a great job.
>
> It helped knowing I wasn't the only one in that position, that there are people out there to help.
>
> I was shaking like a leaf the whole time until the advocate came and talked with us.
>
> I think it was terrific . . . I am impressed and grateful.

When inquiries come from other states and countries about what changes we have made over the years to become more effective, I describe five: (1) For lack of services, we received commitment from the top; (2) for uncoordinated responses, we developed court-based and community roundtables; (3) for inconsistent intervention, we specialized staff; (4) for insensitivity, we did in-house and community training; and (5) for societal acceptance, we did prevention in the schools.

With any program initiative, we must ask, "Does it work?" The fact that the city of Quincy had no domestic homicides for over 10 years is one answer. In addition, a study was done comparing Quincy District Court with an adjacent jurisdiction similar in demographics. Women who sought protection at Quincy Court followed their cases through nearly two-and-a-half times more often than did women who used the other court. In addition, those who used the other court were reabused over twice as often as the Quincy women (Hardeman, 1994). Quincy Court has the lowest drop rate for restraining orders in the state.

After many years of consulting with communities nationwide and internationally about domestic violence prevention, I have found that one of the consistent problems leading to gaps in life-saving intervention is the lack of interagency and interdepartmental coordination. Even simple communication was not always available. If all players don't talk to one another, some services are duplicated whereas others are not provided; this leaves holes in the system and animosity among the groups. I have observed that once existing groups of service providers and criminal justice personnel were assisted in pulling together, enormous strides were made in filling in the gaps, and victims were less likely to get lost in the shuffle.

Prevention of Domestic Violence

Although the above-mentioned level of training is essential for effective intervention, most professional interaction is after the fact—the violence has already begun, if not escalated to dangerous proportions. Not only must we all become educated about this issue as professionals, but we need to be activists and have a positive impact on the people's lives we touch in our chosen profession. We must also see the need to attack this problem before it starts, with more proactive prevention.

The key to long-term change in our society is prevention through education of our youth. If we can reach our children in high school, junior high, and even elementary school with the messages that "Domestic violence is a crime," "There are consequences to domestic violence," and "There are alternative ways to deal with feelings and conflict," we just might create a new generation of thinking and responding to violence in relationships. When young people are asked if they have ever seen warning signs or actual violence in dating relationships, virtually every student raises a hand. It is up to all of us as citizens to encourage our schools to do something to educate our youth about this issue. A variety of curricula are available for school children in your local resource center. Make it your job to get involved.

Another form of prevention is mentoring programs. One such program, the MVP Project (Mentors in Violence Prevention), was established at Northeastern University to institutionalize greater participation of athletes in campus-based efforts to prevent dating violence, sexual harassment, rape, and all forms of male violence against women. MVP works with both male and female student athletes, educating them about their roles and responsibilities while inspiring them to take active leadership roles on these critical issues.

Other efforts were initiated by the surviving family members of a victim of teen dating violence that ended tragically in homicide. *The Yellow Dress*, a skit performed by a young actress that dramatically portrays the victim's abusive teen dating relationship from courtship to the end of her life, has been very well received by student groups. Discussion groups follow the presentation to provide information and support to the young viewers. The purpose of offering this presentation to hundreds of high schools across Massachusetts is to heighten awareness among teens and intervene before another life ends prematurely. Deanna's Fund, the organizaion that produces *The Yellow Dress* also offers theater performances as an educational tool for younger students. *Remote Control, Doing the Right Thing,* and *All Starz* are performances available for kindergarten through junior high school students (see Appendix 8).

Other activities that have been extremely useful in working with young people are mock trials. Students play all the parts of an actual trial about domestic abuse to learn more about the issue of domestic violence and the realities of the court system. A peace walk; a discussion group after viewing a teen dating violence video, skit, or case scenario; public service announcements produced with teens; cable talk shows; community panel discussions; open forums; youth-group fundraisers; and training sessions for students and school personnel are also creative ways to teach youth and get them involved with the issue. Student alliances and coalitions along with teen hotlines and student counseling groups for both teen victims and perpetrators are also effective in the educational process.

Conclusion and Implications

Every one of the model domestic violence programs highlighted by the National Council of Juvenile and Family Court Judges draws on the entire community to work together. This community networking is missing in most communities. Since this problem affects us all, including our children and our future generations, we all must accept the challenge: Every person needs to make a personal and professional commitment to combat domestic violence in her or his community. Speak up at home. Speak up at work, in school, and also in religious settings. Speak up with your friends, family, neighbors, and co-workers. Speak out against domestic violence, and we will see change. Call for further changes in legislation against abuse—contact your legislators and representatives.

Model programs should be replicated; a system should be established to monitor professionals or other certified organizations responding to domestic violence for their compliance with applicable laws and standards of practice. Professionals should be held accountable for their actions or inactions, and government leaders and policymakers should adopt and articulate a strong commitment to end domestic violence. This commitment should produce long-term funding; intense community and student education about the problem; and the message to the public that this is a societal problem that will no longer be tolerated.

Batterers abuse successfully over long periods of time because they can. Most of what has been done to stop the violence has been done by women, many of whom are also survivors of domestic violence. Silence speaks loudly. If we don't become a society of men and women, young and old, who consistently condemn domestic violence, and if we don't take steps to mobilize our communities to eradicate this spiraling social epidemic, we will continue to bandage and bury many more members of our society in the years to come. "In 1995, at the United Nations World Conference for Women in Beijing, China, domestic violence was declared the number one human rights violation facing women and children around the globe. Please, we need everyone to help stop this violence" (Gordon and Kabat, 2000).

APPENDIX 1

The Power and Control Wheel

The Power and Control Wheel was designed to help illustrate how batterers control their partners. It is useful for victims of domestic abuse to review this with a domestic violence specialist from the criminal justice system, a shelter, or a social service agency.

Source: Domestic Abuse Intervention Project, Duluth, Minnesota. Reprinted by permission.

APPENDIX 2

The Equality Wheel

The Equality Wheel demonstrates what qualities a nonabusive, noncontrolling relationship can contain. It is recommended that victims of domestic abuse review this information with a domestic violence specialist from the criminal justice system, a shelter, or a social service agency, to learn more about healthy relationships.

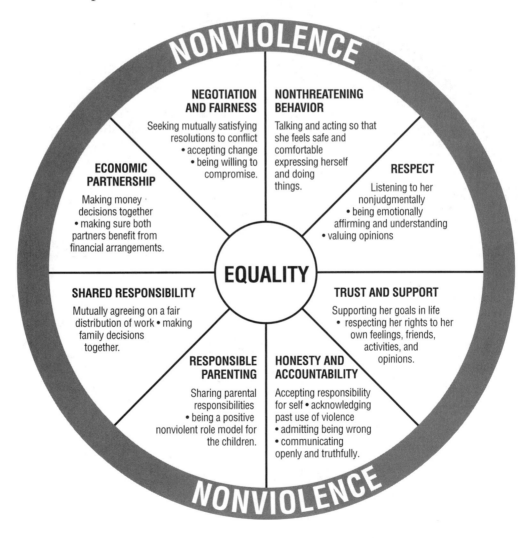

Source: Domestic Abuse Intervention Project, Duluth, Minnesota. Reprinted by permission.

APPENDIX 3

Violent and Controlling Behavior Checklist

Psychological and Economic Abuse:

Instructions: Check off each type of abuse (circle each specific behavior) that you have done in the past 3 months.

___ Yelling, swearing, being lewd, using angry expressions or gestures, outshouting.

___ Criticism (name-calling, mocking, put downs, ridicule, accusations, blaming, use of trivializing gestures).

___ Threats (verbal and nonverbal, direct or implied).

___ Harassment (uninvited visits or calls, following her around, checking up on her, embarrassing her in public, not leaving when asked to, bothering her at work).

___ Isolation (preventing her or making it difficult for her to see or talk to friends, relatives, or others, e.g. criticizing her friends, making jealous comments or accusations, not helping out with the children when she wants to work or go out).

___ Pressure Tactics (rushing her to make decisions, using guilt or accusations, sulking, making threats to have affairs, withholding financial support, manipulating the children, turning friends against her).

___ Economic Abuse (withholding money, the car, credit cards). Making her account for her spending, overspending on yourself, using the legal system against her, using money for drugs or alcohol.

___ Claiming "The Truth," being the authority, defining her behavior, manipulating logic.

___ Lying, withholding information, being unfaithful.

___ Withholding help on childcare or housework, not doing your share, not following through on agreements.

___ Emotional Withholding (not giving support, validation, attention, compliments or respect for her feelings, opinions, and rights). Not showing your feelings other than anger.

___ Not taking care of yourself, abusing alcohol or drugs, staying out late, being reckless, not asking for help.

Physical Violence:

___ Slap, punch, grab, kick, choke, push, finger poking, pull hair, pinch, bite, twist arm.

___ Rape (use of force, threats, or coercion to obtain sex).

___ Use of weapons, throwing things, keeping weapons around to frighten her.

___ Intimidation (blocking her exit, threatening or scary gestures, use of size to intimidate, standing over her, driving recklessly, outshouting, punching walls, banging the table, knocking things around.

___ Damaging or destroying her possessions, abusing the pets, damaging or destroying joint possessions.

___ Restraint (disabling her car, blocking her exit, locking her in a room, sitting on her, preventing her from using the phone, taking her car keys.

Source: ©EMERGE: A Men's Counseling Service on Domestic Violence, 2380 Massachusetts Avenue, Suite 101, Cambridge, MA 02140. Used by permission.

APPENDIX 4

Assessment of the Lethality of a Batterer

Has your partner:

- ever prevented you from leaving home, working, or going to school?
- destroyed your possessions or things of value to you?
- monitored your activities or phone calls?
- followed you or stalked you?
- accused you of being unfaithful?
- ever threatened to commit suicide?
- ever threatened to injure you or those close to you?
- ever hit, slapped, pushed, or kicked you?
- ever owned a weapon, had access to weapons, or attacked you with a weapon?
- ever threatened to kill you?
- ever told you how you would be injured or killed?
- had a history of violent behavior outside the home?
- had a criminal record involving violence toward you or others?
- ever engaged in reckless behavior?
- ever forced you to have sex or to participate in sexual relations that made you uncomfortable?
- had a history of depression, paranoia, or other mental illness?
- ever said, "If I can't have you, no one will"?
- abused drugs or alcohol?

Has the violence become worse over time?

Has the violence become more frequent over time?

APPENDIX 5

Domestic Violence Safety Plan

Safety During an Explosive Argument

- If an argument seems unavoidable, try to have it in a room or area with an exit and *not in the bathroom, kitchen, or anywhere near weapons.*
- Practice how to get out of your home safely. Identify which doors, windows, elevators, or stairs would be best.
- Have a packed bag ready and **keep it in a secret place** so you can leave quickly.
- Identify a neighbor you can tell about the violence and ask them to call the police if they hear a disturbance coming from your home.
- Devise a code word to use with your children, family, friends, and neighbors when you need the police.
- If the situation is very dangerous, **use your own instincts and judgments to keep yourself and your children safe.** Call the police as soon as it is safe to do so.

Safety When Preparing to Leave

- Determine who will let you stay with them or lend you some money.
- Always try to take your children with you or make arrangement to leave them with someone else.
- Leave money, extra keys, copies of important documents, and clothes with someone you trust.
- Open a savings account **in your own name** to establish or increase your financial independence.
- Keep the shelter numbers close by and keep change or a calling card with you at all times.
- Review your safety plan with a domestic violence advocate to plan the safest way to leave your batterer.

Safety on the Job and in Public

- At work, decide who you will tell about your situation. This should include office or building security. (Provide a picture of your batterer if possible.)
- Arrange to have someone screen your telephone calls if possible.
- Devise a safety plan for when you leave work. Have someone escort you to your car, bus, or train. Use a variety of routes to go home if possible. Think about what you would do if something happened while going home.

Safety with a Restraining Order

- When criminal charges are filed against your batterer, be sure to let the police and court know if you want a restraining order.
- **After court hours, the police can get an emergency order from a judge on call that will be in effect until the next court day.**
- Restraining orders don't last forever—be sure you know when yours expires and renew it.
- Keep your restraining order with you at all times; leave extra copies at work, with a friend, in your car, etc.
- Call the police immediately if your partner breaks the restraining order.
- Think of alternative ways to keep safe if the police do not respond right away.
- Inform family, friends, neighbors, and people at work that you have a restraining order in effect.
- Try to avoid places where your batterer may go.

Safety in Your Home

- Inform neighbors and landlord that your partner no longer lives with you, and they should call the police if they see your abuser near your home.
- Rehearse a safety plan with your children for when you are not with them.
- Inform your children's school or daycare about who has permission to pick up your children.
- Give school authorities a copy of your restraining order.
- Change/add locks to your doors and windows as soon as possible.
- Change your telephone number.

Your Safety and Emotional Health

- If you are thinking of returning to a potentially abusive situation, discuss an alternative plan with someone you trust.
- If you have to communicate with your partner, determine the safest way to do so.
- Have positive thoughts about yourself and be assertive with others about your needs.
- Plan to attend a support group for at least two weeks to gain support from others and learn more about yourself and the relationship.
- Decide who you can call freely and openly to give you the support you need.
- Read articles, books, and poetry to help you feel stronger.

Source: Weymouth Police Department, Weymouth, Massachusetts. Reprinted with permission.

APPENDIX 6

Intervention/Treatment Issues for Victim of Domestic Violence

Presenting problem: physical, emotional, psychological, economic, and/or sexual abuse

1. Make safety planning the number one priority.
2. Allow the victim to vent and understand her ambivalence.
3. Express unconditional acceptance and offer extensive support.
4. Help victim identify/label her feelings and fears.
5. Help victim normalize/generalize her feelings.
6. Educate the victim on: dynamics of violence, cycle of abuse, definition of abuse, power and control, affects of abuse on her and her children, obstacles to leaving, the batterer, role of alcohol or drugs, legal and other options, and resources available to her and her children
7. Defeat misconceptions: that the victim is responsible, that there are external excuses, that the abuser is "out of control," that couples counseling is best, that a restraining order solves everything, that abuse happens only in certain economic/social groups, that appearances are accurate, that she has no options, that there is a quick fix, that things are not so bad if she stays.
8. Build the victim's self-esteem and independence.
9. Develop and strengthen the victim's skills: social, job, community networking, asssertiveness, parenting, problem solving, decision making, financial management, etc.
10. Formulate goals and plans for change.
11. Be supportive with follow-through and setbacks.
12. Predict feelings, the batterer's behavior, and the realities of the court process.
13. Set up a support system with local resources, family, and friends.

With consistent support from the criminal justice system and local social service systems on these treatment issues, the victim no longer feels powerless. She feels in control of her life.

Note: Group work is the most powerful and effective mode of treatment. Individual counseling is helpful when the above issues are addressed, but couples work is never appropriate. It is not safe for a victim to disclose the abuse in front of the perpetrator, and couples work reinforces the misconception that the abuse is equally the victim's and batterer's responsibility.

APPENDIX 7

How Do I Know If the Abuser Is Changing?

The victim is the best judge of whether the abuser is changing or not; if your gut feeling is that he has not changed, trust that feeling regardless of other signs. Some of the things that batterers' treatment providers look for are:

- Has he completely stopped saying and doing things that frighten you?
- Can you express anger toward him without being punished for it?
- Does it feel safe to bring up topics that you know upset him?
- Can he listen to your opinion and respect it even when he disagrees?
- Can he argue without being abusive or domineering?
- Does he respect your wishes about sex and physical contact?
- Has he stopped expecting you to do things for him?
- Can you spend time with friends without being afraid that he'll retaliate?
- Can you do other things that are important to you, such as go to school or get a job, without feeling intimidated?
- Are you comfortable with the way he interacts with the children? Do you feel safe leaving them alone with him?
- Is he being supportive and respecting you? Does he listen well to you?
- Do you feel comfortable having friends /family around him?
- Are the extreme jealousy and possessiveness behaviors gone?
- Has he stopped blaming you and others for his feelings and problems?

Source: "What You Should Know About Your Violent Partner," published by ©EMERGE, a Massachusetts Certified Batterer's Intervention Program in Cambridge, Massachusetts. This brochure was meant for the partners of male batterers attending EMERGE. It could apply to all relationships if it were made gender neutral. Reprinted with permission.

APPENDIX 8

Resources

Reading Material

Breaking Free from Partner Abuse: Voices of Battered Women Caught in the Cycle of Domestic Violence, by Mary Maracek. Buena Park, CA: Morning Glory Press, 1993.

Chain Chain Change, for Black Women Dealing with Physical and Emotional Abuse, by Evelyn White. Seattle, WA: The Seal Press, 1985.

Escape: A Handbook for Battered Women with Disabilities, by the Volunteers of F.I.N.E.X. House. Jamaica Plain, MA.

For Shelter and Beyond: Ending Violence against Battered Women and Their Children, 2nd ed. Boston: MA Coalition of Battered Women Service Groups, Inc., 1990.

In Love & In Danger: A Teen's Guide to Breaking Free of Abusive Relationships, by B. Levy. Seattle, WA: Seal Press, 1993.

Keeping the Faith: Questions and Answers for the Abused Woman, by Marie Fortune. New York: Harper & Row, 1987.

Mejor Sola Que Mal Accompanada: Para Le Mujer Golpeada (For the Latina in an Abusive Relationship), by M. Zambrano. Seattle, WA: The Seal Press, 1985.

Men Who Beat the Men Who Love Them, by D. Island and P. Letellier. Center City, MN: Haworth Press, 1991.

Naming the Violence: Speaking Out against Lesbian Battering, ed. by Kerry Lobel. Seattle, WA: The Seal Press, 1986.

When Love Goes Wrong: What to Do When You Can't Do Anything Right, by Ann Jones and Susan Schechter. New York: Harper Collins, 1992.

"Why Do Men Batter Their Wives?" by James Ptacek. In *Feminist Perspectives on Wife Abuse,* ed. by M. N. Bograd and K. Yllo. Beverly Hills, CA: Sage, 1988.

You Can Be Free: An Easy-to-Read Handbook for Abused Women, by Sue Davidson and Ginny NiCarthy. Seattle, WA: The Seal Press, 1989.

Curriculum, Videos, and Performances

Creating a Public Response to Private Violence: Educating & Training Materials. Duluth, MN: National Training Project of the Duluth Domestic Abuse Intervention Project, 1993.

Defending Our Lives. Cambridge, MA: Cambridge Documentary Films, Inc., 1993.

Family Violence: State-of-the-Art Court Programs. Reno, NV: National Council of Juvenile & Family Court Judges, 1992.

Heart on a Chain: The Truth about Date Violence. Northbrook, IL: Advance American Communications, distributed by Coronet/TI Film & Video, 1993.

MVP (Mentors in Violence Prevention) Playbook. Boston: Northeastern University, Center for the Study of Sport in Society, 1994.

Program Manual: First Stage Groups for Men Who Batter, by D. Adams, L. Bancroft, T. German, and C. Sousa. Cambridge, MA: EMERGE, Inc., 1992.

The Quincy Court Model Domestic Abuse Program Manual. Cambridge, MA: Polaroid Corporation, 1995. Polaroid Information Service, PO Box 100, Penfield, NY, 14526–9958.

Teen Dating Violence and Abuse Prevention Act. Boston, MA: MA Department of Education, 2000.

Teen Dating Violence Curriculum, by C. Sousa, L. Bancroft, and T. German. Cambridge, MA: Dating Violence Intervention Project, 1992.

Violent No More: Helping Men End Domestic Violence, by M. Paymar. Alameda, CA: Hunter House, 1993.

The Yellow Dress, Remote Control, Doing the Right Thing, and *All Starz* (teen dating violence theater production). Pastiche Productions, Deana's Fund, Woburn, MA: 1995.

National Hotlines and Resources

Department of Justice Battered Women's Justice Project: 1–800–903–0111

Health Resource Center on Domestic Violence: 1–888–792–2873

National Coalition Against Domestic Violence: 1–303–839–1852

National Domestic Violence Hotline: 1–800–799–SAFE or 1–800–787–3224 (TDD)

National Gay and Lesbian Task Force: 1–202–332–6483

National Resource Center on Domestic Violence: 1–800–537–2238

Rape Abuse and Incest National Network: 1–800–656–HOPE

Resource Center on Domestic Violence: Child Protection and Custody: 1–800–52–PEACE

References

American Medical Association. (1996). *Family Violence: Building a Coordinated Community Response.* New York: American Medical Association.

Browne, A. (1993). Violence against women by male partners: Prevalence, outcomes, and policy implications. *American Psychologist, 48,* 1077.

Buel, S. M. (1990, May). *An Integrated Response to Family Violence: Effective Intervention by Criminal and Civil Justice Systems.* J. D. thesis, Harvard Law School, Cambridge, MA.

Commonwealth Fund. (1993, July). *First Comprehensive National Health Survey of American Women.* New York: Commonwealth Fund.

Commonwealth v. McAfee. (1871). Massachusetts General Laws, Chapter 458.

Day, R. (1994, July 3). Domestic violence: Assault on the home front. *Oregonian,* 5(13): 1.

Eagan, Margery. (1991, October 24). Battered women deserve unconditional protection. *Boston Herald,* p. 12.

Gordon, M., and Kabat, S. (2000). *Domestic Violence: The Facts.* Jamaica Plains, MA: Peace At Home, Inc.

Guarino, H. (1985). *Delinquent Youth and Family Violence: A Study of Abuse and Neglect in Homes of Serious Juvenile Offenders.* Commonwealth of Mass Publication No. 14, 020–74–2–86–CVC. Boston: Boston Department of Youth Services.

Hamberger, L., Saunders, D., and Hovey, M. (1992, May/June). Prevalence of domestic violence in community practice and rate of physician inquiry. *Family Medicine, 24,* p. 4.

Hardeman, J. (1994). *Implementation of the 209A Abuse Prevention Act.* Unpublished study, Brandeis University, Waltham, MA.

Harlow, C. (1991). *Female victims of violent crime.* Washington, DC: U.S. Department of Justice, Bureau of Justice Statistics.

Hilton, Z. (1992). Battered women's concerns about their children witnessing wife assault. *Journal of Interpersonal Violence, 7,* 77–86.

Jaffe, P., Wolfe, D., and Wilson, S. (1990). *Children of Battered Women.* Newbury Park, CA: Sage.

Kramer, R. (1989). *Alcohol and victimization factors in the histories of abused women who come to court: A retrospective case-controlled study.* UMI, Dissertation Information Service. Ann Arbor, MI.

League of Women Voters of Minneapolis. (1990, April). *Breaking the cycle of violence: A focus on primary prevention efforts.* (p. 8). Minneapolis, MN: League of Women Voters of Minneapolis.

Levy, B. (Ed.). (1990). *Dating violence: Young women in danger.* Seattle: Seal Press.

Lewis, D. (1994, October 13). A bottom line for violence. *Boston Globe,* pp. 41,43.

Massachusetts Coalition of Battered Women's Service Groups. (1990). *Fact Sheet.* Boston: Massachusetts Coalition of Battered Women's Service Groups.

———. (1992). *For shelter and beyond: Ending violence against battered women and their children.* Boston: Massachusetts Coalition of Battered Women's Service Groups.

Massachusetts Department of Public Health (1995).*Massachusetts Guidelines and Standards for the Certification of Batterer Intervention Programs.* Boston: Massachusetts Departmnet of Public Health.

Massachusetts Department of Social Services. (1995, February 13). *Domestic violence protocol* (Appendix C) 180.

Massachusetts Medical Society. (1992, October). *Partner Violence, How to Recognize and Treat Victims of Abuse: A Guide for Physicians.* Waltham: Massachusetts Medical Society.

Meyer, H. (1992, January 6). The billion dollar epidemic. *American Medical News,* p. 7.

National Resource Center on Domestic Violence. (1996). *Fact Sheet.* Washington, DC: National Resource Center on Domestic Violence.

Peled, E., Jaffe, P., and Edleson, J. (Eds.). (1995). *Ending the Cycle of Violence—Community Responses to the Children of Battered Women.* Thousand Oaks, CA: Sage.

Senate Judiciary Hearings. (1990). *Violence Against Women* Act. Washington, DC: U.S. Senate Judiciary Hearings.

Straus, M. B. (1991, September). *Children As Witnesses to Marital Violence: A Risk Factor for Lifelong Problems among Nationally Representative Sample of American Men and Women.* Paper presented at the Ross Roundtable on Children and Violence, Washington, DC.

Straus, M. B. (Ed.). (1990). *Abuse and Victimization Across the Life Span.* Baltimore: Johns Hopkins University Press.

Straus, M. B., Gelles, R. J., and Steinmetz, S. K. (1980). *Behind Closed Doors: Violence in the American Family.* New York: Doubleday.

Till death do them part? (1994, July 4). *U.S. News & World Report,* p. 25.

U.S. Bureau of Justice. (1993). *Report to the Nation on Crime and Justice.* Washington, DC: U.S. Bureau of Justice.

U.S. Department of Justice. (1994, November). *Bureau of Justice statistics—Violence between intimates.* NCJ–149259. Washington, DC: U.S. Department of Justice.

Winsten, J. (1993, June). *Commonwealth of Massachusetts Attorney General Scott Harshbarger and Associate Dean and Director of Center for Health Communication Jay A. Winsten. Report on domestic violence: A committment to action.* Boston: Harvard School of Public Health.

CHAPTER 8

Treatment and Recognition for Victims of Terrorism

Jeremy Spindlove

Those who make peaceful revolution impossible will make violent revolution inevitable.
   —John Fitzgerald Kennedy

Introduction

The difficult question of how best to define terrorism is discussed in this chapter. Victims of terrorism have always been readily apparent, since their immediate plight provides powerful and vivid news footage. Who are these victims and how do they cope with the effects and aftereffects of such devastating and traumatic events? In this chapter, I discuss some landmark events that focus attention on the manner in which victims handle the trauma and psychological tribulations of specific events, such as the Stockholm syndrome, the abduction of Patty Hearst, and the siege of the Iranian embassy in London. Although these events are markedly dissimilar, the behaviors involved and responses of the players are similar. How do those who come face-to-face with the immediate effects of terrorist acts of violence handle the psychological impact? I will give an account of my own experience and how the vividness of those acts affected me personally. I will also analyze how far the determination of who really is a victim of terror can be done. Terrorism affects the lives of nearly all of us in some form or another and did so extensively for the last 40 years of the twentieth century: Take any airline flight, and you experience the preboard passenger screening process at airport security, a direct outgrowth of the acts of terror perpetrated on civil aviation in the late 1960s. A trip to the revamped World Trade Center in New York prior to September 11, 2001, revealed large planters of shrubs strategically placed to prevent another truck bomb attack like the one in February 1993. The streets of London today are dotted with CCTV cameras that record vehicle movements into and around the city, surveillance measures that grew out of efforts to combat Provisional IRA attacks on London's business center.

In 1998, when the U.S. embassies in Nairobi and Dar es Salaam were bombed, and 2000, when the USS *Cole* was struck by a boat packed with explosives as it lay in the Yemen port of Aden, most Americans still considered terrorism an overseas problem, despite the Oklahoma City and 1993 World Trade Center bombings. Then, on September 11, 2001, the myth of safety from terrorist acts on U.S. soil was abruptly shattered when three commercial aircraft were hijacked and then flown into both towers of the World Trade Center and the Pentagon; a fourth hijacked flight, reportedly on course for the White House, was brought down in Pennsylvania, apparently by passengers on board. These attacks, masterfully coordinated (allegedly by the Al Qaeda and Osama bin Laden) and executed by suicide bombers, were a harrowing wake-up call to the threat of terrorism . . . anywhere and at any time. At this writing, the war on terrorism is ongoing; the Al Qaeda and Taliban are on the run in Afghanistan, and the worldwide coalition of free countries against terrorism is hanging together to, as President George W. Bush declared, "root out, track down, and destroy terrorists throughout the world" (CNN, 2001).

Terror groups would have us believe that there are no innocent victims of terrorism. In fact, the opposite is the sad reality, as will be shown in this chapter. Many more people die in natural disasters than at the hand of terrorists, but that is more understandable then the evil and obscene atrocities of terrorism.

Terrorism: The Search for a Definition

There exists today no universally accepted definition of the term "terrorism," in spite of the vast number of books on the topic. The lack of definitional clarity and the inappropriate use of the word "terrorism" continue to prompt wide-ranging debate on the topic. There are literally hundreds of definitions.

The U.S. Federal Bureau of Investigation (FBI) defines terrorism thus:

> Terrorism is the unlawful use of force or violence against persons or property to intimidate or coerce a government, the civilian population, or any segment thereof, in furtherance of political or social objectives. Editors "FBI Counterterrorism Responsibilities." (FBI website, Appendix 2)

From this we can deduce that not only individuals but also property, entire governments, and civil populations can be victims of terrorism.

Other notables define terrorism more broadly:

Terrorism is the use or threatened use of force designed to bring about political change. (Brian Jenkins, quoted in Simonsen and Spindlove, 2000, p. 19)

Terrorism constitutes the illegitimate use of force to achieve a political objective when innocent people are targeted" (Walter Laqueur, quoted in Simonsen and Spindlove, 2000, p. 19)

Terrorism is the premeditated, deliberate, systematic murder, mayhem, and threatening of the innocent to create fear and intimidation in order to gain a political or tactical advantage, usually to influence an audience. (James M. Poland, quoted in Simonsen and Spindlove, 2000, p. 19)

In 1986 the Vice President's Task Force on terrorism defined terrorism as

the unlawful use or threat of violence against persons or property to further political or social objectives. It is usually intended to intimidate or coerce a government, individuals or groups, or to modify their behavior or politics. (Terrorism Research Center, 1996)

These definitions are very broad and attempt to encompass the entire spectrum of violence that is terrorism.

If defining terrorism is difficult, then society's ability to respond to it is even tougher. Laws did not exist in the 1960s to deal with terrorism. INTERPOL, the international police organization set up to transcend national borders, had its own charter that precluded it from involvement in issues of a religious, ethnic/racial, and political nature, yet modern-day terrorists invariably launch their attacks on the basis of just such issues. Therefore INTERPOL defined the acts of terror organizations as criminal by nature. Assassination became murder, hostage taking was kidnapping, and so on.

No doubt the definitions by both the Task Force and the FBI have political expedience. Renowned expert Cindy Coombs (1997) frames terrorism in political as much as legal or military terms, and notes that a modern definition has been slow to take shape, despite hundreds of available definitions. According to Coombs, few attempts to describe terrorism meet the standard of legal scholarship necessary for use in international law, and most definitions that do meet a legal standard are not sufficiently ambiguous to satisfy politicians.

HISTORICAL TERRORISM

The first use of the word "terrorism" dates back to the French Revolution, 1792–1794, when the Reign of Terror swept France. At this time more than 400,000 "suspects" were put to death by guillotine. The end of the Terror came with the "assassination" of Robespierre and his council. As the French experience shows, terror can be used for political gain and to maintain a political system through fear and intimidation.

Applying the word "terrorist" to groups or individuals is, not surprisingly, one-sided. The groups who use terror for their goals like to call themselves "freedom fighters," a "workers' army," an "army of liberation," and the like, but never "terrorists."

Terror tactics are used in war as well as during peacetime and can be an effective weapon. Combating and preventing terror attacks because of their very unpredictable nature can turn peace into war. The assassination in Sarajevo of Archduke Franz Ferdinand was the event that began World War I.

CONTEMPORARY TERRORISM

Political assassination: Assassination attempts against heads of state were more prolific in the early part of the twentieth century than at the conclusion. With the modern technical and intelligence networks available, the success of the political assassin is not assured; however, the assassination of Yitzak Rabin, prime minister of Israel, and, before him, of Anwar Sadat, president of Egypt, remind us that such attacks can be successful. Attacks against less significant figures have also taken place.

Drugs, religious fanaticism, and political murders: Drugs in the twentieth century were used to ultimate effect in realizing the politically motivated goals of zealots and fanatics. Today, drugs are used to finance the lethal expeditions of religious zealots, whose targets are not only those of another community within their region but also whole nations or groups of nations whose citizens are regarded by the zealots as legitimate targets for murder. This opens up complete nations to terror attacks by religious fundamentalist groups who espouse the death and destruction of their perceived opponents (Simonsen and Spindlove, 2000).

Piracy: Not such a common practice, with only one remarkable event—the hijacking of the *Achille Lauro* and the murder of an elderly Jewish American passenger in October 1985, by members of the Palestine Liberation Front. Piracy has continued as a criminal activity predominantly in the South China seas, where roving shiploads of pirates have attacked "boat people" escaping from Vietnam. The modern-day version of piracy is the onslaught of air piracy beginning in the 1960s.

State-sponsored terrorism: Government support in the form of money or sanctuary for terror groups has become foreign policy to many governments in their attacks on nation states. Sponsoring and financing insurgent groups either based in the target state or from without became popular in the last 30 years of the twentieth century.

DICTIONARY DEFINITIONS OF TERRORISM

Here is how some dictionaries define "terrorism":

1. The act of terrorizing; use of terror, especially the systematic use of terror by a government or other authority against particular persons or groups.
2. A condition of fear and submission produced by frightening people. (Thorndike and Barnhart, 1990).

OTHER DEFINITIONS

Simple: Violence or threatened violence intended to produce fear or change.

Legal: Criminal violence violating criminal codes and punishable by the state.

Analytical: A specific political and social factor behind individual terrorist acts.

State-sponsored: Terrorist groups used to attack Western interests.

State: Power of the government used to terrorize its people into submission. (U.S. Army Field Manual, 1993)

Statistics

The number of victims of terrorist attacks around the world grows on a daily basis. Not a day goes by when some form of terror attack is not reported in the news, be it in Northern Ireland, India, South Africa, South America, Eastern Europe, or the Middle East. Clearly the scope of terrorism in the twenty-first century is wide.

To begin to appreciate the levels of violence, it is helpful to look at who gets killed and the numbers involved. One of the best modern-day examples is Northern Ireland, where the Protestants and Catholics were at each other's throats for most of the last century and where since the 1960s the Troubles have brought about violence and terror of a magnitude that seems almost incomprehensible for today's Western society. There has been a general acceptance by both sides in this conflict that violence is the inevitable and expected outcome at every turn. During the most violent period of the Troubles, 1969–1983, there were 29,853 shooting incidents, 11,336 bombings, and 1,478 incendiaries (Royal Ulster Constabulary, 1984). That's an average of eight incidents of a terrorist nature every day for 14 years! In a more telling comparison, if the same terror actions were taking place in the United States proportionate to population, there would have been 345,000 dead and over 2.55 million injured. Whether that would be accepted in the United States is but a conversation topic and not relevant to the issues here. Terrorism and terrorists have likely and unlikely targets. Viewing television news footage of the protection afforded heads of state such as the president of the United States gives some indication of the level of protection for the proposed victim (the president). However, the everyday man, woman, or child in the street is not afforded such luxury, and unfortunately the bulk of many terror attacks is against what are frequently referred to as "soft targets"—the general public. So victims are varied and many. On a worldwide scale, the number of terrorist attacks noted by the U.S. State Department for 1999 totaled 392, with 233 victims killed. North America counted 2 attacks, while Latin American countries counted 121 attacks with three fatalities. Asia led the list of regions with 141 dead from a total of 72 attacks. The attacks on September 11, 2001, resulted in 3,000–4,000 deaths—clearly the most deadly example of terrorism in modern times.

State Terrorism: Kidnap Victim Umaru Dikko

Is state terrorism a recent phenomenon? Probably it goes as far back as the execution of Marie-Antoinette on October 16, 1763, and the guillotining of enemies of the French Revolution—death by illegal, violent, and irregular means. State terrorism today refers to a state's practicing terror on its own defenseless citizens, usually by some covert state agency (Simonsen and Spindlove, 2000).

An example of this is the case of Umaru Dikko, a former politician from the African state of Nigeria. Democracy in Nigeria was dealt an untimely blow by a military coup on December 31, 1983, which brought to an end the Second Republic. The previous government election had had the definite smell of election rigging about it, and although the president felt that he enjoyed an overwhelming majority support from the Nigerian populace, this actually was not the case—particularly with the military. After the coup and during his New Year's statement to the people of Nigeria, Major General Buhari spoke of "the propensity of the outgoing civilian administration to mismanage our financial resources . . . the last general elections were anything but free and fair." He stressed that party activities were characterized by "thuggery and rigging" and that the leadership was "corrupt, inept and insensitive" ("Buhari's New Year's Broadcast," 1984).

The military coup and the demise of a democratic system of government were cause for concern both locally and internationally. Umaru Dikko was the former president's right arm, perceived as the "strongman" in the civilian government and a voice of influence to be listened to. While traveling in Europe and the United

States, he granted interviews to journalists that were becoming more threatening to the military government of Nigeria, boasting that he had set aside US$300 million to finance a mercenary-led invasion of Nigeria with an army of 150,000 (more than the total number of men in the Nigerian armed forces) (Okolo, 1987). These verbal jousts had a definite impact on the military rulers: He was the most wanted man in Nigeria. His actions and threats, which included proclaiming a *jihad,* or holy war, against Nigeria, were perceived by the state as terroristic in nature and were to almost cost Dikko his life. Dikko was kidnapped as he stepped out of his London residence on July 5, 1985. But for the quick actions of his secretary, who witnessed the events, Dikko would most likely now be a permanent statistic of state terror tactics. Dikko was drugged and transported to Stanstead Airport in Essex; there the trussed-up Dikko and his handlers were to be shipped by crate on a Nigerian Airways flight from London. British Customs and Excise intercepted the consignment, however, and Dikko was freed (Okolo, 1987). He was alive thanks to the actions of the authorities in England. The state of Nigeria's involvement in this action is only slightly hidden by the activists involved; most of them had some political or business advantage to gain by taking on the kidnap duty for their homeland. Had the Nigerian government been aware of it, they might have been able to effect Dikko's removal from the U.K. by means of extradition if, as they believed, he had also plundered Nigeria of millions of dollars in oil revenues.

Once we accept that terrorism is simply a means to an end, we can apply the term without the inclusion of moral beliefs and sociological or political mumbo-jumbo. The operatives of the PLO are terrorists, but that fact alone does not mean that their aims and objectives are without validity. IRA members can be described as freedom fighters, but they must also accept being called terrorists, given their methods of reaching their goal (Simonsen and Spindlove, 2000).

Victims

There have been many victims of terror, but who are they and how do they become victims? Who are those 233 dead victims from 1999? Depending on the region of the globe, you can get a relatively clear picture as to which group or society is targeted for terrorism. In Northern Ireland you can become a victim in several different ways. Factional infighting occurs within the established terror groups operating in Northern Ireland, through sectarian violence between Catholic and Protestant, and what is interesting is that victims are sometimes random and belong to either the Catholic or Protestant Church, but the actual victim's death has little or no effect on the cause of either terror group in either a united or separated Ireland. Should the terror attack occur in an African nation, it is likely one clan or tribe against another, and again the victims are innocents who play no part in the achievement of the terrorist goals. Islamic fundamentalists, on the other hand, view the United States as the Great Satan, thus advancing the theory that all U.S. facilities and citizens are fair targets in their holy war! The attacks on the U.S. embassies in Nairobi and Dar es Salaam were considered attacks on soft targets, and a large number of those killed were victims either because they worked at the embassies or because they might have been U.S. citizens.

THE OKLAHOMA CITY EXPERIENCES

The bombing in Oklahoma City in 1995 ranks as one of the worst terrorist atrocities perpetrated on the civilian population of the United States in the twentieth century. The ravaging long-term effects of what took place are still being counted and are no doubt similar for survivors or victims at other high-stress incidents occurring around the world. However, this was the first on U.S. soil with such a high death toll, and by an American terrorist. The graphic CNN news coverage showed us how devastating that explosion was to a building of such magnitude, collapsing like a pack of cards in a scene reminiscent of aerial bomb damage of European cities during World War II. Many of the victims were employees of state and federal agencies.

Natural disasters occur frequently throughout the world, but traumatic events such as the airborne attacks of September 11, 2001, seem more extreme and have a different psychological impact for victims than other disasters. The outpouring of grief and support was immediate and effective in both human and monetary terms for the families and businesses affected by the September 11 attacks (they will always be referred to as "9–11"). The long-term psychological impacts, particularly on the rescue workers who have been working continuously in search and recovery efforts, may never be fully appreciated.

LONG-TERM REQUIREMENTS OF VICTIMS

The emotional and psychological effects of incidents like the Oklahoma bombing require government and society to provide support structures and systems to address the emotional conditions and assist with intervention programs supporting those involved in the disaster as a whole. Oklahoma has made strides to address victims' long-term needs, identified as the following:

- Long-term mental health assistance to cope with the immediate post-traumatic stress of the ongoing criminal nature of the event.
- Programs to assist workers as well as employers returning to their workplace in the critical areas of post-traumatic stress.
- The recognition of restitution for the victims.
- Dissemination of information regarding posttrial events.

Substance abuse, rage, domestic violence, and stress-related physical disorders are all by-products of the events that took place in Oklahoma City, and this disaster will continue to affect the lives it touched that day. Night terrors, nightmares, a sense of fear, and short-term memory loss are some of the symptoms reported by those whose lives were relatively untroubled prior to the bombing. Not only the victims and their loved ones but also the rescue workers were affected, working in the extreme situation and spending many long and arduous hours collecting remains and body parts. Nearly 12,984 rescue workers were involved in the rescue and recovery operation, and experts believe that perhaps 20% will suffer some form of post-traumatic stress disorder, and need help with the psychological impact of the Oklahoma bombing.

The press coverage that we devour with our breakfast cup of coffee is but a prelude to our day. We move on to our cocoon of normalcy. For those involved in such an emotionally scarring trauma, returning to normalcy is a very difficult and stressful accomplishment. The Oklahoma community will require long-term health care, particularly in the area of mental health.

Specialists in the field of mental health identify four phases in the recovery process for victims of disasters. The first and probably not the most likely phase is the "heroic" phase. Acts of extreme courage at the time of the incident typify this phase, and, not surprisingly, are portrayed in news media in glowing terms. The next phase is described as the "honeymoon," during which time the individual receives a great deal of attention as well as assistance and feels somewhat optimistic. The third is the "disillusionment" phase, when the reality sets in that things may never be the same again and loved ones are lost forever. The length of each phase is not determined by medical science, but the experts in this field believe that victims need to reach the fourth phase within five years of the incident. The final phase is the "reconstruction" phase. Efforts to help with these long-term symptoms include special services for first responders, consideration of some form of restitution for the victims, and post conviction notification of victims if a perpetrator is identified, arrested, brought to trial, and convicted for his or her crime.

VICTIMS' LEGAL RIGHTS: *UNITED STATES V. TIMOTHY MCVEIGH AND TERRY NICHOLS*

As part of the grieving process, many victims need not only the closure of a trial for those responsible but also the right by law to witness the federal court proceedings. When the court venue for the Oklahoma bombing was moved to Denver, Colorado, which is a considerable distance from the scene of the crime, many of the victims detailed their needs and had them addressed by both Oklahoma City and Denver. These needs included the ability to observe the trial, accommodations for travel and housing, accommodations for closed-circuit television (CCTV) broadcasting, support services during evidence and testimony, a separation of the victims' and defendants' families at the trial, and a process of notification that informs the victims of the ongoing criminal justice process. As a result of the venue change, two important items of legislation were enacted in this regard:

- A new federal statute established that when a federal court changes the trial venue out of the state in which the case was initially brought by more than 350 miles from the location in which the proceedings originally would have taken place, the court must order closed-circuit televising of the proceedings to be broadcast at the original location to permit victims who qualify under the statute to watch the trial proceedings (42 U.S.C. # 10608).
- Congress passed legislation prohibiting the U.S. district judge from ordering victims excluded from the trials of the defendants because the victim may testify or make a statement during the sentencing about the effect of the offense on the victim and the victim's family (18 U.S.C. # 3593).

Denver became the scene of frenzied activity with the local community's overwhelming desire to literally open up their homes to those victims wishing to travel to the trial. Over 600 people volunteered rooms in their homes for relatives of victims, and survivors of the bombing. As with all legal cases of such magnitude, the worlds' press corps were on hand to cover each and every aspect of the trial, so it became very apparent early on that a safe haven for the victims and families was needed. This was provided when the Federal Aviation Administration offered their secure facilities and auditorium to the victims.

The rebuilding of shattered lives from the Oklahoma bombing continues, and the emotional experiences that were encountered will no doubt be called on to help to respond and deal with future disasters. Some closure was finally given the survivors and families of the Oklahoma City Bombing, when Timothy McVeigh was executed on June 11, 2001.

NATIONS AS VICTIMS

If individuals can be victims of terror, then why not entire populations or countries?

The IRA

The Provisional Irish Republican Army took its fight with the British government across the Irish Sea to the British mainland and engaged in terror attacks in London and in provincial cities, targeting mainly soldiers and the pubs and establishments they were known to frequent. In the 1970s and 1980s mainland Britain saw unprecedented terror bombings, the like of which had not been seen since World War II. How did the general populace act? Well, you might expect a society to turn on all persons Irish, but that did not happen. The British public went stoically about their daily routines and left the matter of policing to the authorities. As victims, the British public did not react in a violent manner and neither did they call for the mass roundup of Irish men and women living on the mainland or seek to have them interned. They did not feel at war with the Irish people as a whole. Publicity is a powerful tool, and the devastation did little to bring support for the cause of the IRA. It did prompt Prime Minister Margaret Thatcher to take an almost Churchillian stand against terrorism. With the skillful use of counterterrorist forces available, Britain went on the offensive and fought fire with fire. These actions did much for the spirit and little for the morale of the IRA, except to give it a few more martyrs to mourn.

A further example of victimized travelers and international airlines is the use by terrorists of hijackings. Although the number of incidents involving hijackings has diminished over the last couple of decades, the more subtle approach has been to bomb airliners. Air travel in the middle half of the twentieth century had been the domain of the wealthy, but as technological advances emerged in the aviation industry, air travel emerged as the foremost and quickest means of transport. Civilian aircraft became a popular target for Palestinian terror groups in the 1960s and 1970s. To fight against this threat, air travel became more regulated, with security sanctions being mandated for both domestic and international flights. Hijackings slowed as airlines introduced passenger screening prior to boarding—this had the effect of closing the barn door after the horse had bolted. As terrorists became more sophisticated in their methods of attack, they searched for a means to attack aircraft in other ways. The long-term effect on the traveling public was that they had unwittingly become victims to terrorism. Passengers are now subject to scrutiny at all airports around the world. Who pays for this? The victims—with higher air tariffs, airport taxes, and surcharges.

Uganda: Idi Amin Dada

This despotic self-styled leader who openly praised Adolf Hitler's attempt to exterminate the Jews goes beyond the realms of a psychopath. In studying the actions of Amin, it is difficult to determine what ideology he used. He certainly embraced the modern-day practice of "ethnic cleansing," his first target being the Asians who were the backbone of the Ugandan economy. Since Uganda was part of the Commonwealth, he kicked out over 60,000 African Ugandans of Asian decent. His actions were an attempt to rid Uganda of his political and social enemies and to return the wealth of Uganda back to true-blooded Ugandans. Under his tyrannical rule he unleashed a reign of terror upon his own people.

Terror tactics more reminiscent of bygone centuries augmented Amin's blood lust, such was the barbarian nature of the terror atrocities he engaged in. He created a series of tunnels linking his own presidential palace to the Bureau of State Research. He established two secret state police organizations, the Public Safety Unit and the Bureau of State Research. The former was empowered to shoot to kill on mere suspicion, while the latter carried out interrogations and torture, usually resulting in the death of the hapless victim. The actual number of Ugandans killed during Amin's reign is not known, but is believed to be as high as *half a million*. As in other regions of Africa, tribal rivalries and old hatreds had a great part to play in the selective genocide. Amin, a member of the Lugbara tribe, set in motion the calculated elimination of all of the Lugbaras' historical tribal enemies. The Acholi and Langi tribes were the primary victims of his wholesale slaughter. Handpicked secret police and interrogation units from the Lugbara tribe were eager participants in this state-sponsored genocide. To say that Amin relished his work would be an understatement. On many occasions, he would observe or indulge or conduct torture personally. One particularly sadistic form of execution was to provide a hammer to a prisoner who was then commanded, at gunpoint, to hammer in the skull of the prisoner next to him. This gruesome procedure was repeated until the last prisoner was dispatched with a gunshot. Many executed prisoners' bodies were returned in mutilated condition to their families; others were dumped in rivers or in forests to be ravaged by predators. Among other atrocities practiced by Amin and his tribesmen was cannibalism (Simonsen and Spindlove, 2000).

Rwanda: Hutu versus Tutsi

This African nation experienced state terror on an unprecedented scale in 1994—a genocidal campaign that the international community felt unable or unwilling to prevent. In 1990, the Tutsi-dominated Rwandan Patriotic Front (RPF) launched attacks on the Hutu-controlled Rwandan government. The civil war that resulted lasted for three years before a cease-fire was reached between the two factions in 1993; in 1994, under the auspices of the United Nations, Rwanda prepared to set up some form of transitional government, with the goal of creating a multi-party democracy. However, a plane crash in April 1994 that killed Rwanda's president triggered a wave of violence that engulfed Rwanda in one of the worst genocides in history. The minority Hutu government, determined to stay in power and rule over the majority Tutsi, embarked on state terror tactics not dissimilar to those of the Nazis. The administration openly advanced its demand that Hutus hunt down and kill Tutsis. The words "terror" and "threat" were repeatedly used in its effort to foment hatred for the Tutsi. In a format reminiscent of South American death squads, the Hutu government set up a civilian militia and trained them in weaponry, hand-to-hand combat, and methods of quickly killing an enemy. This organization was called the *Interahamwe*, which means, "those who attack together." The bloodletting of the Tutsi was not counted as a criminal activity, but to the observer it was the most callous use of state power and terror against a weak, unsupported majority. The exact number of victims has never been determined, but graphic news footage following the UN withdrawal showed entire townships of Tutsi massacred by Hutu militiamen. Rwanda has continued to face the problems of millions of refugees and recurring outbreaks of violence between the Hutu and Tutsi because of their unresolved political conflicts.

SPECIFIC VICTIMS OF TERRORISM

Victims of terror attacks have been clearly and substantially depicted in media coverage as true and innocent victims of terror, from IRA car bombings in city centers to the destruction of the Alfred P. Murragh building in Oklahoma City by Timothy McVeigh, to the explosion of the Pan Am Boeing 747 over Lockerbie, Scotland. With regard to individuals, there have been the activities of the Symbionese Liberation Army (SLA) and their abduction, torture, and possible indoctrination of Patty Hearst; the abduction of Terry Waite, the Archbishop of Canterbury's special envoy in Beirut; and the cowardly murder for terrorist gains of Leon Klinghoffer by Palestinians on board a cruise ship in the Mediterranean.

Patty Hearst

Patricia Hearst, granddaughter of the famous newspaper magnate William Randolph Hearst, was abducted by members of the SLA in February 1974. She was brutalized, raped, tortured, and forced to participate in illegal acts, beginning with the San Francisco bank robbery for which she was later convicted. The traumatic kidnapping and subsequent two months of torture produced in her a state of emotional regression and fearful compliance with the demands and expectations of her captors. This was quickly followed by the coerced transformation of Patty into "Tania," her revolutionary alter-ego, and subsequently (and less well known to the public) into "Pearl," after additional trauma over a period of many months. Tania was merely a role imposed on Hearst on pain of death; it was Pearl who later represented the pseudo-identity found on psychiatric examination shortly after Hearst's arrest by the FBI. Chronic symptoms of PTSD were also prominent in this case.

Hearst's kidnapping and subsequent involvement in a bank robbery with the SLA show the classic symptoms of what has been termed the "Stockholm syndrome," discussed in the next section. It is not related only to hostage or terror incidents. Provided the following conditions are present, any one of us can experience this syndrome:

- Perceived threat to survival and the belief that one's captor is willing to act on that threat,
- The captive's perception of small kindnesses from the captor within a context of terror,
- Isolation from perspectives other than those of the captors,
- Perceived inability to escape (Trigiani, 1999).

No doubt from the moment of Hearst's capture and subsequent torture and abuse all the above conditions were met. Long before the term "Stockholm syndrome" was coined, difficult-to-explain feelings of sympathy and even identification with one's captors were recounted by former prisoners. One of these was Hungary's late Cardinal Mindszenty, who was arrested, tried, and imprisoned from 1948 until the 1956 uprising in Budapest. In his memoirs, Mindszenty (1974) wrote that within two weeks of his arrest, under constant coercive interrogation he found himself thinking along different lines than before and seeing things from his captors' point of view. His judgment, reasoning, and sense of self became distorted. "Without knowing what had happened to me, I had become a different person" (West and Martin, 1994, p. 114).

Patty Hearst's ordeal was further magnified after her release from the SLA by her subsequent arrest, trial, and conviction for her involvement in the armed robbery. The notoriety that the media pinned on her, and her jail term, were a terrible price to pay for being kidnapped by urban terrorists. There can be little doubt that Hearst's judgment, reasoning, and self-belief became severely distorted during her captivitiy and that she was in fearful compliance with the captors who held the fragile thread of her life in their hands.

The Stockholm Syndrome

The Stockholm syndrome describes the emotional transformation and psychological changes that occur in captives, and was first applied after a botched robbery at a bank in Stockholm, Sweden, in 1974. Three females and one male were taken hostage in the robbery by two ex-convicts who made threats to kill them but at the same time appeared to show a form of kindness and consideration to them. The high levels of stress that formed in the minds of the hostages led them on a path to survival, one that allowed them to identify with them. This identity took on an almost surreal aspect. The behavior of the captives and the bonding that occurred indicate strong motivational forces for survival. However in the Stockholm incident one of the female captives supposedly fell in love with one of her captors and after her release was vociferously critical of the handling of the operation by the Swedish government. Whether this type of response is typical of all incidents is not easily discernable. Certainly the effects are clear to see from the Stockholm incident. This is not the first time such psychological change has been noticed in captives' behavior.

The Iranian embassy siege in London in April 1980 is another example of Stockholm syndrome being part of a terrorist attack. Six Iranian gunmen, unhappy with the Ayatollah Khomeini's regime, forced their way into their embassy and took 26 people—embassy employees and tourists, mostly—hostage. The gunmen held the embassy for five days, but released a number of hostages during that time. The embassy was eventually stormed by the elite Special Air Service (SAS) of the British military. Although the rescue was swift and effected the release of the hostages, it did not go as smoothly as planned—two hostages were killed. After the SAS entered the building, the terrorists who had not already been killed threw down their weapons and hid themselves among the hostages. Those who were identified by their captives were shot instantly, apparently to prevent the detonation of any explosive devices. Once the terrorists were removed from the embassy, one terrorist was still unaccounted for; he was hiding with the hostages and had not been given up by them. However, he was identified by veteran BBC correspondent Sim Harris, a hostage, who was probably not as traumatized as the rest because of his profession. Again it seems strange to an observer that the terrorist would not be given up, considering the brutality of the terrorists' actions during this particular siege.

Pan Am Flight 103

One of the world's worst airline tragedies of the twentieth century was perpetrated on December 21, 1988, when a bomb exploded in the baggage compartment of a Pan Am Boeing 747. Bombings of airliners was not a new event—after all, an Air India 747 previously had been destroyed over the Irish Sea. What singled out this tragedy for special mention is the fact that the airliner disintegrated over land, in this instance the quiet Scottish town of Lockerbie. Casualties resulted on the ground as well as on the aircraft. Without going into a dissertation on the Libyan court case that resulted from this attack, we will concentrate on the victims alone. Many of those in the aircraft probably died almost immediately. Many fell to the ground in the seat rows in which they were assigned. As for the town of Lockerbie, one portion of it was destroyed when parts of the burning fuselage crashed onto rowhouses in Sherwood Crescent, setting them ablaze. The total number killed on the ground was a staggering 11. Among them were three members of the Flannigan family, four from the Sommerville family, and two from the Henry family. In such a small and tightly woven community as Lockerbie the immediate and catastrophic loss would be etched on the community for many years. In life there is one true certainty, and that is death. Yet in contemporary Western society, death is an unwelcome intruder, and, despite the certainty of death for all of us and the inevitable loss of friends and family, many of us deny and ignore it—and thus remain unprepared. When someone close to us dies, in whatever manner, we are psychologically upended (Vetter and Perlstein, 1991).

The shock, horror, and utter amazement at what occurred that night in Lockerbie scarred the populace. The town became a victim, as did the relatives of the lost loved ones on the ill-fated airliner. Perhaps many could have avoided becoming victims had they been made aware of the following threat posted by the U.S. embassy in Moscow. This message was posted on bulletin boards in all sections of the U.S. embassy in Moscow. Also journalists, businesspeople, and students of American origin in Moscow were notified about this warning. The FAA sent the warning to all U.S. carriers and airlines, including Pan Am.

ADMINISTRATIVE NOTICE
American Embassy, Moscow
December 13, 1988

To: All Embassy Employees
Subject: Threat to Civil Aviation

Post has been notified by the Federal Aviation Administration that on December 5, 1988, an unidentified individual telephoned a U.S. diplomatic facility in Europe and stated that sometime within the next two weeks there would be a bombing attempt against a Pan American aircraft flying from Frankfurt to the United States.

The FAA reports that the reliability of the information cannot be assessed at this point, but the appropriate police authorities have been notified and are pursuing the matter. Pan Am also has been notified.

In view of the lack of confirmation of this information, Post leaves to the discretion of individual travelers any decisions on altering personal travel plans or changing to another American carrier. This does not absolve the traveler from flying an American carrier.

(signed) William C. Kelly, Administrative Counselor

How many heeded that warning and how far it was disseminated is not altogether clear and at this time is probably a moot point.

In coming to terms with the loss, the victims of Pan Am 103 went about their grieving in the limelight of the world's media attention. Now some 13 years after the event, the memories are still there, but new generations are growing up in the community of Lockerbie, the families and friends of those lost remember the dead in memorial services, and American and British families share their common grief. In Scotland today there are memorial locations for remembering those who died in the terrorist attack: a stained glass window set in Lockerbie Town Hall, a memorial at Dryfsedale Cemetery, and a Remembrance Room at Tundergarth Church.

Certain victim groups have emerged from the grief of Pan Am 103. One group calling itself the Victims of Pan Am 103 has set the following goals:

- Discover the truth behind the bombing,
- Seek justice for our loved ones,
- Ensure that the airline industry maintains and improves safety measures,
- Educate the public about this incident,
- Support one another.

You might think that the victims prioritized it in reverse order. No doubt closure for some has been extremely difficult and is exacerbated by a court case that dragged on over two decades. On January 1, 2001, the Lockerbie trial came to its conclusion with one of the Libyan defendants being acquitted and the other, Abdel Basset al-Megrahi, being found guilty and receiving a sentence of life in prison with no consideration of parole for a minimum of 20 years.

Many of the victims on the flight were returning to the U.S. for Christmas, among them 35 students from Syracuse University. For the victims' friends and colleagues at the university, the healing process has included the dedication of a Place of Remembrance and also a Garden of Remembrance. Annual memorial services, as well as a scholarship fund set up to honor them, are also in place at Syracuse University.

The Families of Pan Am 103, Lockerbie, which was founded in 1989, is seeking restitution from the Libyan government and has filed a controversial wrongful death lawsuit for billions of dollars. A more extreme group calling itself Terrorism Watch: Pan Am 103, created in 1995, demands that the United States place a naval blockade on Libya.

The following is a transcript from sessions at the House of Representatives concerning the U.S. response to supporting the victims and related topics concerning the protagonists in the case of the Pan Am Flight 103 bombing:

<hr>

1st Session
H. R. 899

To provide for the liquidation of Libyan assets to pay for the costs of travel to and from the Hague of families of the victims of the crash of **Pan Am** flight **103** for the purpose of attending the trial of the terrorist suspects in the crash.

IN THE HOUSE OF REPRESENTATIVES
March 2, 1999

Mr. ANDREWS (for himself and Mr. LOBIONDO) introduced the following bill; which was referred to the Committee on International Relations

<hr>

A BILL

To provide for the liquidation of Libyan assets to pay for the costs of travel to and from the Hague of families of the victims of the crash of **Pan Am** flight **103** for the purpose of attending the trial of the terrorist suspects in the crash.

Be it enacted by the Senate and House of Representatives of the United States of America in Congress assembled,

SECTION 1. SHORT TITLE.

This Act may be cited as the "**Pan Am** Flight **103** Witness to Justice Act."

SEC. 2. VESTING AND LIQUIDATION OF LIBYAN ASSETS FOR COSTS OF TRAVEL TO THE HAGUE.

The President shall vest and liquidate so much of blocked Libyan assets as is necessary to pay for the reasonable costs of travel to and from the Hague, Netherlands, by immediate family members of United States citizens who were victims of the crash of **Pan American** flight **103** in 1988, for the purpose of attending the trial of those individuals who are suspected of terrorist acts causing the crash.

SEC. 3. DEFINITIONS.

As used in this Act:

(1) BLOCKED LIBYAN ASSETS—The term "blocked Libyan assets" means property and interests in property of the Government of Libya, its agencies, instrumentalities, and controlled entities and the Bank of Libya that are blocked pursuant to the International Emergency Economic Powers Act (50 U.S.C. 1701 et seq.).

(2) IMMEDIATE FAMILY MEMBER—The term "immediate family member" of an individual means his or her parents, siblings, children, spouse, or a person who stood in loco parentis or to whom he or she stood in loco parentis.

SEC. XX. SENSE OF CONGRESS REGARDING THE TRIAL IN THE NETHERLANDS OF THE SUSPECTS INDICTED IN THE BOMBING OF PAN AM FLIGHT 103.

(a) **Findings:** Congress makes the following findings:

(1) On December 21, 1988, 270 people, including 189 United States citizens, were killed in a terrorist bombing on Pan Am Flight 103 over Lockerbie, Scotland.

(2) Britain and the United States indicted 2 Libyan intelligence agents—Abdel Basset Al–Megrahi and Lamen Khalifa Fhimah—in 1991 and sought their extradition from Libya to the United States or the United Kingdom to stand trial for this heinous terrorist act.

(3) The United Nations Security Council called for the extradition of the suspects in Security Council Resolution 731 and imposed sanctions on Libya in Security Council Resolutions 748 and 883 because Libyan leader, Colonel Muammar Qadaffi, refused to transfer the suspects to either the United States or the United Kingdom to stand trial.

(4) The sanctions in Security Council Resolutions 748 and 883 include a worldwide ban on Libya's national airline, a ban on flights into and out of Libya by other nations' airlines, a prohibition on supplying arms, airplane parts, and certain oil equipment to Libya, and a freeze on Libyan government funds in other countries.

(5) Colonel Qadaffi has continually refused to extradite the suspects to either the United States or the United Kingdom and has insisted that he will only transfer the suspects to a third and neutral country to stand trial.

(6) On August 24, 1998, the United States and the United Kingdom proposed that Colonel Qadaffi transfer the suspects to the Netherlands, where they would

stand trial before a Scottish court, under Scottish law, and with a panel of Scottish judges.

(7) The United States–United Kingdom proposal is consistent with those previously endorsed by the Organization of African Unity, the League of Arab States, the Non-Aligned Movement, and the Islamic Conference.

(8) The United Nations Security Council endorsed the United States–United Kingdom proposal on August 27, 1998, in United Nations Security Council Resolution 1192.

(9) The United States Government has stated that this proposal is nonnegotiable and has called on Colonel Qadaffi to respond promptly, positively, and unequivocally to this proposal by ensuring the timely appearance of the two accused individuals in the Netherlands for trial before the Scottish court.

(10) The United States Government has called on Libya to ensure the production of evidence, including the presence of witnesses before the court, and to comply fully with all the requirements of the United Nations Security Council resolutions.

(11) Secretary of State Albright has said that the United States will urge a multilateral oil embargo against Libya in the United Nations Security Council if Colonel Muammar Qadaffi does not transfer the suspects to the Netherlands to stand trial.

(12) The United Nations Security Council will convene on October 30, 1998, to review sanctions imposed on Libya.

(b) **Sense of Congress:** It is the sense of Congress that—

(1) Colonel Qadaffi should promptly transfer the indicted suspects Abdel Basset Al–Megrahi and Lamen Khalifa Fhimah to the Netherlands to stand trial before the Scottish court;

(2) the United States Government should remain firm in its commitment not to negotiate with Colonel Qadaffi on any of the details of the proposal approved by the United Nations in United Nations Security Council Resolution 1192; and

(3) if Colonel Qadaffi does not transfer the indicted suspects Abdel Basset Al–Megrahi and Lamen Khalifa Fhimah to the Netherlands by October 29, 1998, the United States Permanent Representative to the United Nations should—

(A) introduce a resolution in the United Nations Security Council to impose a multilateral oil embargo against Libya;

(B) actively promote adoption of the resolution by the United Nations Security Council; and

(C) assure that a vote will occur in the United Nations Security Council on such a resolution.

FOREIGN OPERATIONS, EXPORT FINANCING AND RELATED AGENCIES APPROPRIATIONS ACT, 1999 (Senate—September 01, 1998)

Mr. LAUTENBERG. Mr. President, today, Senator **Kennedy** and I join together, as we have in the past, in a ceaseless effort to provide some degree of justice for the families of the victims of the terrorist attack on Pan Am 103. This flight was brought down over Lockerbie, Scotland, on December 21, 1988. 259 people on the plane and 11 others on the ground were killed. Most of the victims were Americans, making it the most fatal terrorist atrocity in American history.

Two Libyan security agents have been charged with this heinous crime. They must be held accountable before a United States or United Kingdom court. The United Nations Security Council has imposed sanctions in an effort to make this happen, but for years this has brought no results.

Recently, Secretary of State Albright proposed that the two suspects in the bombing of Pan Am 103 be tried in a Scottish court, under Scottish law, with a panel of Scottish judges, but physically located in the Netherlands. Libyan authorities have publicly accepted this proposal while calling for negotiations.

I remain skeptical of Libya's willingness to cooperate with the international community in bringing terrorists to justice. But I also remain hopeful that the families of the victims will soon be able to end their painful wait for justice. I therefore believe we should give this potential solution an opportunity to work, while remaining determined to see the indicted terrorists brought to trial.

The amendment we are introducing today therefore sets a reasonable time limit for action. It also calls for the imposition of additional multilateral sanctions measures, even including an embargo on oil exports, if Libya fails to turn over the bombing suspects for trial.

The families of the victims of the Pan Am 103 bombing understand that nothing will bring back their loved ones. Nothing we do here can change that. But by adopting this resolution today we send the clear message that we are determined to see justice served and we will continue to increase international pressure on Libya until that happens.

Mr. KENNEDY. Mr. President, I sent this amendment to the desk on behalf of myself and Senators **Lautenberg, D'Amato,** and Torricelli.

Mr. President, ten years ago, in December 1988, 270 people, including 189 Americans, were killed in the terrorist bombing of Pan Am Flight 103 over Lockerbie, Scotland. As a result of the intense and skillful investigation that followed, Britain and the United States indicted 2 Libyan intelligence agents.

The leader of Libya, Colonel Muammar Qadaffi, refused to extradite the suspects to either the United States or the United Kingdom to stand trial. As a result, the international community, acting through the United Nations Security Council, imposed economic sanctions on Libya. The sanctions include a worldwide ban on Libya's national airline and a ban on flights into and out of Libya by the airlines of other nations. They also include a prohibition on supplying arms, airplane parts, and certain oil equipment to Libya, and a freeze on Libyan Government funds in other countries.

Despite these sanctions, Colonel Qaddafi has refused to turn over the suspects to either the United States or the United Kingdom. He has said, however, that he will transfer them to a third country to stand trial.

A week ago, in a major development in this case, the United States and the United Kingdom proposed that Colonel Qaddafi transfer the suspects to the Netherlands to stand trial before a Scottish court, under Scottish law, and with a panel of Scottish judges. Last Thursday, the United Nations Security Council endorsed this proposal and called on Colonel Qaddafi to transfer the suspects promptly.

The Administration has told Colonel Qaddafi that this is a take-it-or-leave-it proposal and that it is non-negotiable. Secretary of State Albright has said that the United States will urge a worldwide oil embargo against Libya in the United Nations Security Council if Colonel Qadaffi rejects this offer and refuses to transfer the suspects to the Netherlands to stand trial. The Security Council is scheduled to conduct the next periodic review of Libyan sanctions on October 30. All of us hope that Colonel Qadaffi will accept this plan before that date.

To send a clear message to Colonel Qadaffi, this resolution calls on him to transfer the indicted suspects to the Netherlands promptly, so that they can stand trial before the Scottish court in the Netherlands. The resolution supports the commitment by the United States Government not to negotiate with Colonel Qadaffi on the details of the proposal. If Colonel Qadaffi fails to transfer the suspects to the Netherlands before the end of October, the resolution calls on the United States Permanent Representative to the United Nations to introduce a resolution in the Security Council to impose a worldwide embargo against Libya and actively seeks its enactment.

The families of the victims of Pan Am 103 have waited too long for justice. The Administration's plan is a reasonable opportunity to end the long impasse over these suspects, and achieve a significant victory in the ongoing battle against international terrorism.

AMENDMENT NO. 3516

Mr. TORRICELLI. Mr. President, I rise today in support of the amendment offered by Senator Kennedy regarding the tragedy of Pan Am Flight 103. This year marks the tenth anniversary of the bombing over Lockerbie, Scotland, which killed 270 people. The memory of the 189 American citizens on board that doomed flight has not faded with the passage of time, but those who want to see justice done have become increasingly frustrated with the amount of time it has taken to try and bring the perpetrators to justice.

Expressing the sense of the House denouncing and rejecting a resolution adopted by Foreign Ministers of the Arab League urging the easing of United Nations sanctions against Libya which . . . (Introduced in the House)

HRES 246 IH

105th CONGRESS

1st Session

H. RES. 246

Expressing the sense of the House denouncing and rejecting a resolution adopted by Foreign Ministers of the Arab League urging the easing of United Nations sanctions against Libya which were imposed because of Libya's refusal to surrender individuals on its territory who are wanted in connection with the 1988 terrorist bombing of Pan Am flight 103.

IN THE HOUSE OF REPRESENTATIVES

September 26, 1997

Mr. LANTOS (for himself, Mr. GILMAN, Mr. SMITH of New Jersey, Mr. ACKER-MAN, Mr. BERMAN, Mr. CARDIN, Mr. DEUTSCH, Mr. FRANK of Massachusetts, Mr. FROST, Mr. GEJDENSON, Mr. LEVIN, Mr. ROTHMAN, Mr. SCHUMER, Mr. SHERMAN, and Mr. WEXLER) submitted the following resolution; which was referred to the Committee on International Relations

---

RESOLUTION

Expressing the sense of the House denouncing and rejecting a resolution adopted by Foreign Ministers of the Arab League urging the easing of United Nations sanctions against Libya which were imposed because of Libya's refusal to surrender individuals on its territory who are wanted in connection with the 1988 terrorist bombing of Pan Am flight 103.

Whereas the United Nations Security Council adopted Resolution 748 on March 31, 1992, imposing an embargo on the sale of arms and on international flights against the state of Libya and in Security Council Resolution 883 on November 11, 1993, further tightened economic sanctions against Libya for its refusal to surrender individuals suspected in connection with the terrorist bombing in 1988 of Pan Am flight 103 over Lockerbie, Scotland, in which 270 individuals were killed and the terrorist bombing in 1989 of the French ATA flight 772 over Niger, in which 160 individuals were killed;

Whereas the Security Council had repeatedly voted to maintain these international sanctions against Libya in view of the persistent refusal of the Government of Libya to hand over for trial the two individuals currently in Libya who are accused of involvement in the terrorist bombing of Pan Am flight 103 and ATA flight 772;

Whereas the United Nations sanctions provide for legitimate humanitarian flights to and from Libya for medical and other reasons, and flights of a religious nature to permit Libyan residents to participate in the Hadj have been approved routinely under the United Nations sanctions;

Whereas Libya has repeatedly violated the United Nations sanctions, most egregiously when an aircraft carrying Libyan leader, Colonel Muammar el-Qadaffi landed in Cairo, Egypt, in July 1996 in order for the Libyan leader to participate in an Arab summit meeting; and

Whereas the Foreign Ministers of the Arab League meeting in Cairo on September 21, 1997, adopted a resolution in which the Ministers invited "Arab countries to undertake measures to ease the severity of the embargo imposed on Libya until a final, peaceful, and just solution to the crisis is reached," "to lift measures freezing Libyan accounts involving money, the source of which is other than the selling or exporting of oil," "to support Libya's right to obtain suitable compensation for human and material damages and losses it sustains as a result of pertinent United Nations Security Council resolutions," and to exempt from sanctions Libyan "flights related to participation of the Libyan political leadership and official delegations in regional and international meetings": Now therefore, be it

Resolved, That the House of Representatives—

(1) denounces and rejects in the strongest terms the resolution adopted on September 21, 1997, by the Foreign Ministers of the Arab League in their conference in Cairo which invites Arab states to take action to ease United Nations sanctions against Libya;

(2) reaffirms the commitment of the United States to support United Nations sanctions against Libya until the two individuals suspected in connection with the terrorist bombing of Pam Am flight 103 and UTA flight 772 are turned over to appropriate judicial authorities in the United States or the United Kingdom and France as required by United Nations Security Council resolutions;

(3) calls upon the President to suspend all United States assistance to all countries which violate United Nations Security Council sanctions against Libya; and

(4) requests that the Secretary of State transmit a copy of this resolution to the government of each country which is a member of the Arab League and express to each government the profound concern of the United States about efforts to undermine the international fight against terrorism by weakening or violating sanctions imposed by the United Nations Security Council.

H.R. 899. A bill to provide for the liquidation of Libyan assets to pay for the costs of travel to and from the Hague of families of the victims of the crash of Pan Am flight 103 for the purpose of attending the trial of the terrorist suspects in the crash; to the Committee on International Relations.

TWA FLIGHT 800

The loss of any aircraft due to a "mishap" is always cause for grave concern. However, the events surrounding the loss of TWA Flight 800 off the eastern seaboard of the United States is still to most observers a mystery. The victims who survive tragic accidents or incidents, particularly this type of disaster, are invariably the friends and family members left behind to grieve. These victims seek closure and a point of contact or place of mourning for their lost loved ones. The other focus after the grieving process is a determination to establish exactly what happened and who was responsible. In the case of TWA Flight 800 the apportioning of blame for the loss on July 17, 1996, is ongoing. Who was actually to blame, if blame is the correct word in this case, is still not entirely clear.

From the outset the casual and not so casual observer could clearly see two U.S. federal agencies at loggerheads over how the investigation would be conducted, namely, the FBI and the National Transportation Safety Board (NTSB). With 1996 being the year of the Olympic Games in Atlanta and reelection time for the Clinton/Gore ticket, there were high stakes. The threat of a terrorist attack on mainland United States was very real, and a clear and present danger no doubt existed in the minds of the Clinton administration as well as those involved in protecting the world stage of the Olympic Games. Do the victims' families have a true understanding and sense of closure for this devastating incident? Is it so easily dismissed as a fuel tank problem and then left to the lawyers at Boeing to settle the litigation issues with the families? Would the hue and cry be louder and last longer and not give a sense of closure if this incident had in fact been the result of a shoulder-fired missile at a civilian airliner? With these speculations in mind, many people point to the U.S. administration as covering up the real events that took place in July 1996.

Salman Rushdie

Salman Rushdie, author of *The Satanic Verses,* became a victim of the fanatical regime of Islamic ruling ayatollahs. Rushdie was perceived as degrading Islamic values and for that the Ayatollah Khomeini issued a *fatwa,* or religious ruling, in February 1989 that permitted the shedding of his blood and called for his execution. Added to that was a bounty of US$2.5 million for anyone carrying out the fatwa. Rushdie went into protective hiding for eight years and was guarded by armed police around the clock. Ayatollah Hassan Sanei offered $2 million for Salman Rushdie's head, and extended the threat of murder to include all supporters of Rushdie, meaning the Rushdie support committees in the West. These groups became increasingly vocal around the February 14 anniversary of the fatwa. One of the latest authoritative pronouncements on the Rushdie affair was made by Mohammad Yazdi, the head of Iran's judiciary, who said (April 1996) the fatwa "will finally be carried out someday." Two days later, the Majlis speaker, Ali Akbar Nouri, reaffirmed his support for the fatwa, saying that he "regretted that Rushdie is still alive."

In September 1997, Iran's new leadership reaffirmed the fatwa on Rushdie, stating once again that revocation is impossible since the author of the fatwa is deceased. There is no indication that Tehran is pressuring the Fifteen Khordad Foundation to withdraw the $2.5 million reward it is offering for executing the fatwa on Rushdie. Rushdie's book had so inflamed Muslim anger around the world that an Iranian religious foundation raised the bounty on his head by $300,000 (Simonsen and Spindlove, 2000).

Rushdie became a victim of freedom of speech, and others associated with *The Satanic Verses* paid with their lives. The Japanese scholar Hitushi Igarashi, who translated the book into Japanese, was murdered in July 1993. William Nygaard, the book's Norwegian publisher, was seriously injured in an assassination attempt in October 1993. The fatwa has not been fulfilled, and it is apparent that the new regime does not support the assassination of Rushdie—however, as the victim in waiting Rushdie must still take extraordinary measures to ensure his public presence is protected.

Terry Waite

In the turbulent years of the 1980s, Beirut was a dangerous place for anyone from a Western country. So it was for the Archbishop of Canterbury's special envoy, Terry Waite, who had been successful as a hostage negotiator in the past, particularly in Africa and the Middle East. Waite went to Beirut on what was termed a humanitarian mission, and he himself became a victim of terrorism and was kidnapped by Islamic terrorists. At first there were wild rumors that he would be released within a short time. For Waite, life was to be an existence of almost solitary confinement in appalling conditions for 1,760 days. A man with very deep religious beliefs, he said of his ordeal and of his captors, "You have the power to break my body, but can't possess my soul." He was deprived of all reading materials for many months and had no knowledge of events unfolding in the outside world. He attributes part of his survival to his strength of mind, something he was not willing to compromise. This allowed him to keep intellectually alive in spite of the deterioration to his physical well-being. Even after five years of captivity, he came across as a strong-willed and positive individual who managed to proffer his own philosophy on these events: his ability to understand and forgive, and the belief that bitterness, although natural, can do more harm to the victim since he or she is eaten up and consumed by it. He believes passionately that forgiveness and justice go together and that people must work together toward understanding their differences and achieving peace.

Terrorists As Victims?

The cyclical nature of the relationship between terrorists and their victims is best illustrated by twentieth-century Northern Ireland. For decades parts of Northern Ireland have been awash with the blood of Catholic and Protestant alike.

Growing up in the North during the turbulent time of the Troubles has a significant impact on the young minds of Northern Irelanders. With troops on the streets and armed checkpoints at every turn, it is not difficult to realize that this would be a fertile recruiting ground for terror organizations. Mairread Farrell grew up in these turbulent times. Her grandfather had been in the IRA and members of the family were strong Catholics and Republicans. Farrell had embraced the Republican cause from an early age and had herself run messages and weapons and explosives for the Provisionals as a teenager. She was eventually sentenced to a long term of imprisonment for her bomb attack on Belfast's Connaught Hotel. After her release 10 years later she went back to the IRA as a heroine of the cause she espoused.

Can terrorists fall victim to their own notoriety and become victims of a state's response to terror? Although Western states do not by law advocate the assassination of terrorists, there are some interesting subjects that are worth discussing. A formal "shoot to kill" policy did not officially exist as part of the British government's response to Irish Republican terrorism. With a highly efficient intelligence network, the British had determined that the Provisional IRA was about to begin a terror campaign in Gibraltar and detonate a bomb during the Changing of the Guard ceremonies. Intelligence reports showed that certain members of the Provisional IRA were on the Spanish mainland with quantities of explosives to complete the task. The would-be terrorists were followed from Spain into Gibraltar. As a part of its campaign to fight terrorism, the British government had turned increasingly to the SAS as its weapon of choice to combat terrorism. The three terrorists who were trailed from Spain were known IRA members Dan McCann, Sean Savage, and Mairread Farrell. Suspected of being about to detonate a bomb, the three were shot dead in a hail of bullets fired by unidentified members of the SAS. All three were killed and later found to have been unarmed. The supposed bomb was not found in their vehicle. The cry of foul play rang loud and clear, particularly from Sinn Fein, but also from Amnesty International, which demanded an independent inquiry into the incident. Had the British conducted a summary execution of the IRA members, and were they no longer to be constrained by the rule of law? Whatever the answer, it was clear that terrorists could become victims. To the IRA, Farrell and her two partners were patriots, to the British they were terrorists, and to their parents they were victims of Irish history.

During the funeral in Belfast for Farrell, McCann, and Savage, a lone Protestant terrorist hurled bombs and fired at the mourners. Sixty were wounded and three were killed. Three days later during the funeral for one of those victims, a car inadvertently ran into the funeral procession. Thinking they were again being attacked by Protestant paramilitaries, the angry mob surrounded the car and viciously beat, stripped naked, and shot both men. It turned out that the two men were off-duty British Army corporals who had lost their way and paid the ultimate price. Out of all the deaths in the North, the Provisional IRA is responsible for 62%, the military for 10%, and the Royal Ulster Constabulary for 2%. In Northern Ireland the doctrine of "an eye for an eye" has left many victims blind.

Critical Incident Stress Reaction

Definitions of critical incidents include the following:

> Any situation beyond the realm of a person's usual experience that overwhelms his or her sense of vulnerability and or lack of control over the situation.

> Any situation faced by emergency service personnel that causes them to experience unusually strong emotional reactions which have the

potential to interfere with their ability to function either at the scene
or later.

A life experience or series of experiences that so seriously upsets the balance of the individual that it creates changes in the persons emotional,
cognitive or behavioral functioning. (Soloman, et al., 2000)

When I worked as a police officer in the 1960s and 1970s, the word *stress* was
almost never heard applied to functions and work experienced by emergency
service personnel. A large number of police forces around the world are male
dominated and paramilitary in style. My experience was that there was no training
on how to handle stressful situations, merely how to apply and define the rule of
law. Stress and emotion were not discussed and the events that happened were
considered part of doing your duties. After four years of service I had been
involved, on the front line so to speak, with all kinds of what would now be termed
stressful incidents: murder, suicide, natural disasters, and terrorist attacks. It is
the last one that I will discuss here and the effect it had on me personally.

The IRA's terror campaign was only just starting on mainland Britain and
I was working in Guildford, a provincial city south of London. The city was
known to be frequented by soldiers from the army camps in Aldershot and the
Scots Guard depot at nearby Pirbright camp. In addition, Guildford is home
to the Women's Royal Army Corp at Stoughton Barracks. Friday and Saturday
nights would see the pubs packed with soldiers and locals enjoying drinking and
socializing. My memory of the following incident is still crystal clear, and my
emotions have always been somewhat under control albeit simmering below the
surface.

An IRA bomb was detonated under a table in the Horse and Groom public
house, located in the heart of the city. I was the first to arrive at the scene, having been parked outside the building some five minutes prior to the explosion.
I do not recall having any conscious thoughts as to my role in this incident
and did not perceive myself as a victim, although my proximity to the blast
could easily have made me one. My duties as I saw them on that fateful night
were to control the scene and assist in the rescue operation of those maimed,
killed, and injured in the blast. After all, at the time no one knew it was a bomb
and the first thoughts were of a gas line explosion. Whatever the cause, I went
straight into that building and saw the devastation firsthand. I entered not as a
spectator but as someone hoping to make a difference, affect a rescue, or hopefully, save a life. My first aid skills were woefully lacking for the injuries I was
about to witness.

The explosion had blown a hole in the wooden floor and taken those around
that table partially into the beer keg cellar below. I went into that cellar and
found two teenage girls with horrendous injuries: Both had had their legs
severely injured by the explosion, and from knee to waist could best be described

as looking like sausage meat. One appeared to be still breathing but with great difficulty from a gaping wound near the upper part of her chest. With the help of a doctor, what could be done for the victims at the scene was done, and they were removed.

I vividly recall standing outside the building after all the dead and wounded had been removed and hearing Sir Peter Mathews, then chief constable, conferring with the local member of Parliament and stating that it was likely a gas main explosion. As he said it we all heard another explosion coming from the direction of Swan Lane some 150 yards down the hill. Why I ran straight down the hill and into the building I do not know—I will put it down to a sense of duty, but at the time the adrenaline was no doubt pumping and thoughts of personal safety never entered my conscious mind. After we removed the landlord from the severely bomb-damaged Seven Stars public house, it began to sink in that the city was in the midst of a bombing campaign. Some hours later after finishing an extended tour of duty I returned to the house I shared with three other single people, two nurses and a local business owner. Unbeknownst to me the two nurses had been at the front line dealing with the appalling injuries as they came into the emergency room. Unable to sleep we all sat around drinking coffee and pouring out our thoughts and tears at what we had seen and what had occurred. That was the moment that we were all able to grieve—and in this instance for people we did not know.

We had all experienced death before, but the previous incidents had not been deliberate mass destruction and maiming. This was altogether new. The next day I returned to normal duty. I did not have any long- or short-term periods of emotional upset that prevented me from performing normal duty. To say that I saw a great many sights during eight years on the force is not an exaggeration. Many of the incidents are long forgotten and many are just faded memories that I am unable to clearly recall. The Guildford pub bombing 27 years ago and what took place that night and exactly where I was, what I did, who was there, and what words were spoken are for me as clear today as they were then. This incident has not played any part in dreams or other areas of my subconscious mind. Perhaps the memory is kept alive and vivid because the incidents of terror and actions of terrorists are an ongoing part of daily news coverage. I do not think of the incident on any regular basis and I can't say that it's a topic of discussion. This is also the first time I have put any thoughts on the subject to print. Although both public houses were rebuilt, I never ventured into either of them again. I revisited both locations in the summer of 1998 to discover with almost sadness that they have both closed down and there is no plaque or sign to commemorate what happened all those years ago, although there is mention of it in the local museum. I find this lack of recognition both sad and puzzling in the circumstances. True, it was not Lockerbie, but it happened and it happened in our city.

As for any critical stress or emotions, I find it somewhat strange that I really have no emotions when remembering the incident. I had many angry thoughts and true hatred for those who had perpetrated these despicable acts but they translated into nothing and had no lasting effect. Have the events had a long-term effect on me? Of course that is difficult to determine. I have never let those events cloud any of my judgments or actions. I believe that at the time my response to the events was measured. Soul searching and grief were not a part of the process. I believe that what happened and what I saw and did was part of my duties. I have thought that, had I stayed outside the pub for a little longer, I could have been killed or injured in the explosion. I did not address that feeling with any seriousness; my personal belief is that one should not dwell on what might have been or what could have happened given a different course of action.

Conceivably the worst terrorist attack of its kind in living memory occurred on September 11, 2001, in New York City at the World Trade Center and in Washington, D.C., at the Pentagon. Commercial aircraft were used as weapons of mass destruction to crash into the Twin Towers and the Pentagon, to impress on the West its clear vulnerability to terrorist attacks, as part of a continuing war being waged by Osama bin Laden and his Al Qaeda movement against the United States. There were over 3,000 immediate victims. Apart from the magnitude of the events that will haunt many of residents of New York and Washington, D.C., the chosen targets were symbolic, striking direct blows at the heart of world trade in New York City and the military power center in Washington, D.C. From an economic standpoint, the victims were many, and the cost of the attacks is now running into hundreds of billions of dollars, including a continuing cost measured in airline failures and other financial repercussions throughout the world.

Victims of terror will continue to hold our attention, and our morbid fascination with the murky world of terrorism has surely entered into a new and ever fearsome dimension.

References

Alexander, Y. (1987). Terroristic murder in Northern Ireland: Who is killed and why. *Terrorism: An International Journal*, 9(4): 243–251.

Auerbach, S., et al. (1994). Interpersonal impacts and adjustments to the stress of simulated captivity: An empirical test of the Stockholm syndrome. *Journal of Clinical and Social Psychology* 13(2): 207–221

Buhari's New Year's broadcast. (1984, January 9). *West Africa,* pp. 56–57.

Coombs, C. C. (1997). *Terrorism in the Twenty-first Century.* Upper Saddle River, NJ: Prentice Hall.

Cooper, H. H. (1978). Close encounters of an unpleasant kind: Preliminary thoughts on the Stockholm syndrome. *Legal Medical Quarterly* 2(2): 100–114

Hacker, F. J. (1976). *Crusaders, Criminals, Crazies: Terror and Terrorism in Our Time.* New York: Norton.

Muraskin, R., and Roberts, A. R. (1999). *Visions for Change: Crime and Justice in the Twenty-first Century.* Upper Saddle River, NJ: Prentice Hall.

Ochberg, F. (1978). The victim of terrorism. *Practitioner* 220, 293–302.

Okolo, J. E. (1987). Nigerian politics and the Dikko kidnap affair. *Terrorism: An International Journal,* 9(4): 326.

President George W. Bush's address to the nation. (2001, September 12). Atlanta, GA: CNN/APN.

Royal Ulster Constabulary. (1984). *Chief Constable Report, 1983.* Belfast: Royal Ulster Constabulary.

Simonsen, C., and Spindlove, J. (2000). *Terrorism Today: The Past, the Players, and the Future.* Upper Saddle River, NJ: Prentice Hall.

Soloman, R., Mitchell, J., Goldfarb, D. A., and Aumiller, G. S. W. (2000, July). Critical Incident Stress Reaction: What is it, how to recognize it, and what to do about it. Available at www.HeavyBadge.com

Soskis, D., and Ochberg, F. (1982). Concepts of terrorist victimization. In D. Soskis and A. R. Roberts (Eds.), *Victims of Terrorism* (pp. 105–135). Boulder, CO: Westview.

Terrorism Research Center. (1996). Definitions. Available at www.terrorism.com.

Thorndike, E. L., and Barnhart, C. L. (Eds.). (1990). *The World Book Encyclopedia.* Chicago: World Book.

Trigiani, K. (1999). Societal Stockholm syndrome. Available at http://web2airmail.net/ktrig246/out_of_cave/sss.html.

U.S. Army Field Manual 100–20. (1993). Combating terrorism. In *Stability and Support Operations.* Washington, DC: U.S. Department of Defense, U.S. Government Printing Office.

Vetter, H. J., and Perlstein, G. R. (1991). *Perspectives on Terrorism.* Belmont, CA: Wadsworth; Brooks/Cole.

Wardlow, G. (1982). *Political Terrorism, Theory, Tactics and Counter-Measures.* Melbourne: Cambridge University Press.

West, L. J., and Martin, P. R. (1994). *Clinical and Theoretical Perspectives.* New York: Guilford.

CHAPTER 9

Hate Crimes Victimization
A Comparison of Bias- and Nonbias-Motivated Assaults

Jack McDevitt and Jennifer Balboni

Introduction

"Hate crimes" are motivated by the offenders' bias toward a particular minority group. Although each state employs a different definition of hate crime, most statutes include groups singled out on the basis of race (such as African Americans or Asian Americans), ethnicity (for example, Latina/Latino), sexual orientation, or disability. Over the last 15 years, there has been a growing legislative push to recognize these crimes as distinct from similar, nonbias offenses. The tragic case of James Bird of Texas, who was dragged to his death behind a pickup truck, solely because of the color of his skin, is one extreme example of a hate-motivated crime. Although such extreme cases are particularly disturbing, more subtle bias crimes, such as assault or vandalism, potentially present a more persistent threat to community safety and cohesiveness.

One response to bias crimes has been to create legislation designed to differentiate crimes on the basis of bias motivation. In the impassioned debate about hate-crime legislation, assertions are made on both sides about the consequences of bias-motivated crimes for their victims. Critics argue that distinguishing hate crime from other comparable crimes is unnecessary because the bias motivation of the offender does not cause additional injurious harm to the

A version of this paper was published in the *Journal of American Behavior Science* (forthcoming 2001).

primary victim. Implicit in this assumption is that bias crimes are not intrinsically different from similar nonbias offenses. Legal scholars Jacobs and Potter (1998) cogently sum up this argument:

> We do not believe that crimes motivated by hate invariably are morally worse or lead to more severe consequences for the victims than the same criminal act prompted by other motivations. (p. 147)

Critics cite the example that "a bias murder victim is just as dead as a nonbias murder victim" as a reason to treat these crimes similarly. Moreover, murderers are sentenced severely, regardless of whether it is bias charge.

Although the "no additional injury" argument is apparently rational, no empirical evidence is available to support it. Furthermore, this assumption about the distinctions between murder victims is misleading because, among other things, it does not address the fact that the overwhelming majority of bias crimes in this country involve intimidation, vandalism, or assault, not murder (UCR Hate Crime Report, 1998). Most people readily would agree that burning a cross on someone's property is different from a typical trespassing or vandalism offense. In this chapter, we focus on differences between bias and nonbias crimes' impact on assault victims, differences that have not been explored fully in prior research. This paper reports the findings of our analysis of survey data from bias and nonbias assault victims regarding the psychological consequences of their victimization experiences. We also discuss a second study on hate-crime reporting patterns for victims.

DIFFERENCES BETWEEN BIAS AND NONBIAS OFFENSES

We propose that hate crimes are inherently more harmful to the social fabric of society than comparable crimes not motivated by bias. Several authors have suggested dimensions of bias crimes that may increase these crimes' impact on their victims. The first unique aspect of bias crimes is the *victim interchangeability* inherent in many of these incidents (Levin and McDevitt, 1993). Interchangeability means that any individual who possesses, or is perceived to possess, a specific trait could be selected as a target. Bias crime victims are chosen because of some actual or perceived status that they are powerless to change.

The second unique dimension of bias crime is *the capacity for secondary victimization.* Bias crime offenders generally intend for their acts to reach far beyond the primary victim and affect all members of a particular minority group. For example, a cross-burning, with its associations with the Ku Klux Klan, not only affects the targeted person or family, but any African American who becomes aware of the incident. Consider the following scenarios:

1. Teenagers scrawl "The Rolling Stones Rock!" on the back wall of their community high school.
2. A white supremacist sprays a swastika on a local synagogue.

Technically, both incidents are vandalism. The first scenario presents a somewhat petty nuisance, whereas the second incident attacks a distinct segment of the population, and attempts to intimidate an entire community. Clearly, the swastika is intended to send a message that Jewish people are not welcome, and further, that violence—even genocide—is an appropriate way to handle differences between groups. It would be difficult to argue that the racial slur does not victimize more people, in a more serious fashion, than the teenagers' prank in the first scenario.

Moreover, the effects of victim interchangability and secondary victimization can interact to disrupt the community in serious and often violent ways. The United States Supreme Court referred to this element of bias crime as "the distinct emotional harm" that such crimes inflict, noting its potential to "incit[e] community unrest" (*Wisconsin v. Mitchell,* 1993). Civil disturbances following highly publicized bias-motivated homicides in Bensonhurst and Howard Beach, New York, as well as the violence and destruction that followed court decisions in the Rodney King case illustrate the Court's fear that bias crimes could exacerbate existing racial tensions to the point of community violence. The Oregon Court of Appeals refers to this elusive attribute of bias crime as the power to "escalate from individual conflicts to mass disturbances" (Harvard Law Review, 1996). Although the Supreme Court and other courts across the country have noted the difference between the two types of crime, research is scant as to precisely *how* bias crime affects its victims.

Next, hate crime victims possess *immutable characteristics* (Levin and McDevitt, 1993). This essentially means that the trait that provoked the crime against them cannot be altered. For instance, an African American person cannot change his or her race after an attack to prevent future victimization; he or she will continue to be African American. Immutable characteristics play a significant role in interpreting the aftermath for bias crime victims.

PRIOR LITERATURE ON HATE-CRIME VICTIMIZATIONS

Research regarding the impact of bias crimes is limited. There has been significant research about the general victimization process, but very little that examines the complex relationship between bias motivation, incidence of crime, and victimization consequences. Moreover, of the few that do examine the extent of psychological and emotional injury suffered by bias crime victims, most fail to provide comparative data for victims of similar nonbias-motivated offenses.

Although numerous studies have been conducted to describe the psychosocial consequences of particular types of victimization (e.g., Kilpatrick and Amick, 1985; Frieze, Greenberg, and Hymer, 1987), only a handful compare symptoms across crime types (Riggs, Rothbaum, and Foa, 1995; Lurigio, 1987; Davis and Brickman, 1996; Wirtz and Harrell, 1987; Resick, 1987) and even fewer are specific to bias crime victimization (Barnes and Ephross, 1994; Ehrlich, Larcom, and Purvis, 1994; Herek, Gillis, Cogan, and Glunt, 1997). In part because of methodological issues, the results of these three studies on bias crime victimization are somewhat inconsistent in their conclusions.

According to Barnes and Ephross (1994), the most prevalent emotional reaction of the 59 bias victim respondents was anger toward the offender, followed by fear. When comparing the victims of bias and nonbias assault, their data indicated that "a major difference in the emotional response of hate violence victims appears to be the absence of lowered self-esteem. The ability of some hate violence victims to maintain their self-esteem may be associated with their attribution of responsibility for the attacks to the prejudice and racism of the perpetrators" (p. 250). This data is notable, but the purposive sampling technique and small sample of respondents raise questions about the findings' generalizability.

Conversely, Ehrlich et al. (1994) in their national telephone victimization survey (2,078 respondents) reveal marked differences in the traumatic effects of hate violence. They indicate that among four subgroups (i.e., nonvictims, group defamation victims, personal crime victims, and bias crime victims), bias crime victims demonstrated the greatest average number of symptoms and behavior variations on a scale of 19 psychophysiological symptoms of post-traumatic stress and 12 social and behavioral changes. The authors reported a clear overall pattern of pervasive consequences in the lives of bias crime victims and conclude that "Ethnoviolence [bias crime] victims suffer greater trauma than do victims of . . . violence which is committed for other reasons" (Ehrlich et al., 1994, p. 27). Specifically, ethnoviolence victims reported experiencing 5.98 negative psychophysiological aftereffects, whereas personal victims had 4.77 and group defamation victims reported 4.02. According to this study, victims of ethnoviolence were also significantly more nervous, lost more friends, had more trouble sleeping or concentrating, had more interpersonal difficulties, and felt angrier than victims of personal crimes (Erhlich et al., 1994).

In a related study by Ehrlich et al. (1994) on the effects of ethnoviolence in the workplace, once again its victims reported the greatest number (5.6) of psychophysiological symptoms on the same 19-point list, whereas personal victims reported only 3.5, and victims of prejudicial insults or jokes reported 5.0 (Barnes and Ephross, 1994). This study's limitation, however, is the broad definition of bias incidents asked of workers during the interview. Participants were asked, "In the past three years, have you ever been mistreated at this company?" They were then asked to determine whether they felt any mistreatment was due to some prejudice.

More recently, Herek et al. (1997) explored the psychological sequelae of gay, lesbian, and bisexual bias crime victims. Recruiting from gay/lesbian community events (such as Gay Pride celebrations), gay bars, or community organizations, the research team got over 2,000 participants to fill out a self-administered questionnaire. This study marks the most expansive empirical effort to include bias crime victims, and although the sample is somewhat skewed toward gays/lesbians who are public about their sexuality (i.e., are able to attend gay/lesbian/bisexual functions, community organizations, etc.), this research is notable for its sample size.

The data indicate that those respondents who reported experiencing a bias crime (compared with victims of nonbias crimes) within the last five years consistently had more intense feelings of adverse psychological sequelae. Statistically significant relationships were found for depressive symptoms, traumatic stress, and anger. One methodological limitation of this study, however, is how the research team coded bias and nonbias events, classifying them by asking respondents whether *they felt* they were victimized because of their sexual orientation. It is possible that this subjective interpretation might be related to other characteristics of the victim, such as the victim's political orientation toward gay, lesbian, and bisexual issues, and thus may also influence the impact of the crime. Despite this limitation, these data support the belief that bias crime victims endure more intense effects of victimization on several levels.

With the exception of these few studies, which represent the first attempt by researchers to quantify the psychological and behavioral impact of bias crime victimization, little is known about the differences between bias and nonbias victimization. The current study attempts to provide further information on some of these issues.

Research Design/Methodology

The present study takes a comparative look into the experience of bias and nonbias victims. A primary goal of the design is to make comparisons possible between similar bias and nonbias crime victims, in an effort to understand if bias crime victims experience differential impacts. To achieve this, the study surveys a comparable group of bias and nonbias violent assault victims identified from law enforcement and advocacy-agency legal records.

When designing this study, the authors estimated that the most powerful data about the victimization experience would be from the victims themselves. To this end, we created a mail survey instrument to be sent to all victims of bias-motivated aggravated assault in the city of Boston[1] between 1992 and 1997, and a random sample of nonbias assault victims.[2] Unfortunately, we had difficulty locating many of these victims, and our response rates suffered, lingering at 23% for the bias victims group and 11% for the nonbias victims group. For this reason, our sample may not be representative of bias victims as a whole. Still, we believe the study's findings shed light on areas of concern for bias crime victims.

Sample Characteristics

A review of the characteristics of the two samples reveals surprising similarities considering the difficulties encountered in obtaining survey responses (see Table 9.1). About 40% of each sample of victims are female (37.8% versus 40%) and the racial and ethnic makeup are similar for the two respondent samples. When we consider the age breakdown of the samples, the bias crime sample is slightly younger, with nonbias victims about twice as likely to be over 45 years old. In addition, the samples are very similar in terms of income and education. Finally, as expected, the bias crime sample is more likely to include victims who identify themselves as gay, lesbian, or bisexual.

CHARACTERISTICS OF INCIDENT

In general, there were few differences between the location of the incident and whether the incident was bias related. It does appear, however, that slightly more of the bias sample were victimized in or near their home (37% versus 30%) and non-bias assaults were more likely to occur at work (14% versus 7%).

Prior research has looked at the impact of location on victimization and subsequent post-traumatic stress disorder. Schepple and Bart (1983) found in their study of sexual assault victims that women who believed they were in a safe place during the attack were more likely to experience severe trauma. The authors speculate that victims attacked in a perceived "safe" place are not able to employ "victim blaming" techniques, and thus have no buffer from the severe psychological impact of victimization. Victim blaming allows the victim to feel that if they had augmented their behavior, they could have prevented the incident; an important corollary is that victims can use this strategy to reduce their fears about future victimization, asserting that if they change their behavior, they can be safe. However, because it is difficult to determine whether our measure of "passing through the area" indicates near the victim's home, we are unable to understand the context of location for a substantial percentage of victims. Although the differences between the bias and nonbias group are not significant, it is notable that a larger percentage of bias victims are victimized near their homes, thus making the victim more vulnerable to the post-incident effects mentioned above.

The one measure that more closely approximates the context of whether the place of victimization is considered safe by the victim is frequency. We asked victims whether they had been to this location (before the incident occurred) "never," "a few times," "quite often," or "almost every day." When we collapse these categories into "never/a few times" and "quite often/almost every day," we find that bias victims are more likely to be victimized in locations that are familiar to them. More than three quarters of the bias group frequented the location where the incident occurred, compared to only two thirds of the nonbias group.

TABLE 9.1 Comparative Statistics Between the Samples of Bias and Nonbias Assault
Victims and Respondents

Demographic Variables Subcategories	Bias Victim Respondents (n=91)	Nonbias Victim Respondents (n=45)
Gender		
Male	62.2	60.0
Female	37.8	40.0
Age		
<8	12.5	11.1
18 to 24	11.4	13.3
25 to 44	62.5	48.9
45 and older	13.6	26.7
Race & Ethnicity		
White	62.2	52.4
Black	23.3	33.3
Asian	6.7	7.1
Other	2.2	2.4
Latino	5.6	4.8
Household Income		
<$20,000	42.7	38.9
$20,000 to $39,999	28.0	22.2
$40,000 to $59,999	8.5	13.9
$60,000 to $79,999	12.2	11.1
$80,000 to $99,999	3.7	8.3
$100,000 or more	4.9	5.6
Education		
<HSN/A	26.1	17.8
HS/Some College	35.2	46.7
College Graduate	22.7	20.0
Post-Graduate	15.9	15.6
Sexual Orientation		
Heterosexual	68.8	94.4
Bisexual	2.5	0.0
Lesbian	6.3	2.8
Gay Male	22.5	2.8
Transgender	0.0	0.0

After the incident, only 28% of the bias victims and 34% of the nonbias victims
returned almost every day. Although these differences are not statistically significant, they are instructive in understanding the context of the crime.

Next, bias crime victims were also more likely to be attacked by a group than our comparison sample of nonbias victims (49% versus 35%). The bias victims had a mean of 2.04 attackers, compared to the nonbias group, which had a mean of 1.84. It is interesting to note that in this sample about one quarter of each group were attacked by a group of four or more offenders (23% versus 25%).

RELATIONSHIP TO OFFENDER/RESPONSIBILITY

Several studies have explored the relationship between victim and offender in cases of sexual assault (Katz, 1991; Koss, Dinero, Seibel, and Cox, 1984; and Ullman and Seigel, 1993). Although these studies focus on different aspects of the healing process, Ullman and Seigel (1993) found that fear and anxiety were more common for women sexually assaulted by strangers. Katz (1991), however, found that these women are more likely to retain a positive self-image than women who are raped by nonstrangers.

In our sample, bias crime victims were significantly less likely to have a prior relationship with the offender than were nonbias victims (83.5% compared to 68.2%). One quarter of the nonbias group reported that they had known their attacker for at least one year, compared to less than 7% of the bias crime victims.

The survey also asked victims how they would describe the nature of the incident. They were asked if the assault was "an unprovoked attack against me," "an ongoing dispute," "a minor disagreement that got out of hand," a case of "mistaken identity," or "a poor response to a situation by the offender." This is important because several critics of bias crime legislation suggest that many so-called bias crimes are simply the result of disputes between individuals of different groups. The data here contradict this assertion: *Nearly all the bias crime assaults were committed by strangers (84%) and most victims reported that the assault was the result of an unprovoked attack (76%).* Only 8% of the bias crime victims reported that the attack was a result of an ongoing dispute. When comparing the two samples, bias crime victims were more likely to have been attacked by strangers (89% versus 68%) and more likely to perceive the attack as unprovoked (76% versus 53%). This supports the prior contention in the literature that bias crime victims are chosen because of their membership in a group, and not because of any prior actions they may have taken. As opposed to many other assault victims, bias crime victims are interchangeable—as far as the offender is concerned, any member of the group could be targeted.

These questions help us understand the qualitative context of the precipitants of the assault; the next set of questions ask the victims to attribute levels of responsibility to the victim, offender, or other individual. Specifically, we asked victims to assess responsibility for the incident on a scale of 0 (victim assumes no responsibility) to 10 (victim assumes full responsibility). Once again, the responses are consistent with the earlier conclusions. Bias crime victims are more likely to report that they had no responsibility for the incident than nonbias crime victims (76% versus 58%). This again fits with prior descriptions of bias crimes in which victims feel that they did nothing to provoke or initiate the attack.

Many nonbias victims reinforced their lack of responsibility for the assault in their qualitative remarks when asked how to reduce or prevent these types of crimes in the future. Whereas bias crime victims often pointed to a community responsibility, *nonbias victims were more likely to respond that the reduction/ prevention of assault was within their own control, inferring they may have precipitated the crime by their own overt actions.* Many nonbias victims' responses involved changing their own behaviors. The following comments were typical for this group when asked what they might do to prevent such crimes in the future:

> "Walk away from the incident."
> "Be polite."
> "Look away, but it is hard not to . . . "
> "Not to settle quarrels physically."

Bias crime victims, conversely, expressed feelings of frustration when asked how to prevent or reduce such crimes in the future. They generally did not indicate that their actions had done anything to provoke or exacerbate a situation, confirming earlier responses about the nature of the assault. Because most bias crime victims did not believe they could do anything to prevent future victimization, they felt frustrated. The following response captures many of the bias crime respondents' feelings about preventing victimization: "Not to be in the wrong place at the wrong time. In other words, it's impossible." *Such remarks indicate that bias crime victims feel powerless to protect themselves in the future.*

Collectively, the responses to questions about the level of responsibility, precipitating incident events, and prior relationship paint a picture of bias crime assaults that differs in many ways from that of nonbias assaults. These events are less likely to involve victims and offenders who are friends or acquaintances or to be precipitated or provoked by any overt actions by the victim, and the onus of responsibility appears to lie much more fully with the offender.

REPORTING PRACTICE

When victims were asked if they had spoken to anyone prior to reporting the crime to the police, bias crime victims were more likely to have sought out someone—in most cases, a family member or a friend—to discuss the incident with before reporting their assault (40% versus 29%). The fact that nearly half of the bias-motivated victims report discussing the attack with someone before going to the police may have important implications for improving the reporting of bias crimes nationally. It may be necessary to broaden outreach efforts to include families of victims as well as the victims themselves, and to increase the availability of victim support programs, where victims can go to obtain support and assistance before they become formally involved in the criminal justice system.

Because the study discussed here deals exclusively with incidents known by the police, we were unable to investigate how many crimes go unreported to the police. A separate study, however, explored this aspect of hate crime victimization (McDevitt et al., 2000). Here, advocacy group members discussed how minority groups are especially hesitant to pursue law enforcement interaction, and may be particularly suspicious of police overall. One representative from an Asian American advocacy group stated that many victims would rather talk with a reporter from an ethnic community newspaper than with the police. The reasons were threefold: the reporter spoke the language and could converse with the victim; he or she was often known throughout the community; and this person was not seen as a potential threat. The gay and lesbian community has a separate set of concerns. Many people within these groups are afraid that police will be either unsympathetic or hostile to them. Many minority groups have long-standing distrust of the police; for this reason alone, it is not surprising that hate crime is overwhelmingly underreported. The underlying theme is that police and minority groups need to work together prior to hate crimes if victims are to feel comfortable soliciting support from law enforcement.

Victim Reactions

BEHAVIORAL REACTIONS

Twelve separate indicators measured post-victimization behavioral changes, each with a dichotomous variable (yes or no). Surprisingly, there were no significant differences between the bias and nonbias groups. Both groups of assault victims appear to take the same steps post victimization: The overwhelming majority of victims in both groups (77.4% for bias, 77.8% for nonbias victims) stated that they pay more attention to where they walk now; try to be less visible after the incident (37.8% for bias, 38.6% for nonbias victims); and had become more active in the community because of the victimization (22% for both). Overall, the similarities in behavior modifications between the groups are striking. The same cannot be said, however, for the psychological consequences of the bias and nonbias victims. We will return to the findings of the behavioral responses during the concluding section of this chapter.

PSYCHOLOGICAL REACTIONS

Using a modified version of a previously established scale[3] to understand some of the psychological sequelae, we asked victims from both groups the same questions about post-event distress. Earlier research (Horowitz, Walker, and Alvarez,

1979) suggests that the psychological themes in this scale can be grouped into two major components: intrusiveness and avoidance. Our scale incorporated one major change from the original; although we used basically the same symptoms, we measured the response differently.[4] In short, our scale attempts to incorporate a measure of both intensity and duration.

Although there are only six items from the psychological scale where *significant* differences exist, every psychological impact measure from this scale had a higher mean value from the bias group than from the nonbias group. This means bias crime victims experienced the adverse psychological sequelae more often than the nonbias control group on every item we measured. Although the levels of significance vary, the direction of the relationship does not; *bias crime victims clearly experienced more negative impacts and experienced these impacts for longer periods of time than the nonbias victim group.*

The psychological impact of crime on the victim is measured in our study by 19 separate scale items. A *t* test was performed between the *bias-motivated* and *nonbias-motivated assault* victim groups on each reaction category. A (moderate) statistically significant difference was detected between the two groups within five (5) of the 19 categories (p<.05). The largest categorical difference was in "feeling angry" with a *t* score of 2.625 and a mean difference of .54 on a 5-point scale (i.e., not at all, days, weeks, months, and years).

All five statistically significant variables at the .05 level are related to Horowitz's intrusiveness theme. Bias crime victims report that they are more nervous, more depressed, have more trouble concentrating, think about the incident when they do not mean to, and feel suicidal more often than nonbias victims. Collectively, we see that the bias victim group has more difficulty coping with the victimization, and that they appear to have additional problems with their recovery process because of increased fear and more frequent intrusive thoughts.

One could, however, argue persuasively that because of imprecise characterization of the mean as an instrument of comparison in the *t* test, we somehow may have blurred the test's significance. To address this, the research team split these variables in several different ways. First, we collapsed the psychological variables into two categories: Either the presence of the symptom (coded as 1) or the absence of it (coded as 0). Collapsing these categories yields very similar results. Once again, feelings of depression, nervousness, difficulty concentrating at work, and feeling ashamed/losing confidence are significantly below the .05 level. These results strongly indicate a relationship between the element of bias in assault that relates to whether the victim experiences these adverse psychological sequelae at all.

At this point in the analysis, the research team wished to test further the bivariate relationships within the psychological sequelae. Specifically, one could argue that the difference between having symptoms "for a few days" and not having them at all is not very remarkable. For this reason, we created a separate dichotomous variable that collapsed categories into "not at all/for a few days" (coded as 0) and "a few weeks, months, years." This division makes the implicit objective assumption that most victims of violence suffer some harm; however, when the impact duration creeps into weeks or months, there is something notable about it.

The results from this analysis are congruent with earlier tests of significance. Four variables: "More nervous than usual," "Thought about when I didn't mean to," "Didn't feel like living any longer," and "Had trouble concentrating at work," all indicated a Pearson value below the .05 level of significance. Again, we see that the level of intrusiveness for the bias crime victim is greater than for the nonbias victims. In this version of the analysis, only "more depressed" falls from being significantly different between the two groups. By nearly every bivariate measure, the bias victims are affected more intensely, with more intrusive psychological sequelae.

FEELINGS OF SAFETY

When asked how safe they feel after the crime, bias crime victims are significantly less likely to feel safe. Almost one half of the nonbias victims reported feeling less safe after the incident (46%), but a significantly higher number of bias crime victims report feeling unsafe after their attack (59%). This increased fearfulness is interesting, as the nonbias attacks were more likely to have involved reported injury. One possible reason for this increased fear may be that bias crime victims are more likely to be concerned that a similar crime may happen in the future, especially because they have experienced previous attacks more frequently. Fully 52% of the bias crime sample reported that they were very concerned about becoming a victim of a similar crime in the future, compared to 37% of the nonbias crime sample. In addition, after the incident bias crime victims were more likely to report that they felt unsafe alone in their neighborhood at night (42% versus 32%) and returning to the area of the incident (52% versus 44%). Taken together, these findings indicate that bias crime assault victims are more likely to experience more fear and reduced feelings of safety after the crime than nonbias crime assault victims.

OTHER VICTIMIZATION CONSEQUENCES

We asked both samples if they had experienced other negative life events since the assault, and in most areas, the bias crime sample reported more negative experiences. For example, they were more likely to have lost a job (50% versus 34%). In addition, bias crime victims reported significant health problems after the assault (48% versus 32%). Conversely, the nonbias group was more likely to experience a divorce or separation (15% versus 7%). It is impossible to determine if these changes are related to the assault that preceded them; it is true, however, that many of the bias crime victims in this sample experienced more traumatic events in their lives following the original assault.

Additionally, we asked each sample a summary question, "Overall, how difficult was it for you to overcome the effects of this incident?" Here again, the bias crime sample was almost three times more likely to report that recovery had been very difficult (36% versus 13%).

Conclusion

Our data has several limitations. First, the limited sample size of the comparative study reinforces the need for replication. Second, the nonrepresentative sample raises questions about generalizability. However, the difficulties we encountered in getting victims to respond, and our efforts to improve responses, can inform future research projects. Both bias and nonbias victim groups were hard to locate, and when correct addresses were found, people were hesitant to respond through the mail. This population may need more intensive efforts, such as interviews instead of self-administered questionnaires, as a methodology to encourage participation in sharing their victimization experiences.

Despite some methodological difficulties, our data confirm several previously posited hypotheses. First, compared to nonbias-motivated assaults, bias crimes tend to be perpetrated by multiple offenders on strangers; and its victims are more likely to be selected only because they belong to a particular group. Bias crimes more often occur in locations familiar to the victim, who is much more likely to experience increased fear after the incident. Additionally, victims of bias assault are more likely to feel the effects of victimization more intensely and for a longer period of time. Whether this is because of the inability to employ traditional coping mechanisms or some other phenomena, bias crime victims suffer more intense intrusive psychological sequelae than do nonbias assault victims.

Although the behavioral responses may initially seem surprising, we believe these also confirm earlier hypotheses. First, victim interchangability injects a unique dynamic into the victimization process. Victims are aware that their overt actions did nothing to precipitate their victimization; being the "wrong person" at the wrong time and place qualifies the bias victim as a target. Therefore, if the impetus for victimization is something that is outside of the bias victim's control before the incident, it is reasonable that there would be little that the victim would do differently subsequent to it. Qualitative responses from open-ended questions on the survey confirmed that victims recognized their distinct vulnerability, whereas nonbias victims believed that their behavior may have encouraged the offender, or exacerbated a tense situation among acquaintances. Psychological sequelae, however, are less easily controlled by the victim. The level of intrusive thoughts created by the incident and the feelings of helplessness associated with bias-motivated victimization all point to a unique victimization process for bias victims. These findings present clues about how criminal justice professionals can better work with hate crime victims.

This research supports the conclusion that bias crimes effect their victims differently from nonbias crimes. Victims of bias crimes are more fearful after the incident and are more likely to experience a series of intrusive thoughts. This is true even if we control on the type of crime—in this case, assaults. Although it is beyond the scope of our study to definitively conclude whether various hate crime legislation is justified, it is clear that bias victims have distinct needs. These conclusions support the claim that bias crimes do in fact affect their victims differently, and that consequently law enforcement and social service agencies should be cognizant of these differences when assisting bias crime victims.

Lastly, this project does not address the impact that bias crimes have on their secondary victims—the community. Because bias crimes have the ability, and often the intent, to reach far beyond the primary victim (attributable to victim interchangability), every member of the targeted minority group who is aware of the crime is affected by this solitary incident. Unfortunately, this is well beyond the scope of the current study. With these considerations in mind, we hope that the research community will both attempt to replicate this research with additional bias victim samples, and tap into the important topic of secondary victimization.

Acknowledgments

This project was sponsored through the National Institute of Justice, grant #97-IJ-CX-0011.

Points of view or opinions in this article are those of the authors and do not necessarily represent the official position of the funding source.

The authors wish to thank Luis Garcia and Joann Gu for their partnership in this project. We also thank Michael Buerer for his very insightful, helpful comments on an earlier draft of this paper.

Endnotes

[1]The city of Boston was selected because of its comprehensive strategies for investigating bias crimes through the Community Disorders Unit (CDU), formed in 1979 in response to heightened racial tensions within the city. Because of this, the research team had access to an extensive database of bias crime offenses.

[2]Child abuse and domestic assaults were excluded from the study. Because both of these categories touch on specific phenomena, the team felt that their inclusion would be inappropriate.

[3]This is the Horowitz "Impact of Event Scale" (1979).

[4]Originally, Horowitz employed a "not at all, rarely, sometimes, often" response framework for each of the scale items, within a time frame of "within the last seven days." Upon the suggestion of our advisory group, we decided to account for differences between the groups while incorporating a time dimension, thus further refining the "sometimes" category of the original scale. In addition, because our sample included victims who had been victimized spanning one month to six years prior to the administration of the survey, asking whether the respondent encountered the adverse stimuli or reaction "always, sometimes, rarely or not at all" as was done in the original Horowitz instrument would conceal the time-sensitive nature of the impact. Respondents were asked whether they experienced the particular emotion or coping technique "not at all," "for a few days," "for a few weeks," "for a few months," or "for a few years."

References

Barnes, A., and Ephross, P. H. (1994, May). The impact of hate violence on victims: Emotional and behavioral responses to attacks. *Social Work*, 39(3): 247–251.

Davis, R., and Brickman, E. (1996). Supportive and unsupportive aspects of the behavior of others toward victims of sexual and nonsexual assault. *Journal of Interpersonal Violence*, 11(2): 250–262.

Ehrlich, H. J., Larcom, B. E. K., and Purvis, R. D. (1994, May). *The Traumatic Effects of Ethnoviolence*. Towson, MD: The Prejudice Institute, Center for the Applied Study of Ethnoviolence.

Ephross, P. H., Barnes, A., Ehrlich, S., Weiss, K. R., and Weiss, J. C. (1986, October). *The Ethnoviolence Project: Pilot Study*. Baltimore: National Institute Against Prejudice and Violence.

Federal Bureau of Investigation. (1999). *Hate Crime Statistics 1998*. Washington, DC: U.S. Department of Justice.

Freedy, J., Resnick, H., Kilpatrick, D., Dansky, B., and Tidwell, R. (1994). The psychological adjustment of recent crime victims in the criminal justice system. *Journal of Interpersonal Violence*, 9(4): 450–468.

Frieze, I. H., Greenberg, M. S., and Hymer, S. (1987). Describing the crime victim: Psychological reactions to victimization. *Professional Psychology: Research and Practice*, 18(4): 299–315.

Greenberg, M., and Ruback, R. B. (1992). After the crime: Victim decision making, *Perspectives in Law and Psychology*, 9, 181–213.

Harvard Law Review. (1996). Penalty enhancement does not punish free speech or thoughts. *Hate Crimes*. B. Leone and P. A. Winters (Eds.). San Diego, CA: Greenhaven Press.

Herek, G., Gillis, J. R., Cogan, J. C., and Glunt, E. K. (1997, April). Hate crime victimization among lesbian, gay, and bisexual adults: Prevalence, psychological correlates, and methodological issues. *Journal of Interpersonal Violence*, 12(2): 195–215.

Horowitz, M., Walker, N., and Alvarez, W. (1979, May). Impact of events scale: A measure of subjective stress. *Psychosomatic Medicine*, 41(3): 209–218.

Jacobs, J., and Potter, K. (1998). *Hate Crime: Criminal Law and Identity Politics*. New York: Oxford University Press.

Janoff-Bulman, R. (1992). *Shattered Assumptions*. New York: Free Press.

Jenness, V., and Broad, K. (1997). *Violence Against Women, and the Law*. New York: Adline De Gruyter.

Katz, B. (1991). The psychological impact of stranger versus nonstranger rape on victims' recovery. In A. Parrot and L. Bechhofer (Eds.), *Acquaintance Rape: The Hidden Crime*. New York: John Wiley and Sons.

Koss, M., Dinero, T., Seibel, A., and Cox, S. (1984). Stranger and acquaintance rape: Are there differences in the victim's experience? *Psychology of Women Quarterly*, 12, 1–24.

Levin, J., and McDevitt, J. (1993). *Hate Crimes: The Rising Tide of Bigotry and Bloodshed*. New York: Plenum Press.

Lurigio, A. J. (1987). Are all victims alike? The adverse, generalized, and differential impact of crime. *Crime and Delinquency*, 33(4): 452–467.

McCann, I., Sakheim, L., David, K., and Abrahamson, D. J. (1988, October). Trauma and victimization: A model of psychological adaptation. *Counseling Psychologist*, 16(4): 531–594.

McDevitt, J. (1986). *Characteristics of Bias-Motivated Incidents in Boston, 1983–1989*. Boston: Center for Applied Social Research; Northeastern University.

McDevitt, J., Balboni, J., Bennett, S., Weiss, J., Orchowsky, S., and Walbolt, L. (2000). *Improving the Quality and Accuracy of Bias Crime Statistics Nationally: An Assessment of the First Ten Years of Bias Crime Data Collection.* Final report submitted to the Bureau of Justice Statistics. Grant #98–BJ–CX–K010.

McDevitt, J., Balboni, J., Garcia, L., and Gu, J. (forthcoming). Consequences for victims: A comparison of bias and non-bias motivated assaults. *The Journal of American Behavior Science.*

Norris, F., and Kaniasty, K. (1991). The psychological experience of crime: A test of the mediating role of beliefs in explaining the distress of victims. *Journal of Social and Clinical Psychology,* 10(3): 239–261.

Resick, P. (1987). Psychological effects of victimization: Implications for the criminal justice system. *Crime and Delinquency,* 33(4): 468–478.

Riggs, D., Rothbaum, B., and Foa, E. (1995). A prospective examination of symptoms of post-traumatic stress disorder in victims of nonsexual assault. *Journal of Interpersonal Violence,* 10(2).

Rothbaum, B., Foa, E., Riggs, D., Murdock, T., and Walsh, W. (1992). A prospective examination of post-traumatic stress disorder in rape victims. *Journal of Traumatic Stress,* 5(3): 455–475.

Sales, E., Baum, M., and Shore, B. (1984). Victim readjustment following assault. *Journal of Social Issues,* 40(1): 117–136.

Schepple, K. L., and Bart, P. B. (1983). Through women's eyes: Defining danger in the wake of sexual assault. *Journal of Social Issues,* 39(2): 63–81.

Ullman, S. E., and Seigel, J. M. (1993). "Victim–offender relationship and sexual assault. *Violence and Victims,* 8(2): 121–133.

Wirtz, P., and Harrell, A. (1987). Victim and crime characteristics, coping responses, and short and long-term recovery from victimization. *Journal of Consulting and Clinical Psychology,* 55(6): 866–871.

Wisconsin v. Mitchell. (1993) 508 U.S. 476.

CHAPTER 10

Victims of Racial Profiling

Amy Farrell and Deborah Ramirez

Introduction

This chapter addresses what happens when individuals are victimized by the police or perceive that the police are targeting them unjustly. One of the most controversial issues around police accountability and integrity is racial profiling, commonly understood as the practice of targeting or stopping a pedestrian or the driver of a motor vehicle primarily on the basis of that individual's race. Aggressive crime control strategies, utilized by police in an effort to reduce crime rates through the late 1990s, have raised concern among community members, particularly within the community of color, that vigorous stop and search practices threaten the civil liberties of citizens. Racial profiling's social and human costs were illustrated by then–United States Attorney General Janet Reno when she stated:

> When citizens do not trust their local police officer, they are less willing to report crime and less willing to be witnesses in criminal cases. When there is a breach of trust, it means people are more distrustful of the police, more tense when there is an encounter, and less likely to cooperate. As a result, police officers are more tense, and they may by more likely to react with more force than necessary. Suddenly a routine encounter can become a deadly clash. (Attorney General's Remarks to the National Press Club, 1999, p. 2)

The perceptions of individuals that they are stopped, searched, and harassed by the police on the basis of their race is a complex and multifaceted problem. Dedicated police officers and professional police practices have contributed greatly to making our communities safer. The overwhelming majority of police officers are hard-working public servants who perform a dangerous job with dedication and honor, but the perception that some police officers engage in racial profiling threatens to create deep distrust of the police in many communities.

The appearance of racial bias in decisions to stop certain individuals arises out of a long history of adversarial relationships between the police and disenfranchised communities. Conflict between police personnel and communities of color has included police enforcement of Jim Crow segregation, including efforts to prevent black voters from registering in the South; the "Zoot Suit" riots between police and navy personnel and Hispanics in Los Angeles in 1943; and the Watts, Detroit, Newark, and other race riots of the 1960s. Recent events, such as the videotaped beating of Rodney King by officers of the Los Angeles Police Department or the Mollen Commission's 1994 report of widespread police brutality against minority citizens in the Bronx, reinforce fears that police officers victimize minorities. The perception of police victimization, whether based on credible evidence or historical anecdotes, often leads to distrust between police agencies and communities of color.

Survey research on public attitudes toward the police has consistently shown that race is one of the strongest predictors of negative perceptions of police (Weitzer, 1999a). For example, in a 1994 survey of police practices in Ohio, nearly half of all African American respondents reported that they had been "hassled" by the police, compared to only 9% of white respondents (Browning, Cullen, Cao, Kopache, and Stevenson, 1994). New research on neighborhood and class differences on group attitudes toward the police highlights that people of color are not homogenous in their general evaluations of police performance. These studies do indicate that the impression that people of color are treated differently by the police remains consistent across neighborhood and class differences (Weitzer, 1999b). In turn, perceptions of racial profiling threaten to erode confidence in the police across many communities of color. Increased attention to individual perceptions of racial profiling and disparate treatment by the police is an important part of the evolving research on race and police integrity.

The Social Costs of Racial Profiling Victimization

In the late 1990s, U.S. news-media coverage exploded with stories on racial profiling. The allegations are now so common that the community of color has labeled the phenomenon with the derisive terms "driving while black" or "driving while brown." Front-page news stories and editorials in both the national and local press illustrated the high social and individual costs associated with the widespread belief that police were engaging in racial profiling.

National surveys confirm that a majority of Americans, regardless of race, believe that racial profiling is a significant social problem. According to a Gallup Poll released on December 9, 1999, over half of Americans believe that the police actively practice racial profiling, and, more significantly, 81% of them say they disapprove of the practice (Gallup Poll, 1999). In this national sample of adults, 59% said that racial profiling is widespread. When the responses to the survey question were broken down by race, 56% of whites and 77% of blacks responded that racial profiling was pervasive. Additionally, the Gallup survey asked respondents how often they had been stopped by the police, on the basis of their race alone. Six percent of whites and 42% of blacks responded that they had been stopped by the police because of their race and 72% of black men between the ages of 18 and 34 believed they had been stopped because of their race.

While polls show that most Americans believe that racial profiling exists and that it is harmful, its personal human costs are often the most striking. Motorists of color frequently cite the fear of being stopped by the police as a motivating factor for changing the way they conduct their everyday tasks, for example, altering their driving patterns to avoid particular parts of town. Other motorists fear the humiliation of repeatedly being asked to step out of their car, or being searched on the road. Above all, black and Hispanic drivers resent being "labeled" criminal solely because of the color of their skin. The words of Keith Smith, an African American resident of Seattle, Washington, illustrate the pain and anger that a perception of racial profiling causes. During a city council hearing on racial profiling, Smith stated "All of us are not thieves, we're not prostitutes, not druggies just because I may feel like putting on a pair of baggie pants or putting my hat on backwards" (Wilson, 2000).

Interviews with African American and Hispanic individuals who believe that they have been victims of racial profiling demonstrate the anger, fear, and resentment that such stops elicit. As with other forms of bias-motivated violations, such as violence against women and hate crimes, the "act" itself is often less traumatic than the fear associated with being targeted for being part of an identifiable group. Interviews conducted by David Harris, a law professor at the University of Toledo, showed that when black drivers were pulled over for traffic violations without a plausible explanation, they were likely to assume that race was a factor in the police officers' decisions to make the traffic stop. As one interviewee noted,

> We just constantly get harrassed. So we just feel like we can't go nowhere without being bothered. But yet I got a cop pull me over says I'm weaving in the road. And I just came from a friend's house, no alcohol, no nothing. It makes you wonder—was it because I'm black? (Harris, 1999, p. 272)

Black and Hispanic drivers often make adjustments in their daily activities to avoid such experience. They avoid driving in particular neighborhoods where they believe they will look "suspicious." Some individuals have reported that they do not buy "flashy" cars that draw the attention of police officers and increase the probability that they will be stopped.

Although individuals often feel the dramatic personal effects of racial pro-filing in their daily activities, the costs of such perceptions within large segments of our society on police–community relationships are staggering. Recent survey data confirms a strong connection between perceptions of race-based stops by the police and animosity toward local and state law enforcement. In addition to gathering data on individual perceptions of stops by the police, the 1999 Gallup poll asked respondents how favorably they viewed the police. Eighty-five per-cent of white respondents had a favorable response toward local police, and 87% of white respondents had a favorable response to state police. However, African American respondents overall had a less favorable opinion of both state (64%) and local (85%) police. The less favorable responses of black respondents toward local and state police may be explained by perceptions of treatment by the police. More than half (53%) of African American men between the ages of 18 and 34 believe that they have been treated unfairly by local police.

Similarly, a 12-city survey conducted by the Department of Justice in 1998 demonstrates that although most people in the African American commu-nity felt satisfied with police services in their neighborhoods, their level of dissat-isfaction was approximately twice that of the white community (Bureau of Justice Statistics, 1999). This wide schism in all 12 of the cities surveyed indicates the need for law enforcement to work harder to restore the confidence of com-munities of color in the critical work being done by law enforcement. Police departments that fail to address the perception of racially discriminatory polic-ing within minority neighborhoods may find their own law enforcement efforts undermined.

How Do We Recognize Racial Profiling? Evaluating Indicators of Disparate Treatment

Although anecdotal and empirical evidence confirm national perceptions about racial profiling's pervasiveness, many question whether racial profiling is actually victimization by the police. To understand why community members interpret racial profiling as police victimization, it is important to understand how police officers make decisions to stop a vehicle or person, and how the actions of the officer during the stop shape an individual's perception that she or he was victimized. This second issue may include questions such as: Are passengers and drivers ordered to step out of the car? Is the suspect treated with respect? Are police questioning the occupants about subjects unrelated to the traffic stop violation? Did the officer request permission to search the car and its contents? How long did the encounter last? Evidence from anecdotal accounts and statistical studies help us understand why certain police stops are perceived as racial profiling.

ANECDOTAL EVIDENCE

Personal anecdotes and stories illustrate the experiences of those who believe they have been stopped because of racial profiling and, in turn, give rise to a set of common concerns about police stop and search practices. A recent report by David Harris (1999a), *Driving While Black: Racial Profiling on Our Nation's Highways,* cites numerous accounts of disparate treatment toward minorities by police from a variety of state and local jurisdictions. A sample of these accounts demonstrates the emotional impact of such incidents.

Reports that police stop drivers because they or their passengers do not appear to "match" the type of vehicle they occupy is common in racial profiling accounts. This "driving in the wrong car" concern is illustrated by the experiences of Dr. Elmo Randolph, a 42-year-old African American dentist, who commutes from Bergen County, New Jersey, to his office near Newark. Since 1991, Randolph says he has been stopped by New Jersey state troopers more than 50 times. Randolph does not drive at excessive speeds and claims he has never been issued a ticket (Hosenball, 1999). Instead, troopers approach his gold BMW, request his license and registration, and ask him, "Do you have any drugs or weapons in your car?" The experience of Dr. Randolph and many other minority drivers on New Jersey's highways led to the recent consent decree and settlement between the State of New Jersey and the Department of Justice. As a result of the settlement, New Jersey State Police are collecting data on the race and ethnicity of persons stopped by state troopers and improving the supervision and training of their officers.

Another common allegation is that police stop people of color from traveling through predominately white areas because the police believe that people of color do not "belong" in certain neighborhoods and therefore may be engaged in criminal activity. This type of profiling was reported by Alvin Penn, the African American deputy president of the Connecticut State Senate. In 1996, a Trumbull, Connecticut, police officer stopped Penn as he drove his van through that predominately white, suburban town. After reviewing Penn's license and registration, the officer asked Penn if he knew which town he was in (Bridgeport, the state's largest city, where African Americans and Latinos are 75% of the population, borders Trumbull, which is 98% white). Penn, recalling that he had been turning around on a dead-end street when the officer stopped him, responded by asking why he needed to know which town he was in. The officer told him that he was not required to give Penn a reason for the stop and that if he made an issue of it, the officer would cite him for speeding (Weizel, 1999). Three years after this incident, Alvin Penn sponsored legislation that ultimately made Connecticut the second state in the nation to collect data on the demographics of individuals stopped by the state police.

By far, however, the most common complaint by members of communities of color is that they are stopped for petty traffic violations such as underinflated tires, failure to signal properly before switching lanes, vehicle equipment failures, speeding less than 10 miles above the speed limit, or having an illegible license plate. One example of this is the account of Robert Wilkins, a Harvard Law School graduate and a public defender in Washington, D.C., who went to a family funeral in Ohio in May 1992. On the return trip, Wilkins, his aunt and uncle, and a 29-year-old cousin rented a Cadillac for the trip home. His cousin was stopped for speeding in western Maryland while driving 60 miles per hour in a 55-miles-per-hour zone of the interstate. The group was forced to stand on the side of the interstate in the rain for an extended period of time while officers and drug-sniffing dogs searched their car. Nothing was found. Wilkins, represented by the ACLU, filed suit, and ultimately received a settlement from the state of Maryland (*Wilkins v. Maryland,* 1993).

Although this small sample of anecdotal evidence does not prove that police officers actively engage in racial profiling, it is representative of the thousands of personal stories cataloged in newspaper articles, interviews, ACLU commentary, and court battles.

EMPIRICAL RESEARCH ON RACIAL PROFILING

In addition to the growing body of individual accounts of racial profiling, scholars have begun an empirical examination of the relationship between police stop and search practices and racial characteristics of individual drivers. The majority of empirical research collected to date has been drawn from expert testimony accompanying lawsuits. *Wilkins v. Maryland State Police* (1993) was one of the first cases to introduce empirical evidence of racial profiling into the court record.

As described in the anecdotal evidence section, the story of Robert Wilkins is a dramatic example of racial profiling and its implications. After being stopped by the police and detained on the side of the road for a lengthy period of time, Wilkins filed suit against the Maryland state troopers who stopped him. In 1995 and 1996, as a result of Wilkins's settlement with the Maryland State Police, the department was forced to turn over data on police searches on I-95 to an academic expert. Using data released by the Maryland State Police pursuant to the settlement, researchers compared the population of people searched and arrested with those violating traffic laws on Maryland highways. To construct a comparison population, the research group designed a violator sample using both stationary and rolling surveys of drivers exceeding the legal speed limit on a selected portion of I-95 in Maryland. This violator survey indicated that 74.7% of speeders were white, whereas 17.5% were black (Harris, 1999b). In contrast, according to Maryland State Police data, blacks constituted 79.2% of the drivers searched. The outside research panel concluded that the data revealed "dramatic and highly statistically significant disparities between the percentage of black I-95 motorists legitimately subject to stop by the Maryland State Police and the percentage of black motorists detained and searched by Maryland State Troopers on this roadway" (Lamberth, 1999).

Empirical data on stop and search practices in New Jersey also originated through actions of the court. In the late 1980s and early 1990s, African American drivers reported being stopped disproportionately by New Jersey state troopers. In response to these complaints, in 1994, the Gloucester (NJ) County Public Defender's office, while representing Pedro Soto and others, filed a motion to suppress evidence obtained in a series of searches, alleging they were unlawful because they were part of a pattern and practice of racial profiling by the New Jersey state troopers (*State of New Jersey v. Pedro Soto*, 1996). As part of that litigation, the defendants received traffic stop and arrest data compiled by the New Jersey State Police in selected locations from 1988 through 1991.[1]

Table 10.1 illustrates the disparities between black drivers' representation in the driving population and their representation among those individuals stopped or searched. Between 1988 and 1991 in New Jersey, African Americans were disproportionally more likely to be stopped and arrested than white drivers. The Superior Court of New Jersey relied upon this data in its decision to suppress the evidence seized by New Jersey state troopers in 19 consolidated criminal prosecutions, and concurred with the assessment of outside researchers that the troopers unlawfully relied on race in stopping and searching motorists on the New Jersey Turnpike.

TABLE 10.1 New Jersey State Police Data: 1988–1991

	Stopped	Searched
White	59%	21%
Black	27%	53%
Hispanic	7%	24%

Source: Adapted from Peter Verniero and Paul Zoubek, *New Jersey Attorney General's Interim Report of the State Police Review Team Regarding Allegations of Racial Profiling (NJ Interim Rep.)*, April 20, 1999.

Recent data collection efforts in New Jersey and New York confirm the independent empirical findings utilized in court cases. In April 1999, the Attorney General of New Jersey issued a report indicating that New Jersey state troopers had engaged in racial profiling along the New Jersey Turnpike (Verniero and Zoubek, 1999). This report tracked the racial breakdowns of traffic stops between 1997 and 1998, and established that people of color constituted 40.6% of the stops made on the turnpike. Although few stops resulted in a search, 77.2% of those individuals searched were people of color. An analysis of these searches' productivity indicated that 10.5% of those involving white motorists and 13.5% involving black motorists resulted in arrest or seizure. Finally, the New Jersey report demonstrates that minority motorists were much more likely to be involved in consent searches than nonminority motorists, accounting for 8 out of 10 consent searches.

In December 1999, the Attorney General of New York, Eliot Spitzer, released the results of an investigation by his office of "stop and frisk" practices in New York City. It showed that African Americans and Latinos were much more likely to be stopped and searched, even when the statistics were adjusted to reflect differing criminal participation rates in some neighborhoods (Flynn, 1999). After reviewing 175,000 incidents in which citizens were stopped by the police during the 15-month period that ended in March 1999, the attorney general found that blacks were stopped six times more often than whites, while Latinos were stopped four times more often. Blacks made up 25% of the city population but 50% of the people stopped, and 67% of the persons stopped by the New York City Street Crimes Unit (New York Attorney General, 1999).

International data suggests that racial profiling is not an isolated U.S. experience. A 1998 study by the British government's Home Office examined the racial and ethnic demographics of the stop and search patterns of 43 police forces in England and Wales. The study indicated that black individuals were, on average, seven and a half times more likely to be stopped and searched and four times more likely to be arrested than whites (Home Office, 1998), in spite of the fact that, according to census population figures, Great Britain is 93% white and 7% ethnic minority. Although the high proportion of searches on people of color has been a constant feature of police searches in London and elsewhere, the proportion of searches that result in an arrest does not differ by race or ethnicity—that is, regardless of whether the search was of a white or black person. In London, the arrest rate was 11.1% for light-skinned Europeans, 11.4% for dark-skinned Europeans, and 11.7% for black people. In the case of Asians, the arrest rate was lowest at 9.4% (FitzGerald, 1999).

Anecdotal and empirical evidence has helped state and local activists, community members, and government officials understand the problem of racial profiling and has raised new questions about police stop and search practices. However, more expansive and systematic data collection is needed to address the concerns surrounding police practices and racial profiling.

Origins of Racial Profiling and the Complexities of Police Discretion

Although empirical research, anecdotal evidence, and survey data confirm that racial profiling victimization exists, many still question how such profiling happens. Throughout all areas of their daily routine, police exercise a great deal of individual discretion. During traffic stops, for example, police must use reasoned judgment in deciding which cars to stop from among the universe of cars being operated in violation of the law. Since a myriad of traffic enforcement and vehicle code laws apply to all cars on the road, and there are more vehicles being operated in violation of the local traffic laws than police have the resources to stop, officers have a wide ambit of discretion in selecting which cars they stop.

Many traffic officers will tell you that by following any vehicle for one or two minutes, they could observe a basis on which to stop it. Many police departments have not developed formal written or standardized criteria directing officers on how to use this discretion. Instead, officers often develop their own ad hoc method of winnowing suspicious from innocent motorists. This intuition, often learned by young officers observing the actions of more experienced officers, can vary widely across individual officers, even within a particular department. Finally, police departments often use traffic stops as a means of ferreting out illicit drugs and weapons. Consequently, some officers routinely use traffic "pretext stops" to track down drug or gun couriers. These discretionary decisions are seldom documented and rarely reviewed. As a result, individual officers are infrequently made accountable for their decisions.

LEVELS OF POLICE DISCRETION

A number of factors may influence an officer's decision to stop and search an individual; the various types of potential scenarios can easily be broken down into high- and low-discretion realms. Traffic and pedestrian stops can be viewed on a continuum of discretion from low-discretion stops, where an officer's discretion is limited, to high-discretion stops, where the decision to stop someone is often a discretionary call based on an officer's experiences in the field.

Low Discretion

Although the nature and scope of low-discretion stops will vary by place and context, they are common in policing and can include those based on externally generated reports of a crime or suspicious activity, such as when a victim describes a particular suspect. In the traffic stop context, particularly in jurisdictions where traffic enforcement is a priority, speeding over 8 to 10 miles above the speed limit or running a red light might also be placed in the category of low-discretion stops. Some jurisdictions have calculated the actual percentage of stops that fall in this low-discretion category. The New York attorney general's "Stop and Frisk" study, for example, shows that only 30% of the stops were based on victims' descriptions. Similarly, in London, only a quarter of searches in selected study sites were considered low discretion (FitzGerald, 1999b).

High Discretion

The complexities of police discretion emerge more often in the high-discretion stop category. In the traffic stop context, these are stops for underinflated tires, safety belt warnings, failure to signal when changing lanes, and other minor vehicle code and nonmoving violations. In the pedestrian stop context, high-discretion stops involve those who may "look suspicious" but are not engaged in any specific criminal violation or activities. These high-discretion stops invite both intentional and unintentional abuse. Police, obviously, are just as subject to racial and ethnic stereotypes they learn from our culture as any other citizen. Unless documented, such stops create an environment that allows the perpetuation of stereotypes to go undetected.

THE PERCEPTION THAT MINORITIES ARE MORE LIKELY TO CARRY CONTRABAND

The perception that African Americans, Latinos, Asian Americans, and other minorities are more likely to carry drugs than whites intensifies the complexities of police discretion in stops and searches.[2] The escalating pressure from the "war on drugs" has led some police officers to target people of color, whom police believed to be disproportionally involved in drug use and trafficking. Although some members of the police community suggest that race-based searches are justified because more minority drivers are found with contraband, the empirical evidence amassed to date calls such assumptions into question.[3] In the analysis of Maryland's Interstate 95 traffic stop data, researchers found that 28% of drivers and passengers—black *and* white—who were searched were carrying contraband. Thus, contraband was found on roughly the same percentage of white and black drivers, regardless of race. According to the New Jersey Attorney General's Interim Report, the "hit rates," or the rates at which contraband was found among individuals who were searched, did not differ significantly by race. Ten percent of the searches of white motorists resulted in an arrest or seizure, compared to 13% of those of black motorists. Similarly, in the New York study of "stop and frisk" practices between 1998 and 1999, the attorney general found that 13% of whites stopped were arrested, compared to only 11% of blacks and Latinos. In a recent United States Customs Service study, nationwide data from customs stops revealed that whereas 43% of those searched were either black or Latino, the "hit rates" for blacks and Latinos were actually lower than those for whites. The study found that 7% of whites, 6% of blacks, and 3% of Hispanics had contraband. This is particularly surprising because the Customs Study does not involve car stops, but rather stops and searches in airports. Presumably, if the perception that drug couriers are more likely to be black or Latino were true, a widespread survey of airport searches should reveal differing "hit rates" (Harris, 1999b). Similarly, in London, the probability of finding contraband as a result of a search did not significantly differ among races. Although sound empirical research on the relationship between race and "hit rates" for contraband is limited, to date the evidence indicates that blacks and Latinos are no more likely than whites to be in possession of narcotics or other contraband.[4]

In many cases, disproportionate minority arrests for drug possession and distribution have fueled perceptions by police and others that race is an appropriate consideration in the decision to stop or search an individual.[5] However, existing data on the productivity of searches across racial groups suggest that stop and search practices have become a game of "search and you will find." Police officers who aggressively and disproportionately search people of color will arrest more people of color than whites, not because of differences in behavior, but because they are stopping and searching many more people of color than whites. Regardless of whether the perception that blacks and Latinos are more likely to be found in possession of contraband could be empirically verified, our laws do not permit race to be used as a basis for stopping and searching individuals.

Conclusion and Strategies to Address the Problem of Racial Profiling

As law enforcement agencies across the United States increasingly work with diverse communities and respond to different needs within these communities, they confront feelings of distrust from some groups within the communities they serve and protect. In turn, many police departments have begun to recognize the potential damage that is done when members of the community they police perceive that they have become victims of illegitimate police practices. In response to allegations of racial profiling, a number of state and local agencies have begun to track the race, ethnicity, and gender of those who are stopped and/or searched by police officers.

On June 9 and 10, 1999, President Bill Clinton, Attorney General Janet Reno, civil rights leaders, police, and other government leaders participated in a Washington, D.C., conference entitled "Strengthening Police–Community Relationships." During the conference, President Clinton called racial profiling a "morally indefensible, deeply corrosive practice" and further stated that, "racial profiling is in fact the opposite of good police work, where actions are based on hard facts, not stereotypes. It is wrong, it is destructive and it must stop" (U.S. Department of Justice, 1999). As a result of increased national concern over racial profiling, Clinton directed federal agencies to begin gathering data on the race and ethnicity of persons stopped, for future analysis.

In addition to the federal data collection efforts, state legislation in Connecticut, North Carolina, Washington, Kansas, Tennessee, Rhode Island, and Missouri has begun requiring state police and/or local police agencies to record and make public the racial and ethnic pattern of their traffic stops. Nationwide, a significant number of law enforcement agencies have begun to voluntarily implement data collection systems.

By providing information about the nature, character, and demographics of police enforcement patterns, these efforts can serve as a catalyst for nurturing and shaping productive community and police discussions. Data collection allows police departments to gather and assess information on the demographics of the population they come into contact with, and to integrate such knowledge into a comprehensive training program. Finally, a data collection system can enable police and the community to assess the quantity and quality of police–citizen encounters. Data collection by itself is not a solution to the complex problem of police use of profiles and the perception of racial bias by the community of color. However, when implemented properly, data collection can be an initial step in a training program to educate officers about the conscious and unconscious use of racial and ethnic stereotypes and to promote courteous and respectful police–citizen encounters.

As we enter the new millennium, the challenge that confronts U.S. police organizations is how to sustain the historic decline in criminal activity rates and, at the same time, enhance police legitimacy in the eyes of the communities being served. Appropriately addressing allegations of racial profiling victimization is central to this new mission.

Endnotes

[1] The stop and arrest information was compiled using patrol charts, radio logs, and traffic tickets for selected dates from April 1988 to May 1991.

[2] This idea has been perpetuated by some police training materials. For example, in the mid-1980s the Florida Department of Highway Safety and Motor Vehicles issued guidelines for the police on common characteristics of drug couriers that warned officers to be suspicious of drivers who do not "fit the vehicle" and "ethnic groups associated with the drug trade." For a discussion of this practice, see O.W. Wisotsky, *Beyond the War on Drugs: Overcoming a Failed Public Policy,* Buffalo, NY: Prometheus Books (1990).

[3] It is important to note that only a limited number of empirical studies have examined the relationship between an individual's race and the probability that the individual is carrying contraband. More research is needed before appropriately addressing such questions.

[4] National research conducted by the Federal Substance Abuse and Mental Health Services Administration (SAMHSA) *National Household Survey of Drug Abuse,* indicates in its 1998 survey that the rate at which blacks use illegal drugs is 8.2%, only slightly higher than the white or Latino

rates (both at 6.1%). This research indicates that the vast majority of people across all racial groups do not use drugs, and subsequently should not be seen as targets of suspicion. Similarly, the National Institute of Drug Abuse found that 12–14% of those who abuse drugs are black. This percentage mirrors the representation of blacks in the general population. For more information, see the National Clearinghouse for Alcohol and Drug Information, Research and Statistics, 1998.

[5]It is true that the racial demographic of arrest statistics for narcotics shows that more blacks, Latinos, and other minorities are arrested on drug charges. However, most drug possession and distribution goes undetected. It is private and conducted outside the ambit of police view. Only a small percentage of these crimes receive law enforcement's attention. Thus, the number of drug arrests may only reflect law enforcement patterns.

References

Attorney General's Remarks to the National Press Club. (1999, April 15) (on file with author).

Browning, S. L., Cullen, F., Cao, L., Kopache, R., and Stevenson, T. (1994). Race and getting hassled by the police: A research note. *Police Studies, 17,* 1–11.

Bureau of Justice Statistics. (1999, May). *Criminal Victimization and Perceptions of Community Safety in 12 Cities* (NCJ 173940). Washington, DC: U.S. Department of Justice.

FitzGerald, M. (1999a). *Final Report into Stop and Search.* London: Metropolitan Police.

———. (1999b). *Searches in London, Interim Evaluation of Year One of the Programme of Action.* London: Home Office.

Flynn, K. (1999, December 1). State cites racial inequality in New York police searches. *New York Times,* p. A22.

Gallup Poll Organization Poll Release. (1999, December 9). *Racial Profiling Is Seen As Widespread, Particularly among Young Black Men,* 1–5. Gallup Poll Organization. Available at www.gallup.com/poll/releases/pr991209.asp

Harris, D. (1999a). *Driving While Black: Racial Profiling on Our Nation's Highways.* New York: American Civil Liberties Union.

———. (1999b). The stories, the statistics and the law: Why driving while black matters. *Minnesota Law Review, 84,* 280–281.

Home Office. (1998). *Statistics on Race and the Criminal Justice System: A Home Office Publication Under Section 95 of the Criminal Justice Act of 1991.* London, England: Home Office.

Hosenball, M. (1999, May 17). It is not the act of a few bad apples: Lawsuit shines the spotlight on allegations of racial profiling by New Jersey state troopers. *Newsweek,* pp. 34–35.

Lamberth, J. (1999, August 16). Driving while black: A statistician proves that prejudice still rules the road. *Washington Post,* p. C1.

National Clearinghouse for Alcohol and Drug Information, Research and Statistics. (1998). *National Household Survey on Drug Abuse.* Washington, DC: Department of Health and Human Services.

Office of New York Attorney General. (1999, December 1). *"Stop and Frisk" Practices: A Report to the People of New York From the Office of the Attorney General.*

State of New Jersey v. Pedro Soto. Superior Court of New Jersey 734 A.2d 350. (1996).

U.S. Department of Justice. (1999). *Attorney General's Conference on Strengthening Police-Community Relationships,* Report on the Proceedings, U.S. Department of Justice, June 9–10, 1–40.

Verniero, P., and Zoubek, P. (1999, April 20). *New Jersey Attorney General's Interim Report of the State Police Review Team Regarding Allegations of Racial Profiling*. New Jersey Attorney General's Office: State of New Jersey.

Weitzer, R. (1999a). Citizens' perceptions of police misconduct: Race and neighborhood contexts. *Justice Quarterly,* 16, 819–846.

———. (1999b). Racialized policing: Residents' perceptions in three neighborhoods. *Law and Society Review,* 34, 129–155.

Weizel, R. (1999, May 2). Lawmaker pushes for racial profiling bill. *Boston Globe,* p. D21.

Wilkins v. Maryland State Police, Civil Action No. CCB–93–483, Md. Federal District Court (1993).

Wilson, K. (2000, August 23). Residents paint a profile of racism for city council. *Seattle Post Inquirer,* p. A1.

PART III

VICTIMS IN ORGANIZATIONAL CONTEXTS

CHAPTER 11

Straight Time
Inmates' Perceptions of Violence and Victimization in Prison

Craig Hemmens and James W. Marquart

Introduction

The stereotype of prison is that of a dangerous place, where strong inmates prey on the weak. According to one inmate–author, fear of assault is so pervasive, "everyone is afraid" (Abbott, 1981, p. 144). In 1992, there were 10,181 inmate-on-inmate attacks that required medical attention, and 66 criminal homicides in state and federal prisons (Camp and Camp, 1993). These statistics indicate that the stereotype of prison is not without a basis in reality. Not surprisingly, research has shown that a feeling of personal safety is crucial in establishing a high quality of prison life (Toch, 1977). Although there has been much study of the relationship between sociodemographic and criminal history characteristics and inmate adjustment to prison (Goodstein and MacKenzie, 1984; MacKenzie, 1987; Wright, 1989, 1991, 1993), relatively little attention has been paid to the relationship between these characteristics and perceptions of violence and victimization in prison.

In this chapter we present results from a survey of 775 recently released adult male inmates regarding their perceptions of violence in prison. Relationships between perceptions of the level of prison violence and individual sociodemographic and criminal history characteristics, such as age at first arrest, number of prior incarcerations, and number of years in prison, are examined.

Life in Prison

What is the effect of incarceration on those subjected to it? There are a number of accounts of prison life, written by prisoners, current (Shakur, 1993) and former (Abbott, 1981); and outside observers (Earley, 1992). These reports can best be described as case studies, anecdotal accounts of life in one institution at one point in time, as experienced by one man. Although they provide an enormous amount of information, and a very real human touch, they are lacking in generalizability.

The sociological literature is rife with studies of prison life and inmate adjustment patterns. Modern sociological research on prison life dates from Clemmer's (1940) pioneering work, *The Prison Community.* He observed that the written rules and regulations of the institution explained only a part of how a prisoner adjusted to life in the "Big House." Equally if not more important was the informal social system created by the inmates. He developed the concept of "prisonization" (p. 299) to explain how a prisoner becomes assimilated into the informal social structure of the prison.

Sykes, in *The Society of Captives* (1958) and elsewhere (Sykes and Messinger, 1960), further developed Clemmer's concept of prisonization, explaining the cause of inmate alienation as a reaction to the "pains of imprisonment" (1958, pp. 63–83), which he identified as loss of one's liberty, loss of material possessions, loss of heterosexual contact, loss of personal autonomy, and loss of personal security. Suffering these pains, Sykes believed, caused inmates to become insecure and bitter and led them to "reject their rejecters" (McCorkle and Korn, 1954, p. 98). The result was that the pains of imprisonment forged an inmate population unified by its shared pains. Prisoners developed their own informal social structure based on their responses to the pains of imprisonment. This subculture reinforced a set of norms and values in opposition to those espoused by the prison staff. This was known as the "inmate code" (Sykes and Messinger, 1960).

The model of prison life developed by Clemmer and extended by Sykes became known as the "deprivation" model (Allen and Simonsen, 1995) or the "indigenous" or "functional" model (Irwin and Cressey, 1964). It focuses on the humiliations and degradations inherent in forced confinement. The model has received mixed empirical support. Research by others has lent some support to the concept of prisonization. Wheeler (1961), Garabedian (1963), Schrag (1961), Wellford (1967), Street (1970), Berk (1968), Grusky (1959), Wilson (1968), and Tittle (1968) tested the deprivation model in a variety of correctional institutions and found at least some support for the concept, although the degree of support varied by institution type.

The deprivation model was challenged by researchers who decried its disregard for the effect of the outside world and individual characteristics on how inmates adjust to prison (Irwin and Cressey, 1964; Irwin, 1970; Carroll, 1974;

Jacobs, 1977). These writers noted that an inmate did not come into prison a blank slate, but rather brought with him the code of the streets, which he used in modified form within the prison walls. This was referred to as the "importation model." Irwin and Cressey (1964) argued that preinstitutional experiences and backgrounds have a major impact on how an inmate adapts to incarceration. There is empirical support for the importation hypothesis (Wood et al., 1968; Thomas, 1977; Faine, 1973; Lawson et al., 1996; Carroll, 1974; Jacobs, 1977).

Later writers suggested that both the deprivation and importation models presented an incomplete picture of inmate life. The "integrated model" (Thomas, 1970, 1977; Zingraff, 1975) incorporated elements of both models in an attempt to provide a more complete picture of inmate adjustment patterns. These writers pointed out that Clemmer acknowledged that preprison experiences play some role in adjustment and that Irwin and Cressey admitted that some inmates are more affected by the prison environment than others.

More recent research has focused on the relationship of selected socio-demographic and criminal history characteristics and inmate adjustment patterns (Goodstein and MacKenzie, 1984; MacKenzie, 1987; Wright, 1989, 1993). The present study extends this trend and includes an understudied group, Hispanic inmates.

Prison Violence

A number of studies have documented the relatively high level of aggression and victimization in prisons. Bowker (1980) provides a comprehensive review of the literature on victimization in prison, including physical, psychological, economic, and social victimization of inmates by other inmates, as well as victimization of inmates by correctional staff. He found that self-report data indicated a much higher level of inmate victimization than did official data. This finding is in line with research on victimization studies in the general population (Bureau of Justice Statistics, 1992).

Research indicates that the vast majority of inmates experience feelings of vulnerability to victimization and attack, creating a mental state in which they are "constantly on guard against danger [they] cannot hope to locate, to anticipate, or to guard against" (Toch, 1977, p. 42). Toch (1977) found that certain inmate characteristics, including physical size and age, are related to the degree of fear experienced. There is also evidence that white inmates have a higher fear of victimization, in part because they are more likely to be victims of interracial assault (Fuller and Orsagh, 1977; Irwin, 1980).

An early study of victimization in North Carolina state prisons by Fuller and Orsagh (1977) found that although victimization was not uncommon, the rate of unprovoked victimization was quite low. Their comparison of official records and self-report data from interviews with approximately 400 inmates indicated that official reports seriously underreported victimization in prison, similar to what occurs in the free world. They also found that victimization in prison was a much more likely occurrence than in the free world: By their estimate, an inmate had a 50% greater chance of being assaulted than did a person in the free world (Fuller and Orsagh, 1977).

Another study found that violence within an institution was largely a function of age (Mabli et al., 1979). The authors studied assault rates in two federal prisons, one for young offenders and one for older offenders, and found that assault rates were higher in the former. When some of the younger offenders were transferred to the prison for older offenders, and some of the older inmates were moved to the prison for younger offenders, assault rates increased in the facility for older offenders and decreased in the facility for younger offenders.

McCorkle (1992, 1993a, 1993b) surveyed inmates of a southern maximum-security facility to determine the impact of living in a violence-prone institution. Whereas prior studies concentrated on victimization rates, McCorkle focused on the effect of victimization on inmates' attitudes and actions. He found that inmates' fear of victimization was higher than fear of victimization in the general population (McCorkle, 1993b), not surprising given the well-documented levels of violence in prisons. The inmates with the highest fear of victimization were the young, socially isolated inmates, who also tended to be the most frequent targets of victimization (McCorkle, 1993b). This finding validates the anecdotal and participant observation literature, which suggested that gang affiliation served to protect inmates (Jacobs, 1977; Fong, 1990; Ralph, 1997), and empirical research that suggests that the inmates most likely to be victimized are those without prior institutional experience (Wright, 1991).

More than half of the respondents in McCorkle's (1993a) study had been the target of a serious threat during their imprisonment, more than a third had been struck by fists, and a quarter of the respondents had been attacked with something more serious, such as a weapon (McCorkle, 1993a). When asked how safe they considered the prison, over half said they considered it at least reasonably safe, and only 14% considered it very unsafe (McCorkle, 1993b). Asked to estimate the chances of being attacked while incarcerated, 44% said low, 41% said medium, and only 14% said high (McCorkle, 1993b). McCorkle (1993a) found a strong association between prior victimization and fear of future victimization, and found that young inmates and white inmates had higher levels of fear (McCorkle, 1993a).

McCorkle points out that it is unclear whether these levels of fear are higher than in the past, since no studies of fear of victimization exist. He suggests, however, that the fear level is probably higher today, because the inmate population has changed, and the control policies of prisons have changed. A study by Crouch and Marquart (1990) of victimization and levels of fear in Texas before, during, and after court intervention provides an excellent explication of this hypothesis.

Before the 1970s Texas prisons were run under what DiIulio (1987) has called the "control model." Inmate activity was regimented and controlled. Correctional staff, severely undermanned as a result of poor funding, used some of the more aggressive, dominant inmates to control the others, a control mechanism referred to as the "building tender" or "BT" system (Marquart, 1986). In this manner correctional officers "co-opted" (Marquart, 1986) many potential discipline problems and were able to oversee a large number of inmates with a small number of staff. Texas prisons were acclaimed as some of the best run and safest institutions in the country (DiIulio, 1987). During the 1970s and 1980s Texas prisons became increasingly overcrowded and the subject of a massive class-action lawsuit alleging unconstitutional practices, *Ruiz v. Estelle* (503 F. Supp 1265 (S.D. Texas 1980)). The BT system was ordered dismantled by the court, and the Texas Department of Corrections (TDC) eventually complied, but failed to provide replacement control measures. At the same time prison gangs increased their dominance and stepped into the power vacuum (Fong, 1990; Ralph, 1997). The result was several years of virtually unchecked violence, culminating in 52 inmate-on-inmate homicides in 1985 (Fong, 1990). Late in the 1980s, the TDC began to regain control of its prisons, hiring additional staff and building units to relieve the overcrowding. Violence decreased, at least according to the official statistics.

Crouch and Marquart (1990) studied inmate perceptions of violence in the TDC during this turbulent period. Contrary to popular perception, they found that inmates did not feel safer during the BT era than during the height of inmate violence during the mid-1980s. Crouch and Marquart surveyed 416 inmates who had been incarcerated in the TDC from between 1978 and 1981 until 1987. Of these, almost 40% had begun serving time before 1978. They asked the respondents to describe how safe they felt in the TDC during several different periods between 1978 and 1987. Their findings were striking. Inmate perceptions of safety did not, on the whole, vary significantly from the control period through the late 1980s, despite the fact that official reports of inmate violence increased dramatically. One would expect inmate fear to increase as prison became more violent, but this did not occur in the aggregate. What Crouch and Marquart did note was that perceptions of safety over time varied on the basis of the race and age of the individual inmate. During the control period, black inmates were much less likely to feel safe than white inmates. During the early reform period, the number of white inmates who reported feeling safe declined dramatically relative to black and Hispanic inmates. During the period of highest institutional violence, the inmates did not indicate any greater fear for their safety.

Crouch and Marquart (1990) provide several explanations for these findings. First, while the control period was marked by low numbers of officially reported violent acts, during this period white inmates comprised the vast majority of the BT population. As the number of black inmates increased and the BT system began to be dismantled, the group in power, the white inmates, began to experience a concomitant increase in their fear. And during the period of high institutional violence, most of the violence occurred in isolated areas, the segregation units where gang members were housed. The average inmate was not involved in the gang violence, and hence had no reason to fear it.

Assuming prison is a dangerous place, what is the impact on the mental and emotional well-being of the inmates? Toch's (1977) research indicates that fear of victimization is high in prison. Others have demonstrated that fear of victimization is associated with higher levels of psychological and physical problems (Zamble and Porporino, 1988). McCorkle (1993a, 1993b) found that older inmates and those incarcerated for a longer time had higher levels of mental health (or what he termed "general well-being"), as did those inmates who had several friends in prison and received visitors regularly. Significantly, he noted that an inmate's level of fear was the strongest predictor of his mental health.

Given that some inmates are more susceptible to attack than others, what can an inmate do to reduce the likelihood of being victimized? McCorkle (1992) found that inmates pursue one of two strategies. The older, more fearful, and more socially isolated inmates often use avoidance behavior, such as "keeping to themselves" (p. 164), avoiding certain areas of the prison, and spending more time in their cell. The second strategy, adopted by younger inmates, is to employ more proactive, aggressive tactics such as using violence, lifting weights, and "getting tough" (p. 165).

Methods

The data for the present study were obtained from a survey administered over a six-week period to 775 men just released from incarceration in the Institutional Division of the TDC (TDCJ–ID). These former inmates, or "exmates," were interviewed at the bus station in downtown Huntsville. There are over 100 prisons in the TDCJ–ID, but virtually all inmates are processed and released through one institution. They are released through the front entrance of the Walls Unit, located in Huntsville, and are provided with their personal belongings, a small check from the state, and a voucher for a bus ticket to their destination. State law requires that persons released from prison must return to the place where they were convicted and sentenced; this requirement ensures that virtually all releasees will in fact go to the bus station upon their release.

As the former inmates approached the bus station to purchase their tickets, the interviewers went up to them and asked them to participate in the survey. No material inducements were offered, and confidentiality was assured. Some exmates agreed to submit to the interview at this time, others agreed to be interviewed after obtaining their bus tickets, and still others agreed to be interviewed after first going to a nearby store or restaurant. Some exmates initially declined to cooperate, but later changed their mind and were interviewed while they waited for the bus to arrive. Some exmates declined to be interviewed or were not approached by the interviewers. Reasons given for not participating included general disinterest in the project ("What do I care about some survey?"), suspicion of the interviewer's motives ("How do I know you don't work for the state?"), and a lack of time ("I just got out of TDC and I want to have some fun, not sit around and answer some dumb survey"). Interviewers did not approach every single exmate because sometimes there were too many exmates and not enough interviewers. The selection of who to interview was random in that interviewers simply attempted to contact as many exmates as possible, given the limited number of interviewers and the large number of exmates.

According to TDCJ–ID data, 1,900 inmates were released during this six-week time period. As mentioned, some exmates elected not to participate, and others were not contacted by the the interviewers because of lack of time and/or interviewers. A total of 775 surveys were completed. None of the completed surveys were unusable, although exmates did occasionally choose not to answer a particular question. This represents a response rate of 41%. This is an acceptable level, but the question remains whether those who did not respond are systematically different from the whole population. If so, then selection bias would exist, which would limit the generalizability and accuracy of the survey results (Maxfield and Babbie, 1995).

Interviewers noted no apparent similarity among those who did not participate—no one racial or ethnic group or age category seemed more likely to decline to participate. It was not possible to determine if certain groups of exmates with similar but unobservable characteristics declined to participate. However, a comparison of demographic variables of the respondents with all TDCJ–ID inmates reveals no appreciable difference between respondents and nonrespondents. Demographic variables compared included race/ethnicity, age, number of prior convictions, length of present sentence, marital status, and education level. This comparison suggests that nonresponse bias is not a significant factor in this research project. Nevertheless, it must be acknowledged that there is the possibility that inclusion of the attitudes and perceptions of the nonrespondents may have altered the findings to some degree.

Another potential sampling problem is selection bias. Selection bias occurs when potential respondents are systematically excluded from participation by actions of the interviewer (Babbie, 1995). Steps taken to limit selection bias in this research project included (1) contacting exmates as soon as possible after their release, so as to reach as much of the population as possible; (2) employing interviewers of differing ages, races, and genders, in an effort to match as closely as possible the demographic characteristics of the exmate population and thus foster a sense of commonality and trust; (3) employing an interviewer who could communicate with Spanish-speaking exmates, so as not to exclude any non–English-speaking members of the population; (4) reading the survey to exmates, so as not to exclude exmates with little or no reading ability; (5) making the survey short and easy to respond to, so as to encourage exmates to participate; and (6) instructing the interviewers on effective techniques, and pretesting to work out any kinks in the techniques.

Findings

SAMPLE CHARACTERISTICS

Descriptive statistics for the sociodemographic and criminal history characteristics of the 775 male exmates in the sample are summarized below. Sample characteristics are similar to Texas and national data regarding sociodemographic characteristics of male inmates in 1994. Blacks are the largest racial/ethnic group in the exmate sample, comprising almost half (48%) of all respondents. Whites account for approximately one third (33.7%) of all respondents, while Hispanics make up 17.2% of the sample. The average age of the exmate sample is 32.98 years. White exmates are slightly older, with a mean age of 33.84, compared with a mean age of 32.67 for black exmates and 32.16 for Hispanic exmates. The difference in mean ages among the three racial/ethnic groups is not statistically significant.

The mean number of years of education completed by the exmate sample is just under eleven (10.96) years, or less than a high school diploma (12 years). Over half (55.4%) of all the exmates have not completed high school. Slightly over one quarter (28.8%) of the exmates have a high school diploma or General Equivalency Diploma (GED), while 15% have at least some college experience. The three groups do demonstrate some difference in education level. Black exmates have the highest mean for years of education, 11.27. Whites have a mean education level of 11.00 years. Hispanic exmates have a mean education level of 10.06 years, over a full year less than black exmates.

Almost half (48.9%) of all exmates report having been arrested before they turned 18. Approximately 11% report being arrested for the first time at age 18, 14.3% report being arrested for the first time between the ages of 19 and 21, 16.5% report being first arrested between the ages of 22 and 29, and 7.2% report their age at first arrest as 30 or older. Hispanic exmates report their first arrest occurring at a younger age than do the white and black exmate groups. Hispanic exmates had a mean age at first arrest of 17.72 years, while white exmates had a mean age at first arrest of 19.11 years and black exmates had a mean age at first arrest of 20.26 years.

Almost half (45.3%) of the exmates were serving their first prison term, 7.9% had served time once before, 27.7% had served time in prison on two prior occasions, 12% report having been incarcerated on three prior occasions, and 7.1% report having served time on four or more prior occasions. White exmates had the highest mean number of prior incarcerations, at 2.58. Black exmates had a mean of 2.40, while Hispanic exmates had a mean of 2.33 prior incarcerations.

Thirty-five percent of the exmates indicate they served between one and two years in prison before their release, 21.7% served between two and three years, 15.6% served between three and four years, and 19.9% served more than five years of their current sentence. Black exmates report serving the longest sentences, with a mean of 38.69 months served on their current offense. White exmates served 35.75 months on average, and Hispanic exmates served 35.33 months on their current offense.

VIOLENCE/VICTIMIZATION

To measure exmates' perceptions of violence and fear of victimization in prison today, interviewers asked them to what extent they agreed with five statements regarding violence and victimization. The possible range of scores for each of these items was 1 ("strongly agree") to 4 ("strongly disagree"). A lower mean score indicates that an exmate tends to agree with the statement; a higher mean score indicates that an exmate tends to disagree with the statement. Table 11.1 presents the scores for each of the three racial/ethnic groups. The group mean, standard deviation, F ratio, and associated probability level are displayed.

Racial/ethnic identity does not appear to be a major factor in perceptions of violence and danger in prison. Comparison of the mean scores on the five items on violence and victimization reveals a statistically significant difference on only one item: "I worried a lot about getting beaten up or attacked while I was in TDC." This item was reverse coded, so a higher mean score indicates agreement with the statement. Black exmates had a mean score of 2.031, white exmates a mean score of 2.204, and Hispanic exmates a mean score of 2.200. The difference in the mean score of black exmates relative to white and Hispanic exmates' mean scores is statistically significant at the .05 levels. Thus, black exmates as a whole are less concerned with being attacked in prison than either white or Hispanic exmates. This lower level of concern may be a function of the numerical superiority that blacks currently have in prison.

The other variables are presented in Table 11.2. These include the sociodemographic variables age and education level and the criminal history variables age at first arrest, number of prior incarcerations, and number of years incarcerated. For these continuously measured variables, the coefficient of correlation (Pearson r) and the associated probability level are displayed.

Age appears to be a major determinant of perceptions of violence and victimization in prison. The age of the exmate, both at first arrest and at the time he completed the survey, shows up repeatedly on the five violence items. As shown in Table 11.2, exmates arrested at an earlier age experience more problems with

TABLE 11.1 Means, Standard Deviations, and F Ratios in Analysis of Variance (One-Way Classification) of Exmates' Responses to Survey Questions about Violence and Victimization

Race/Ethnicity	N	M	SD	F	p
Item 15: "I worried a lot about getting beaten up or attacked while I was in TDC"					
White	260	2.204	0.634		
Black	360	2.031	0.733		
Hispanic	132	2.200	0.691	6.261	.002
Item 19: "I almost never had any problems with other inmates while in TDC"					
White	260	2.400	0.752		
Black	363	2.284	0.768		
Hispanic	133	2.316	0.722	1.823	.1622
Item 20: "There are enough guards to provide safety and security for the inmates"					
White	259	2.568	0.776		
Black	362	2.547	0.773		
Hispanic	130	2.592	0.723	0.178	.8366
Item 39: "Inmates attack other inmates very often"					
White	258	2.508	0.690		
Black	356	2.477	0.737		
Hispanic	130	2.646	0.703	2.683	.069
Item 42: "Overall it is pretty safe in TDC"					
White	254	2.504	0.664		
Black	355	2.559	0.736		
Hispanic	133	2.639	0.644	1.926	.146

other inmates, do not believe there are enough guards to provide safety and security, are more likely to agree with the statement "Inmates attack other inmates very often," and perceive prison as less safe overall than do exmates who were older at first arrest.

Younger exmates are generally more likely than older ones to perceive prison as a dangerous place. While exmate age does not have a statistically significant influence on fear of being attacked, it does have significant influence on all of the other items. Younger exmates indicate they have more problems with other prisoners, are less likely to believe there are enough guards to ensure inmate safety, are more likely to agree with the statement "Inmates attack other

TABLE 11.2 Correlations between Continuous Variables and Exmates' Responses to Survey

Variable	r	p
Item 15: "I worried a lot about getting beaten up or attacked while I was in TDC"		
Age	−.0328	.364
Education level	−.1110	.002
Age at first arrest	−.0657	.071
Time served (years)	.0414	.400
Number of prior sentences	−.0472	.334
Item 19: "I almost never had any problems with other inmates while in TDC"		
Age	−.2528	.000
Education level	−.0173	.632
Age at first arrest	−.1405	.000
Time served (years)	.0379	.440
Number of prior sentences	−.0406	.405
Item 20: "There are enough guards to provide safety and security for the inmates"		
Age	−.1635	.000
Education level	−.0020	.956
Age at first arrest	−.1259	.001
Time served (years)	.0394	.425
Number of prior sentences	−.0620	.205
Item 39: "Inmates attack other inmates very often"		
Age	−.2476	.000
Education level	−.0774	.034
Age at first arrest	−.1432	.000
Time served (years)	.0555	.262
Number of prior sentences	−.0637	.195
Item 42: "Overall it is pretty safe in TDC"		
Age	−.2447	.000
Education level	−.0510	.162
Age at first arrest	−.1824	.000
Time served (years)	.1399	.005
Number of prior sentences	.0504	.305

inmates very often," and perceive prison as more dangerous overall than older exmates. Clearly, age matters, at least in regard to an exmate's perception of the level of violence and danger in prison. Younger exmates are consistently more likely than older exmates not to believe violence is common but to have actually experienced problems while incarcerated. These findings are in accord with anecdotal accounts and news reports that suggest that younger inmates are more often involved in disputes and altercations resulting in disciplinary action.

Interestingly, although younger exmates as a whole describe prison as more dangerous than do older exmates, they do not admit to being worried about being attacked at a greater rate than older exmates. There are several possible explanations for this phenomenon. Younger exmates may have a false sense of personal security, despite being aware of the violence in prison. This may be because they are members of inmate gangs that provide their membership with protection from assault, or it may be because they still possess youthful belief in their own invulnerability.

The other criminal history variables, number of prior incarcerations and number of years spent in prison, seem to have little relationship with perceptions. Other criminal history variables not presented in Table 11.2 also fail to reveal any statistically significant difference in group means. These include whether the exmate was incarcerated for a new offense or a parole violation, current sentence length, and time served on this sentence.

The variables that most frequently had a statistically significant relationship with perceptions of violence include exmate age, race/ethnicity, and age at first arrest. The impact of these variables on exmates' perceptions of violence when other variables are controlled for is next examined, using logistic regression procedures. Logistic regression, or logit, is useful for analysis of dichotomous variables that are not normally distributed, and the relationship between the dependent and independent variables is not linear. Logistic regression allows the researcher to perform a regression-like analysis of data when the dependent variable is dichotomous rather than continuous. Multiple regression is not robust against the assumption of the continuous linearity of the dependent variable.

Logistic regression produces values similar to and different from those of multiple regression. The Wald statistic is a test of statistical significance, and has a chi-square distribution. The –2 log likelihood (–2LL) figure assesses how likely the observed results are, given the parameter estimates. The model chi-square value is determined, variables are added to the equation, and the –2LL value is obtained again. Any improvement on the model chi-square is revealed in the new –2LL value and by the significance level of the model chi-square. Model fit can also be assessed by using a classification table to determine how many correct predictions were made with the model. If the new –2LL is statistically significant, the null hypothesis that the model with the variables added does not improve our prediction is rejected (Menard, 1995). Exp(B) is the odds ratio, the number we multiply by the odds of an increase in the dependent variable for each 1-unit increase in the independent variable. An odds ratio greater than

1 indicates that the odds increase when the independent variable increases; an odds ratio less than 1 indicates that the odds decrease when the independent variable increases.

Stepwise logistic regression is useful in two contexts: predictive research and exploratory research (Menard, 1995). Backward regression prevents the exclusion of variables involved in suppressor effects. A suppressor effect occurs when a variable appears to be statistically significant only when another variable is controlled. With backward elimination, since both variables are already in the model, there is less risk of failing to find a relationship when one in fact exists.

Logistic regression was chosen for these data because the narrow range of answers (1 to 4 on a modified Likert scale) tended to produce very clear response patterns—exmates either agreed or disagreed with most statements. Consequently, exmate responses were recoded into two categories—agree/disagree— and logistic regression was performed. A backward elimination procedure was run to determine which variables remained in the model.

Table 11.3 displays the results of the logistic regression on the five items related to violence and victimization in prison. All five items resulted in at least one variable's remaining in the logistic regression equation. Age was the sole remaining variable in three equations. Exmate age is highly predictive of perceptions of violence generally. For items 19, 20, and 39, as exmate age increased, the likelihood of agreeing with the statement increased. With each of these, the predictive ability for a one-year change is slight, but the predictive ability of the model increases when age categories are compared. For each increase in age category, exmates are almost twice as likely to disagree with the statement "I almost never had any problems with other inmates while in TDC" (item 19). For each increase in age category, exmates are approximately one and a half times more likely to disagree with the statement "There are enough guards to provide safety and security for the inmates" (item 20). For each increase in age category, exmates are approximately one and a half times more likely to disagree with the statement "Overall, it is pretty safe in TDC" (item 42). Interestingly, however, for each increase in age category, exmates are approximately twice as likely to disagree with the statement "Inmates attack each other very often" (item 39). These findings parallel the analysis of variance findings, which indicate that younger exmates are not as concerned with violence in prison as older exmates but acknowledge nonetheless that it is a violent place.

Race plays a prominent role in only one model. White exmates are 1.47 times more likely than black exmates to agree with the statement "I worried a lot about getting beaten up or attacked while I was in TDC." Hispanic exmates are 1.2 times more likely than black exmates to agree with that statement. The difference between white and Hispanic exmates was not statistically significant. This item suggests that race may play some role in victimization. In the next section, the findings regarding perceptions of race relations are discussed.

TABLE 11.3 Logistic Regression on Selected Perception of Violence Items

	B	Wald	Sig.	R	Odds Ratio
Item 15: "I worried a lot about getting beaten up or attacked while I was in TDC"					
Race (B/W)	.3867	5.869	.0492	.0538	1.47
Educ. (B/W)	−.1052	5.287	.0215	−.0713	1.11
Age (H/W)	−.3430	5.918	.0150	−.0933	1.41
Race (H/B)	−.4843	4.111	.0426	−.0651	1.20
Item 19: "I almost never had any problems with other inmates while in TDC"					
Age (B/W)	−.5429	20.318	.0000	−.1522	1.72
Age (H/W)	−.6198	17.549	.0000	−.1755	1.86
Age (H/B)	−.7364	27.567	.0000	−.2044	2.10
Item 20: "There are enough guards to provide safety and security for the inmates"					
Age (B/W)	−.2805	6.882	.0087	−.0764	1.32
Age (H/W)	−.3599	8.960	.0028	−.1150	1.43
Age (H/B)	−.3976	11.436	.0007	−.1198	1.50
Item 39: "Inmates attack other inmates very often"					
Age (B/W)	−.6091	31.0585	.0000	−.1880	1.84
Age (H/W)	−.5489	16.449	.0000	−.1658	1.73
Age (H/B)	−.7053	12.899	.0000	−.2078	2.02
Item 42: "Overall, it is pretty safe in TDC"					
Age (B/W)	−.5209	20.976	.0000	−.1524	1.68
Age at first arrest (B/W)	−.0409	7.347	.0067	−.0809	1.04
Age (H/W)	−.6705	22.088	.0000	−.1962	1.96
Age at first arrest (H/W)	−.0646	7.857	.0051	−.1059	1.07
Age (H/B)	−.4278	11.343	.0008	−.1197	1.53
Age at first arrest (H/B)	−.0531	8.250	.0041	−.0979	1.05

B = black, W = white, H = Hispanic.

Conclusion

The present study suggests that inmates' perceptions of the level of violence and victimization do vary and that a substantial portion of this variance can be explained by certain sociodemographic and criminal history characteristics. Age is a particularly important variable. Analysis of variance reveals that exmate age, both at the time interviewed and at time of first arrest, are significantly related to perceptions. The regression model confirms this analysis.

As a group, over half of all exmates agree with the statement "Overall, it is pretty safe in TDC." Slightly over 10% strongly disagree with the statement. Yet it appears that there is some degree of fear, and an awareness that prison is a dangerous place. This is in accord with prior research by McCorkle (1993b). Over half the inmates he surveyed considered prison at least reasonably safe, while only 14% considered it very unsafe, despite the fact that a significant percentage of the inmates reported having been victimized while in prison.

Inmates react to incarceration differently, based on a number of factors. Sociodemographic characteristics appear highly correlated with perceptions of the institutional experience generally, and the present results confirm the importance of factors such as race and age. Further research is needed to determine how the differential response to incarceration may be used by correctional administrators to improve institutional security.

References

Abbott, J. (1981). *In the Belly of the Beast.* New York: Bantam.

Allen, H. E., and Simonsen, C. E. (1995). *Corrections in America.* Upper Saddle River, NJ: Prentice Hall.

Babbie, E. (1995). *The Practice of Social Research* (6th ed.). Belmont, CA: Wadsworth.

Berk, B. B. (1968). Organizational goals and inmate organization. *American Journal of Sociology,* 71, 522–534.

Bowker, L. H. (1980). *Prison Victimization.* New York: Elsevier.

Bureau of Justice Statistics. (1992). *Drugs, Crime, and the Criminal Justice System.* Washington, DC: Department of Justice.

Camp, G. M., and Camp, C. G. (1993). *Corrections Yearbook.* South Salem, NY: Criminal Justice Institute.

Carroll, L. (1974). *Hacks, Blacks, and Cons.* Lexington, MA: Lexington.

Clemmer, D. (1940). *The Prison Community.* New York: Holt, Rinehart, and Winston.

Crouch, B. M., and Marquart, J. W. (1990). Resolving the paradox of reform: Litigation, prisoner violence, and perceptions of risk. *Justice Quarterly,* 7, 103–123.

DiIulio, J. J. (1987). *Governing Prisons: A Comparative Study of Correctional Management.* New York: Free Press.

Earley, P. (1992). *The Hot House: Life inside Leavenworth Prison.* New York: Bantam.

Faine, J. R. (1973). A self-consistency approach to prisonization. *The Sociological Quarterly,* 14, 576–588.

Fong, R. S. (1990, March). The organizational structure of prison gangs: A Texas case study. *Federal Probation,* 54, 36–43.

Fuller, D. A., and Orsagh, T. (1977). Violence and victimization within a state prison system. *Criminal Justice Review,* 7, 35–55.

Garabedian, P. G. (1963). Social roles and processes of socialization in the prison community. *Social Problems,* 139–152.

Goodstein, L., and MacKenzie, D. L. (1984). Racial differences in adjustment patterns of prison inmates—prisonization, conflict, stress, and control. In D. Georges-Abeyie (Ed.), *The Criminal Justice System and Blacks* (pp. 313–339). New York: Clark Boardman.

Grusky, O. (1959, July). Organizational goals and the behavior of informal leaders. *American Journal of Sociology,* LXV (1):59–67.

Irwin, J. (1970). *The Felon.* Englewood Cliffs, NJ: Prentice Hall.

———. (1980). *Prisons in Turmoil.* Boston: Little, Brown.

Irwin, J., and Cressey, D. R. (1964). Thieves, convicts and the inmate culture. *Social Problems,* 10, 142–155.

Jacobs, J. B. (1977). *Stateville.* Chicago: University of Chicago Press.

Lawson, D. P., Segrin, C., and Ward, T. D. (1996). The relationship between prisonization and social skills among prison inmates. *The Prison Journal,* 76, 293–309.

Mabli, J., Holley, C., Patrick, J., and Walls, J. (1979). Age and prison violence: Increasing age heterogeneity as a violence-reducing strategy in prisons. *Criminal Justice and Behavior,* 6, 175–186.

MacKenzie, D. L. (1987). Age and adjustment to prison: Interactions with attitudes and anxiety. *Criminal Justice and Behavior,* 14, 427–447.

Marquart, J. W. (1986). Prison guards and the use of physical coercion as a mechanism of prisoner control. *Criminology,* 24, 347–366.

Maxfield, M. G., and Babbie, E. (1995). *Research Methods for Criminal Justice and Criminology.* Belmont, CA: Wadsworth.

McCorkle, L., and Korn, R. (1954). Resocialization within the walls. *Annals of the American Academy of Political and Social Sciences,* 293, 88–98.

McCorkle, R. C. (1992). Personal precautions to violence in prison. *Criminal Justice and Behavior,* 19, 160–173.

———. (1993a). Fear of victimization and symptoms of psychopathology among prison inmates. *Journal of Offender Rehabilitation,* 19, 27–41.

———. (1993b). Living on the edge: Fear in a maximum-security prison. *Journal of Offender Rehabilitation,* 20, 73–91.

Menard, S. (1995). *Applied Logistic Regression Analysis.* Newbury Park, CA: Sage.

Ralph, P. H. (1997). From self-preservation to organized crime: The evolution of inmate gangs. In J. W. Marquart and J. R. Sorensen (Eds.), *Correctional Contexts: Contemporary and Classical Readings* (pp. 225–250). Los Angeles: Roxbury.

Ruiz v. Estelle, 503 F. Supp 1265 (S.D. Texas 1980).

Schrag, C. (1961). Some foundations for a theory of correction in the prison. In D. Cressey (Ed.), *The Prison.* New York: Holt, Rinehart, and Winston.

Shakur, S. (1993). *Monster: The Autobiography of an L. A. Gang Member.* New York: Atlantic Monthly Press.

Street, D. (1970). The inmate group in custodial and treatment settings. *American Sociological Review,* 33, 40–55.

Sykes, G. M. (1958). *The Society of Captives: A Study of a Maximum Security Prison.* Princeton, NJ: Princeton University Press.

Sykes, G. M., and Messinger, S. L. (1960). The inmate social system. In R. Cloward (Ed.), *Theoretical Studies in Social Organization of the Prison.* New York: Social Science Research Council.

Thomas, C. W. (1970). Toward a more inclusive model of the inmate contraculture. *Criminology,* 8, 251–262.

———. (1977). Theoretical perspectives on prisonization: A comparison of the importation and deprivation models. *Journal of Criminal Law and Criminology,* 68, 135–145.

Tittle, C. R. (1968). Inmate organization: Sex differentiation and the influence of criminal subcultures. *American Sociological Review*, 30, 492–504.

Toch, H. (1977). Social climate and prison violence. *Federal Probation*, 4, 21–25.

Wellford, C. (1967). Factors associated with adoption of the inmate code: A study of normative socialization. *Journal of Criminal Law, Criminology and Police Science*, 58, 197–203.

Wheeler, S. (1961). Socialization in correctional communities. *American Sociological Review*, 26, 697–712.

Wilson, T. P. (1968). Patterns of management and adaptations to organizational roles: A study of prison inmates. *American Journal of Sociology*, 71, 146–157.

Wood, B. S., Wilson, G. G., Jessor, R., and Bogan, J. B. (1968). Troublemaking behavior in a correctional institution: Relationship to inmates' definition of their situation. *American Journal of Orthopsychiatry*, 36, 795–802.

Wright, K. N. (1989). Race and economic marginality in explaining prison adjustment. *Journal of Research in Crime and Delinquency*, 26, 67–89.

———. (1991). The violent and the victimized in the male prison. *Journal of Offender Rehabilitation*, 16, 1–25.

———. (1993). Prison environment and behavioral outcomes. *Journal of Offender Rehabilitation*, 20, 93–113.

Zamble, E., and Porporino, F. J. (1988). *Coping, Behavior, and Adaptation in Prison Inmates.* New York: Springer–Verlag.

Zingraff, M. T. (1975). Prisonization as an inhibitor of effective resocialization. *Criminology*, 13, 366–388.

CHAPTER 12

Victims of School Violence

*April J. Berry-Fletcher
and John D. Fletcher*

Introduction: Public Discourse and Personal Understanding of School Violence

In violence research one often comes across essays on the pervasiveness of violent behavior in contemporary American society and advice on how to minimize the risk of becoming a victim. One sincerely written volume, *Everyday Violence* (Stanko, 1990), empathically came to terms with the threat of violence through collected firsthand experiences and distinguished this perspective from one that may be gathered from less personal information:

> We gather our knowledge of danger and of violence in private, yet it is in the public domain that the thinking about crime and violence take [*sic*] place. The public debate about crime, in too many respects, wrongly silences our private understandings about personal danger. And the way in which anxiety about safety is publicly expressed serves to separate the fear of crime from our private knowledge about danger. (p. 145)

Private or personal knowledge can be considered an understanding of what is ordinary in life or what can be expected in certain circumstances. We privately may know, for example, that driving through a particular neighborhood at night carries greater risks than traveling through another one with different characteristics. We may know to cross the street if we suspect someone is following us.

Personal knowledge or awareness of violence is developed over time. It is not something that is strongly based on prevalence statistics or other types of information that is publicly available; it is much more grounded in childhood experience, things our parents taught us, and the common sense that grows out of countless life experiences.

In the past few years, public awareness and, hence, much of public discourse about school violence has centered on extraordinary and horrific incidents. One such event has been the Columbine High School tragedy of April 20, 1999, in which two teenaged students went on a shooting rampage that killed 12 students and one teacher.

Numerous commissions and researchers have cited events such as the Columbine tragedy as a point of departure for a more thorough examination of the causes and prevalence of school violence (e.g., Kaufman et al., 1999). It has been often noted that although horrific events such as the Columbine shootings compel public attention, our knowing the details about them adds little to our understanding of the true breadth and depth of school violence.

The public discourse falls short in another important way. In our private knowledge of risks at school, we intuitively know that school is an environment that is defined not only by discrete violent events but by the conditions that perpetuate or put a stop to them. In such an environment, there are victims of events and conditions that instill fear and create a private sense of danger, and also efforts to control violence that mitigate those fears.

> If you took the same instances [of violence] and applied it to adults, it would be considered a crime, you know. People turn around and say, "This is kids." We're just growing up. Yeah, I would say it's a crime because I've seen [violence], I've experienced [it], I know what kids are like. I'm not bemoaning, you know, some of the shit that I went through as a kid, 'cause it toughened me in ways now or it's helped me change or opened my eyes to things now that might not have if I hadn't gone through that. And I wouldn't go through that again for all the tea in China, no way, no how. (Stanko, 1990, p. 111)

In this chapter we approach the topic of school violence in two ways. The first course, through published material on the prevalence and precursors to youth violence and the numbers of victims, is a well-trod one, though much remains to be learned through additional research. The second course, from the perspective of students who are the targets of violence and are coming of age in school environments in which they must find a way to keep safe, has been less intensely studied. We know far more about perpetrators than we know about victims, and we know the least about how children's development is shaped in environments that they perceive as unsafe. In discussing this topic, I supplement published material about victims with firsthand accounts shared by students in counseling.

Prevalence of School Crime

THE JUVENILE POPULATION

Since 1995 the Office of Justice Programs, U.S. Department of Justice, has annually published juvenile crime data, and the volume *Juvenile Offenders and Victims: 1999 National Report* (Snyder and Sickmund, 1999) was the principal source for this section on school crime prevalence. Unless otherwise noted, the statistics on the juvenile population and crime prevalence were taken from this publication.

In 1998, there were 70.2 million Americans under the age of 18. This was approximately 26% of the population. Juveniles age 15–18 years, an age cohort that has been associated with two thirds of juvenile crime, numbered approximately 10.5 million. This age group has been on the decline since the 1970s, but has recently begun an upward swing and is expected to reach a level similar to that recorded in the 1970s within the next decade. Juvenile crime could be expected to increase commensurately.

A disproportionate percentage of juveniles lived in poverty as of 1999. Although persons under the age of 17 constituted 26% of the total population, they made up 40% of all persons living below the poverty line. The number of white juveniles living in poverty has been increasing more rapidly than that of minority populations. The percentage of the black juvenile population living in poverty did, in fact, decline by 2% from 1988 to 1997.

JUVENILE VIOLENCE

Between 1980 and 1997, nearly 38,000 juveniles were murdered. Approximately one fourth involved a juvenile perpetrator, but a very small number of incidents occurred in school. According to the National School Safety Center (2000), the number of school-related homicides has ranged from a low of 21 incidents in the 1994–1995 academic year to a high of 53 in both 1992–1993 and 1993–1994. In every year since 1991, shooting has been the cause of death in at least three out of four incidents.

Murders are committed hours, days, or even longer after a precipitating offense or insult, actual or perceived. Most crimes against juveniles, including murders by youth, occur within four hours after school, but the statistics may not tell us the full story of school violence, because only those murders that occur during the school day or when students are on the way to and from school are counted.

The category "serious violent crimes," as defined in the *1999 National Report,* included such incidents as sexual assault, robbery, and aggravated assault. In one year, 1996, school children ages 12–18 years were the victims of 671,000 incidents, of which 225,000, or about one third, occurred in school.

The rates for serious violent crimes were twice as high for males as for females (10 versus 5 per 1,000 students), and almost twice as high for the 12- to

14-year-old cohort as for the 15- to 18-year-old group (10 versus 6 per 1,000 students). Urban schools had six times as many serious violent crimes as rural schools (12 versus 2 per 1,000 students); suburban schools had 8 incidents per 1,000 (Kaufman et al., 1999).

A related index of the level of serious school violence is students' reports of physical fights, particularly those that result in injury. In 1991, 42.5% of surveyed high school students reported that they had been in a fight, and 4.4% indicated that fighting had caused injury. In 1997, both percentages had declined: 36.6% were involved in fights and 3.5% suffered an injury from a fight (Brener et al., 1999).

Theft seems to be the most common crime in school. In 1996, there were 2.1 million in-school victims of theft in the 12- to 18-year-old age group, compared with 1.6 million incidents outside of school.

Two recent studies by Singer and his colleagues at Case Western Reserve University published in 1995 and 1997 are the most comprehensive assessments to date of the prevalence of school violence that is below the level at which it is considered a reportable crime. In the 1995 study, a sample of 3,700 high school students from a "small city" and from an "urban" area were asked if they had ever been beaten, slapped, or threatened or had witnessed someone else being victimized in these ways. The 1997 study asked the same questions of elementary school students and added a rural subsample.

Among high school students, about 3 out of 4 from both small cities and urban areas had witnessed someone being beaten, and about 9 out of 10 had witnessed someone being slapped or threatened. Urban males reported a higher incidence of being beaten up, 9.8%, than did males in small cities, 5.6%. Females were less likely to report that they had been a victim of this type of assault (4% of the small city subsample and 4.4% of the urban setting).

Among elementary school students, an interesting finding was that about half of the rural males reported having been hit or slapped at school, while 41% of the urban males indicated that this had happened to them. Rates for males' being beaten up were about the same for the small city, rural, and urban areas (13.8%, 14.1%, and 14.7%, respectively), but for females going to school in urban areas the rates were twice as high as those reported by females from either small cities or rural areas (10.3% versus 5.5 and 4.7%).

Similar findings have been reported in the School Crime Supplement to the National Crime Victimization Survey, 1995 (Kaufman et al., 1999). Among students ages 12–19 years, 4% reported being the victim of a violent crime, and 8% reported being threatened or injured by a weapon.

The percentage of students who carry a weapon on school grounds is an index of both a crime and students' perception of danger in school. In 1991, 11.8% of the high school students surveyed said that they had carried a weapon, and this figure had fallen to 6.9% in a 1999 survey (Brener et al., 1999).

Bullying was described for young survey takers as "picking on others a lot or making other students do things" (an informal definition that varies from other studies) in the National Household Education Survey of 6th- to 12th-graders for the 1992–1993 school year. Of the total sample, 8% reported being a victim. The highest percentage was for 6th-graders (13%), and the lowest was for 12th-graders (3%). Anecdotal information suggests that these numbers may be a low estimate of the prevalence of bullying in schools. A recent report by the National Association of Attorneys General (2000) titled *Bruised Inside* concluded that bullying was a major cause of violence in the schools. At some schools, they found, "bullying occurs constantly" (p. 25).

Students are not the only targets of juvenile violence. Between 1993 and 1997, teachers were the victims of approximately 1,114,000 thefts and 657,000 violent crimes. On average, 38 teachers per 1,000 were the victims of violent crimes each year. Male teachers were more likely to be the victims of violent crimes than were female teachers (45 versus 27 per 1,000), and urban teachers were more likely to be victims than were suburban or rural teachers (39 versus 22 and 26 per 1,000).

Correlates of Juvenile Violence in the Schools

Violent behavior, however unexpected and shocking, is largely determined by life history. Perinatal problems and differences in temperament appear to be important factors for about 3–5% of excessively aggressive individuals, but for most, violence appears to be learned (Flannery, 1997). In this section we examine four categories of precursors to juvenile violence in the schools: characteristics of the individual child, characteristics of the family, characteristics of the school, and American culture.

CHARACTERISTICS OF THE INDIVIDUAL CHILD

Excessive aggressivity, particularly of the impulsive sort, is maladaptive in most situations. Children who are prone to acting violently in school may achieve some marginal and fleeting status with peers, but more often their behavior is "out of synch" with their circumstances. Youth who are persistently violent are often referred to as "antisocial" in the broad sense that their behavior does not take into account the feelings of other people or the norms of society.

One of the most remarkable findings in behavioral research is that the majority of conduct-disordered adolescents and violent adults had significant behavior problems in early childhood (Eron and Huesmann, 1993; Henry et al., 1996). Aggressive behavior has an early onset and is tremendously stable over time.

Historically, research psychologists have looked for explanations in both nature and nurture. For some time there was a spirited debate between theorists as to which was more important, biology or environment, but the contemporary view is that there is developmental interplay between the two.

On the nature side of the equation, many studies point to an association between childhood aggression and low intelligence and other cognitive deficits. IQ scores for conduct-disordered adolescents are approximately eight points lower than those for their better adjusted peers, a finding that holds up even when other factors, such as economic status and race, are controlled (Goodman et al., 1995; Rowe, 1994). There is a strong relationship between low verbal IQ, which includes social comprehension and social problem skills, and aggression (Moffitt, 1993).

Aggressive elementary school children tend to act on limited interpersonal information and to overly attribute hostile motives to other people in social situations (Dishion et al., 1984). Errors in social judgment and lack of social skills result in peer rejection, which limits opportunity to learn more adaptive social cognitive skills (Coie et al., 1992), so the interplay between cognitive factors (nature) and social experience (nurture) begins quite early and cannot be meaningfully separated.

Additional nature variables found to be associated with delinquency include attention deficit–hyperactivity disorder, oppositional-defiant disorder, and depressive symptoms. These psychological problems are associated with neurophysiological deficits, some of which are due to birth complications, but also with preschool history, so there is no contemporary claim that individuals with a particular psychological disorder are predestined to be violent. Werner (1994), for example, followed a large group of children into adulthood and consistently noted that "the developmental outcome of virtually every biological risk condition was dependent on the quality of the rearing environment" (p. 136).

Like individual differences in IQ, the tendency to be impulsive, restless, antagonistic, moody, or withdrawn can be a serious handicap for a child in a school that highly values behavioral conformity and a predictable pace of achievement. Failure in academics and the inability to relate to peers and adults increase the risk of aggressive behavior, which leads to further failure, and so on.

The FBI's National Center for the Analysis of Violent Crime recently published *The School Shooter: A Threat Assessment Perspective* (O'Toole, n.d.), which examined 18 school shootings in an attempt "to develop a better understanding of these events—the incident itself, and the shooter, his background, and other social dynamics which may have influenced the crime" (p. 2). While this assessment focused on the most horrendous of violent crimes in a school setting, the range of personality characteristics identified are undoubtedly of some interest, and future research may find that they are generalizable to other types of youth crime.

The personality traits and behavior of school shooters include:

- Leakage ("occurs when a student intentionally or unintentionally reveals clues to feelings, thoughts, fantasies, attitudes, or intentions that may signal an impending violent act. These clues can take the form of subtle threats, boasts, innuendoes, predictions, or ultimatums. They may be spoken or conveyed in stories, diary entries, essays, poems, letters, songs, drawings, doodles, tattoos, or videos" [O'Toole, p. 16]),

- Low tolerance for frustration,
- Poor coping skills,
- Lack of resiliency,
- Failed love relationship,
- Injustice collection ("The student nurses resentment over real or perceived injustices. No matter how much time has passed, the 'injustice collector' will not forgive or forget those wrongs or the people he or she believes is responsible. The student may keep a hit list with the names of people he feels have wronged him" [p. 17]),
- Signs of depression,
- Narcissism ("The student is self-centered, lacks insight into others' needs and/or feelings, and blames others for failures and disappointments" [p. 18]),
- Alienation ("The student consistently behaves as though he feels different or estranged from others" [p. 18]),
- Dehumanization of others ("He characteristically views other people as 'non persons' or objects to be thwarted" [p. 18]),
- Lack of empathy,
- Exaggerated sense of entitlement ("The student constantly expects special treatment and consideration, and reacts negatively if he doesn't get the treatment he feels entitled to" [p. 18]),
- Attitude of superiority,
- Exaggerated or pathological need for attention,
- Externalization of blame ("The student consistently refuses to take responsibility for his or her own actions and typically faults other people, events or situations for any failings or shortcomings" [p. 19]),
- Masking of low self-esteem,
- Anger management problems,
- Intolerance,
- Inappropriate humor ("Jokes or humorous comments tend to be macabre, insulting, belittling, or mean" [p. 19]),
- Seeking to manipulate others,
- Lack of trust,
- Closed social group,
- Changes of behavior,
- Rigidity and opinionatedness,
- Unusual interest in sensational violence,
- Fascination with violence-filled entertainment,

- Negative role models ("The student may be drawn to negative, inappropriate role models such as Hitler, Satan, or others associated with violence and destruction" [p. 21]),
- Behavior that appears relevant to carrying out a threat ("The student appears to be increasingly occupied in activities that could be related to carrying out a threat—for example, spending unusual amounts of time practicing with firearms or on various violent web sites" [p. 21]).

FAMILY CHARACTERISTICS

Family characteristics are conventionally referred to as the nurture part of the equation, but when the life course of children who are violent in school is studied, referring to their upbringing as "nurture" seems sadly ironic. The risk of youth violence is dramatically increased by the presence of a number of negative family factors, as one would expect. It is in the home that children are initially socialized, and the child's personality is formed around behaviors that are reinforced in early childhood.

The development of aggressive behavior in children is significantly associated with parental substance abuse and limited education, and a particularly strong relationship has been found with antisocial or criminal behavior. Economic disadvantage and dependency on transitional financial assistance are also significant correlates (Farrington, 1998).

Many researchers are interested in child-rearing practices as predictors. Youth violence and delinquency have been associated with homes in which discipline was inconsistent, and there was more punishment for misbehavior than reward for appropriate behavior. The failure to consistently define and reinforce positive, prosocial behavior thwarts the development of the child. Since disciplinary thrusts can be parried by the child with an equally aggressive display, opposition to adult authority, rather than cooperation, will be learned and then generalized to the school setting.

Patterson (1992) has identified a reciprocally coercive style of interaction that can develop between parent and child.

> A coercive style of parent–child interaction can develop when parents reinforce coercive child behavior and are inadvertently reinforced themselves—by giving in to their coercive child, they are rewarded when the child stops yelling or trying to manipulate them. Children learn that aggressive behavior often leads to parents' giving them what they want. (Farrington, 1998, p. 4)

Harsh disciplinary practices and parental rejection are also associated with the development of aggression in childhood (Fraser, 1996). When such mistreatment reaches the level at which state social service involvement is justified, there is a dramatically increased likelihood that the child will become delinquent in adolescence. One of the most frequently cited studies of child physical abuse and neglect as predictive factors was conducted by Widom (1989). This longitudinal study of 900 abused children and 700 nonabused children showed that mistreatment predicted later arrests for violence independently of all other variables. The mistreated children were 38% more likely than the nonabused children to be arrested for a violent crime as adults.

Thornberry (1994) considered the influence of three kinds of violence in children's homes—marital partner violence, a climate of hostility, and child abuse—and found that exposure to all three more than doubled the risk of youth violence.

The FBI study (O'Toole, n.d.) on the individual characteristics associated with students who had shot others at school or had been foiled in such an attempt were cited earlier. Although these characteristics pertained to only a small group of the most violent individuals, the personality traits are of interest and research may show that many of them are generalizable to other types of aggressive behavior. The study also identified the "family dynamics" of school shooters:

- Turbulent parent–child relationship ("The student's relationship with his parents is particularly difficult or turbulent. This difficulty or turbulence can be uniquely evident following a variety of factors, including recent or multiple moves, loss of a parent, addition of a step parent, etc. He expresses contempt for his parents and dismisses or rejects their role in his life. There is evidence of violence occurring within the student's home" [O'Toole, p. 21]),
- Acceptance of pathological behavior ("If contacted by school officials or staff about the child's troubling behavior, the parents appear unconcerned, minimize the problem, or reject the reports altogether even if the child's misconduct is obvious or significant" [p. 21]),
- Lack of intimacy,
- Student's ruling the roost,
- No limits or monitoring of TV and Internet use.

The psychological mechanisms by which parental mistreatment is translated into aggressive behavior by the child seem patently obvious, but their influence is far from clear. Although the correlations between abuse and delinquency are significant, they do not explain why many children who are mistreated do not develop into violent or antisocial adolescents. Abuse and neglect appear to be risk factors that may signify the presence of "chronic psychosocial adversities" (Rutter et al., 1998, p. 188) in some homes but not others.

There are also "protective factors" (Farrington, 1998, p. 451), some of which may be present in the family and home, that mitigate the influence of risk factors. Werner and Smith (1982), for example, found that the protective factors for children who possessed four or more risk factors but did not develop delinquent behavior included being the first born, exhibiting affection as infants, having a small family size, and receiving attention from parents and others.

Variation in the development of antisocial and aggressive behavior can also be explained by the presence of individual strengths that compensate for adversity. There has been strong research interest in the development of resilience in children, but consideration of this literature goes beyond the scope of this chapter. It is important to note in passing, however, that the prevalence of violence cannot be ascribed to single factors, such as parenting, which are beyond influence.

SCHOOL CHARACTERISTICS

The school can play a significant role in the development of childhood aggression and the display of violence. Children with IQ deficits, limited capacity for impulse control, and poorly developed social skills have at least the potential for growth. The school has the opportunity to interrupt the causal chain to violent crime that often begins before the child first enters the building. The school, within the limitations of community policy, also has latitude in constructing a disciplinary system that is intolerant of violent behaviors.

Since the Columbine killings, many state governments have convened blue ribbon panels of some sort to examine the problem of school violence and recommend policies to contain and reduce it. In the Commonwealth of Massachusetts, for example, a Governor's Advisory Council on Youth Violence had already been created by executive order in June 1998 but published its recommendations in August 1999 in the wake of Columbine. Its mission was to "review, recommend and report to the Governor, policies and programs necessary to ensure safe schools across the Commonwealth, including violence prevention initiatives and emergency response protocol" (Governor's Advisory Council, p. 4). The council's recommendations were grouped into five main areas: inventory, evaluation, and compilation of existing youth violence programs; education; prevention; critical incident response and management; and proposed safe school legislation.

> A safe environment comes from the establishment of a framework that includes violence prevention, a comprehensive safety and crisis plan, and the combined efforts of schools, law enforcement, human service officials, as well as families, to respond to the needs of potentially violent children. . . . Successful plans and strategies include a continuum of efforts from violence prevention to intervention and alternative strategies. (p. 4)

Regarding youth violence programs, the council recommended that current programs be cataloged, communication among educators be encouraged, and best practices be selected on the basis of measured outcomes. There is a wide range of youth violence programs, but they have a common purpose of teaching prosocial skills to children who most seem to need them either through an established curriculum or in vivo through conflict mediation.

With regard to education, the council recommended greater efforts to reach disruptive and behaviorally disordered children; institution of a character development curriculum; and collaborative efforts among various state agencies, community leaders, and, of course, the public schools. Of these recommendations, the intention to do more for troubled children seems to follow most directly from the literature on risk that has been cited in this chapter.

The council's prevention recommendations included a plan to identify youth who "present a risk of serious antisocial behavior" through the sharing of information across state agency lines and the development of safety plans. Sharing information would presumably improve the response to such children, but the agencies involved were not instructed to collaborate by the council.

The intent of recommendations regarding critical incident response and management was to create a "controlled, coordinated response plan," and the section on proposed legislation recommended stiffer penalties for violent behavior but did not propose additional funding. The success of the Massachusetts plan, like that of others, is yet to be determined.

AMERICAN CULTURE

No assessment of youth violence is complete without a discussion of the influence of the media. There is no doubt that television, movies, and music routinely feature violence as entertainment. In 1993, the American Psychological Association estimated that by the age of 18, the typical child has witnessed 33,000 murders on television alone.

Exposure to media violence does increase the risk that a child will engage in aggressive behavior. Children who are exposed to high levels of violence are more accepting of it and tend to act more aggressively after watching violent programs. Chronic exposure appears both to desensitize children and to increase their fear that they will be a victim, because they come to view the world as a dangerous place, and its effect is greatest on children who have a preexisting tendency to be aggressive.

The Vermont National Education Association, in an examination of youth violence, considered media violence in a broader cultural context and offered a couple of interesting observations. The first is that contemporary "culture associates children with violence. . . . Violence sells. Violence sells to children; associating children with violence sells to both adults and children. Our national cultural romance with violence may extend to school yards and classrooms" (n.d., p. 6). Second, at the same time as violence is glorified, there has been a movement toward harsher penalties for juvenile crime and away from policies that are supportive of families and children.

The Victims

In this section we examine the impact that specific violent actions have on the victims and their schoolmates. Sexual harassment, rape, bullying, and gang violence are examined, because being the victim of these crimes has a profound impact on a child. As we will show, these crimes also create an environment in which all of the children in the school are indirectly victimized, because children identify with their peers. Children instinctively recognize that they are like one another. As a result, when one child is a victim, all children are vulnerable.

In victimology research, the individual at whom the violent act is directed is usually referred to as the "direct" victim. The relatives, friends, and peers of the direct victim are viewed as the "indirect" victims. Here we examine the ramifications of bullying, gang behavior, rape, and sexual harassment not only for direct victims, but also for the school as a whole, or the indirect victims.

BULLYING AND GANG VIOLENCE

Olweus (1999) defined bullying as situations in which a person is exposed, repeatedly and over time, to negative actions by one or more persons. This definition excludes situations in which peers of equal strength or size are fighting. Bullying is characterized by an imbalance in strength and power; it can include the use of words, gestures, or physical contact to carry out the harassment.

In the case of youth gangs, the increased power and strength that a group of youths represents creates an atmosphere of intimidation and danger for all who do not belong to the gang. Hence, gang presence in schools is seen as an aspect of bullying behavior and a major contributing factor to students' perception of danger in schools.

Bullying behavior perpetrated by an individual acting alone or as a member of a gang is considered a major cause of school violence. In schools where there are a number of children who use bullying to negotiate conflict, a higher degree of aggression and violence ensues (Szyndrowski, 1999). The recent report of the National Association of Attorneys General (2000) states that "bullying and the way peers treat each other" is the second major cause of youth violence (p. 32). When children feel the environment is unsafe, they may be more likely to overreact to threats or to arm themselves for protection, thereby increasing the risk of violence overall.

Effects of Bullying or Gang Violence on Indirect Victims

As this report suggests, the effects of bullying behavior extend far beyond the direct victims. Indirect victims—students who directly witness the aggression as well as those who simply hear about it—are also affected in complex ways. In many schools, students are known to antagonize children who are fighting in order to escalate the conflict.

This group behavior is often at odds with their individual reports of their reactions to school violence. For example, the National Association of Attorneys General (2000) conducted a series of focus groups in which students in various age groups were encouraged to discuss their reactions to school violence. Respondents consistently objected to the presence of violence in schools. Students identified violent behavior patterns in their homes as a major cause of their and others' bullying behavior. They reported that their own violence was related to their family's use of intimidation, threat, and force to resolve conflict.

As noted, the victimization of some students by bullying behavior escalates the risk of violence for all children. According to a student quoted in the report by the National Association of Attorneys General, "One kid brings a gun, another kid feels unsafe and then he brings a knife" (p. 33). Hence, the perception of danger escalates the risk of violence not only through each child's carrying a weapon in reaction to the other, but in the recognition by the students as a group that their peers are armed and wary.

In many cases, students' perception that the environment is unsafe leads to the creation of gangs. A group of children who socialize together on the basis of shared interests is often referred to as a "clique." When racial or ethnic minorities form cliques in the interest of safety, this grouping is often termed "gang behavior." In essence, the difference between the terms "clique" and "gang" can be based more on race, class, or ethnicity than on the bases for forming a social group (Barovick et al., 1999).

Regardless of which term is used to refer to this social behavior, students travel in groups to avoid appearing vulnerable or alone. The gangs associated with typical middle and high school social behavior have a stronger, survival-oriented basis when the reason for relating to particular peers is not a shared interest in sports but rather a shared interest in managing the effects of an unsafe school environment.

The overall effect of school violence on the indirect victims can create a vicious cycle of victimization. Students who perceive the environment as unsafe often gravitate toward social groupings for protection. These social groupings, or gangs, are likely to perpetrate violence against particular students. Let's now examine the characteristics of victims of violence.

Effects of Bullying and Gang Violence on Direct Victims

Victims of bullies often fear school because they see it as an unsafe place. As many as 7% of America's eighth-graders stay home at least once a month because of bullies. Being bullied tends to increase a student's isolation, because his or her peers do not want to lose social status by associating with the student or do not want to increase the risks of being bullied themselves. Being bullied often leads to problems that can continue into adulthood (Olweus, 1999). One student who was harassed by bullies, who were also gang members, for several months gave her counselor the following account of her experiences:

I started the school year later than the other kids. I got a locker in the basement and I didn't know that was the area that the tough kids hung out in. I just put my stuff in there. They broke the lock. Then they took all my stuff. I couldn't pass in my homework. I didn't know the teachers and I didn't know any of the other kids except some kids who said "hi" to me in homeroom. They started following me to classes. They would be outside the door, looking in the window and giving me the finger and telling me they were going to beat me up. They did it all day, all the time. Then they started to follow me home and if they caught up with me, they would beat me up. They would all surround me and one girl would say that I called her something and push me. The other girls would push me and they would start beating me up.

One of the disturbing trends this story illustrates is the growing participation of girls in gang activity and the overall increase in girls' use of violence. According to Konopka (1966), girls are widely believed to have better social skills and stronger social networks than boys. However, as girls are increasingly exposed to violent role models in the media and in their daily lives, the incidence of fighting, aggression, and violent crimes among them is increasing.

Many direct victims report that their parents did not know or ask about bullying. The victims often feel that adults will not or do not intervene and that reporting this problem may lead to retaliation. Students find that teachers seldom or never talk to their classes about bullying (Charach, Pepler, and Ziegler, 1995). School personnel may view bullying as a harmless rite of passage that is best ignored unless verbal and psychological intimidation crosses the line into physical assault or theft.

Dishion et al. (1984) found that in schools in which a number of students exhibit bullying or aggressive behavior, group norms are likely to be accepting of aggression. In addition, they note that preadolescent children who form friendships with antisocial peers appear to be at heightened risk for later antisocial behaviors, including delinquency, drug abuse, and dropping out of school.

This research not only validates many parents' concern that associating with the "wrong crowd" can have negative effects on children, but also points out that unchecked behaviors such as intimidation, threats, and extortion can shift group norms in a school toward a higher acceptance of violence.

Characteristics of Individual Victims of Bullying and Gang Violence

Individual children who are the victims of bullies, either in gangs or individually, are perceived as unlikely to defend themselves or retaliate when confronted by those who bully them (Coie, 1990). Many victims share other characteristics, such as poor social skills or social isolation. They are reported to be close to their parents and may have parents who can be described as overprotective. The major physical characteristic of victims is that they tend to be weaker than their peers; other physical characteristics—such as weight, dress, or wearing eyeglasses—do not appear to correlate significantly with victimization (Batsche and Knoff, 1994; Olweus, 1999).

Bullying and Hate Crime

Crimes that are motivated by perceived differences or by bias against a group are usually referred to as hate crimes when they are committed by adults. In schools that have a tendency toward violence and also have a racial or ethnic mix, youths who gravitate toward one another because of common characteristics are at risk for developing hostile and stereotyped views of other groups. This dynamic creates a vulnerability to expressions of hatred toward minority groups.

The responses of individual victims of hate crimes include intense feelings of vulnerability, anger, and depression as well as physical ailments, learning problems, and difficult interpersonal relations. Like most crime victims, the victim of hate crime experiences a group of symptoms similar to post-traumatic stress disorder (as described in the *Diagnostic and Statistical Manual of Mental Disorders,* 1999). Victims of hate crimes are more intensely affected, because they are targeted for violence on the basis of aspects of themselves that they are likely unable to change.

Hate crimes in schools are especially problematic because of adolescents' sense of vulnerability. As noted, it is common in high schools for students to be divided along racial, religious, or gender lines. These separations emphasize the differences in race, class, ethnicity, sexual orientation, and other demographics that can divide students. If students sense that they are vulnerable to violence, this segregation can create tensions between groups that are, in turn, expressed as hate crime.

RAPE

The rape of a child is at odds with our cultural beliefs regarding the innocence of childhood and the importance of protecting it. For the individual child and her peers, the incidence of rape shatters the perception of the world as a safe place.

Although we sanctify childhood, when rape happens at school, a subtle and gradual blurring of the terms "victim," "child," and "rape" often ensues. According to Bayley (1991), a victim is (1) a person who has suffered a loss or a significant decrease in well-being unfairly or undeservedly and in such a way that the person was helpless to prevent the loss; in addition, (2) the loss has an identifiable cause, and (3) the legal or moral context of the loss entitles the sufferer to social concern.

The girl rape victim—who, according to *Uniform Crime Reports* (Federal Bureau of Investigation, 2000), is generally between the ages of 12 and 14—is initially seen as a child. In this image, she satisfies Bayley's (1991) criteria that she be helpless. However, this image of the rape victim as a girl often evolves into a "young woman" who is, over time, referred to as the "alleged victim." Although this phrasing is intended to protect the accused, it has the subtle effect of disqualifying the victim.

Victims of sex crimes face a prejudice that other crime victims don't often experience: the widely held belief that they contribute to their own victimization. Victims find their choices—to wear a particular outfit, to go out alone, to accept a ride—scrutinized and second-guessed.

Gibbs (1984) notes that even liberals and feminists are known to be harsh and skeptical when dealing with rape victims, particularly when the girls are from lower socioeconomic backgrounds or are victimized in date rape. In the case of the adolescent victim, the ambivalence is even more pronounced. Perhaps this ambivalence is grounded in the definition of victim as being helpless to prevent the crime. Often, adolescent victims of sexual mistreatment behave in ways that compromise our sympathy. They are frequently angry, hostile, truant, uncooperative with authorities, and untrusting. These behaviors are the very opposite of our expectations of victims.

Individual victims of rape in schools, like rape victims in general, are often revictimized by the way the crime is dealt with by the police and the courts. The erosion of support for and increasing skepticism regarding the veracity of the victim's story not only revictimize the individual student, but also send a message to other students about how such matters are viewed.

The following is a counselor's account of an incident involving rape in a high school in suburban Massachusetts. (Names and identifying details have been altered to preserve privacy.)

> At first Karen [the school principal] had been sympathetic. She had heard from Lisa's friends that Lisa was really upset and afraid to press charges. Karen felt that Lisa simply needed some support and hoped that I [as the school counselor] could be of assistance. I met with Lisa, who had known the boy who raped her. She was, in our sessions, all of the things you expect a victim to be. She was fearful of retaliation by the boy and his crowd, hurt that some of the girls did not believe her and confused by the insistence by so many of her friends that she report the rape when she did not feel she could handle the investigation and trial.
>
> Later, Karen called me and said, "This is no innocent little victim like I thought at first. She had a lot more to do with this than we originally thought." I thought, "Here we go again." I cannot remember a time when a girl at this school has reported a rape that she did not then become more on trial than the rapist.

In this case, Lisa had offended the school officials and some of her teachers by behaving in angry, uncooperative ways and by seeking contact with her perpetrator. She reported to me that she needed to know why he had raped her. Lisa acted on her anger and indignation and sought out her perpetrator to confront him. Even those who initially supported Lisa found her behavior inconsistent with that of a victim. She was not acting in a manner that reflected the passive injury of a victim and the wish to avoid the assailant at all costs. Instead, she was behaving aggressively, by defying authority in seeking out her rapist. Because Lisa's behavior was at odds with conventional perceptions of how a "good victim" behaves, she was gradually viewed as at least partially culpable for the rape.

In a study of the emotional impact on victims of violent acts ranging from domestic abuse and sexual assault to political terror, Herman (1992) found that all victims share some common emotional reactions and that the credibility of the victim can be compromised by her emotional reaction:

> The ordinary response to atrocities is to banish them from consciousness. . . . Atrocities, however, refuse to be buried. Equally as powerful as the desire to deny atrocities is the conviction that denial does not work. Folk wisdom is filled with ghosts who refuse to rest in the grave until their story is told. The conflict between the will to deny horrible events and the will to proclaim them aloud is the central dialectic of psychological trauma. People who have survived atrocities often tell their stories in a highly emotional, contradictory, and fragmented manner which undermines their credibility. (p. 393)

SEXUAL HARASSMENT

School personnel may respond to rape in inconsistent ways, but the existence of rape as a social issue is widely recognized. Less acknowledged acts, such as unwanted fondling, grabbing, and touching of girls, known as sexual harassment, also contribute to students' perception of school as a dangerous place.

A young woman from an overcrowded urban junior high school in Massachusetts whom I interviewed for this chapter recounted the following anecdote about her experience of school violence:

> When I was in junior high, the . . . boys used to grab your ass or grab your boobs and . . . you know other parts and stuff. They would do it when we were in the halls at school and we were all crowded down the halls, like changing classes or something. They would push into the girls and start grabbing at you and act like they weren't really doing it. I told my mother after it happened at first and she said to tell the principal. So, one day when we were going out the building and I saw the principal, I said that some of the boys were grabbing at the girls in private places. He said

to look to see who it was next time and to tell him. But I couldn't really tell. There were so many boys I didn't know and they would all run away after. Plus, if I told, they would beat me up. So I skipped school. I skipped a lot.

This student's experience illustrates many of the issues common to school violence in general. The girls were singled out by a group of boys who, as a group, normalized the sexual harassment of the girls. As this student points out, she and her friends began to arm themselves against the boys.

It started when one girl, I can't remember who, stuck one of the boys with a safety pin she had on her shirt. She stuck it right in his hand. I guess his sister pushed her on the stairs the next day and her friends started following his sister around. Then we all started to follow his sister. We had to get back at someone.

This situation illustrates the vigilante nature of children's management of their experience of danger. The girl told her mother and principal of the problem, but found this ineffective. A peer retaliated against the aggressive acts, and groups of children gravitated toward one another in the interest of safety, protection, and revenge.

The presence of these violent acts in their school, combined with the lack of an effective response by school officials, resulted in an escalation of violence. The girls formed a gang-type presence and singled out a victim to retaliate against for their victimization. The lack of an appropriate adult response furthered the risk, because the girls had to manage the situation for themselves with limited experience and a great deal of fear and anger.

Conclusion

The problem of school violence has been associated with extreme acts of violence, such as school shootings that capture the headlines. Although these horrific incidents are important to understand, they are among many threats of violence that students perceive in schools.

Statistics are regularly compiled as serious acts of violence, such as school shootings and assaults with weapons as well as property crime, but they reflect only a fraction of the risk students feel at school. From the perspective of students, the violent acts of rape, sexual harassment, bullying, and gang violence have a profoundly personal impact.

Violent incidents in the school not only have a profound effect on the individuals involved, but also define the environment for all children. Fear of crime causes some students to bring weapons to school, for others it encourages gang membership, and for all it contributes to a sense of unease and fear, because these measures tend to escalate tension and risk.

Clearly, adult response to violence plays a central role in reducing the risk. Teachers, administrators, parents, and others associated with schools can respond to victimization in a manner that not only aids the direct victim but also assures indirect victims that violence is not acceptable or tolerated.

References

American Psychiatric Association. (1999). Diagnostic and Statistical Manual of Mental Disorders. (DSM-IV) (4th ed.). Washington, DC: American Psychiatric Association.

American Psychological Association. (1998). *Hate Crimes Today: An Age-Old Foe in Modern Dress.* Available at http://www.apa.org/pubinfo/hate.

Barovick, H., Philadelphia, D., and Rivera, E. (1999, May 3). A curse of cliques. *Time,* pp. 44–46.

Batsche, G. M., and Knoff, H. M. (1994). Bullies and their victims: Understanding a pervasive problem in the schools. *School Psychology Review,* 23(2): 165–174.

Bayley, J. E. (1991). *To Be a Victim.* New York: Plenum.

Brener, N. D., Simm, T. R., Krug, E. G., and Lowry, R. (1999). Recent trends in violence-related behaviors among high school students in the United States. *Journal of the American Medical Association,* 282, 440.

Charach, A., Pepler, D., and Ziegler, S. (1995). Bullying at school: A Canadian perspective: A survey of problems and suggestions for intervention. *Education Canada,* 35(1): 12–18.

Coie, J. (1990). Toward a theory of peer rejection. In S. Asher and S. Coie (Eds.), *Peer Rejection in Childhood.* Cambridge, England: Cambridge University Press.

Coie, J. F., Lochman, J. E., Terry, R., and Hymna, C. (1992). Predicting early adolescent disorder from childhood aggression and peer rejection. *Journal of Consulting and Clinical Psychology,* 60, 783–792.

Dishion, T. J., Loeber, R., Stouthamer-Loeber, M., and Patterson, G. R. (1984). Skill deficits and the male delinquency. *Journal of Abnormal Child Psychology,* 12, 37–54.

Eron, L. D., and Huesmann, R. (1993). The stability of aggressive behavior—even unto the third generation. In M. Lewis and S. M. Miller (Eds.), *Handbook of Development Psychopathology* (pp. 147–156). New York: Plenum.

Farrington, D. P. (1998). Predictors, causes, and correlates of male youth violence. In M. Tonry and M. H. Moore (Eds.), *Youth Violence.* Chicago: University of Chicago Press.

Federal Bureau of Investigation. (2000). *Uniform Crime Reports.* Available at www.fbi.gov/ucr/ucr.htm.

Flannery, D. J. (1997). *School Violence: Risk, Preventive Intervention, and Policy.* Educational Resources Information Center (ERIC): Clearinghouse on Urban Education. Available at http://eric-web.tc.columbia.edu/monographs/uds109.

Fraser, M. W. (1996). Aggressive behavior in childhood and early adolescence: An ecological development perspective on youth violence. *Social Work,* 41, 347–361.

Gibbs, J. T. (1984). Black adolescents and youth. *American Journal of Orthopsychiatry,* 54, 6–21.

Goodman, R., Simonoff, E., and Stevenson, J. (1995). The relationship between child IQ, parent IQ, and sibling IQ on child behavioral deviance scores. *Journal of Child Psychology and Psychiatry,* 36, 409–425.

Governor's Advisory Council on Youth Violence. (1999). *Prevention and Response.* Available at www.state.ma.us/eops/council_report.htm.

Herman, J. L. (1992). *Trauma and Recovery.* New York: Basic Books.

Kaufman, P., Chen, X., Choy, S. P., Ruddy, S. A., Miller, A. K., Chapman, C. D., Rand, M. R., and Klaus, P. (1999). *Indicators of School Crime and Safety.* NCES 1999–057/NCJ–178906. Washington, DC: U.S. Departments of Education and Justice.

Konopka, G. (1966). *The Adolescent Girl in Conflict.* Englewood Cliffs, New Jersey: Prentice Hall.

Moffitt, T. E. (1993). The neuropsychology of conduct disorder. *Development and Psychopathology,* 5, 135–152.

National Association of Attorneys General. (2000). *Bruised Inside: What Our Children Say about Youth Violence, What Causes It, and What We Need to Do about It.* Available at www.Naag.org/features/bruised_inside.pdf.

National School Safety Center. (2000). *School Associated Violent Deaths.* Available at http://www.nsscl.org/savd/savd.pdf.

Olweus, D. (1999). *Bullying at School: What We Know and What We Can Do (Understanding Children's Worlds).* Cambridge, England: Blackwell.

O'Toole, M. E. (n.d.). *The School Shooter: A Threat Assessment Perspective.* Washington, DC: Critical Incident Response Group, National Center for the Analysis of Violent Crime, FBI Academy.

Patterson, G. R. (1992). Developmental changes in antisocial behavior. In R. D. Peters, R. J. McMahon, and V. L. Quinsey (Eds.), *Aggression and Violence throughout the Lifespan* (pp. 52–82). Newbury Park, CA: Sage.

Rowe, D. (1994). *The Limits of Family Influence.* New York: Guilford Press.

Rutter, M., Giller, H., and Hagell, A. (1998). *Antisocial Behavior by Young People.* Cambridge, England: Cambridge University Press.

Singer, M. (1997). The mental health consequences of children's exposure to violence. Cleveland, OH: Case Western Reserve University, Mandel School of Applied Social Sciences.

Singer, M., Anglin, T., Song, L., and Lunghofer, L. (1995). Adolescents' exposure to violence and associated symptoms of psychological trauma. *Journal of the American Medical Association,* 273, 477–482.

Snyder, H. N., and Sickmund, M. (1999). *Juvenile Offenders and Victims: 1999 National Report.* Washington, DC: Office of Juvenile Justice and Delinquency Prevention.

Stanko, E. (1990). *Everyday Violence.* London: Pandora.

Szyndrowski, D. (1999, Fall). The Impact of Domestic Violence on Adolescent Aggression in the Schools. *Preventing School Failure,* 44(1):9.

Thornberry, T. P. (1994). *Violent Families and Youth Violence.* Washington, DC: Department of Justice, National Institute of Justice, Office of Justice Programs.

Vermont National Education Association. (n.d.). *School Violence Report.* Available at http://www.vtnea.org/vio-4.htm.

Werner, E. E. (1994). Overcoming the odds. *Development and Behavioral Pediatrics,* 13, 131–136.

Werner, E. E., and Smith, R. S. (1982). *Vulnerable but Invincible: A Longitudinal Study of Resilient Children and Youth.* New York: Adams, Bannister, and Cox.

Widom, C. S. (1989). The cycle of violence. *Science,* 244, 160–166.

CHAPTER 13

Victims of Campus Violence

April J. Berry-Fletcher

Introduction

In May 1995, the coroner's van stood outside an ivy-covered brick dormitory at Harvard University. Oblivious, joggers and bicyclists ventured along the banks of the Charles River, and shoppers strolled along the brick sidewalks. The few passersby who did take notice of the van assumed that one of the panhandlers often seen in nearby Harvard Square had drunk or drugged himself to death.

In fact, a female college student had stabbed her roommate to death and then committed suicide. This shocking case illustrates the central issue associated with campus violence. Harvard, like many colleges, is characterized by bucolic green lawns, an atmosphere of contemplation, and, most of all, a sense of safety. Grisly violent events are not associated with college life.

In this chapter, I examine three main issues related to campus violence. First, I consider problems related to attaining reliable prevalence data, specifically, the debate around underreporting or not reporting campus crime and the measures the federal government has taken to address this issue.

I then explore the many reasons that college campuses are at risk for violence: the age of most college students, the prevalence of substance abuse on campuses, the crowded living conditions, and a recent increase of violence in American culture, especially in high schools, among others. Theories about how these issues create an environment vulnerable to crime are considered.

The chapter concludes with an examination of the most common crimes on campus. The crimes often are not reported to college officials, are difficult to address, but have a profound impact on the victims.

Violence on Campus

In the early morning of April 5, 1986, Jeanne Clery was brutally raped and murdered in her dorm room by a fellow student at Lehigh University.

It was later noted by Jeanne's parents that the university had not advised students and faculty about 38 violent crimes that had occurred in the three years preceding her murder. They launched an aggressive lobbying movement that resulted in the Campus Security Act of 1992. Prior to this act, colleges and universities were not required to maintain statistics regarding crime on campus. Congress renamed this law the Clery Act in 1998 in memory of Jeanne Clery.

The Clery Act stipulates that colleges and universities must distribute an annual security report detailing the incidences on their campuses of murder, sex offenses, robberies, aggravated assaults, burglaries, motor vehicle thefts, and arrests for weapons possession and liquor and drug abuse violations. Schools must publish and disseminate an annual campus security report containing various security policies and three years' worth of crime statistics. They must also issue timely warnings about crimes that pose an ongoing danger. These warnings usually involve alerting the campus community in writing that a particular crime has taken place. According to the Clery Act, schools with a police or security department of any kind must also maintain a public crime log of all crimes reported to that department. This information must be made available to all students and employees.

The purpose of the Clery Act is to ensure that all members of a college community are aware of the crime risk. Many colleges have argued that these reporting requirements put urban or inner-city colleges at a disadvantage, because the likelihood of crime is higher by virtue of the location. In addition, college-owned property, such as hospitals, social service agencies, and the like are considered part of the campus despite the minimal contact most students have with these sites. The concern is that students will avoid schools with higher reported crime rates.

Another debate associated with the Clery Act is whether Jeanne Clery's family or other families would choose another school or substantially change their behavior if made aware of the previous crimes. Knowledge that crime exists does not necessarily lead to different behavior. This tendency to ignore risk is considered to be especially high among college-aged students.

For individual victims of campus crime, the publication of these statistics can have mixed results. For example, in the case of sexual assault, alerting the campus community that the crime has taken place can have the effect of lessening the victim's sense of isolation. Some victims report that there is a certain validation of their experience in the public announcement of the crime. The publication of safety information that accompanies the notification of campus crime, such as how to prevent an assault, causes other victims to feel that the community is indirectly blaming them for their victimization. As one student phrased it, "It's like they are saying this wouldn't have happened to me if only I had followed the safety instructions they gave us at Orientation." Or, as another student who had been raped stated, "They tell you not to go to a guy's room alone, but if you make the mistake of trusting some one and something bad happens, does that mean it's your fault you got raped?"

Although the effect of the Clery Act on individual victims varies, the overall goal of the act is to establish reliable information regarding crimes that occur on college campuses. However, as I show in this chapter, the types of crime that the Clery Act requires colleges to report are not entirely the same as those that pose the greatest risk to students.

Students are at greatest risk of interpersonal violence that is perpetrated by a student who knows them. The vast majority of instances of violence of this kind are not reported to college officials and are seldom prosecuted. Crimes that college students are likely to be victims of, such as hazing, stalking, and simple assault associated with dating relationships, are not reported in an organized

TABLE 13.1 Campus Crime Statistics: Incidents on Campuses of 481 Colleges and Universities with More Than 5,000 Students

Crime	1998	1997	1-year change
Murder	20	18	+11.1%
Manslaughter	1	2	−50.0%
Forcible sex offenses	1,240	1,114	+11.3%
Nonforcible sex offenses	159	125	+27.2%
Robbery	1,068	1,100	−2.9%
Aggravated assault	2,267	2,205	+2.8%
Burglary	13,745	14,565	−5.6%
Motor vehicle theft	4,160	4,272	−2.6%
Arson	539	461	+16.9%
Hate crimes	179	155	+15.5%
Arrests			
Liquor law violations	23,261	18,708	+24.3%
Drug law violations	8,844	7,964	+11.1%
Weapons law violations	972	967	+0.5%

The numbers include sex offenses reported both to campus police officers and to other campus officials. The schools reported the data in compliance with federal laws.

way. In fact, date rape and most other acts of interpersonal violence are the least likely crimes to be reported to college officials. Consequently, official statistics regarding these crimes are unreliable.

Along with crime that occurs among individuals who know one another, crimes against women are the most common (Neft and Levine, 1997). In some cases, college-age women may be less safe in a college dormitory than in many other living situations, because of the many issues discussed in the next section: substance abuse, crowded living quarters, the presence of fraternities, the age of students, hazing rituals, and other variables that create an environment of increased risk for violence on campus.

What Factors Lead to Campus Violence?

There are four main issues that contribute to the risk of campus violence. The first is the theory that traditional college-aged students are desensitized to violence. The second is the age of college students: Most college students are late adolescents and young adults, and this age group is more likely than any other age group to be the victim of or to commit a crime. The third issue is the high incidence of alcohol and other drug abuse on campuses. Lastly, the stress and social complexity of dormitory or community living situations are considered as they relate to the risk of violence.

DESENSITIZATION TO VIOLENCE

Desensitization to violence is described by Fenske and Hood (Hoffman et al., 1998), who point out that the permeation of violence in American schools, in the media, in film, and in other influential aspects of American culture serves to desensitize the present generation of college-aged students to violence. According to this theory, an individual who is repeatedly exposed to horrific or otherwise unacceptable events or behaviors comes to view these events as normal. For example, youths who have seen guns featured in television programs and movies daily over weeks and years may be more accepting of weapons.

The current generation of college students has been exposed to a great deal of direct and brutal violence on television, in video games, and in daily life. The theory of desensitization proposes that because of this overexposure, this generation is less reluctant to use violence as a problem-solving strategy.

AGE COHORT

The Federal Bureau of Investigation's (1998) statistical report of crimes and their victims indicates that 67% of all violent crimes in the United States were perpetrated by individuals between the ages of 12 and 20 years old. Sixty-two percent of all robberies were committed by this age group, and 69% of all assaults were committed by them.

Traditional-aged college students (17–23 years old) are not only more likely than older adults to commit crimes, but also more likely to be the victim of a violent crime. In fact, according to a Department of Justice report (1998), a person age 16–19 is four times more likely to be victimized than a person age 35–49.

According to the *Chronicle of Higher Education's (CHE's)* 1999 *Annual Report on the Freshman Class,* 94.3% of entering freshmen were between 18 and 19 years old. When this is considered in conjunction with the Bureau of Justice statistics, college-aged students are at high risk for being the victim or the perpetrator of a violent crime. According to the *CHE's* report, 60% of entering freshmen planned to live in a college dormitory, and over half moved from 50 to 500 or more miles from college to home. This means that over half of the youths entering college in 2000 lived on campus.

ALCOHOL AND OTHER DRUGS

Other factors that contribute to the likelihood of becoming the victim of campus violence involve the use of both licit and illicit drugs and alcohol. A recent survey by Towson State University's Center for the Study and Prevention of Campus Violence ("A Look at Campus Crime," 2000) asked 1,085 undergraduates at colleges across the country about crimes such as sexual assault, armed robbery, theft, and vandalism. About 36% of the respondents reported having been victims of crimes while at college, and 8% reported having committed crimes. Forty-six percent of the students who said they had committed crimes said they had been using alcohol at the time. Nearly 10% said they had used drugs before they broke the law, and 6.5% said they had used both alcohol and drugs.

This survey offers a concrete, statistical relationship between alcohol and drug use and crimes on and around campuses. Common wisdom holds that the decreased inhibition that results from substance use leads to criminal or aggressive behavior. The Towson University study begins to support the suspicion that drugs and alcohol are important components of both becoming a victim of violence in college and committing a crime during college.

In June 2000, the *CHE* related that many colleges reported increased arrests for drug and alcohol use. While some college officials indicated that changes in reporting requirements accounted for the increase in arrests, many note that there is an increase in drug use. Of particular concern are new designer drugs such as ecstasy and Rohypnol.

According to the National Institute on Drug Abuse (NIDA), unlike the current encouraging trend toward stabilized or decreased use of other illicit drugs, such as cocaine and heroin, the use of ecstasy is increasing, particularly on college campuses. The NIDA reports that ecstasy shares the chemical properties of hallucinogenic (LSD-like) and stimulant (amphetaminelike) drugs. Structurally, it is similar to the stimulant methamphetamine and the hallucinogen mescaline.

The use of these and dozens of other licit and illicit drugs, with or without alcohol, creates moods and settings conducive to violence. In the case of ecstasy, highly agitated individuals who are actively hallucinating are at risk for becoming victims of violence or perpetrating violence, whereas Rohypnol and other sedating or amnesiac drugs put women at high risk for sexual assault.

DORMITORY LIVING, STRESS, AND VIOLENCE

According to Palmer (1993), one factor that increases the likelihood of becoming a victim of campus violence is students' physical proximity to one another. Residence halls conform to local and state laws regarding acceptable numbers of occupants, but the number of residents per square foot is generally greater than in any other type of living situation.

Most college students are not accustomed to community living in such congested situations. Palmer points out that many students are similarly unaccustomed to sharing rooms, toilets, televisions, computers, and meals with a large crowd of virtual strangers. The noisy, crowded conditions of residence halls are experienced by many students as a source of stress. As Palmer notes, even under the best circumstances (such as within a loving relationship and under ideal living conditions), people who live together get on one another's nerves. The tension produced by crowded, noisy living environments can escalate to violence, particularly if drugs or alcohol is involved.

Although dormitory living presents students with stressful circumstances that increase the likelihood of violence, the rate of reporting of violent crimes does not always reflect the incidence. Palmer, in a 1993 report, found that 374 resident assistants (RAs) from 12 institutions identified a total of 5,472 incidents that had victimized them and students on their floors during their tenure as RAs (an average of two semesters). This yields an average of 14.6 incidents per RA per academic year.

Palmer also states that of the violent incidents described as the most serious and in which gender was identified, 90% of the perpetrators were male, whereas 75% of the victims were female. The most serious incidents of men's violence against women generally took the form of sexual violence (such as battery), involved victims and perpetrators who knew one another, occurred in private, and were not reported to institutional officials or the police.

Palmer's research indicates that over the course of an academic year, violent crimes that are known by residence life staff but are not reported to college officials are committed about every two weeks. Most of the victims of these violent crimes were women. In fact, Palmer points out that many female victims minimize the violence or attribute it to their own errors or misjudgment.

These findings reflect three central aspects of campus violence: Women are the primary targets of campus crime. Female victims tend not to report crime and to instead blame themselves for failing to prevent it. A vast number of violent crimes go unreported on campuses.

Specific Types of Crimes

In this section I explore crimes including but not limited to those that colleges are required to reported under the Clery Act. Crimes that students report privately, to each other, faculty members, residence life staff, or their parents, are considered in order to understand the students' subjective sense of safety or lack thereof on campus.

RAPE

According to Fossey and Smith (1996) the films *Animal House* and *Revenge of the Nerds* portray fraternity men engaging in acts toward women that would probably be viewed as criminal offenses if they were to actually occur. On the one hand, the sexual antics of college men are satirized as harmless, humorous, and playful. On the other, college administrators have come to see the effects of sexual assault on victims, both male and female, as physically and psychologically harmful. The fact that these actions are simultaneously humorous and criminal illustrates the tremendous ambivalence Americans feel toward aggressive sexual behavior on college campuses.

Although there are no specific predictors of sexually assaultive behavior, Bohmer (1993) found that fraternity members are more likely than nonfraternity members to engage in nonphysical pressure and to use drugs and alcohol as a means of facilitating sex, but they are no more likely than other campus males to use physical force.

In addition to fraternity men, student athletes have a high propensity for committing campus-related rape, perhaps because of their privileged position on campus. Although rapes take place in a variety of settings, they often occur at parties, especially fraternity parties, and alcohol is frequently a factor.

For the victims, the experience of being raped at college is complicated by the social setting. In many cases, the assault is not reported. The assailant is likely to be a peer with whom the victim attends classes, eats meals, and shares common friends. This proximity is problematic, because most rape victims wish to avoid contact with their assailants. For the college victim, avoidance is seldom possible.

In cases in which the victim has told other students of the assault or in which rumors have spread, the victim often finds herself the subject of harsh judgment by peers. Many female students judge the victim as being careless, having poor judgment, or blatantly lying about the incident. Victims often find themselves, rather than the alleged assailant, on trial in the court of public opinion.

Prevalence

There are wide disparities in the prevalence data for rape. According to the FBI's (1998) *Uniform Crime Report,* there were 102,560 reported rapes or attempted rapes in 1990. The Bureau of Justice Statistics (1998) estimates that 130,000 women were victims of rape in 1990. A Harris poll (Hoff, 1998) sets the figure at 380,000 rapes or sexual assaults for 1993.

According to a study by the National Center for Victims of Crime (1996), there were 683,000 completed forcible rapes in 1990. The Justice Department says that 8% of all American women will be victims of rape or attempted rape in their lifetime. Neft and Levine (1997) describe rape as the most underreported of all crimes in the United States, with estimates ranging from 310,000 to 680,000 rapes and sexual assaults on women every year. They also note that by the early 1990s rape was known as the most common violent crime on U.S. college campuses and that 82% of rape victims are assaulted by an acquaintance.

Paludi (1996) and DeFour (1996) cite a research study in which approximately one third of all American college students report using or being victims of courtship violence, with pushing, grabbing, shoving, slapping, and throwing objects being the most common types of violent behavior (Follingstad et al., 1992).

As these disparate numbers suggest, reliable statistics regarding rape on college campuses are difficult to establish. As noted earlier, rape victims are very unlikely to report the assault. Once a sexual assault is reported, it is often reduced to a "he said, she said" conflict. Consequently, it can be very difficult to prove that the female did not consent to sexual relations.

In response to college men's complaints that an accusation of rape by a female student can have devastating effects on a man's reputation, many college rape prevention programs emphasize the importance of men's getting clarification on the sexual intentions of women. For the protection of both men and women, men may benefit from assuming that women do not want to be intimate. If men assume that a woman's behavior means no, they will be more likely to pursue an explicit yes. The message of such programs is that misunderstanding is less likely when communication about sexual intention is made clear.

Effects on Victims

Because women vary greatly in their reactions to rape, it is difficult to predict how an individual woman will respond to rape on campus. A woman's immediate response to being raped often includes fear of being alone, and fear that the perpetrator may return. This fear can generalize to fear of all men, especially if the assailant was a stranger and the attack was violent.

In cases of acquaintance rape (often referred to as date rape) women may doubt their judgment about who is a good partner and whether they can ever again date safely. Intimate situations that resemble the circumstances of the assault can cause a great deal of anxiety. As a result, a woman's feelings about sexual relations can be negatively affected.

Unfortunately, some women also suffer negative reactions from friends and family. Boyfriends often feel angry and may misdirect this anger at the victim. Questions of how she reacted and behaved during the rape often serve to suggest that she shares the blame for the assault. This blaming can be damaging to the victim and illustrates why many women choose to avoid reporting the assault.

As noted earlier, many victims who do report rape and prosecute find themselves on trial. Many states prohibit the admission of a woman's previous sexual behavior as part of the criminal trial, but her relationships and substance abuse history, if any, are often the topic of courtroom discussion. If the assault is not reported to the police, the victim's prior sexual behavior and subsequent reactions are often evaluated to assess her responsibility for the crime.

SEXUAL HARASSMENT

Sexual harassment of students in college settings is considered sexual discrimination. This type of discrimination is prohibited under Title IX of the 1972 Educational Amendments Act, which prohibits discrimination in colleges on the basis of sex. This law applies to all colleges that receive federal funding.

Most legal definitions of sexual harassment include some or all of the criteria outlined by the Equal Employment Opportunity Commission. These criteria define sexual harassment as unwelcome sexual advances, requests for sexual favors, and other verbal or physical conduct of a sexual nature when any one of the following criteria is met:

- Submission to such conduct is made either explicitly or implicitly a term or condition of the individual's employment;
- Submission to or rejection of such conduct by an individual is used as the basis for employment decisions affecting the individual;
- Such conduct has the purpose or effect of unreasonably interfering with an individual's work or creating an intimidating, hostile, or offensive work environment.

Prevalence

According to Paludi (1996) and DeFour (1996), some researchers have found that approximately 50% of undergraduate women and approximately 10% of college men experience sexual harassment from at least one of their instructors during their four years of college.

Studies demonstrate that black and Asian women are more likely than white women to experience sexual harassment. Other findings show that the most typical harassment involves sexually suggestive comments, rubbing up against students, inviting students for drinks, and other seductive behaviors.

In my own research, one student recalls that she had difficulty in a course from the first day. She had found the professor sympathetic and sought out his help during office hours. She found that he did not answer her questions in their first meeting and that he instead talked at length about his wife and friends. She scheduled a second meeting in the hopes of getting answers about specific problems. During the second meeting, the professor described his friend as a "horny guy" and a person who would "make it with a tree."

The student later reported privately that she had been very uncomfortable. She wondered if the instructor would issue a passing grade if she simply tolerated his sexualized rambling. She did not schedule additional appointments and instead sought the help of a tutor. The professor often referred to her and called on her often during lectures, heightening her discomfort. However, his comments in class were not inappropriate.

Weeks later, she learned that other female students had similar experiences when seeking extra help. Only one of the four students who stated they had felt harassed agreed to file a complaint with the college. This student also reported somewhat vague, sexualized talk that was not consistent with the purpose of the meeting. This complaint was not deemed sufficient to pursue because of its vagueness and because her grades had not been affected.

Although colleges have taken sexual harassment by professors very seriously in the past decade or so, this case exemplifies the complexities of sexual harassment. The students involved were unable to obtain needed help and instead were subjected to inappropriate, sexualized conversation. However, their experiences were not technically considered harassment.

The effect on the victims usually depends on the nature and extent of the harassment. Sexual harassing behaviors that involve physical coercion and are perpetrated by a professor who is significantly older than the student can have serious psychological effects. Some faculty have compared this relationship to that of a psychotherapist and patient. Using this model, the effects of sexual harassment on the student are similar to those of sexual harassment of a patient by a therapist.

In cases of harassment that do not involve physical coercion, many students attempt to cope in a variety of ways, including denying the behavior, ignoring it, minimizing its impact, confronting the harasser, reporting the harassment, and leaving school.

AGGRAVATED ASSAULT

Aggravated assault usually involves an attack by one person on another in which the offender uses or displays a weapon in a threatening manner or the victim suffers severe injury. According to the Campus Security Act, aggravated assault generally requires an intention to do great bodily harm, usually with weapons, but it is not necessary for injury to result. In contrast, assault is defined as a crime that occurs when one person tries to physically harm another in a way that makes the person under attack feel immediately threatened. Actual physical contact is not necessary; threatening gestures that would alarm any reasonable person can constitute an assault.

As discussed earlier, it is believed that college students may be more likely to resort to violence as a problem-solving strategy than to use verbal negotiation. Because statistics on less violent offenses, such as battery or assault, are not routinely reported, some college officials may not be aware of the prevalence of these classes of violence on campus.

As Palmer (1993) noted, residence life personnel are exposed to the high incidence of aggressive conflict between students. Individual colleges have developed creative and effective strategies to prevent or reduce the incidence of interpersonal violence. At Mount Ida College in Newton, Massachusetts, strategies include training resident assistants and resident directors in conflict management or mediation skills that they then teach to students.

Other efforts to reduce the likelihood that students will use violence for problem solving include a conflict management group that meets continually throughout the semester. Students mandated to attend the group are encouraged to discuss the situation that preceded the aggression and to consider alternative responses to conflict. A surprising finding from the anger management group at Mount Ida College is the high incidence of women's use of the group. In fact, during the 1999–2000 academic years, more females used the group than males. This finding may reflect a growing social trend wherein females are more likely to resort to violence as a problem-solving strategy.

An aspect of assault on campus that has not been explored in the research is domestic violence. Anecdotal evidence suggests that the incidence of violence between college students who are dating is increasing. This type of violence is characterized by a great deal of secrecy and denial by not only the victim and perpetrator but also students and residence life staff, who are unsure how to intervene.

STALKING

A recent increase in stalking crimes throughout the country has resulted in greater awareness of these crimes on college campuses. According to the National Center for Victims of Crime (1999a), stalking activity generally escalates from what initially may be bothersome yet legal behavior to obsessive, dangerous, violent, and potentially fatal acts.

The National Center for Victims of Crime (1999b) also found stalkers may or may not know their victims. In some cases, the stalker may be an estranged partner. However, in many cases, the stalker may have met the victim only briefly or not at all. The feelings of the stalker toward the victim can be obsessively affectionate or extremely hostile. In some cases, the stalker may suffer from a mental illness, and is delusionally convinced that the victim is in love with him or her. Any action by the victim is misperceived as evidence of the victim's interest.

Victims may be subjected to a range of behaviors, such as nonconsensual communication, following, telephone calling, or watching from a distance. Victims of these acts on college campuses may find it difficult to prove that they are being stalked. By definition, a college campus is a finite geographical area where individuals come into frequent contact and spend a great deal of time in common areas such as the library or cafeteria.

Victims of stalking often have limited recourse. Colleges can issue "Stay Away" orders requiring students to avoid contact and maintain a specified distance from one another. However, enforcing either a "Stay Away" order issued by the college or a protection order issued by a judge is difficult. Because most places on campus are community living spaces or academic classrooms, accidental encounters are nearly unavoidable.

Prevalence

Because stalking is not often reported and colleges are not required under the Clery Act to report such crime data, reliable statistics specific to colleges are unavailable. However, data from the National Center for Victims of Crime indicate the prevalence of this crime nationally.

- One in 12 (8,156,460) women and one in 45 (2,040,460) men have been stalked at some time in their lives;
- Approximately 1,000,000 women and 400,000 men are stalked annually in the United States;
- Most stalking cases involve victims and offenders who know each other (23% of female victims and 36% of male victims are stalked by strangers), and about half of all stalking victims file a report with police;
- Thirty percent of female stalking victims and 20% of male stalking victims seek psychological counseling following their victimization (Tjaden, 1998).

Effects on Victims

The effects of stalking on the victim can be profound. The sense that one is being watched or observed can cause a great deal of fearfulness, anxiety, and guardedness. The victim of a stalker cannot know when the stalker is watching. Threats can be direct or indirect, and the subtlety of the comments can make it difficult to prove they are a threat.

One freshman woman reported that she had once gone with a young man to the college carnival, where they both rode the Ferris wheel, walked around, and played some games. One game involved throwing darts at partially inflated balloons. When her date pretended to stab her with a dart, she was surprised and frightened. She ended the relationship because she thought he was "too weird."

When she later found a balloon in the mail that was cut open and had red ink oozing from it, she was frightened and confused. Later, a bloody dart was left in front of her door. Campus police were reluctant to pursue the matter on such limited and speculative evidence. As a result, the victim was forced to wait until another clue or threat was issued.

This student's experience is not unlike those of many stalking victims. The stalker uses innuendo and suggestion of threat. Often the victim is the only person who understands the significance of the stalker's message. This leaves her isolated and wondering if she is simply reading too much into these messages. She often finds that others are unable to help her end this behavior, because most, if not all, of it is legal.

HAZING

Hazing is generally defined as violence or emotionally abusive behavior directed at specific individuals as part of the initiation process to join a student organization or become a member of the college at large. It includes physical or emotional harassment of prospective members. The point is that the student has to endure punishment if she or he wants to become a group member. Although student groups that are recognized by colleges are prohibited from receiving college funds if they practice hazing, students who are the most likely to become hazing victims are those who are involved in athletic activities or join social or Greek organizations or other college-related clubs.

Prevalence

Alfred University (Suggs, 1999) published a study based on responses from more than 2,000 athletes and 1,600 coaches and administrators. Suggs's (1999) research found that 79% of athletes said they had either hazed another athlete or been hazed themselves during their college careers. Nearly two thirds of the athletes admitted participating in what Suggs categorized as "questionable" activity, such as being forced to wear objectionable clothing or drink something disgusting. More than a quarter said they had participated in at least one dangerous or criminal act, such as stealing or taking first-year athletes off the campus and abandoning them.

Nuwer (1999) likened hazing to cult indoctrination. For example, emotional control and isolation of newcomers are techniques used by both cults and fraternities and sororities that engage in hazing. Nuwer points out that some campus clubs order pledges to avoid relationships with others outside the chapter as well as with their families. New members or pledges are subjected to strange rituals such as not bathing and wearing odd clothing.

The intention of these hazing rituals, like those of the cult, is to increase the new member's sense of dependence on and investment in the group by manipulating the student through humiliation. Sleep deprivation, hunger, social isolation, and intimidation are also common. The effects on victims resemble those on other individuals or groups who have been isolated and subjected to threats, degradation, and constant harassment.

Athletic teams seek to improve cohesion through secret initiation rituals. Female athletes are almost as likely as male athletes to participate in hazing: 68% of male athletes and 63% of female athletes took part in "questionable" initiation activities. However, only 16% of the women participated in what the researchers described as "unacceptable" hazing, whereas 27% of the men did so (Suggs, 1999).

As noted earlier, according to the *CHE's* 1999 *Annual Report on the Freshman Class*, 77% of freshman college students reported that they would be living on campus. Over half of them would live 101 to 500 miles from their homes. This distance leaves freshmen without an immediate source of social and emotional support.

Students participate in campus groups such as sororities, fraternities, and athletic groups as a means of replacing or enhancing the social and emotional supports they left at home or to gain supports they never had. Student groups offer fraternal (brotherly) and sorority (sisterly) relationships and an instant network of intensely related peers. The tendency of clubs to use a sibling model illustrates the students' urge to create a family in which they feel a sense of belonging and a shared, common history.

It appears that students resort to hazing activities in an effort to accelerate and intensify these bonds. The more hardship the student endures to belong, the more valued the membership is. The more intense the hazing experience, the more involved the shared history. Through this shared experience, students can begin to feel a sense of belonging. Unfortunately, the rituals involved can be extremely dangerous.

It is widely believed that several binge-drinking deaths in recent years at schools such as the Massachusetts Institute of Technology were associated with fraternity behavior and possibly hazing rituals. Such alcohol-related initiation rituals are often ignored or accepted because they are so common. However, young adults subjected to toxic levels of alcohol and other drugs frequently find themselves in local hospital emergency rooms because of nearly lethal blood alcohol levels.

What Can Colleges Do to Reduce Hazing?

Given that hazing rituals are the means by which students seek to create intense emotional bonds, colleges would be wise to offer alternative safe initiation rites to student groups. For example, team-building activities involving physical challenges that require group cohesion and cooperation can serve similar emotional and social functions at school, as they do in other sectors of society. Many corporate training programs involve an Outward Bound model of team building wherein mutual trust, team cohesion, and identification of the individual strengths of each team member are emphasized. These positive, demanding activities can replace injurious hazing rituals.

Effects on Victims

Although the extent to which victims of hazing have suffered violence, degradation, social isolation, and related trauma closely resembles that of survivors of cults, natural disasters, or violent assault, colleges have not developed a concerted, institutional response to address victim reactions.

One reason for the lack of a concerted response from colleges is that most students willingly participate in hazing rituals. In fact, they become invested in hazing and inflict similar harm on the next group of initiates. Despite the social isolation and physical and emotional abuse, students continue to identify strongly with hazing rituals.

Although students often willingly participate in their own victimization, they should receive an evaluation of the medical, psychological, and social effects that have resulted from these processes. On the basis of this assessment, colleges should make efforts to assist students in reintegrating into college life. Students may need support and assistance from student clubs and organizations that do not involve negative initiation rituals but offer a sense of safety and community. Similarly, the medical needs of hazing victims should be carefully assessed. Hazing victims may minimize injuries or illnesses because of fear of rejection or retaliation.

The social, psychological, and academic implications of hazing should also be treated. College counseling centers are often skilled in responding to critical incidents such as sudden death, suicide, and sexual assault. Many of the clinical issues associated with hazing resemble these psychologically traumatic events, and a comprehensive intervention may be coordinated through the counseling service.

HATE CRIME

The legal definition of hate crime varies by state. In Massachusetts, for example, a hate crime is defined by the Governor's Task Force on Hate Crime as "any criminal act coupled with overt actions motivated by bigotry and bias including, but not limited to, a threatened, attempted, or completed overt act motivated at least in part by racial, religious, ethnic, handicap, gender or sexual orientation prejudice, or which otherwise deprives another person of his constitutional rights by threats, intimidation or coercion, or which seek to interfere with or disrupt a person's exercise of constitutional rights through harassment or intimidation" (Massachusetts General Laws, 1997).

A hate crime is widely considered to be the behavioral manifestation of prejudice. According to Ehrlich (1992) many hate crimes are not limited to nasty talk or pranks, but include physical assaults and even murder.

Ehrlich (1992) found in his review of hate crime statistics that significant rates of what is termed ethnoviolence against all minority groups, along with a keen awareness of such incidents by minority students and a contrasting lack of awareness by majority students, is common. Ehrlich states, "There can be no doubt . . . that ethnoviolent behavior is a significant part of intergroup relations at American universities" (p. 15).

Why Do Hate Crimes Happen on College Campuses?

Although any attempt to explain unacceptable, illegal, or immoral behavior can resemble an attempt to justify such actions, this examination of the reasons hate crimes occur on campus should not be taken as such. The effort is made to identify the aspects of campus life that create a vulnerability to hate crime.

Racially, ethnically, and socially integrated campuses are generally agreed upon and valued goals for American colleges. At the same time, most college students were raised in relatively segregated communities. For most college students of any age, the transition to college represents the first intimate exposure to individuals of different backgrounds, abilities, sexual orientation, races, and other demographics.

Traditional-aged college students often find it challenging to adapt to the diversity that many campuses offer. In fact, there are no similar social circumstances in which citizens are expected to immediately assimilate to a variety of new cultures, languages, and norms of behavior. In addition to adapting to the cultures of others, the student is adapting to the ethos of the college campus.

This adaptation occurs in the context of a highly competitive environment. Athletics, dating, and course work pit student against student. Meanwhile, the cost of attending college has reached astronomical heights while financial aid has dwindled in recent years. Many students are acutely aware of grants that are available to minority students and resent that race or ethnicity is the basis of financial aid. Many students also resent what they view as preferential treatment of minority applicants.

These circumstances, among others, create a college environment that is vulnerable to hate crimes. The emotional climate can become extremely hostile, with minority students becoming the target of majority students' misunderstanding, anger, and resentment. Colleges generally assume that the civility and acceptance that are valued aspects of academia will inoculate the campus against expressions of hate. Unfortunately, hate crimes in academia reflect the social reality that integration is a complex and emotionally charged phenomenon.

Prevalence

According to the *Chronicle of Higher Education* ("A look at campus crime," 2000), among colleges with enrollments of over 5,000 students the incidence of hate crimes in 1997 and 1998 was 155 and 179, respectively. Numbers for schools with smaller enrollments are not available. The Hate Crimes Prevention Act of 1999 highlighted the rise of anti-gay hate crimes. Hate crimes committed against gays, lesbians, and bisexuals make up the third highest category of hate crimes reported to the FBI, currently representing almost 14% of all hate crimes (Massachusetts General Laws, 1997). The National Coalition of Anti-Violence Programs (1999), an umbrella organization for local groups that monitor anti-gay violence, reported that while violent crime continues to decrease nationally, the number of actual or suspected anti-gay murders in reporting cities, states, and regions was 33 in 1998, up from 14 a year before.

Effects on Victims

Whereas the motivations for hate crimes may be understood, the implications of these acts for victims are less well understood. Like any group, victims of hate crimes react differently to different criminal acts.

As noted earlier, victims of hate crimes share similar characteristics with regard to race, gender, sexual orientation, or ethnicity. The violence directed at the victim is based on aspects of the person that she or he is usually unable to change.

Hate crimes are similar to terrorism in that they usually come from an unknown perpetrator and are simultaneously deeply personal and completely impersonal. The attack is personal because it targets a significant aspect of the victim's identity. It is impersonal because it is usually committed by a relative stranger through secretive means.

These attacks cause a sense of distrust and fear in the victim. Because the perpetrator is not known, all members of the college community are suspect. In some regards, the effect that hate crimes have on their victims is similar to the effect of stalking. A case example from a small New England college is illustrative:

> During a school dance, a black campus police officer noted a white male student frequently entering and exiting the bathroom. The officer followed the student in the bathroom and witnessed the student receiving money from another male. The officer suspected drugs were sold and asked the student to leave the premises.
>
> As he was leaving, the student shouted racial slurs at the officer. Later that evening, the same student returned to the dance and slipped back into the bathroom. He used a bar of soap to write racist statements on the bathroom mirrors. He proceeded to the college dormitories, where he continued to write racist slurs about Jews, African Americans, and homosexuals with soap and spray paint on various areas of the dormitory and

bathrooms. The college had installed surveillance cameras in the halls, and the student was captured on film committing the acts.

A number of Asian, Hispanic, and African American students approached college officials about the incident to express their fear and anger. They believed that the college needed to improve relations between groups. They pointed out that students tended to self-segregate and that this issue was not overtly addressed by the college.

The college responded by instituting a series of performing arts programs in which dance, music, and food from different cultures were shared. A local gay/lesbian speakers bureau was invited to campus to provide students an opportunity to meet and question homosexual students. Through these efforts and the support expressed by other students, the victims of this hate crime reported feeling less isolated and fearful. While the injury of this attack could not be reversed, the college managed the problem in a manner that directly addressed group differences. As a result, the issues of diversity in the college community became the focus of attention and interest. Copycat crimes and a culture of fearfulness and secrecy that supports hate crime were avoided.

According to Fenske and Gordon (in Hoffman, Schuh, et al., 1998), the challenge for colleges is to develop policies and programs that balance the interests of academic freedom, First Amendment rights, and political correctness, which many campuses have been faulted with overemphasizing. They report that a successful method of preventing or responding to hate crimes involves the introduction of extracurricular activities that expose different groups to one another. Through such experiences the mysteriousness of "others" is reduced and differences can be explored. In addition, the college curriculum should reflect the diversity of human history.

MURDER

Hoffman, Summers, and Schoenwald (1998) cite a 1993 Centers for Disease Control (CDC) study in which 1 in 13 high school students responded that they had carried a weapon to school and said that they did so for two main reasons. One was that they felt an increased sense of danger and having a weapon allowed them to feel less vulnerable. The second was that weapons were a source of self-esteem or respect.

If students are armed at the age of 16 or 17 for high school, there is little reason to believe that they are less likely to be armed by the age of 18, when they enter college. In fact, several incidents involving shootings in college settings have involved firearms belonging to students.

In 1998 at colleges with enrollments under 5,000 students, there were 22 murders reported. This figure does not include murders that occurred off campus. Hoffman, Summers, and Schoenwald (1998) suggested that college violence is best understood as workplace violence. That is, colleges are the workplace for students, faculty, and staff alike. While many students live on campus, their purpose is to work on a degree. Consequently, viewing the issue of murder on campus as a workplace issue offers a useful perspective.

According to the National Institute of Occupational Safety Hazards (NIOSH) (1990), during the period 1980–1989, nearly 7,600 U.S. workers were victims of homicide in the workplace. NIOSH reported that homicide was the leading cause of occupational death from injury for women and the third leading cause for all workers. Guns were used in 75% of all occupational homicides from 1980 to 1989. Knives and other types of cutting and piercing instruments accounted for 14% of these deaths during this period (NIOSH, 1990).

At this time, there are no uniform reporting requirements regarding the method by which murders were committed, the relationship between the assailant and the victim, or the age and gender of the victim. As a result, little can be said about the victims of murder on campus.

Conclusion

The issue of violence on U.S. college campuses has received greater attention in the past decade because of several high-profile, violent murders. The murders and subsequent lobbying by parents of the victims resulted in the passage of the Clery Act, which mandated that all colleges eligible for funding by the federal government collect and publicize annual crime statistics.

The Clery Act calls for uniform reporting of murder, rape, robbery, aggravated assault, and hate crimes; information on other types of violent crime is less accessible. The acts of hazing, stalking, and some types of sexual assault as well as suicide are not covered by the act. Consequently, information on the prevalence of these violent events on campuses is not readily available.

This is of concern, because college-aged student data gathered since 1990 reflects trends toward increased violence on campuses at the same time that violence in the general population declined. Some of this increase can be attributed to increased reporting and greater uniformity in campus crime reports attributable to the Clery Act.

At the same time, demographic, social, and environmental conditions on college campuses create an environment at high risk for violence. The close proximity of individuals between the ages of 18 and 24 in an environment that is competitive heightens the risk of violence.

According to the U.S. Department of Justice (1994), 8 out of 10 murder victims were killed by someone they knew. Women represented 51% of the total freshman class in 1999 ("A Look at Campus Crime," 2000). These statistics mean that women living in close proximity to men are at greater risk to become homicide victims. Women are also more likely to be victims of rape, assault, battery, and aggravated assault. Therefore, women on college campuses may be at higher risk for murder than other groups of women. Likewise, men are more likely to be victims of violent hazing rituals and to complete suicide.

Colleges are aware of many of these issues and are developing creative strategies to address them. The victims of these crimes, however, often leave college. Future directions for research in this area should emphasize a close investigation of the reasons for attrition. Many students drop out of school, change housing, or transfer because they were victims of crime that went unreported. While the Clery Act and other efforts begin to track campus violence, many victims remain unrecognized and their injuries go unaddressed.

Colleges are increasingly concerned with attrition rates. Most colleges gather data on a standard set of reasons for leaving or changing schools. These reasons generally include family problems, medical problems, financial problems, or problems with course schedules. The question of victimization is seldom considered.

As this chapter has shown, the confluence of factors including the age of students, the crowded conditions of residence halls, a competitive environment, a tendency toward the use of violence to solve problems, and the prominence of drugs and alcohol puts college campuses at high risk for violence.

It is noteworthy that many of the crimes that occur on college campuses, with the exception of hazing and hate crime, are targeted at women. In some respects, college campuses can be dangerous places for young women.

Awareness of risk and a strong commitment to prevention and education can aid colleges in avoiding violence against all students. When violence does occur, prompt, comprehensive interventions that respond to the victim's range of needs are encouraged. A model of intervention that considers the social, emotional, medical, and academic implications of violence is needed to most effectively respond to victim needs.

APPENDIX

Campus Sexual Assault Victim's Bill of Rights, Excerpted from the Campus Security Act, 20 U.S.C. 1092(f)

(8)(A) Each institution of higher education participating in any program under this subchapter and part C of subchapter I of chapter 34 of title 42 shall develop and distribute as part of the report described in paragraph (1) a statement of policy regarding—

  (i) such institution's campus sexual assault programs, which shall be aimed at prevention of sex offenses; and

  (ii) the procedures followed once a sex offense has occurred.

  (B) The policy described in subparagraph (A) shall address the following areas:

  (i) Education programs to promote the awareness of rape, acquaintance rape, and other sex offenses.

  (ii) Possible sanctions to be imposed following the final determination of an on-campus disciplinary procedure regarding rape, acquaintance rape, or other sex offenses, forcible or nonforcible.

  (iii) Procedures students should follow if a sex offense occurs, including who should be contacted, the importance of preserving evidence as may be necessary to the proof of criminal sexual assault, and to whom the alleged offense should be reported.

  (iv) Procedures for on-campus disciplinary action in cases of alleged sexual assault, which shall include a clear statement that—

    (I) the accuser and the accused are entitled to the same opportunities to have others present during a campus disciplinary proceeding; and

    (II) both the accuser and the accused shall be informed of the outcome of any campus disciplinary proceeding brought alleging a sexual assault.

  (v) Informing students of their options to notify proper law enforcement authorities, including on-campus and local police, and the option to be assisted by campus authorities in notifying such authorities, if the student so chooses.

  (vi) Notification of students of existing counseling, mental health or student services for victims of sexual assault, both on campus and in the community.

  (vii) Notification of students of options for, and available assistance in, changing academic and living situations after an alleged sexual assault incident, if so requested by the victim and if such changes are reasonably available.

(C) Nothing in this paragraph shall be construed to confer a private right of action upon any person to enforce the provisions of this paragraph.

References

Adams, J., Kottke, J., and Padgitt, J. (1983). Sexual harassment of university students. *Journal of College Student Personnel, 24*, 484–490.

Andrews, A. B. (1992). *Victimization and Survivor Services: A Guide to Victim Assistance.* New York: Springer.

Annual report on the freshman class. (1999). *Chronicle of Higher Education.* p. A1.

Baron, S. A. (1993). *Violence in the Workplace.* Ventura, CA: Pathfinder.

Bohmer, C. (1993). *Sexual Assault on Campus: The Problem and the Solution.* New York: Lexington.

Bureau of Justice Statistics. (1998). Criminal offender statistics. Washington, DC: U.S. Department of Justice, Bureau of Justice Statistics.

Cage, M. C. (1992, November 18). More students seek counseling, but less is available. *Chronicle of Higher Education,* p. A26.

Campus drug arrests. (1997). In A.M. Hoffman et al. (Eds.), *Violence on Campus: Defining the Problems, Strategies for Action.* Gaithersburg, MD: Aspen.

DeFour, D. C. (1996). The interface of racism and sexism on college campuses. In M. A. Paludi (Ed.), *Sexual Harassment on College Campuses: Abusing the Ivory Power* (pp. 49–55). Albany: State University of New York Press.

Department of Justice, Federal Bureau of Investigation, Criminal Justice Information Services (CJIS) Division Uniform Crime Reports. (1995). *Hate Crime.* Available at www.fbi.gov/ucr/hatecm.htm.

Ehrlich, H. (1990). The ecology of anti-gay violence. *Journal of Interpersonal Violence, 5*(3), 359–365.

Federal Bureau of Investigation. (1998). *Uniform Crime Report.* Washington, DC: U.S. Department of Justice.

Follingstad, D. R., Wright, S., Lloyd, S., and Sebastian, J. A. (1991). Sex differences in motivations and effects of dating violence. *Family Relations, 40*, 51–57.

Fossey, R., and Smith, M. (1996). An administrator's guide for responding to campus crime: From prevention to liability. *New Directions for Higher Education.* San Francisco: Jossey–Bass.

Hoff Sommers, C. (1998). The real issue: Researching the "rape culture" of America: An investigation of feminist claims about rape. Available at http://www.leaderu.com/real/ri9502/sommers.html.

Hoffman, A. M., Schuh, J. H., Fenske, R. H., and Hood, S. (1998). *Violence on Campus: Defining Problems, Strategies for Action.* Gaithersburg, MD: Aspen.

Hoffman, A. M., Summers, R. W., and Schoenwald, I. (1998). Violent crime and the university workplace. In A. M. Hoffman et al. (Eds.), *Violence on Campus: Defining the Problems, Strategies for Action.* Gaithersburg, MD: Aspen.

Kuh, G. D., and Arnold, J. C. (1993). Liquid bonding: A cultural analysis of the role of alcohol in fraternity pledgeship. *Journal of College Student Development, 34*, 327–334

A look at campus crime: Crime on campuses with more than 5,000 students. (2000, June 9). *Chronicle of Higher Education.*

Massachusetts General Laws. (1997). Available at www.state.ma.us/massgov.htm.

National Center for Victims of Crime. (1999a). June 8, 1998, testimony of Gwendolyn Puryear Keita, Ph.D., on behalf of American Psychological Association on Violence against Women Act II. New York: John Jay College.

———. (1999b).Stalking statistics. Available at www.ncvc.org/stalking-center.htm.

National Coalition of Anti-Violence Programs (1999). Hate crime, 1999. Available at www.edc.org/nvpp/who.html.

National Institute for Occupational Safety and Health (NIOSH). (1990). Current intelligence bulletins on workplace hazards. Available at www.niosh.gov.eg/.

Neft, N., and Levine, A. D. (1997). *Where Women Stand—An International Report on the Status of Women in 140 Countries, 1997–1998.* New York: Random House.

Nuwer, H. (1999). *Wrongs of Passage: Fraternities, Sororities, Hazing, and Binge Drinking.* Bloomington: Indiana University Press.

Office of Civil Rights. (1997). *Policy Guidance.* Washington, DC: U.S. Department of Education.

Palmer, C J. (1993). *Violent Crimes and Other Forms of Victimization in Residence Halls.* Asheville, NC: College Administration Publications.

Paludi, M. A. (Ed.). (1996). *Sexual Harrassment on College Campuses: Abusing the Ivory Power.* Albany: State University of New York Press.

Project on the Status and Education of Women. (1978). *Sexual Harassment: A Hidden Issue.* Washington, DC: Association of American Colleges.

Rape Statistics (1999). *Sexual assault information page.* Available at http://www.cs.utk.edu/~bartley/sa/stats.html.

Sank, D., and Caplan, D. (1991). *To Be a Victim.* New York: Insight Books, Plenum.

Siegel, D. (1994). *Campuses Respond to Violent Tragedy.* Phoenix, AZ: Oryx Press.

Suggs, W. (1999, September 3). 79% of college athletes experience hazing, survey finds. *Chronicle of Higher Education,* p. A83.

Tang, C., Yik, M., and Cheung, F. (1996). Sexual harassment of Chinese students. *Archives of Sexual Behavior,* 25, 201–215. In A.M. Hoffman et al. (Eds.), *Violence on Campus: Defining the Problems, Strategies for Action.* Gaithersburg, MD: Aspen.

Tjaden, P. (1997, November).The crime of stalking: How big is the problem? Washington, DC: U.S. Department of Justice, National Institute of Justice.

U.S. Department of Justice. (1994). *Annual report.* Washington, DC: U.S. Department of Justice. Available at www.usdoj.gov/ag/index.html.

U.S. Department of Justice, Violence against Women Office. (1998, November). Prevalence, Incidence, and Consequences of Violence Against Women: Findings from the National Violence Against Women Survey. Available at www.ojp.usdoj.gov/vawo/laws.

CHAPTER 14

Workplace Violence
The Sexual Assault and Rape of Jane Doe

Norman F. Lazarus

Introduction

The risks of exposure to workplace violence have increased tremendously as more women have entered the workplace over the last 50 years. Unfortunately, the results a victim seeking legal or administrative redress for sexual harassment and/or sexual assault can expect often depend on differing interpretations as to how the courts apply existing law to a specific set of facts.

> Workplace violence has emerged as an important safety and health issue in today's workplace. In its most extreme form, homicide is the second leading cause of fatal occupational injury in the United States. Nearly 1,000 workers are murdered, and 1.5 million are assaulted in the workplace each year. According to the Bureau of Labor Statistics Census of Fatal Occupational Injuries (CFOI), there were 709 workplace homicides in 1998, accounting for 12% of the total 6,026 fatal work injuries in the United States. (Warhol, 1998, accessible at www.bls.gov/iif/oshcfoi1.htm)

According to research compiled by Steve Kaufer and Jurge W. Mattman (2001) in an article titled "The Cost of Workplace Violence to American Business,"

> the phenomenon of workplace violence began generating concern among public and private sector organizations in the United States in

early 1990, and the awareness has increased steadily. While perceived as a threat to employees, no statistical information existed to permit the proactive development of prevention programs and policies. At that time, statistics maintained by governmental agencies such as OSHA and state-level programs tracked employees that were injured or killed in a work environment, but provided no breakdown of deaths or injuries that were caused by current or former employees. In September of 1993, a Chicago based National Safe Workplace Institute released a study pegging the cost of workplace violence at $4.2 billion annually. They estimated that in 1992, 111,000 violent incidents were committed in work environments, resulting in 750 deaths. The Workplace Violence Research Institute, from its ongoing experience working with companies and government agencies, believed that the true cost was greater than $4.2 billion. In 1994, we began a research project that would first identify the myriad of elements that comprise the loss to American businesses and agencies, and then develop specific costs for each type of incident.

The results of the research project showed that workplace violence actually resulted in a $36 billion annual loss. The study was released in April of 1995 and received national attention and validation. The dramatic increase in estimated costs over the 1993 study by the National Safe Workplace Institute were not indicative of an 850% increase in incidents. Rather it proved that an incident of workplace violence has a far-reaching financial impact on an organization, when all the cost factors are considered. The results of the 1996 project showed a slight decrease in the total dollar cost of about 2.3 percent. This brought the annual cost to approximately $35.4 billion for 1995. The Workplace Violence Research Institute attributes most of the drop to increased awareness and employee training. Many survey participants indicated that during 1994 and 1995, they implemented training for supervisors and managers, with some conducting mandatory training for all levels of employees. The Institute's definition of workplace violence includes threats, harassment and intimidation, wording that has found its way into workplace violence prevention policy language of thousands of business organizations in the United States. This shift to a broader definition has also mandated a change in the training for employees. (Accessible at www.workviolence.com)

Fear of humiliation and retaliation by the employer and/or perpetrator are the principal reasons that rape and sexual assault are among the most underreported incidents in the workplace. This is especially true when the victim is forced to accuse a supervisor who directly controls her working conditions. This chapter explores some of the extraordinary and contradictory phenomena found in the amalgam of cases that have formed the basis of case law on workplace violence and employment relations. Some of these court decisions and patterns of fact are influenced by outside factors such as political influence, media coverage (or lack of it) and most important, whether a victim and her attorney have the financial resources to battle an employer that is usually far better financed, and the ability to deal with the psychological, physical, and mental stress of fighting a large corporation that is often experienced in flexing its economic muscle against an often unfortunate victim who might find herself in the wrong place at the wrong time.

Many of the problems victims of workplace violence encounter can be illustrated by the long battle for justice waged by a client of mine, "Jane Doe," who was the victim of a brutal rape by the assistant store manager at the supermarket where she worked in a Greater Boston suburb.

A Middlesex Superior Court summary judgment, dated October 17, 1994, summarized the case's factual background as follows:

> This case arises out of an alleged rape that occurred at defendant Purity Supreme, Inc. ('Purity'). Plaintiff, Jane Doe, alleges that Purity's employee, whose identity was impounded by the Court due to his threats of physical violence to the victim and her husband and children is referred to in this chapter by his Court appointed pseudonym, Assistant Store Manager ("ASM"), raped her and seeks to recover on a medley of common law and statutory claims for her injuries. (*Jane Doe v. Purity Supreme, Inc.*, 1994, p. 609)

Without even referencing the effect of Purity/Stop & Shop's knowledge of ASM's prior discipline, in May 1996 the Massachusetts Supreme Judicial Court (SJC) ruled, in essence, that rape by a supervisor previously disciplined for sexual harassment, yet retained as a supervisor, is nothing more than an "industrial accident" (an injury suffered by an employee that "arises out of the employment" which is compensable under a statutory scheme, regardless of fault, but results in a limited form of compensation).

In *Jane Doe v. Purity Supreme, Inc.* (1996) the SJC decided a number of issues under a summary judgment standard, without a trial on the merits, and rejected all of the plaintiff's claims. The SJC, ruling on a case of first impression resolving a conflict in decisions by lower court judges, held that since she did not file a Complaint with the Massachusetts Commission against Discrimination (MCAD) within six months, she had lost her rights to sue Purity Supreme. Previously there was a split in authority between judges in the Massachusetts Trial Court as to whether a victim could proceed directly to court under a subsequently enacted Massachusetts Statute with a three-year statute of limitations that prohibited sexual harassment (Massachusetts General Laws, 1996, c.214, §1C.) Indeed, although it was noted in the Verified Complaint (signed under oath), the SJC did not even discuss the fact that Jane Doe did not come forward sooner because she was so intimidated by the rapist's threats of "[d]eath . . . [and burning her] house down." It took Doe 13 months and the assistance of two priests to tell her husband that she was a rape victim. That alone speaks volumes about the fear, intimidation, and "hostile and abusive work environment" that Purity allowed ASM to create in that particular store.

The SJC held that,

> The Assistant Store Manager, [ASM] who was not scheduled to work, sent home every employee but Doe. While Doe and the assistant store manager were working in the manager's office, the assistant store manager sexually assaulted and raped Doe. Prior to this incident, Purity had disciplined the assistant store manager several times for sexual harassment. Moreover, several Purity employees had complained of the assistant store manager's inappropriate conduct. Purity subsequently terminated the assistant store manager. (*Jane Doe v. Purity Supreme, Inc.,* 1996, p. 565)

The SJC went on to hold that because Jane Doe missed the six-month statute of limitations (even though her claims were filed within the three-year statute of limitations allowed for most civil actions seeking money damages), her only valid claim against Purity Supreme was for a workers' compensation injury. The SJC ruled that since her injuries happened at the hands of another employee, all she had suffered was a workers' compensation injury because it "arose out of the employment" (Massachusetts General Laws, c.152, §24).

One of the leading treatises on the subject was a law review article written in 1993 by a University of Arizona law professor, Jane Korn, "The Fungible Woman and Other Myths of Sexual Harassment," her detailed analysis of workplace sexual harassment cases throughout the country. The title stems from a Colorado case, *Tolbert v. Martin–Marietta Corp.* (1988), in which the plaintiff, Donna Tolbert, was walking to the company cafeteria when she was accosted by another Martin–Marietta employee, whom she did not know, who forced her into a room and forcibly raped her. The court held that, because both the perpetrator and the victim were employees of the defendant corporation, Tolbert's injuries were covered by the state workers' compensation act. In essence, the court appeared to be saying that she was in the wrong place at the wrong time, and that virtually any woman who had the misfortune to have walked by the perpetrator at that moment would have been a rape victim. Professor Korn found that "recent studies indicated that sexual harassment and sexual assault occur in the workplace with distressing frequency, and that 50% of working women may be victimized by harassment or assault at some point in their working lives" (Korn, 1993, p. 1365).

Title VII of the Civil Rights Act of 1964 provides that "[i]t shall be an unlawful employment practice of an employer . . . to discriminate against any individual with respect to his compensation, terms, conditions, or privileges of employment, because of such individual's race, color, religion, sex or national origin" (78 Stat. 255, as amended, 42 U.S.C. §2000e 2[a][1]). The United States Supreme Court has held that this not only covers "terms" and "conditions" in the narrow contractual sense, but "evidences a congressional intent to strike at the entire spectrum of disparate treatment of men and women in employment" (*Meritor Savings Bank, FSB v. Vinson, et al.,* 477 U.S. 57 [1987]). "When the workplace is permeated with discriminatory intimidation, ridicule and insult that is sufficiently severe or pervasive to alter the conditions of the victim's employment and create a hostile and abusive working environment, Title VII is violated" (*Harris v. Forklift Systems, Inc.,* 510 U.S. 17, 21 [1993]). Title VII does not preempt state common law tort claims (*Bernstein v. Aetna Life & Casualty, Inc.,* 343 F.2d 359 [9th Cir. 1988]).

Equal Employment Opportunity Commission (EEOC) guidelines and judicial decisions interpreting Title VII have, in turn, recognized two distinct types of claims for sexual harassment. One type has been labeled "quid pro quo" sexual harassment; the other, "hostile environment" sexual harassment (*Meritor Savings Bank, FSB v. Vinson,* 477 U.S. 57, 65 [1986]). These two terms—which do not appear in the statutory text of Title VII—first appeared in academic literature and were later noted by the Supreme Court in *Meritor,* and *Burlington Industries v. Ellerth,* 118 S. Ct. 2257 (1998).

Quid pro quo sexual harassment occurs when (1) an employee is subjected to unwelcome sexual harassment in the form of sexual advances or requests for sexual favors, and (2) submission to the unwelcome advances is an express or implied condition to receiving job benefits or of continued employment. However, in order to establish employer liability for quid pro quo sexual harassment, the employee must establish a third element: that the employee's refusal to submit to a supervisor's sexual demands results in a tangible job detriment. Examples of tangible job detriment include a refusal to hire, dismissal, denial of a raise or promotion, demotion, withholding or withdrawal of benefits, docking of pay, and undesirable reassignment or transfer resulting in a significant change in an employee's duties (*Burlington Industries,* 1998). Under the quid pro quo theory, an employer is held strictly liable "for the conduct of the supervisory employees having plenary authority over hiring, advancement, dismissal and discipline" (*Highlander v. KFC National Management Company,* 805 F.2d 644, 648 [6th Cir. 1998]).

The other kind of actionable harassment under Title VII—hostile environment harassment—is conceptually different from quid pro quo and is governed by different rules. The main distinguishing feature between the two forms of sexual harassment is that under the hostile environment theory, the employee need not show a tangible job detriment to hold the employer liable under Title VII.

The substantive standards for hostile environment claims were set forth by the Court in *Meritor* and later reaffirmed in *Teresa Harris v. Forklift Systems, Inc.,* 510 U.S. 17, 21 (1993). Under these decisions, sexual harassment is actionable if it is sufficiently "severe or pervasive" to alter the terms and conditions of the plaintiff's employment. A hostile or abusive work environment is created when a reasonable person would find it hostile or abusive, and the victim subjectively perceives it as such. Unlike quid pro quo harassment, the discriminatory alteration in the terms and conditions of plaintiff's employment is "constructive" as opposed to "explicit," and the employee must prove the offending conduct was "severe or pervasive" (*Harris v. Forklift Systems, Inc.*, 510 U.S. 17, 21 [1993]).

The sporadic use of abusive language, gender-related jokes, and occasional teasing are not deemed to be severe or pervasive, but rather, "ordinary tribulations of the workplace" (*Faragher v. City of Boca Raton*, 118 S. Ct. 2275 [1998]). "Moreover, to be considered pervasive, incidents of environmental harassment must be more than episodic; rather they must be sufficiently continuous and concentrated" (*Faragher v. City of Boca Raton*, 1998). Title VII does not prohibit genuine, but innocuous differences in the ways men and women continually interact with members of the same or opposite sex, and simple teasing, offhand comments, and isolated incidents, unless extremely serious, will not amount to discriminatory changes in the terms and conditions of employment (*Oncale v. Sundowner Offshore Services, Inc.*, et al, 523 U.S. 75 [1998]).

Rather, the Court has made it abundantly clear that Title VII should not be made the functional equivalent of a "general civility code," and conduct must be extreme before it will be deemed sufficiently severe as to give rise to an actionable hostile work environment claim (*Oncale v. Sundowner Offshore Services Inc.*, 1998).

Jane Doe

After Jane Doe exhausted all of her appellate rights in the Massachusetts Courts, she did proceed with her workers' compensation case, which finally resulted in a five-day hearing in 1997. In November 1997, a 49-page opinion by Industrial Accident Judge Douglas Bean held Purity Supreme/Stop & Shop liable for the rape of Jane Doe by their ASM, whom they had previously disciplined for sexually harassing women at other Purity stores. Jane Doe's testimony before Judge Bean described in horrific detail an event that is many women's worst nightmare. One of the witnesses at the Department of Industrial Accidents hearing, a coworker at the time, confirmed her earlier deposition testimony that she saw bruises "like finger marks" around both of Jane Doe's wrists shortly after the rape, before Purity conducted its investigation. Indeed, to further verify Jane Doe's credibility on the issue of "fresh complaint" of the rape, Judge Bean had before him the affidavit from her parish priest (who had subsequently moved to another state) with regard to her confidential communications to him shortly after the rape and long before he and another priest helped her overcome her fears of the ASM's threats to kill her and burn down her house and finally tell her husband why she had become so depressed and despondent, required so much medical attention, and caused so much additional trauma to her family as well as herself (*Jane Doe*, Mass. DIA, Case No. 08441590, Bean, J. [1997]).

Jane Doe endured many psychiatric hospitalizations as a result of her rape trauma syndrome. One of her psychiatrists, who testified at the hearing, confirmed that his interviews and prior test results were consistent with the vicious attack that she suffered.

The judge found that in July 1990, the defendant Store Manager asked Jane Doe to talk with "Mary Moe," a woman who worked part-time in the store, regarding allegations that the ASM had sexually harassed and/or attacked her. Mary Moe initially denied the allegations and Jane Doe reported that information back to the store manager (*Doe,* 1997). Approximately two months later, Mary Moe came to Jane Doe and told her that she had been sexually attacked by the ASM but had not reported it previously because of his threats that he would "burn her house down" if she told anyone. Jane Doe reported this information to the store manager, who later informed Jane Doe that he had talked to the ASM, who had denied the allegations. The store manager did not report this information to any senior management at Purity, and they continued to retain the ASM with all of his supervisory powers (*Doe,* 1997).

As a result of a sexual harassment complaint to Purity's senior management by another female employee about two months after Jane Doe was raped, Purity commenced an investigation into allegations of sexual harassment by the ASM and learned about the attacks on Jane Doe, Mary Moe, and the harassment of many other female Purity employees in that store (Doe, 1997, pp. 810–843).

Indeed, it is undisputed that Purity provided no sexual harassment training to any employees of the store in question after their detailed investigation! Judge Bean found that the rape was an act of retaliation against Jane Doe for having reported the sexual assault on Mary Moe to the store manager, who apparently never reported it to management.

The judge held that the rapes of Jane Doe and Mary Moe and the ASM's sexual harassment of many other female Purity employees at the same store were not revealed by the victims to Purity management until January 1991. Indeed, the judge ruled that Jane Doe was raped by the ASM in large part as retaliation for having reported his oral rape of Mary Moe, a then 16-year-old high school girl who worked at Purity after school. Judge Bean imposed the most severe sanction that he could under the Massachusetts Workers' Compensation Act, "double damages" for Purity's intentional wrongdoing (see generally Massachusetts General Laws, 1997, c.152, §28).

After months of additional negotiation and further litigation in the state court to enforce the workers' compensation judgment, which had not been honored in full by the supermarket, the case was settled and the supermarket's appeal withdrawn in a settlement agreement. It included a confidentiality agreement requiring Jane Doe to state only that "the workers' compensation claim filed by Jane Doe pending at the Department of Industrial Accidents has been settled. The terms are confidential." However, settling the case took a great deal of organization and pressure from Jane Doe, her attorney, local women's groups, as well as a press conference in front of the supermarket's corporate headquarters with public remarks by Jane Doe and others, including the state senator who was one of the sponsors of the remedial legislation.

In *Burlington Industries v. Ellerth* (1998), the plaintiff, Kimberly Ellerth, alleged that she was forced to resign her salesperson position because Ted Slowik, a vice-president with one of Burlington's divisions, was sexually harassing her on a very frequent basis. When Slowik interviewed Ellerth for a promotion, he questioned her likelihood of being selected because she was not "loose enough." Ellerth did receive the promotion, however, although she alleged that she was the victim of numerous instances of unwelcome advances. Ellerth resigned without referring to the alleged sexual harassment. However, she did complain to a superior about Slowik in a subsequent letter a few weeks after her resignation.

The U.S. Supreme Court held that an employee who refused a supervisor's sexual advances, but suffered no tangible job detriment, may recover against the employer without showing the employer to be negligent or otherwise at fault, subject to an affirmative defense. The Supreme Court began by assuming that a trier of fact could find that Slowik made numerous threats to retaliate against Ellerth if she denied him sexual liberties. The Court decided the case as a hostile work environment claim, requiring a showing of severe or pervasive conduct.

The *Ellerth* Court decided that "[w]hatever the exact contours that aided in the agency relation standard, its requirements will always be met when a supervisor takes a tangible employment action against a subordinate" (*Burlington Industries v. Ellerth*, 1998). The Court focused on the issue of "[w]hether the agency relation aids in commission of supervisor harassment which does not culminate in a tangible employment action" (*Burlington*, 1998).

When a supervisor claims he or she can make an employee's job difficult, they are applying the very type of leverage and power that their position gives them vis-à-vis lower-level employees. Clearly, such supervisors' behavior is made easier by virtue of the agency relationship with the employer, who has invested the supervisor with her or his power. The *Burlington Industries v. Ellerth* Court held, "[a]n employer is subject to vicarious liability to a victimized employee for an actionable hostile environment created by a supervisor with an immediate (or successively higher) authority over the employees" (1998).

The Supreme Court outlined an affirmative defense that employers may assert in hostile environment litigation:

> When no tangible employment action is taken, a defending employer may raise an affirmative defense to liability or damages, subject to proof by a preponderance of the evidence. The defense comprises two necessary elements: (a) that the employer exercised reasonable care to prevent

and correct promptly any sexually harassing behavior and (b) that the plaintiff employee unreasonably failed to take advantage of any preventive or Corrective opportunities provided by the employer or to avoid harm otherwise. . . . No affirmative defense is available, however, when the supervisor's harassment culminates in a tangible employment action, such as discharge, demotion, or undesirable reassignment. (*Burlington Industries v. Ellerth,* 1998)

Although there were eight separate opinions written by the various justices, the Court apparently compromised by paying attention to Congress's directive to determine employer liability under agency principles, and also providing an affirmative defense for employers who take a decidedly proactive approach to preventing harassment in the workplace (*Burlington Industries v. Ellerth,* 1998). In *Faragher, supra,* the Court rejected the argument that Terry and Silverman were acting within the scope of their employment, citing a number of appellate court decisions establishing that harassment by supervisors is conduct outside the scope of their employment (*Burlington Industries v. Ellerth,* 1998). If Jane Doe's rape had occurred in Florida, as Beth Faragher's did, or in most other states, Purity would have been held liable for all of their ASM's wrongful conduct committed through the use of his authority as a supervisor.

The Court recognized the tension between its holding in *Meritor,* 477 U.S. 64, that an employer is not "automatically" liable for harassment by a supervisor who creates a hostile environment, and its current position that a supervisor's misconduct, aided by supervisory authority, subjects the employer to vicarious liability. To ameliorate this tension, the Court reaffirmed the same two-prong affirmative defense previously described in *Ellerth* (see generally 118 S. Ct. 2257 [1998]).

First, it is clear that in quid pro quo harassment, the employer will be held strictly liable regardless of whether it knows or should know of the harassment. However, there must be a tangible job detriment or there is no liability for quid pro quo harassment. It is evident, following *Ellerth,* that unfulfilled threats of an adverse employment action will not be sufficient to establish liability for quid pro quo harassment. However, negligence on the part of the employer is not a prerequisite to liability and the affirmative defense is unavailable when an adverse employment action occurs.

Second, an employer will be vicariously liable when a legally sufficient hostile work environment claim has been established based upon supervisory conduct, irrespective of a negligence, but will be allowed to assert the affirmative defense recognized in *Ellerth* and *Faragher.*

Third, with regard to hostile environment harassment perpetrated by co-employees who do not occupy a supervisory position, the employer will be liable only if it knew or should have known of the harassment and failed to take reasonably prompt and appropriate action to stop the harassment.

Fourth, in rare cases, the harassment may be motivated, at least in part, by a purpose to serve the employer, and thus the employee may be deemed to be acting within the scope of employment. For example, the employer may desire to have fewer female employees and an employee's harassment against the female employees may assist in effectuating that goal, resulting in vicarious liability. (Gunter and Rattray, 1998, pp. 96–97)

In *Oncale v. Sundowner Offshore Services, Inc., et al,* (1998), a unanimous Supreme Court held that sex discrimination consisting of same-sex sexual harassment is actionable under Title VII. Title VII's prohibition of discrimination "because of . . . sex" protects men as well as women (*Newport News Shipbuilding & Dry Dock Co. v. EEOC,* 1983, 462 U.S. 669, 682) and in the related context of racial discrimination in the workplace this Court has rejected any conclusive presumption that an employer will not discriminate against members of his own race (*Castaneda v. Partida,* 1977, 430 U.S. 482, 499).

Recognizing liability for same-sex harassment will not transform Title VII into a general civility code for the American workplace, since Title VII is directed at discrimination because of sex, not merely conduct tinged with offensive sexual connotations; since the statute does not reach genuine but innocuous differences in the ways men and women routinely interact with members of the same, and the opposite, sex; and since the objective severity of harassment should be judged from the perspective of a reasonable person in the plaintiff's position, considering all the circumstances.

Title VII's prohibition of discrimination "because of . . . sex" protects men as well as women, *Newport News Shipbuilding & Dry Dock Co. v. EEOC,* 462 U.S. 660, 682 (1983) and in the related context of racial discrimination in the workplace we have rejected any conclusive presumption that an employer will not discriminate against members of his own race. "Because of the many facets of human motivation, it would be unwise to presume as a matter of law that human beings of one definable group will not discriminate against other members of that group." *Castaneda v. Partida,* 430 U.S. 482, 499 (1977). See also *Id.*, at 515–516 n. 6 (Powell, J., joined by Burger, C. J., and Rehnquist, J., dissenting). In *Johnson v. Transportation Agency, Santa Clara Cty.,* 480 U.S. 616 (1987), a male employee claimed that his employer discriminated against him because of his sex when it preferred a female employee for promotion. Although we ultimately rejected the claim on other grounds, we did not consider it significant that the supervisor who made that decision was also a man. *See Id.*, at 624–625. If our precedents leave any doubt on the question, we hold today that nothing in Title VII necessarily bars a claim of discrimination "because of . . . sex" merely because the plaintiff and the defendant (or the person charged with acting on behalf of the defendant) are of the same sex.

Courts and juries have found the inference of discrimination easy to draw in most male–female sexual harassment situations, because the challenged conduct typically involves explicit or implicit proposals of sexual activity; it is reasonable to assume those proposals would not have been made to someone of the same sex. The same chain of inference would be available to a plaintiff alleging same-sex harassment, if there were credible evidence that the harasser was homosexual. Harassing conduct need not be motivated by sexual desire to support an inference of discrimination on the basis of sex. A trier of fact (judge or jury) might reasonably find such conduct to be discriminatory. For example, if a female victim is harassed in such sex-specific and derogatory terms by another woman as to make it clear that the harasser is motivated by general hostility to the presence of women in the workplace. A same-sex harassment plaintiff may also, of course, offer direct comparative evidence about how the alleged harasser treated members of both sexes in a mixed-sex workplace. Whatever evidentiary route the plaintiff chooses to follow, he or she must always prove that the conduct at issue was not merely tinged with offensive sexual connotations, but actually constituted "discrimina[tion] . . . because of . . . sex."

There is another requirement that prevents Title VII from expanding into a general civility code: As we emphasized in *Meritor* and *Harris,* the statute does not reach genuine but innocuous differences in the ways men and women routinely interact with members of the same sex and of the opposite sex. The prohibition of harassment on the basis of sex requires neither asexuality nor androgyny in the workplace; it forbids only behavior so objectively offensive as to alter the "conditions" of the victim's employment. "Conduct that is not severe or pervasive enough to create an objectively hostile or abusive work environment—an environment that a reasonable person would find hostile or abusive—is beyond Title VII's purview." *Harris,* 510 U.S., at 21, citing *Meritor,* 477 U.S. at 67. We have always regarded that requirement as crucial, and as sufficient to ensure that courts and juries do not mistake ordinary socializing in the workplace—such as male-on-male horseplay or intersexual flirtation—for discriminatory "conditions of employment." We have emphasized, moreover, that the objective severity of harassment should be judged from the perspective of a reasonable person in the plaintiff's position, considering "all the circumstances." *Harris, supra,* at 23. In same-sex (as in all) harassment cases, that inquiry requires careful consideration of the social context in which particular behavior occurs and is experienced by its target. A professional football player's working environment is not severely or pervasively abusive, for example, if the coach smacks him on the buttocks as he heads onto the field—even if the same behavior would reasonably be experienced as abusive by the coach's secretary (male or female) back at the office. The real social impact of workplace behavior often depends on a constellation of surrounding circumstances, expectations, and relationships which are not fully captured by a simple recitation of the words used or the physical acts performed. Common sense, and an appropriate sensitivity to social context, will enable courts and juries to distinguish between simple teasing or roughhousing among members of the same sex, and conduct which a reasonable person in the plaintiff's position would find severely hostile or abusive. (*Oncale v. Sundowner Offshore Services, Inc., et al*, 523 U.S. 75 [1998])

Similar results have been reached in many state courts considering the same issue, such as *Melnychenko v. 84 Lumber Co.* (1997), in which the Massachusetts SJC ruled that the prohibitions against sexual harassment applied equally when the alleged perpetrator and victim were of the same sex.

Workers' Compensation

Workers' compensation was designed as a no-fault system that evolved in the first half of the twentieth century as workers began to organize and lobby for some small measure of equality in the workplace. Previously, workers, especially those not represented by a union or other collective bargaining agent, had few rights—certainly not protection from overt acts of harrassment and discrimination—little job security, often no health insurance, and usually could be terminated by their employer with or without a good reason.

The purpose of workers' compensation acts is to provide a no-fault system of benefits for victims of industrial accidents, not to provide an escape hatch for employers' liability for sexual harassment/assault in the workplace. As Professor Korn notes in "The Fungible Woman," workers' compensation was set up as a no-fault system so as to spread the risk of injury among all employers through a shared system of insurance. As additional proof that the workers' compensation system was not intended to make sexual assault/harassment in the workplace a no-fault injury, recent Massachusetts precedent has held that an employer's liability policy does not provide coverage for sexual assault/harassment by an employee (*Rideout v. Crum & Forster, Inc.*, 417 Mass. 757 [1994]); see also, *Worcester Insurance Co. v. Fells Acre Day School, Inc.*, 408 Mass. 393 [1990]). Currently, many insurance carriers offer a separate liability rider for employers, commonly known as Employers Practices Liability Insurance, which usually requires training for employees.

"The Fungible Woman" illustrates the purpose of workers' compensation laws, relating it to the evolving laws on sexual harassment:

> I conclude that workers' compensation statutes never were intended to cover injuries resulting from sexual harassment or sexual assault. Rather, they were enacted to provide benefits to employees who were injured by risks inherent in the workplace. . . . Sexual harassment is not a risk inherent in the workplace. To limit compensation of sexual harassment victims to a workers' compensation scheme wrongly suggests that sexual harassment and sexual assault are risks of working which women must cope with, the way all workers have to put up with the risk of being injured by malfunctioning equipment or slipping on a wet floor. (Korn, 1993, p. 1370)

Liability for sexual harassment should be fault-based (Korn, 1993, pp. 1370–1371, 1418).

Rape by a supervisor previously disciplined for sexual harassment, is **not** an "industrial accident." According to my research, Massachusetts is the only state to have its highest Court rule that the rape of an employee by a supervisor previously disciplined for sexual harassment, but retained as a supervisor, is nothing more than an industrial accident that "arises out of the employment." For Jane Doe, this interpretation left her with no right to sue her employer for their wrongful conduct in retaining their ASM and knowingly exposing their employees to harm. Rape should never be treated as the same type of employment risk as slipping on a wet floor (see Korn, 1993, p. 137)!

The SJC holding in *Doe, supra,* sends the wrong message to those who harass women. If you scare your victim into silence for six months, you can get away with it. *Doe v. Purity* presents several issues, however, some of Constitutional dimension, that were briefed and argued, but not addressed by the SJC. They relate to the unique facts of this case, on the false imprisonment and other issues relating to Purity's active culpability, and not just vicarious liability. Sexual harassment violates the Equal Protection Clause of the Fourteenth Amendment to the U.S. Constitution. Sexual harassment accomplished by threats, intimidation, or coercion constitutes precisely the kind of conduct proscribed by the Act. The SJC also failed to consider the effect of the threats and intimidation on Jane Doe, and the fact that she could not cope with her fear and intimidation (*O'Connell v. Chasdi,* 400 Mass. 686 [1987]).

In this chapter, the term "workers' compensation exclusivity" is used frequently in cases; it means that workers' compensation laws in every state have a provision whereby the employee implicitly accepts the benefits of being able to obtain workers' compensation benefits for any injury in the workplace, regardless of proving fault, in exchange for accepting the more limited benefits for lost wages, "loss of function" (disability), and payment of causally related medical treatment. A plaintiff in an ordinary civil action can normally recover compensation for so-called pain and suffering, over and above actual out-of-pocket damages, and for the full amount of actual lost wages. The "exclusivity" provisions of the Massachusetts Workers' Compensation Act (c.152, §23–24) provide that employees can, in fact, exempt themselves from the Workers' Compensation Act and retain their common law and/or statutory rights to sue their employer *only* if they give their employer "written notice that at the time of contract that they claim such a right" (Massachusetts General Laws, ch. 152, §23–24). The Massachusetts Supreme Judicial Court rejected my arguments on behalf of Jane Doe that Purity's failure to provide a safe working environment and properly protect its employees should be viewed as a violation of public policy and a breach of Purity's implied covenant of good faith and fair dealing, the violation of which also constitutes a violation of Massachusetts General Laws, c.93A (*Anthony's Pier Four, Inc. v. HBC Associates,* 1991). Furthermore, it is not likely that an employer would hire an individual who insisted on retaining his common-law rights and opting out of the workers' compensation system that covers all other company employees.

Nonetheless, on similar, but less outrageous patterns of fact, many state courts have taken a position like that of the Florida Supreme Court:

> Public policy now requires that employers be held accountable in tort for the sexually harassing environment they permit to exist. . . . If we are to deter sexual harassment, employers must realize the seriousness of the problem; monetary damages are an effective means to accomplish this end. One of the primary goals of tort law is to deter certain conduct and thus tort liability may provide the needed incentive to defendants to change their behavior. In contrast, limiting employer's liability to workers' compensation will do little to encourage them to eliminate sexual harassment and assault in the workplace. (*Byrd v. Richardson–Greenshields Securities, Inc.,* 552 So.2d 1099, 1104 [Fla. 1989])

Jane Doe spoke out publicly for the very first time on April 13, 1997, when we both appeared at a New York City press conference held by Congresswoman Carolyn Maloney (D–NY), announcing legislation to prevent employers from using a workers' compensation "arising out of the employment" relationship defense in a sexual assault case where the victim is an employee of the company. Congresswoman Maloney's legislation was initially inspired by a New York case against Saks Fifth Avenue where an employee was raped at one of their stores, and the company asserted a workers' compensation defense because the rape happened on the premises. In that instance, public pressure, including articles in the *Wall Street Journal*, forced Saks Fifth Avenue to drop their workers' compensation defense, settle the case without further litigation, and actually publicly support Congresswoman Maloney's legislation (which unfortunately did not pass).

Over the course of this ordeal, Jane Doe has grown stronger in speaking out for her rights. On April 30, 1997, she and I testified before the Massachusetts Judiciary Committee on behalf of legislation sponsored by a number of legislators and women's groups to increase the short six-month statute of limitations claims to three years, the same as most other civil actions. The bill was approved unanimously by the Judiciary Committee and sent to the Massachusetts House Ways and Means Committee. This is where the opponents of the bill were able to do their lobbying for big business behind closed doors. Shortly before the end of the legislative session, the women's groups met with the chairman of the Ways and Means Committee and were told that if they would agree to a 300-day as opposed to 3-year change in the statute of limitations, the Ways and Means Committee would report the bill out to the floor of the House with a favorable recommendation, in time for it to become law before the end of the legislative session. After the women's groups agreed to this change, the bill never was reported out by the Ways and Means Committee.

So as not to confuse the reader with these concepts, I should note that so-called third-party lawsuits are permitted under the various workers' compensation laws. What this means is that, for example, if a supermarket employee is sitting in the company lunch room on a break and the chair she is sitting in collapsed as a result of a defect in the manufacture or design of the chair, the injured employee can sue the manufacturer of the chair for the full value of her injuries.

False Imprisonment

The tort of false imprisonment consists of the intentional and unjustified confinement of a person, directly or indirectly, whereby the person confined is conscious of or is harmed by such confinement (*Baker v. McCollan* [1979]). In Jane Doe's case there can be no question that before even enduring the violent rape, she was falsely imprisoned when the ASM confined her to the store manger's office when they were alone in the store after midnight.

The SJC opinion in *Doe v. Purity, et al.* affirmed its prior holding that false imprisonment, slander, alienation of affections, and invasion of the right to privacy were exceptions to the exclusivity provisions of the workers' compensation statute. The SJC held that the false imprisonment exception to workers' compensation exclusivity, which should have applied, could not be enforced against Purity Supreme, because "rape and sexual assault were not within the scope of [his duties]" and not in his job description. The SJC opinion did not discuss the effect of Purity's prior knowledge of his conduct and their investigation into prior complaints of sexual harassment by female employees.

Simply stated, it is difficult to think of any right more personal to a woman than the right to be free from rape and sexual assault. It is shocking to the conscience to allow an employer who makes a conscious decision to retain a supervisor, with all of his authority, after several complaints from female employees, to benefit from the fact that the supervisor chose the store manager's desk rather than the back seat of a car to commit the atrocity. It strains credulity to argue that rape and sexual assault are the kind of actions that the legislature intended to be encompassed by the exclusivity provisions of the act and that slander and alienation of affections are not (*Foley v. Polaroid,* II, 1987).

> With regard to the false imprisonment issue, the SJC ignores the effect of Purity's knowledge of the prior course of conduct of their Assistant Store Manager and their failure to take any remedial action regarding subsequent complaints made by employees about inappropriate conduct by the Assistant Store Manager (see Doe, *supra,* at 565). In denying Jane Doe's claim for false imprisonment the SJC cites *Worcester Ins. Co. v. Fells Acre Day School, supra,* at 404. However, the SJC ignored Jane Doe's argument regarding that portion of the case requiring a factual inquiry to determine whether the abuse and/or wrongful intent of staff members could be imputed to the corporation (*Id.* at 408–409). "If it could be shown that a workplace practice was so routine as to constitute a general practice or policy, the practice could be imputed to the employer, even if it was not for the benefit of the corporation." (*Worcester Ins. Co.,* 1990, pp. 408–409)

In reaching its decision, the SJC relied on a Federal District Court case stating:

> Considerations of this kind led a court to conclude that, although a corporate insured was covered for negligent supervision claims when its principals had sexually harassed employees, the insurance company had no responsibility "for the corporation's intentional or discriminatory acts." (*Worcester Ins. Co.,* 1990, p. 409, citing *Seminole Point Hosp. Corp. v. Aetna Casualty & Sur. Co.,* 675 F. Supp. 44, 47 [D.N.H. 1987])

In *Seminole* (1990) female employees filed claims in New Hampshire Federal Court alleging that during the course of their employment they were subjected to sexually suggestive remarks, requests for sexual favors, and acts of assault and battery, including inappropriate touching by directors and employees of the hospital corporation. They further alleged that Seminole Point knew of this conduct but took no steps to prevent such activities. As a result of the continual sexual harassment, the female employees alleged that they were forced to leave their employment. Aetna issued a Workers' Compensation and Employers' Liability Insurance Policy to Seminole Point, its president, and its executive director. Aetna denied that it was obligated to defend or indemnify Seminole Point for the intentional acts of sexual harassment and assault and battery. In its analysis, the *Seminole* court said:

> Employers have an affirmative duty to investigate claims of sexual harassment and deal appropriately with the offending personnel under the Civil Rights Act of 1964, because failure to investigate gives tacit support to the discrimination and because the absence of sanctions encourages abusive behavior (citing *Munford v. James T. Barnes & Co.*, 441 F. Supp. 459, 466 (E.D. Mich. 1977). Thus, *Seminole Point may be liable for [its directors'] alleged wrongdoings for its own negligent supervision and failure to undertake an investigation to find out what was taking place.* (emphasis added, *Seminole*, 190, p. 47)

Employers are deemed to have knowledge of sexual harassment that is openly practiced in the workplace or is well known among employees, as is often the case when there is more than one harasser or victim (*Lipsett v. University of Puerto Rico*, 1988).

> [I]f the employer becomes aware of sexual harassment misconduct in the workplace and does nothing to stop it, the employer, by acquiescing, may have brought the supervisor's actions within the scope of his or her employment. . . . An employer is not insulated from liability by the fact that its supervisor was acting entirely for his own benefit. Moreover, an employer can be held liable when "it was the employer's delegation of authority that empowered the supervisor to act." [A]n employer is liable for the discriminatorily abusive work environment created by the supervisor if the supervisor uses his actual or apparent authority to further the harassment, or if he was otherwise aided in accomplishing the harassment by the existence of the agency relationship. (Turner, 1994, pp. 43–44)

Now a judge has heard live testimony on the merits, reviewed many exhibits and confidential medical records, and determined that Purity Supreme/Stop & Shop are indeed responsible for the "heinous" conduct of their ASM.

The obvious question that comes to mind is, What happened to the criminal case against the ASM for rape? As noted in the course of this chapter, the ASM's conduct and criminal threats so intimidated Jane Doe that she did not even seek legal counsel until the three-year statute of limitations for civil actions was close to expiring. When I first explained these rights to Jane Doe and her husband, it is hard to forget the look of fear that came over her face and the tears that followed. When she was finally able to muster the courage to talk with the district attorney's office, she was not encouraged and the prosecution was then less than vigorous. It was suggested to Jane Doe that she did not want to subject her family to the trauma of reliving these events "right before Christmas." Jane Doe also had the right to sue the ASM personally for money damages. However, she would not do so because of the ASM's threats to her and her family. The day after my first face-to-face meeting with Purity's attorney, Jane Doe's house was broken into in the middle of the afternoon and the only things taken were her jewelry, which was not insured. (The local police knew about Jane Doe's claims, but were not able to find proof of any wrongdoing by any individual, although the break-in nearly intimidated Jane Doe from going forward with her suit.)

Negligent Hiring

Negligent hiring and negligent retention has led to many lawsuits when store management fails to screen, investigate or check references on the people it employs. The difference between the two relates to when the employer becomes aware that the employee is unfit for the job. Negligent hiring occurs when, prior to hiring, the employer knew or should have known that a particular applicant was not fit for the job. Failure to adequately screen applicants results in a liability for the employer. Negligent retention occurs when an employer becomes aware of an employee's unsuitability—or should be aware of it—and fails to act on that knowledge. At least two other theories of law may become involved. They are "respondeat superior" and "negligent entrustment." Respondeat superior is the notion that a master–servant relationship exists between the employer and the employee, in which the employer may become liable for the behavior of an employee acting as the employer's agent. Negligent entrustment is particularly pointed at guard firms. It generally involves the improper use of a weapon. The plaintiff must prove that the employer knew the employee or officer was incompetent or inexperienced in the use of the weapon, but failed to provide training to offset the employee's lack of knowledge. A business may face challenges from more than one of these theories if involved in litigation. Unlike the theory of respondeat superior, negligent hiring and retention allows the employer to be held liable for actions of employees outside the scope of their duties. It is only necessary to prove that the employer was negligent in hiring and retention practices. Hiring and retention suits are not limited to employees who injure customers. Violence against fellow employees may also result in litigation. While such violence by a disgruntled worker may be viewed as a random, unpreventable act, the employer's failure to foresee the potential of that act may be called into play in a lawsuit. According to "Duty of Care

Standards, an employer has a responsibility to provide a safe work environment. (Kaufer, 1998, available at www.workviolence.com)

Foreseeability—an employer's knowledge of the potential for threats of violence—is an integral part of the organization's duty to protect. Conversely, the random killing of 21 customers at a McDonald's restaurant in the San Diego, California, area was held by the court in *Lopes v. McDonald's* (1987) to be the homicidal acts of a "maniacal suicidal person" and not foreseeable. Another landmark case in negligent hiring came in 1979 with a $750,000 award against Avis Rent-A-Car. Avis management failed to check the application of a man before hiring him, and the employee subsequently raped a coworker. Had the company checked, it would have discovered that during the time the applicant listed as being in high school and college, he was actually serving a three-year prison sentence on a robbery conviction. In another case, an Amtrak employee shot and seriously wounded his supervisor. The court awarded the supervisor $3.5 million from Amtrak. The action, *Smith v. Amtrak* (1987), was brought because of Amtrak's alleged failure to discipline the employee for previous action that indicated violent tendencies.

> Various studies reveal that certain industries are more prone to violence than others. High-risk businesses include convenience stores, restaurants and bars, service stations, taxi services, and hotels, motels or inns. Mortality figures in these occupations are higher than in police work, studies show. Hospitals are also at risk, particularly from violence carried out by gang members. Women are increasingly at risk. While comprising 43 percent of the workforce, women account for 53 percent of workplace homicides, according to a 1987 study. Many women work in the retail industry, which has the highest homicide rate, primarily from robberies. (Kaufer, 1998, available at www.workviolence.com)

Jane Doe's case is not a situation wherein an individual with an unblemished employment record suddenly committed illegal or violent acts that the employer had no duty to foresee (see *Foster v. The Loft, Inc.*, 1988). "The employer's knowledge of past acts of impropriety, violence or disorder on the part of the employee is generally considered sufficient to forewarn the employer who selects or retains such employee in his service that he may commit an assault" (*Foster*, 26 Mass. App. Ct., 1998, pp. 290–291).

In *Meritor v. Vinson,* the Supreme Court indicated that sex between a supervisor and a subordinate employee accomplished without physical force can still be sexual harassment, or worse, with the employer being liable under respondeat superior and related principles (*Karibian v. Columbia*, 1994; *Kelly-Zurian v. Wohl Shoe*, 1994; *Henson v. Dundee*, 1982; *Mary M. v. City of Los Angeles*, 1991).

In *Karibian*, Columbia University was liable to the plaintiff who had sex with her supervisor for two years during off hours and outside of the workplace before complaining to her employer. The innocent employer was still liable for a "hostile environment" sexual harassment claim under Title VII. The court held that if a supervisor creates a hostile environment and was aided in doing so because he was a supervisor, the employer is automatically liable even if it had no knowledge of the problem and acted quickly and appropriately once it found out.

If the supervisor used his actual or apparent authority to further the harassment, or if he was otherwise aided in accomplishing the harassment by the existence of the agency relationship, the employer is absolutely liable (see *Karibian*, 1994). In reaching its decision, the court relied on principles of agency and respondeat superior. The Supreme Court of California reached a similar decision in the case of *Mary M. v. Los Angeles*, which involved an on-duty police officer who misused his powers by raping a woman he had detained. The city that employed him was held liable, with the court rejecting the argument that the officer's conduct was so out of the ordinary that there should not have been vicarious liability charged against the employer (*Mary M. v. Los Angeles*, 1991).

Indeed, the concept of negligent retention of an employee was recently expanded by the Minnesota Court of Appeals in a case in which a man shot a coworker to death at her home 18 days after quitting his job as a custodian. This result was reached despite the fact that the murder was motivated by personal reasons. The woman had rebuffed her former coworker's romantic overtures. The court held that the focus in a negligent retention suit is whether the employer was on notice that the employee posed a threat and failed to take steps to ensure the safety of others, not whether the action occurred at the work site (*Yunker v. Honeywell, Inc.*, 1993).

Harrison v. Edison Brothers Apparel Stores, Inc. (1989) involved allegations of an unpermitted touching of the plaintiff and sexually suggestive remarks and requests for sex. That court held that where the plaintiff suffered severe mental and emotional distress from the sexual harassment by her supervisor, it was not a natural risk of employment, and thus not the exclusive remedy under North Carolina's Workers' Compensation Act.

That court did not bar the plaintiff's claim for negligent retention of the supervisor. The court noted that an injury is:

> deemed to arise out of the course of employment when it is a natural and probable consequence or incident of the employment and the natural result of one of its risks, so there is some causal relation between the injury and the performance of some service of the employment. . . . Sexual harassment is not a risk to which an employee is exposed because of the nature of the employment, but is a risk to which the employee could

be equally exposed outside employment. [Citation omitted] Therefore, plaintiff's claim is neither covered nor barred by the Workers Compensation Act. (*Harrison v. Edison Brothers Apparel Stores*, 1989, p. 1188)

Busby v. Truswal Systems Corp. (1989) involved workers' compensation issues arising out of claims under Alabama's statute prohibiting the tort of outrageous conduct and invasion of privacy. Similar to the right of privacy in Massachusetts, the Alabama court held that these claims are not barred by that state's Workers' Compensation Act.

Like Purity's ASM, the supervisor in *Busby* was charged with having done and/or said many rude and crude things to female employees. The court held that "conduct constituting the tort of outrageous conduct cannot reasonably be considered to be within the scope of the act" (*Busby*, 1989, p. 325). In a concurring portion of his opinion, Justice Kennedy noted, *"sexual harassment in the workplace should be viewed, as it is in many jurisdictions, as a flagrant violation of public policy. The threat of economic coercion in sexual harassment as well as the abusive power by supervisory personnel should be sufficient to sustain a cause of action for the tort of outrage.* The Court cited cases in a number of jurisdictions in accord with this position" (*Busby*, pp. 328–329, emphasis added).

College-Town v. MCAD (1987) involved rude and crude remarks by a supervisor similar to Purity's ASM. The court noted that "a work environment pervaded by harassment or abuse, with the resulting intimidation, humiliation, and stigmatization, poses a formidable barrier to the full participation of an individual in the workplace" (*College-Town*, p. 162). The Court went on to discuss other aspects of the supervisor's sexual harassment and addressed a number of cases in other jurisdictions. In a footnote, the court cites Justice Marshall's comments in his concurring opinion in *Meritor v. Vinson*, stating that the company should be liable for the discriminatory work environment created by its supervisor. The court held that College-Town is

> vicariously liable for the acts of its agents—its supervisory personnel. . . . Supervisors who create a sexually harassing environment present a serious barrier to that goal [removing discrimination from the workplace]. Harassment by a supervisor stigmatizes an employee and appears to reflect an attitude of the employer that the employee is not considered equal to other employees. In addition, harassment by a supervisor carries an implied threat that the supervisor will punish resistance through exercising supervisory powers, which may range from discharge to assignment of work, particularly exacting scrutiny, or refusal to protect the employee from co-worker harassment. . . . It is the authority conferred upon a supervisor by the employer that makes

the supervisor particularly able to force subordinates to submit to sexual harassment. . . . We do not think that the legislature intended employers to be liable for the supervisor's discriminatory acts in exercising their supervisory powers only after the employee complained to the employer. We are not insensitive to the fact that employees are understandably reticent to complain or to try to prove affronts of such a personal and debasing nature [as sexual harassment]. (*College-Town,* 1987, pp. 165–167)

As noted in "The Fungible Woman" and other treatises, some appellate courts have concluded that rape between two employees, if it occurs in the workplace, is a workers' compensation injury (*Tolbert v. Martin-Marietta Corp.,* 1988). However, many of these appellate courts were adopting that view because it was the only way the rape victim could recover any benefits.

If there is no wrongful conduct on the part of the employer, workers' compensation may arguably be the only way to compensate the victim. Some states have held that a victim of sexual harassment can make a tort claim against the employer and bring a claim for workers' compensation benefits at the victim's election (*Cremen v. Harrah's Marina Hotel & Casino,* 1988).

There can be no question that women are at a far greater risk of being victims of rape, sexual assault, and sexual harassment. They are placed at risk not because of the nature of their duties and responsibilities, but because of their gender. Injuries caused by intentional actions of a supervisor in sexually assaulting an employee are "plainly beyond anything the legislature could have contemplated as entitling the employee to recover only under the Workers' Compensation Act" (*Cremen v. Harrah's,* 1988, p. 151).

In that case, the plaintiff was a cocktail waitress at the defendant's casino. Similar to the facts in Jane Doe's case, Harrah's supervisor propositioned the plaintiff after he brought her into his office and closed the door behind them. He then forced the plaintiff to the floor and sexually assaulted her. On those facts, the court held that they were not willing to say that simply because the plaintiff was required to wear what could be described as sexually provocative clothing because of her job, she consented to the supervisor's assault or that it was a risk she assumed as part of her job (*Cremen v. Harrah's,* 1988, pp. 151–153).

Furthermore, the court held that the plaintiff could recover for her common law remedies and under the New Jersey Workers' Compensation Act. The court held that Harrah's could not use the Workers' Compensation Act to shield itself from liability for the intentional acts of one of its supervisory employees. The court went on to note that where "the employer is a corporation, the employer can act only through its employees, so for practical purposes, actions taken by certain corporate officers and supervisors are actions taken by the corporate-employer" (*Cremen v. Harrah's,* 1988, pp. 151–153, 156, 158).

Jane Doe's case is not a situation in which an otherwise exemplary employee suddenly went off the deep end. Purity was or should have been fully aware of their ASM's proclivities and prior course of conduct. Indeed, a review of Purity's investigation into the manager's pattern of sexual harassment involving many female Purity employees at the store in question reads like a nightmarish textbook example of what the U.S. Supreme Court had in mind when it talked about "unwelcome advances" (*Meritor v. Vinson*, 1986; *Harris v. Forklift Systems, Inc.*, 1993; *Jane Doe v. Purity Supreme and Stop & Shop*, 1997).

Over the years there have been many studies in legal and psychological journals regarding the effects of sexual harassment and workplace violence. A recent study by Dr. Jeremy Rose (2000), who has worked as a consultant for the National Jury Project, shows "there may be a tendency to think that women who have experienced unwelcome sexual advances may be automatically sympathetic to the plaintiff, but this is often not true. Research shows that women in jobs where unwelcome conduct is common, such as waitresses or those who work in male-dominated fields such as construction, are often hardened by the experience and expect a woman to know how to handle the situation" (p. 847).

Several major cases decided on June 26, 1998, by the U.S. Supreme Court further delineated the extent of management liability for sexual harassment. In *Faragher v. City of Boca Raton* (1998) and *Burlington Industries v. Ellerth* (1998), the Court ruled that employers cannot plead ignorance or look the other way and thereby avoid liability for the discriminatory behavior of their employees.

Both *Faragher* and *Burlington Industries* involved situations where the victims alleged "hostile environment and sexual harassment." Beth Faragher was a lifeguard employed by the city of Boca Raton, Florida. Although a victim of sexual harassment that included remarks such as "Date me or clean the toilets for a year," she did not complain to higher management or suffer a tangible job detriment. However, she alleged that she was forced to resign because of the sexually abusive work environment. Likewise, Kimberly Ellerth did not inform anyone in authority at Burlington Industries about her sexual harassment, despite knowing that it was against written company policy.

The Supreme Court determined that employers will be held vicariously liable for actionable sexual harassment caused by a supervisor. As stated by the Court in both of the decisions, "an employer is subject to vicarious liability to a victimized employee for an actionable hostile environment created by a supervisor with immediate (or successively higher) authority over the employee" (*Burlington Industries*, p. 2270; *Faragher*, pp. 2242–2243). Thus, regardless of whether the employer knew or should have known of its supervisor's misconduct, it will be held responsible and vicariously liable for the conduct of the supervisor on whom they conferred the authority that contributed to the wrongful conduct.

The plaintiff was held to have met her burden of proof on probable cause, pretext, and constructive discharge in a recent unanimous opinion of the U.S. Supreme Court, *Parent v. Spectra Coating Corp.* (Lawyers Weekly No. 2205100–2000; see also *Reeves v. Sanderson Plumbing Products., Inc.*, 2000). In that case, the Court held that a showing of pretext alone may be sufficient evidence of discrimination to meet the plaintiff's burden of proof. Many of the current cases allow victims to meet their burden of proof under *Faragher* and *Burlington Industries*, and held that they can demonstrate the hostile and abusive work environment and the respondents' frequent use of pretext to justify discriminatory and/or abusive treatment in the workplace.

Recent cases have held that it is *"our experience that more often than not people do not act in a totally arbitrary manner, without any underlying reasons, especially in a business setting. Thus, when all legitimate reasons . . . have been eliminated as possible reasons for the employer's actions, it is more likely than not the employer, who we generally assume acts only with some reason, based his decision on an impermissible consideration"* (emphasis in original; *Blare v. Husky Injection Molding Sys. Boston, Inc.*, 419 Mass. 437, 446 [1995], quoting *Furnco Constr. Corp. v. Waters*, 438 U.S. 567, 577 [1978]).

> A showing that the employer's reasons are untrue gives rise, therefore, to an inference that the plaintiff was a victim of unlawful discrimination. That inference, together with the elements described in stage one, establishes a prima facie case sufficient to withstand a motion for directed verdict under Mass. R. Civ. P. 50 (a), 365 Mass. 814 (1974). Together they provide sufficient basis for the jury to return a verdict for the plaintiff. The employer may counter the effect of this evidence by showing that, even if his articulated reason for the adverse action is untrue, he had no discriminatory intent, or that his action was based on a different, nondiscriminatory reason. Correspondingly, the plaintiff is not limited to the falsity of the employer's articulated reasons in proving discrimination. (*Blare*, 1995, p. 446)

In *Reeves v. Sanderson Plumbing Products, Inc.* (2000), the U.S. Supreme Court affirmed the principle that "once the employer's justification has been eliminated, discrimination may well be the most likely alternative explanation, especially since the employer is in the best position to put forth the actual reason for its decision. . . . In appropriate circumstances, the trier of fact can reasonably infer from the falsity of the explanation that the employer is dissembling to cover up a discriminatory purpose. . . . The Court resolved the conflict among the federal appeals courts, and concluded that a plaintiff's prima facie case combined with a rejection of the employer's "nondiscriminatory explanation for its decision" is adequate to sustain a finding for intentional discrimination" (*Reeves,* 2000, p. 2098).

As in "The Fungible Woman," as well as in life, Jane Doe and Donna Tolbert were in the wrong place at the wrong time and the legal system did not grant them the justice and full recompense they deserved. Yet in many other cases throughout the country victims have been able to effect far more substantial judgments and settlements.

Even comparing the appellate holdings in analogous cases in Massachusetts, although Jane Doe's case was eventually investigated by the local district attorney's office, they took no legal action, civilly or criminally, against the supermarket. Yet Massachusetts has seen one of the most notorious manslaughter convictions of a businessperson in *Commonwealth v. Welansky* (1944). In that case, Bernard Welansky, the owner of the Cocoanut Grove nightclub, scene of a tragic fire over 50 years ago in which over 300 people died, went to jail for manslaughter, even though he was not even on the nightclub's premises that night. The court held that the club was being operated in accordance with his management practices, which included blocking some of the exits so that patrons could not get out of the club without paying for their drinks.

Looking toward the future on this issue of workplace violence, it is certainly hoped by virtually any fair-minded person that the result in Jane Doe's case on the legal issues argued and briefed before the Massachusetts SJC is a true anomaly. For whatever reason, sometimes "good cases make bad law."

There is a related concept that is attracting increasing attention in this area. It is often referred to as "workplace bullying," and, as the name implies, it is usually more subtle, coercive, and psychological than overt sexual harassment and actual workplace violence. Often these people are viewed with favor by management because they are forceful and intimidating and produce well for the company's raison d'être, the bottom line.

Most experienced human resources management people are aware that most people do not lose their jobs because of an inability to perform at an acceptable level of competence; they lose their jobs because of a personality conflict with their supervisor.

Conclusion

There is obviously a greater sensitivity to victims of workplace violence. However, victims must also overcome the subtle backlash created by insurance companies and large conservative corporations with regard to people who cry wolf or stretch the truth to obtain a better financial settlement. Victims who are not inured to the rough and tumble of business psychology are often surprised to learn that the media make the news as often as they report it. We hear about the cases in which a victim recovers nothing for a serious injury. We also hear about the cases like the one in which a California jury made a huge punitive damage award against Ford Motor Company, after the jury found out that Ford made a business decision that it was cheaper to pay all the damage awards they lost on the negligent design of the exploding gas tanks on the Ford Pinto, which resulted in many deaths and injuries, than it was to recall all the Pintos then on the road and replace their gas tanks.

More recently, many people are familiar with the large jury verdict in the McDonald's "hot coffee" burning injury case. What often escapes significant public attention is when cases such as these either have the verdict substantially reduced on appeal or victims have to settle for a modest percentage of their claim to recover anything at all. Both of those verdicts were reduced on appeal, with little media attention.

Employers need to be more sensitive to the physical and psychological well-being of their employees in the workplace. Good people skills on the part of corporate management and greater public awareness can go a long way toward fostering better morale in the workplace. This will hopefully bring about increased productivity and improved working conditions and still generate a positive effect on a company's bottom line.

References

78 Stat. 255, as amended, 42 U.S.C. §2000e 2(a)(1).

Anthony's Pier Four, Inc. v. HBC Associates, 411 Mass. 451 (1991).

Baker v. McCollan, 443 U.S. 137, 146 (1979).

Bernstein v. Aetna Life & Casualty, Inc., 343 F.2d 359 (9th Cir. 1988).

Blare v. Husky Injection Molding Sys. Boston, Inc., 419 Mass. 437, 446 (1995).

Bureau of Labor Statistics. (1998). *Census of fatal occupational injuries (CFOI).* Washington, DC: U.S. Department of Labor, Bureau of Labor Statistics.

Burlington Industries v. Ellerth, 118 S. Ct. 2257 (1998).

Busby v. Truswal Systems Corp., 551 So.2d 322 (Ala. 1989).

Byrd v. Richardson–Greenfields Securities, Inc., 552 So.2d 1099, 1104 (Fla. 1989).

Castaneda v. Partida, 430 U.S. 482, 499 (1977).

College-Town v. MCAD, 400 Mass. 156 (1987).

Commonwealth v. Welansky, 316 Mass. 383, 55 N.E. 2d 902 (1944).

Cremen v. Harrah's Marina Hotel & Casino, 680 F. Supp. 150 (N.J. 1988).

Estrich, S. (1991). Sex at work, *Stanford Law Review,* 43, 813, 821–822.

Faragher v. City of Boca Raton, 118 S. Ct. 2275 (1998).

Foster v. The Loft, Inc., 26 Mass. App. Ct. 289 (1988).

Foley v. Polaroid, 508 N.E.2d 72 (Mass. 1987).

Furnco Constr. Corp. v. Waters, 438 U.S. 567, 577 (1978).

Theresa Harris v. Forklift Systems, Inc., 510 U.S. 17, 1993.SCT.46674 <http://www.versuslaw.com>; 114 S. Ct. 367, 126 L. Ed. 2d 295, 62 U.S.L.W. 4004 (1993).

Gunter, J. L., and Rattray, T. L. (1998, October). Recent developments in employer liability for sexual harassment—Ellerth and Faragher. *Florida Bar Journal* 72(95), 94–98.

Harrison v. Edison Brothers Apparel Stores, Inc., 724 F.Supp. 1185 (M.D.N.C. 1989).

Henson v. Dundee, 682 F.2d 897 (11th Cir. 1982).

Highlander v. KFC National Management Company, 805 F.2d 644, 648 (6th Cir. 1998).

Jane Doe v. Purity Supreme and Stop & Shop, Mass. DIA, Case No. 08441590, Bean, J. (1997), 2000 L.W. USA 847.

Jane Doe v. Purity Supreme, Inc., 422 Mass. 563, 1996. MA. 805 <http://www.versuslaw.com>, 664 N.E.2d 815 (1996).

Jane Doe v. Purity Supreme, Inc., 2 Mass. L. Rptr., No. 30, 609 (1994, December 5), Middlesex Superior Court, Civil Action No. 93–6530, October 17, 1994 (Gershengorn, J.).

Johnson v. Transportation Agency, Santa Clara County, 480 U.S. 616 (1987).

Karibian v. Columbia, supra, Kelly–Zurian v. Wohl Shoe, 27 Cal. Rptr. 457 (1994).

Kelly-Zurian v. Wohl Shoe, 27 Cal. Rptr. 457 (1994).

Kaufer, S. (2001). Corporate liability: Sharing the blame for workplace violence. In *The Complete Workplace Violence Prevention Manual.* Santa Ana, CA: St. James Press. Available at www.workviolence.com.

Kaufer, S., and Mattman, J. W. (2001). The cost of workplace violence to American business. In *The Complete Workplace Violence Prevention Manual.* Santa Ana, CA: St. James Press. Available at www.workviolence.com.

Korn, J. (1993). The fungible woman and other myths of sexual harassment. *Tulane Law Review,* 67, 1363.

Lipsett v. University of Puerto Rico, 864 F.2d 881 (1st Cir. 1988).

Lopes v. McDonald's (1987), as cited by S. Kaufer, *Corporate Liability: Sharing the Blame for Workplace Violence,* infra.

Mary M. v. City of Los Angeles, 814 P.2d 1341 (Cal. 1991).

Massachusetts General Laws, c.93A. (1967).

Massachusetts General Laws ch. 152, §23 et seq. (Worker's Compensation Statute).

Massachusetts General Laws ch. 214, §1C.

Massachusetts R. Civ. P. 50(a).

Melnychenko v. 84 Lumber Co., 424 Mass. 285 (1997).

Meritor Savings Bank, FSB v. Vinson et al., 477 U.S. 57, 106 S. Ct. 2399, 91 L. Ed. 2d 49, 54 U.S.L.W. 4703, 1986.SCT.42670 <http://www.versuslaw.com> (1986).

Munford v. James T. Barnes & Co., 441 F.Supp. 459, 466 (E.D. Mich. 1977).

National Crime Victimization Study. (1996). *Workplace violence, 1992–1996* (Report No. NCJ–168634).

Newport News Shipbuilding & Dry Dock Co. v. EEOC, 462 U.S. 669, 682 (1983).

O'Connell v. Chasdi, 400 Mass. 686 (1987).

Oncale v. Sundowner Offshore Services, Inc., et al., 523 U.S. 75 (1998).

Parent v. Spectra Coating Corp. (Lawyers Weekly No. 2205100–2000).

Reeves v. Sanderson Plumbing Products, Inc., 120 S. Ct. 2097, 197 F.3d 688 (2000).

Rideout v. Crum & Forster, Inc., 417 Mass. 757 (1994).

Rose, J. (2000, September 18). Research shows sexual harassment jurors don't react the way lawyers might expect. *Lawyers Weekly USA.*

Seminole Point Hosp. Corp. v. Aetna Casualty & Sur. Co., 675 F.Supp. 44, 47 (D.N.H. 1987), as cited by *Worcester Insurance Co. v. Fells Acre Day School, Inc.*

Smith v. Amtrak (1987), as cited by S. Kaufer, *Corporate Liability: Sharing the Blame for Workplace Violence.*

Title VII of the Civil Rights Act of 1964, 42 U.S.C. §2000e 2(a)(1).

Tolbert v. Martin-Marietta Corp., 759 F.2d 17 (Colo. 1988).

Turner, N.J. (1994, December). Employer liability for acts of sexual harassment in the workplace: Respondeat superior and beyond. *Florida Bar Journal,* 43–44.

United States Constitution, as amended.

Warhol, G. (1998). National census of fatal occupational injuries. Washington, DC: U.S. Department of Labor. Available at www.bls.gov/iif/oshcfoi1.htm.

Worcester Insurance Co. v. Fells Acre Day School, Inc., 408 Mass. 393, 558 N.E.2d 958 (1990).

Yunker v. Honeywell, Inc., 496 N.W.2d 419 (Minn. Ct. App. 1993).

CHAPTER 15

Victims of Victimless Crimes

John D. Fletcher

Introduction

Addressing the Provincial Legislature of Gauteng in South Africa that was considering decriminalization of prostitution in 1996, the Reverend Yajn de Plessis beseeched the assembled lawmakers:

> Prostitution is the most expressive case of an abuse of power—something South Africa is not unaccustomed to. . . . Most black people in South Africa knows [*sic*] how power can be abused, and many a black person can remember how they had to prostitute their dignity, values, and customs to the previous regime—just to survive.
>
> Commercial prostitution is also a classic patriarchal crime and speaks volumes about the inequality of women and children in our society. . . . How does society view the prostitute? Men and women are culturally conditioned to place all the blame for prostitution on women. Well, this is like saying that black people were powerless in the previous regime because they liked it. (de Plessis, 1996, p. 1)

The reverend argued against decriminalization of prostitution, a prohibited activity which is often classified as a "victimless crime." Victimless crimes are activities that are prohibited even though they do not infringe on the rights of others. De Plessis's arguments bring us to the core of the continuing socio-political controversy over whether crimes can be truly "victimless" by calling attention to the fact that, in his country, behavior can be coerced even as it appears voluntary, and can harm the persons involved, however willing they might be.

What Are "Victimless Crimes"?

In the seminal treatise in the field, *Victimless Crimes: Two Sides of a Controversy* (Schur and Bedau, 1974), the sociologist Edwin Schur posited that "Victimless crimes are created when we attempt to ban through criminal legislation the exchange between willing partners of strongly desired goods or services" (p. 6). He held that these activities were victimless in the sense that "the persons involved in exchanging (illicit) goods and services *do not see themselves* as victims" (p. 7).

The prohibited activities that can be classified by academicians or political activists as victimless crimes are quite extensive. Lists vary, but "much of the apparent disagreement in these lists is owing to nothing more than selective discussion and illustration" (Schur and Bedau, 1974, p. 60). As the definition of victimless crimes is quite general, lists will expand and contract depending not only on personal selection but also on changes in culture and law. Most frequently cited are:

- Prostitution
- Abortion
- Drug use
- Gambling
- Homosexuality

Less frequently mentioned and less thoroughly examined victimless crimes in the literature are:

- Bribery
- Private fighting
- Public drunkenness
- Vagrancy
- Suicide
- Public nudity

In our time, one can add downloading MP3s and Internet censorship laws.

Are Victimless Crimes Truly Victimless?

Whether people are victims needs to be addressed in two ways. First, how is the term "victim" to be conceptualized? Is it, as Schur argues, that people who do not see themselves as victims are not victims? Or can one be a victim because of sociopolitical pressures that are more powerful than individual choice, as de Plessis suggests? Second, we need to consider the disparate activities that have been classified as victimless crimes separately to fully appreciate the issues involved.

According to Feinberg (1984), the English word "victim" is derived from the Latin "victima," which referred to an animal or person killed as a sacrifice in a religious rite. In this original sense, it is interesting to note that being selected as a sacrifice was considered a high honor. One might even say that, even though these people were victims, they did not see themselves as such.

The word "victim" has developed two additional definitions that Feinberg (1984) describes. "It can refer to a person who suffers any kind of serious misfortune (and not just death or physical injury), whether through cruel or oppressive treatment by other persons, or from any kind of circumstances" (p. 117), and finally as "a person who suffers harm by being swindled" (p. 118).

Applying these definitions of victim to the question of victimless crimes, Feinberg (1984) reaches an elegant and amusing conclusion:

> Now that the senses of the word "victim" have been clearly laid out on display, there is no point in further discussion of the fruitless quibbles over whether certain crimes are "victimless" or not, except insofar as those controversies rest on genuine disagreements over the empirical facts. In the first sense, all crimes *except* the killing of living things (animals or people) as sacrificial offerings to a deity are "victimless." In the second sense, only those disapproved actions which harm no one at all are victimless. (p. 118)

What Is the Basis for Prohibiting "Victimless Crimes"?

It is worthwhile and well within the science of victimology to first consider the empirical evidence of harm as the consequence of a range of activities referred to as "victimless crimes." It is more difficult and controversial but still necessary to compare the harm of specific actions (prostitution, drug use, and so on) with the harm caused by prohibition itself. Claims of relative harm or victimhood are inextricably linked to the moral and legal foundations of societies. The boundary between the study of victimology and political action has reached a pivotal point, where a decision is made to move beyond comparing options to making a choice. This is a decision that every citizen makes in the political process, but taking sides is something this chapter will avoid.

Criminal law "rests on the enforcement of public morality" (Richards, 1982, p. 4). It is not, as some might claim, that victimless crimes are defined by a set of values that are privileged, for example, the Judeo-Christian tradition, and the rest of criminal law is based on the protection of the individual. However, the position taken by those opposed to such laws is that there is an overreaching of authority. The roots of this position can be traced to John Stuart Mill's (1859) *On Liberty,* which used the "harm principle" to limit the scope of criminal law. "Acts may properly be made criminal only if they inflict concrete harms on assignable persons" (Richards, 1982, p. 3). To a demonstrable if controversial extent, laws against prostitution, homosexuality, gambling, and so on are based on "concrete harm." For virtually every "victimless crime" there is at least a claim of concrete harm, and usually some evidence to support it.

Sometimes, however, a prohibition continues to exist even after the harm caused by the behavior has been controlled through other means. For example, the prohibition against prostitution can be linked to sincere efforts to control the spread of venereal disease (Walker, 2000), which is now better addressed through preventive education and medical treatment. The criminal penalties may continue even as more effective ways of reducing harm are identified. For example, criminal prosecution of drug offenses may be more costly and less effective than treatment as a means of reducing substance use and abuse. The prohibition remains in the culture, even as it has lost its link to the protection of individuals from harm.

Of concern to others is that "overcriminalization," or defining acts that are personal moral choices as criminal, creates laws that are practically unenforceable and potentially harmful to both individuals and society as a whole.

> The first intent of laws
> Was to correct the effect, and check the cause
> And all the ends of punishment
> Were only future mischeifs to prevent. (Defoe, 1703, p. 225)

The general rubric of victimless crimes includes those activities that many people feel they have the right to undertake and are strongly motivated to commit. Unlike crimes against persons or property, victimless crimes occur between consenting individuals who are unlikely to report their behavior. Enforcement is difficult, costly, and often requires intrusion into private lives through such means as wiretapping, use of informants, and "sting" operations.

Victimless Crimes? Prostitution, Drug Use, Gambling, and Suicide

The four areas selected for in-depth consideration have in common several characteristics. They are prevalent; in other words, a significant number of people are not dissuaded by law from engaging in them. Second, their social importance has given rise to sufficient research to be able to move beyond the polemics of the opposing viewpoints on legalization and examine such activities' consequences and potential for harm.

PROSTITUTION

Prevalence

Prostitution is illegal everywhere in the United States except within 15 of Nevada's 17 counties. In Storey County, Nevada, houses of prostitution are licensed; elsewhere, simply tolerated (Geis, 1972). Despite prohibition, the number of persons estimated to have worked as prostitutes ranges as high as 1,000,000 by the legalization advocacy group, Prostitutes' Education Network. In 1972, Geis estimated the number to be between 100,000 and 500,000. The number of children involved in prostitution has been estimated at 100,000 (UNICEF, 1997).

Arrest statistics are slightly more informative, but record-keeping methods vary among municipalities. Some include juvenile arrests and others do not. In 1997, there were 20,909 arrests for prostitution in Los Angeles, and 7,350 in New York City (Advocacy Committee, 1999). Of those arrested, most (70–80%) are female prostitutes, 20–30% are male prostitutes, and only 10% are male customers (Prostitutes' Education Network, 2000). Street prostitution constitutes 10–15% of this type of criminal activity in the United States; the remaining 85–90% occurs in brothels, massage parlors, out-call services, and so on.

History of Prohibition

Richards (1982), following Scott (1936), observed that prostitution emerged as a commercial enterprise with the development of urban centers in the mid-nineteenth century. There was a brief period in American history before the turn of the century when licensing was considered, but the arguments for expansion of this practice were rejected by political movements that attacked both prostitution and alcoholism. In Europe, there was a longer period of licensing prior to World War I, but "feminist arguments against the degree to which licensing unjustly regulated and stigmatized the lives of prostitutes led to . . . abolition" (Richards, 1982, p. 91).

The prohibition of prostitution in the United States was not initially based on concerns about harm to individuals through the transmission of disease, proliferation of other crimes, and so on, but on moral precepts. The "purity leagues" that spearheaded the prohibition of prostitution were founded on Calvinistic ideas that a woman's role was as an "intensely spiritual wife (who) would purify and elevate the husband's coarser worldly nature" (Richards, 1982, p. 91). Although the spread of venereal disease was a concern, particularly in Victorian England, the driving force in that country was the "regulation of female moral behavior," which if left unregulated meant that "the stable condition of the British nation was open to social upheaval. Purity was therefore looked upon as an essential condition of female citizenship" (Walker, 2000, p. 1).

Prostitution among adults is a classified misdemeanor subject to local enforcement. Enforcement is difficult and it tends to be sporadic and only marginally successful in containing this activity.

Harm as a Consequence of Prostitution

Prostitution is believed to cause a wide range of social and health problems. According to Richards (1982), the arguments most often heard in support of continued prohibition define prostitution as a harmful, immoral activity that causes other crimes (criminogenesis), spreads venereal disease, and is self-destructive. Of these arguments, criminogenesis is supported by the observation that prostitution frequently occurs in concert with other crimes, but whether it causes other crimes is another matter. Richards believes "'criminalization' itself fosters these evils by forcing prostitutional activities into the clandestine criminal underground" (p. 92), and one can add that an association between prostitution and other crimes has not been reported in countries where it is legal. On the other hand, drug addiction among prostitutes has been found to be as high as 71%, and sex as barter for drugs is common (Fullilove et al., 1992).

The incidence of sexually transmitted diseases, and specifically AIDS, has not been shown to be higher among prostitutes than comparison groups in some studies (Lambert, 1988), but has in others (Parriott, 1994, cited in Raymond, 1998). Richards (1982) cited data in Winick and Kinsie (1971) that indicated that prostitutes take more precautions than do "promiscuous amateur(s)." The San Francisco Task Force on Prostitution *Final Report* (1996) stated that the incidence of HIV infection among female prostitutes was not significantly higher than for other females seeking treatment in health centers.

The incidence rate of HIV infection, however, varies widely, and the role of prostitution as a variable is confounded by its co-occurence with IV drug use. The task force noted that the Centers for Disease Control conducted a study from 1987 to 1989 in which women were recruited from brothels, clinics, treatment programs, and the street. HIV infection rate was zero among brothel workers in Nevada but ranged as high as 47.5% among women in a methadone maintenance program. In Africa and other developing areas, the incidence of STDs, including HIV/AIDS, that can be linked to prostitution is significantly higher (Simonsen et al., 1990). Jacobson (1992) estimated that "70 percent of female infertility . . . is caused by sexually transmitted diseases that can be traced back to their husbands or partners" (p. 10), who had frequented prostitutes.

The psychological health consequences of prostitution are significant across all studies, including those of women working in brothels. Prostitution is an illegal, low-status endeavor, not an acceptable career choice in contemporary American society. The vast majority of females who become prostitutes suffered abuse and/or neglect as children (Advocacy Committee for Women's Concerns, 1999; San Francisco Task Force, 1996). Estimates of incestuous abuse as children range from 35% to 85%.

Violence is a major problem for female prostitutes, particularly those on the street. Among this group, studies consistently find that 80% report being physically assaulted (Farley and Hotaling, 1995; Prostitutes' Education Network, 2000). Drug use is consistently higher among prostitutes. A 1994 study of 68 prostitutes in the Minneapolis–St. Paul area (Parriott, 1994) found that almost all of the women categorized themselves as chemically addicted. In the San Francisco Bay area, a survey of homeless street prostitutes indicated that 67% were in need of drug and alcohol treatment. According to the Prostitutes' Education Network, 50% of street prostitutes are addicted.

Substance abuse may precede prostitution (James, 1977), and dependence can develop as an interaction among a constellation of personal and situational variables. The current state of research is that there is comorbidity, but the kinds of research that could permit any statement that drug use was a consequence of prostitution simply do not exist. It is more likely that the causality is the other way around; drug use and addiction cause prostitution and then interact to perpetuate it, in much the same way as other coexisting conditions, such as homelessness and poverty, may.

Emotional disorders, particularly depressive suicidal thoughts, are strongly linked to prostitution (Raymond, 1998). In the Minneapolis–St. Paul survey, 46% of prostitutes had attempted suicide. The majority of respondents in the San Francisco Bay area studies stated that they were in need of psychological treatment for themselves and their children. Mental health issues, like substance abuse, can be correlated with prostitution, but the role of prostitution as causal agent is not clear. The politics of the issue divide on whether continued prohibition or legalization would lessen the harms of drug use, violence, mental disorders, and suicide.

To the extent that women and men are the victims of their circumstances, which include prostitution, it is an open question whether prohibiting one "choice," prostitution, would lessen the probability of other choices, such as drug use. A view that is more comprehensive and consistent with research to date is that a number of harmful behaviors are co-occurring, and that the response to the victim should address a range of needs.

Prostitution is driven by harmful preconditioning factors that are pervasive in our culture today. Pornography, drug abuse, economic hardship, child abuse, racism, sexism, as well as an inability to establish satisfying perennial relationships are all pervasive influences within our culture. Failure to recognize these influences as roots of prostitution results in both superficial understanding and either an ineffective or total lack of response to the problem. (Advocacy Committee for Women's Concerns, 1999, p. 4)

DRUG USE

Prevalence

In everyday language, a "drug" is a substance that can have recreational use but is prohibited, whereas alcohol is something else not defined. Only among treatment professionals is alcohol correctly classified as a drug. The "substances" that can be "abused" or that one can develop a "dependence" on that are listed in the *Diagnostic and Statistical Manual, IV–TR,* include cannabis, caffeine, cocaine, hallucinogens, inhalants, nicotine, opioids, phencyclidine, sedatives, hypnotics, and anxiolytics (American Psychiatric Association, 2000).

The singling out of one substance for toleration and others for prohibition has happened throughout history. Richards (1982) recalled Benjamin Rush, a prominent physician who wrote *An Inquiry into the Effects of Ardent Spirits upon the Human Body and Mind* in 1814. In this work, which was based on careful observation but was also influenced by his religious background, Rush renounced hard liquor but regarded fermented beverages—beer and cider—as well as opium to be less harmful. If Rush's views had held sway, this section on drug use prevalence would then be concerned with segregating hard liquor use, the prohibited substance, from beer and opium use, the permitted substances. This is not to say that all substances are equally harmful or benign so that any differentiation among them is an accident of history, but it is to note at the outset that when the harmful effects of drug use are examined, the results may not align themselves neatly with law.

Comparably better prevalence statistics are available for drug use than for other victimless crimes because the federal government funds surveys and enforcement as well as treatment. The activities of measurement and prevention or containment are obviously intertwined. The Drug Enforcement Administration of the U.S. Department of Justice (2000) posits that "there has been an alarming increase in drugs" since the 1960s. Citing the National Household Survey on Drug Abuse, which is conducted annually, they note that in 1962, 4 million had tried an illegal drug but by 1998 the number had risen to 78.1 million. This number is roughly half of all Americans over the age of 12. According to the Office of National Drug Control Policy (2001), lifetime prevalence for heroin use has been estimated to be 2.8 million; cocaine, 23 million; marijuana, over 72 million; and nearly 19 million report some drug usage within the past year.

Overall illegal use has increased, but the pattern of usage has changed over the past decade. For some substances and for some age groups, patterns of usage have actually decreased. The National Household Survey of 1999 (Office of Applied Studies, 2000) that reached 70,000 individual respondents included the following highlights:

- An estimated 14.8 million Americans were current users of illicit drugs in 1999, meaning they used an illicit drug at least once during the 30 days prior to the interview. By comparison, the number of current illicit drug users was at its highest level in 1979, when the estimate was 25 million.
- Of youths aged 12–17, 10.9% reported current use of illicit drugs in 1999. Marijuana is the major illicit drug used by this group; 7.7% of youths were current users of marijuana in 1999.
- In 1999, 105 million Americans aged 12 and older reported current use of alcohol, meaning they used alcohol at least once during the 30 days prior to the interview. About 45 million of this group engaged in binge drinking, meaning they drank 5 or more drinks on one occasion during that 30-day period; 12.4 million were heavy drinkers, meaning they had 5 or more drinks on one occasion 5 or more days during the past 30 days.
- An estimated 2.3 million persons first used marijuana in 1998. This translates to about 6,400 new marijuana users per day. More than two thirds of these new users were under the age of 18. The rates of marijuana initiation for youth during 1995–1998 are at their highest levels since the peak of the late 1970s. The rate had increased between 1991 and 1995 from 46 per thousand potential new users in 1991 to 80 per thousand potential new users in 1995; that is, use of marijuana by youths who had never previously used the substance doubled during that time period. However, the 1998 rate for youth (81.0) was significantly lower than the 1997 rate (90.8).
- There were an estimated 149,000 new heroin users in 1998, not statistically different than the 189,000 new users in 1997 or the 132,000 new users in 1996. Estimates of heroin incidence are subject to wide variability and usually do not show any clear trend.

Addiction to a substance is said to occur when an individual is unable to control consumption, when the level of use adversely affects health, safety, or other important aspects of life functioning, and when there are both increased tolerance and withdrawal symptoms (APA, 2000). Addiction, or more precisely dependence, can develop for any drugs, including alcohol. Most users do not become addicted. The addiction rate for alcohol has been estimated to be 1 out of 5, and the addiction rate for other illicit substances, including heroin and opiates, appears to be about 1 out of 10 (Heyman, 1996).

History of Prohibition

King (1957) wryly observed about controlling narcotics that "addicted persons have enjoyed the appellation 'dope fiend' for only some forty years, while the 'pusher' of pre–World War I society was usually the local pharmacist, grocer, confectioner, or general store keeper" (p. 1). Opiates, like alcohol, were tolerated until the mid- to late-nineteenth century, but were eventually restricted because of identical religious and political forces that led to the passage of the Nineteenth Amendment prohibiting "the manufacture, sale, or transportation of intoxicating liquors" (Constitution of the United States, Amendment 19, Section 1).

The Prohibition movement was rooted in the Protestant reformist zeal that emerged in the late 1800s, and it rapidly became a powerful political movement for "public morality" and the purification of politics. The movement, discussed earlier in the section on prostitution, targeted behaviors that detracted from family life ideals, which included a spiritual home that could be corrupted by unchaste women or patronage of saloons (Richards, 1982).

The major legal impetus for the control of drugs, other than alcohol, was the Harrison Act of 1914. This act was not a criminal but a regulatory statute that set excise taxes on opium and, thus, could severely restrict sale or distribution to only those individuals who were "lawfully entitled." A similar act was passed to control marijuana in 1937 (King, 1957).

These laws and, particularly, the zeal with which these restrictions were implemented were fueled by the temperance movement that already had been so effective in restricting alcohol sales. Restrictions often went far beyond their original legislative intent. The Prohibitionists' efforts coupled with the medical community's failure to speak up at the time to clarify use and misuse, meant that much of the legal apparatus was firmly in place before due consideration to different types of drugs was given (Richards, 1982).

Current drug enforcement is based on a network of federal and state laws and international agreements. Among the most important of these are the Comprehensive Drug Abuse Prevention and Control Act of 1970 and the establishment of the Office of National Drug Control Policy in 1988. The Comprehensive Drug Abuse Prevention and Control Act of 1970 divides drugs into five "schedules." Drugs with the most potential for abuse and for which no medical use is expected are listed in Schedule I. Heroin and marijuana, among others, are listed on this schedule. Schedule II–IV drugs may be used medically. Schedule II includes cocaine, morphine, and amphetamine-type stimulants, such as Ritalin. Schedule III drugs are considered to have less potential for abuse, and so the penalties for misuse are substantially reduced. This schedule includes nonamphetamine-type stimulants and barbiturates. Schedule IV includes sedatives, both barbiturate and nonbarbiturate. Schedule V is made of compounds that have trace amounts of drugs listed in Schedules II–IV.

The Act has been repeatedly amended, and enforcement legislation connected to it. A recent addition in the news was the passage of the Hillory J. Farais and Samantha Reid Date-Rape Drug Prohibition Act of 2000. The young women for whom this legislation was named died as the result of being given "club drugs" that acted as central nervous system depressants. This statute added Rohypnol, GHB, and Ketamine to Schedule III, as well as outlining enforcement strategies to prevent their use for date rape and other crimes.

The Office of National Drug Control Policy (ONDCP) was established by Congress in 1988. The ONDCP is part of the Executive Office of the President, and its mission has been to "lead the Nation's counter narcotics efforts by developing policies and coordinating, promoting, and implementing initiatives to successfully reduce the supply, the use, and the social acceptance of Drugs in the United States" (Bennett, 1997). Drug control policies are set in four areas: treatment, prevention, domestic law enforcement, and international law enforcement.

Enforcement of drug laws is costly. The Fiscal Year 1999 budget for the ONDCP alone was $450.7 million. Funding for the drug control function of all federal agencies totaled $17 billion that year (ONDCP). One function, interdicted international drug traffic, has cost $150 billion since 1981, according to the American Civil Liberties Union.

Harm as a Consequence of Drug Use

With the possible exception of marijuana, all controlled drugs have potentially toxic effects and most are addictive. This is also true of alcohol, of course. These drugs have secondary effects that are most plausibly related to the fact that they are prohibited, and there is no regulation over dosage concentration, quality, or administration. According to ONDCP compiled data, about half of all emergency room patients present with alcohol and/or other drug complications. Intravenous drug injection is associated with higher risk for hepatitis C and HIV infection. The availability of clean needle exchange programs is believed to reduce these risks.

Addiction (or dependence) is a serious health problem that can be attributed to substance use in combination with other factors. Use and abuse do not lead directly to addiction, but are mediated by gender, culture, cost of various substances, and reinforcement contingencies (Heyman, 1996). The prevailing theoretical model among treatment specialists is that addiction is a disease process. This model was popularized in contemporary times by E. M. Jellineck in a series of papers leading up to the publication of the now classic text, *The Disease Concept of Alcoholism* (1960), but the notion that excessive alcohol consumption was better understood as a disease rather than a vice was actually a guiding principle of the temperance movement. While the anticipated outcome of temperance was to be a better society, Prohibition was necessary because people fell prey to alcohol's powerful effects.

Like other diseases, alcohol addiction strikes some people but not others. The disease is characterized by a loss of control. Substance ingestion becomes compulsive, and withdrawal or prolonged abstinence from the drug of choice is avoided at often extreme cost to the individual. In the disease model, addicts are victims:

> As a victim, the afflicted has no control over the onset and progression of the disease if left untreated. In the disease concept of alcoholism (and drug addiction) the cardinal feature is loss of control over the use of alcohol, manifested by a a preoccupation with acquiring, continued use despite adverse consequences, and a pattern of relapse to alcohol. The loss of control, which can actually be inherited, is the sine qua non for alcoholism (and drug addiction) as qualifying for the disease state. The loss of control signifies a victim state that reflects an alteration of brain function by alcohol or drugs that is not under the conscious volitional control of the individual. (Heyman, 1996, p. 9).

Heyman contended that an addict's characteristic compulsive behavior does not constitute a loss of control, in that addicts are able to adjust their behavior to environmental changes, such as price increases, drug availability, and other factors. He theorized that drug use constitutes a preference, but it is powerfully influenced by "perverse conditions created by substances that, when consumed in large amounts, decrease their own future value and the future value of other activities" (p. 22).

The disease model remains the dominant theoretical framework because it most successfully explains why drug use becomes compulsive with such disastrous results for individuals, families, and communities. Although chemically addicted persons may have choices, they are not easily made ones, and pursuit of abstinence can be a lifetime struggle.

The question that has been raised by opponents to the criminalization of drug use (meaning those drugs other than alcohol) is whether people would be harmed less. One type of harm, clearly, is addiction. The other types of harm include the transmission of disease, drug use's association with violence and date rape, and miscellaneous criminal activities surrounding drug distribution, individual procurement, and use.

In regard to addiction, the role of drug availability is unclear. Alcohol is the most prevalent—but legal—drug, and more people are dependent on it than any other drug. The position of the American Civil Liberties Union (2000) is that "prohibition fosters the sale and consumption of more potent and dangerous forms of drugs" and "would not *necessarily* [italics added] increase drug abuse" (p. 4). They have also raised the "forbidden fruit" hypothesis, and point to the decline in the Netherlands' adolescent marijuana consumption from 10% to 6.5% in the decade following legalization there in 1976.

A significant relationship between alcohol/drug consumption and rape has been found (Levine and Kanin, 1987). "Loss of control" because of alcohol/drug use has been a common justification by men who physically abuse their wives, but domestic violence intervention specialists almost uniformly view such explanations as excuses for violent behavior that is better understood as a deliberate means of exercising control over spouses.

There has been a wide range of criminal and self-injurious behavior related to drug use. The U.S. Department of Justice describes the drug–crime relationship in three categories: (1) drug-defined offenses, such as cultivation, possession, production, and sales, (2) drug-related offenses, such as violent behavior because of drug use, stealing to get money to buy drugs, crimes against competitive drug dealers, and (3) drug-using lifestyle, which lends itself to a range of illegal activity (Office of Justice Programs, 1994). Among the findings of the Justice Department is that many arrestees test positive for recent illegal drug use. For example, 68% of men and 63% of women arrested for burglary in 1991 and 48% of men and 65% of women in homicide arrests tested positive for drugs. And recalling the previous section on prostitution, 47% of men who are arrested and an astonishing 85% of women test positive for drug use (Office of Justice Programs, 1994).

There is no reasonable way, however, to separate the harm caused by specific drug types and that caused by criminalization (and lack of regulation) that is responsible for variations in drug quality, concentration, toxicity, drug prices and procurement through a distribution underworld, and so on. Central to the range of harms caused by drugs, however, is the disease of addiction and its many victims.

GAMBLING

Prevalence

People gamble in many different ways, from the purchase of lottery tickets to playing bingo at the neighborhood parish to visiting a casino. Over 80% of U.S. adults gamble at some time in their lives (Committee on the Social and Economic Impact of Pathological Gambling, 1999), and indications are gambling's acceptance as a pastime is increasing.

Gambling, unlike prostitution and drug use, is a permitted activity that becomes a crime only when it occurs outside of state-sanctioned outlets. As all but three states have some form of legalized gambling, and casinos are located in 21 states, it may be becoming increasingly difficult to commit this type of victimless crime. How prevalent is illegal gambling? Arrest statistics may be the best estimate of the extent of the problem. In 1995, there were 12,800 reported arrests for gambling out of a total number of 14,528,300 arrests (Sourcebook of Criminal Justice Statistics, 1995).

History of Prohibition

Over the course of American history, gambling has been at times considered by the general public to be sport or harmless diversion, and at other times it is has been viewed as a true vice because of its harm to families and society as a whole. Our time is characterized by fairly widespread acceptance, but this acceptance has grown rapidly within one or two generations from a post-war period in which gambling was outlawed in all but one state, Nevada. There currently are government-sponsored lotteries in all but a handful of states, and casinos have been built or are being considered throughout the country.

In colonial America, gambling was permitted everywhere except in New England, where Puritan ethics prevailed, and Pennsylvania. The Puritans believed that people should prosper solely because of good character that was evidenced in their hard work and not because of good luck while enjoying themselves.

By the mid-eighteenth century, financial problems in all colonies led to the establishment of state lotteries. Public acceptance of gambling was elevated to public appreciation for this form of revenue. "Playing the lottery became a civic responsibility" (Dunstan, 1997, p. 3).

Lotteries continued to be popular through the War of Independence, but there were increasing incidents of fraud. For example, one private lottery set up by Congress to beautify Washington, D.C., in 1823 ended in its operators' running off with the proceeds. Scandals such as this were evidence to social reformers that people, particularly the poor, were being victimized by lottery operators.

By 1840, lotteries were abandoned in all U.S. states, and although they returned briefly after the Civil War in the southern states, they were completely abolished by state and federal laws by the mid-1870s. Casinos flourished in the mid- to late-nineteenth century in major population areas, such as New York City and California communities enriched by the Gold Rush. Toward the end of the nineteenth century, most states passed laws to first outlaw specific games, then penalized those who ran the games, and finally made it illegal to gamble at all.

Gaming returned at the height of the Great Depression. In 1933, several states took the lead in legalizing horse racing. At the same time, there was a crackdown on the illegal gambling that had flourished under organized crime families in major metropolitan areas. Concerns with organized crime prevented almost all states from legalizing gambling. Only Nevada permitted the operation of casinos from 1931 until 1978, when it was joined by New Jersey, with its Atlantic City casinos.

In 1964, New Hampshire reestablished a state-run lottery, followed by New York in 1967. All but three states operate lotteries presently as a means of avoiding tax increases.

Harm as a Consequence of Gambling

As in alcohol/drug use, some people who gamble will develop an addiction to it. As described in the *Diagnostic and Statistical Manual IV–TR* (American Psychiatric Association, 2000), "pathological gambling" is a "persistent and recurrent maladaptive behavior" (p. 283) that is characterized by such symptoms as preoccupation, the need "to gamble with increasing amounts of money in order to achieve the desired excitement" (p. 283), loss of control over gambling, and the development of serious problems in family or work life. Its onset is gradual, the disease process is selective, and treatment consists largely of supported abstinence.

The prevalence of pathological gambling over a lifetime has been estimated to be 1.5% of the population (Committee on the Social and Economic Impact of Pathological Gambling, 1999). There have been some studies that indicate that the prevalence of pathological gambling increases with exposure, and, as expected, the states in which casinos have been in operation the longest seem to have the highest numbers of adults who are addicted (Dunstan, 1997).

The consequences of addiction to gambling can be severe. Pathological gambling often occurs with other emotional problems, such as substance abuse and depression, and gambling losses and debts can lead to criminal activity, the ruin of families, and suicidal despair.

Even the legalized form of gambling is associated with crime. The crime rate in communities where casinos have been located was 84% higher than the national average in 1994, and it has been rising as the national average has fallen (Shapiro, 1996).

Although regulation of the new wave of casinos has been thought effective in keeping out organized crime, the large amounts of cash involved continue to attract criminal interest. Skimming, loan sharking, money laundering, and robberies of people leaving casinos are crimes that can be expected to occur with greater frequency near casinos (Dunstan, 1997).

One of the major concerns about lotteries throughout their history has been that people with limited means are victimized by the offering of a slim chance to escape impoverishment. The fears of reformers in the early 1800s find credibility in numerous studies of state-developed lotteries at the end of the twentieth century, which have been most attractive to individuals who can least afford to gamble on the minuscule chance offered (Borg, Mason, and Shapiro, 1991). A study of Pennsylvania lottery sales by the Pittsburgh *Tribune-Review* (Houser, 1999) is representative. Among their findings were:

> In Allegheny County, the most recent lottery records available show stores in neighborhoods with per capita incomes lower than $20,000 sold more than twice as many tickets per resident as those in neighborhoods where average incomes exceeded $30,000.
>
> Regular players are more likely to be poor than those who play less than once a week, according to the lottery's latest marketing study. (p. 1)

ASSISTED SUICIDE

Prevalence

Assisted suicide, also known as "voluntary euthanasia" or "physician-assisted suicide," in contemporary usage usually refers to the practice of ending the life of a terminally ill person. The numbers of people who have or would assert that they have a right to this practice is much smaller than the number of people who commit suicide because they are emotionally despondent or for other reasons. It has been estimated that over 31,000 kill themselves each year (Hoyert et al., 1999). It is the eighth leading cause of death in the United States (National Institute of Mental Health, 2000). Approximately 750,000 people, or 2.9% of the population, attempt suicide each year (Clark, 1992; Suicide and Crisis Center, 2000).

The decision to end one's life is typically made after a prolonged, intense personal struggle, and not because of a single, acute event. Of the people who attempt suicide, 95% suffer from a diagnosable mental illness; 50% suffer from major depression (Task Force on Life and the Law, 2000). The 1997 suicide rates for people aged 75–84 and 85–94 years were the highest—19.3 and 20.8 persons per 100,000 respectively, compared to the average of 11.4 per 100,000 (Hoyert et al., 1999). Senior citizens must cope with declining health and other losses, which may explain their higher rates.

Terminally ill patients make up 2–4% of suicides (Clark, 1992). This population does not include patients who may be assisted by physicians and others illegally, and it does not include passive suicide—death caused by the removal of life supports. The wish of terminally ill patients to die does not seem to be directly attributable to pain and suffering. Several studies of patients with severe pain and disability found that the majority do not wish to die. There has been a much stronger relationship established between the presence of mental illness, particularly depression, within this group than in the general population (Task Force on Life and the Law, 2000).

Physician-assisted suicide appears to be widespread despite being against the law in most states. A survey of Oregon physicians prior to that state's 1997 legalization found that 7% had assisted patients and 60% would. A study of oncologists at the Dana Farber Cancer Institute in Boston, published in 1997, reported that 57.2% had been asked by their patients with cancer to assist them in committing suicide, and 13.6% had acceded to their request (Facts on File, 1997).

History of Prohibition

Assisted suicide has very much been in the news lately, and the debate has intensified because of successful efforts to legalize it in Oregon and the actions of Dr. Jack Kervorkian in flouting the law. Notwithstanding the events over the past 5 or 10 years, assisted suicide is prohibited in 49 states.

Current statutes are historically rooted in English common law. It was considered "self-murder." William Blackstone asserted "the suicide is guilty of a double offense; one is spiritual, in invading the prerogative of the Almighty, and rushing into his immediate presence uncalled for; the other temporal, against the king, who hath an interest in the preservation of all his subjects" (quoted in Task Force on Life and the Law, 2000, p. 12).

In American colonial times, the practice was considered a "grave public wrong" which could result in imprisonment if one survived the attempt. In the early twentieth century, suicide was decriminalized in all states, but this did not convey a "right" to the act upon which assisted suicide laws might stand.

At present 32 states have specific statutes prohibiting assisted suicide, and in the remaining 17 states, persons may be subject to prosecution for murder or manslaughter (Smith, 1997). In New York state, for example, a person who assists in a suicide may be guilty of second-degree manslaughter, but if there was duress or deception, the finding could be second-degree murder. No person has ever been convicted of either offense in New York.

A nationwide Gallup poll in 1996 reported that 75% of respondents were in favor of permitting physicians to aid in ending the lives of their terminally ill patients, which would seem to indicate that the legislative tide would begin to flow in the direction of passage of statutes allowing the practice. There has been legislative activity in virtually all states, but proposals have been defeated consistently across the country (Facts on File, 1997).

In 1997, the Supreme Court heard two cases, *Vacco v. Quill* and *Washington v. Glucksberg,* in which state laws prohibiting assisted suicide were upheld. Although the rulings in these cases did not define a Constitutional right to die and to be assisted in this act, the Court did not bar individual states from passing legislation to define the practice.

In upholding the Washington state law, Chief Justice Rehnquist wrote the 8 to 0 majority opinion:

> The history of the law's treatment of assisted suicide in this country has been and continues to be one of the rejection of nearly all efforts to permit it. That being the case, our decisions lead us to conclude that the asserted "right" to assistance in committing suicide is not a fundamental liberty interest protected by the Due Process Clause.
>
> The Constitution also requires, however, that Washington's assisted suicide ban be rationally related to legitimate government interests. This requirement is unquestionably met here. . . . First, Washington has an "unqualified interest in the preservation of human life. . . . "
>
> The State has an interest in preventing suicide, and in studying, identifying, and treating its causes. . . . Research indicates, however, that many people who request physician-assisted suicide withdraw that request if their depression and pain are treated. . . .
>
> Next, the State has an interest in protecting vulnerable groups— including the poor, the elderly, and disabled persons—from abuse, neglect, and mistakes. . . . If physician-assisted suicide were permitted, many might resort to it to spare their families the substantial financial burden of end of life health care costs. . . .

The State's assisted suicide ban reflects and reinforces its policy that the lives of terminally ill, disabled, and elderly people must be no less valued than the lives of the young and healthy, and that a seriously disabled person's suicidal impulses should be interpreted and treated the same way as anyone else's. . . . (Rehnquist, 1997, p. 18)

Harm as a Consequence of Assisted Suicide

Proponents of assisted suicide laws argue that the practice is occurring, but for arbitrary reasons it is available to some patients and not to others. A well-crafted law would ensure equal access and institute important safeguards. They further argue that many patients are in chronic pain or suffer from disabilities so severe that death is a reasonable alternative that should not be denied.

Over the course of the ongoing debate, several victims of progressively crippling and terminal conditions have come forward so that people can see beyond the abstract principles at issue. Barbara Oskamp, who suffered from an inoperable brain tumor, spoke during the Oregon debate: "I'm so afraid of pain and being dependent, of not having my body parts work. I don't know if I could do it or would do it. But I want the feeling of having a choice of ending what may be a horrible situation" (Kolata, 1997, p. C4).

The continuing opposition to legislation has appeared to be based on four main arguments:

1. Pain and suffering can be relieved for most terminally ill patients. It is maintained that far fewer patients would request assistance in suicide if both their pain *and* related depression were effectively treated.
2. The contention that patients are rational when they make the decision to end their lives is questionable. As noted, most terminal patients who attempt suicide, like the general population, are suffering from a mental illness (Task Force on Life and the Law, 2000).
3. There is a world of difference between passive suicide and voluntary euthanasia. Passive suicide, through living wills and other means, allows for life supports to be removed. Euthanasia places the act within the hands of medical practitioners, whose decision making may be corrupted by influences other than the patient's will.
4. Assisted suicide and euthanasia will be practiced through the prism of social inequality and prejudice that characterizes the delivery of services in all segments of society, including health care. Those who will be most vulnerable to abuse, error or indifference are the poor, minorities, and those who are least educated and least empowered. (Facts on File, 1997)

This is the "slippery slope" that has been persuasively argued by Wesley Smith in *Forced Exit: The Slippery Slope from Assisted Suicide to Legalized*

Murder (1997). The core of this argument is not the intent of physicians, health care institutions, and managed care organizations to intentionally inflict concrete harm, but that the values and priorities of these constituencies are potentially harmful and need to be curtailed.

Conclusion

The term "victimless crimes" has referred to a wide variety of consensual activities that proponents of legalization contend are basic rights that should not be abridged. The term has been found to be a misnomer, because a victim is someone who suffers harm. A central question to consider from the perspective of victimology is the relative harm caused by different courses of action—in this instance legalization versus prohibition.

The excerpt from a speech by Reverend de Plessis which opened this chapter addressed a specific victimless crime, prostitution, but his comments have larger significance and connect us to earlier efforts to create a humane society. The Reverend calls attention to social conditions that profoundly affect individual choice and the harm that is caused when these oppressive and deceptive processes are not limited by law.

If the chapter had begun with comments by social reformers in early American history, it would have been easier to dismiss the views as paternalistic, religiously grounded nonsense that have little bearing on a contemporary society, which has increasingly broadened its definition of individual rights. The temperance movement, for example, was shaped by the religious and cultural views of the time, but, at its heart, it was an attempt to grapple with real social problems related to alcohol, which continue to this day. Likewise, the chapter could have opened with a condemnation of gambling: "The entire history of legalized gambling in this country and abroad shows that [it] brought nothing but poverty, crime and corruption, demoralization of moral and ethical standards, and ultimately a lower living standard and misery for all the people" (Geis, 1972, p. 229).

Such strongly stated views about upholding social "moral and ethical standards" distract the reader from the core tenet that laws create standards of behavior which are often intended to protect people and not to simply to keep them in the fold of one religious group or another.

In considering in detail four victimless crimes—prostitution, drug use, gambling, and assisted suicide—the question of harm and the debate between individual rights and state interests in preserving standards could be concretely understood. In contemporary terms, the debate over prostitution concerns women's status in society and the decisions that people may be given a right to make, but which are shaped by childhood sexual abuse, drug dependence, and lack of legitimate options. The question of legalizing more drugs most clearly raises the issue of whether legal controls, however inspired by public health concerns, might cause more harm than would decriminalization. In considering gambling, one issue first raised two centuries ago is the victimization of the poor by state-run lotteries. Finally, in considering legalization of assisted suicide, the needs of the terminally ill for a dignified death were weighed against the position that legalization would lead to further victimization of the poor and disempowered.

None of these issues gives rise to easy solutions except within a political polemic. There really are no victimless crimes, but there are political decisions that are made by every generation that must not only fully take into account the harm to specific individuals but also define society in the future as both as a protector and creator of victims.

References

Advocacy Committee for Women's Concerns to the 211th General Assembly. (1999). *Prostitution in the United States.* Available at www.horeb.pcusa.org/oga/diversity/advocom.htm.

American Civil Liberties Union. (2000). *ACLU Briefing paper: Against drug prohibition.* Available at www.aclu.org/library/pbp19.html.

American Psychiatric Association. (2000). *Diagnostic and Statistical Manual–IV–TR.* Washington, DC: American Psychiatric Association.

Bennett, W. (1997). In Close Up Foundation. *U.S. drug policy.* Available at www.closeup.org/drugs.htm.

Borg, M. O., Mason, P. M., and Shapiro, S. L. (1991, July). The incidence of taxes on casino gambling: Exploiting the tired and poor. *American Journal of Economics and Sociology,* 50(30): 323–332.

Clark, D. C. (1992). Rational suicide and people with terminal conditions or disabilities. *Issues in Law and Medicine,* 8, 147–166.

Committee on the Social and Economic Impact of Pathological Gambling. (1999). *Pathological Gambling: A critical review.* Available at www.nap.edu/html/pathological_gambling.

Defoe, D. (1703). *A Hymn to the Pillory.* Reprinted in J. T. Boulton (Ed.) (1975), *Selected Writings of Daniel Defoe.* London: Cambridge University Press.

de Plessis, Y. (1996). *The prostitution dilemma: International trends facing up to it.* Available at yesunet.org/nagcs/p/dilema.htm.

Dunstan, R. (1997). *Gambling.* Available at www.library.ca.gov/CRB/97/003.

Facts on File News Services. (1997, July 3). Justices uphold states' rights to ban doctor-assisted suicide. *Facts on File World News Digest.*

Farley, M., and Hotaling, N. J. (1995, April 16). Research study of prostitutes. *San Franciso Examiner,* 485.

Feinberg, J. (1984). *Harm to Others.* New York: Oxford University Press.

Fullilove, M. T., Lown, A., and Fullilove, R. (1992). Crack ho's and skeezers: Traumatic experience of women crack users. *The Journal of Sex Research,* 29, 275–287.

Geis, G. (1972). *Not the Law's Business?* Rockville, MD: National Institute of Mental Health.

Heyman, G. M. (1996). Resolving the contradictions of addiction. *Behavioral and Brain Sciences,* 19, 561–610.

Houser, M. (1999, August 22). Most-loyal bettors have least to spare. *Tribune–Review.* Available at www.triblive.com/news/lottery/lott0822.html.

Hoyert, D. L., Kochanek, K. D., and Murphy, S. L. (1999). Deaths: Final data for 1997. *National Vital Statistics Report,* 47(19). Hyattsville, MD: National Center for Health Statistics.

Jacobson, J. L. (1992, May/June). The other epidemic. *World Watch,* 10–17.

James, J. (1977). *Prostitutes and Prostitution.* New York: General Learning.

Jellineck, E. M. (1960). *The Disease Concept of Alcoholism.* New Haven, CT: Hillhouse.

King, R. (1957, Winter). Narcotic drug laws and enforcement policies. *Law and Contemporary Problems.*

Kolata, G. (1997, June 24). Anguished debate: Should doctors help their patients die? *New York Times,* C4.

Lambert, B. (1988, September). AIDS in prostitutes, not as prevalent as believed, studies find. *New York Times,* C1.

Levine, E. M., and Kanin, E. J. (1987). Sexual violence among dates and acquaintences: Trends and their implications for marriage and family. *Journal of Family Violence,* 2, 55–65.

Mill, J. S. (1859). *On Liberty.* London: Classic Library.

National Institute of Mental Health. (2000). In harm's way: Suicide in America. NIH Publication No. 01–4594. Available at http://www.nimh.nih.gov.

Office of Applied Studies, Substance Abuse and Mental Health Administration (SAMHSA). (2000). *Summary of findings from the 1999 National Household Survey on Drug Abuse.* Available at www.health.org/pubs/nhsda/99hhs.

Office of Justice Programs, United States Department of Justice. (1994, September). *Drugs and Crime Data,* NCJ–149286. Washington, DC: U.S. Department of Justice.

Office of National Drug Control Policy. (2001). Drug facts. Available at http://www.whitehouse-drugpolicy.gov/drugfact/index.html.

Parriott, R. (1994). Health experiences of Twin Cities women used in prostitution. In J. G. Raymond (1998), *Health effects of prostitution.* Available at www.uri.edu/artsci/wms/hughs/catw/health.htm.

Prostitutes' Education Network. (2000). *Prostitution in the United States—The statistics.* Available at www.bayswan.org/stats/htm.

Raymond, J. G. (1998). *Health effects of prostitution.* Available at www.uri.edu/artsci/wms/hughes/catw/health.htm.

Rehnquist, W. J. (1997, June 27). The State has an interest in preventing suicide . . . and treating its causes. *Washington Post,* 18.

Richards, D. A. J. (1982). *Sex, Drugs, Death, and the Law.* Totowa, NJ: Rowman and Littlefield.

San Francisco Task Force on Prostitution. (1996). *Final report 1996.* Available at www.bayswan.org/7quality.html.

Schur, E. M., and Bedau, H. A. (1974). *Victimless Crimes: Two Sides of a Controversy.* Englewood, NJ: Prentice Hall.

Scott, G. (1936). *A History of Prostitution from Antiquity to the Present Day.* New York: AMS.

Shapiro, J. P. (1996, January 15). America's gambling fever. *U.S. News and World Report,* 58, 60.

Simonsen, J. N., Plummer, F. A., Ngugi, E. N., Black, C., Kreiss, J. K., Gakinya, M. N., Waiyaki, P. D., Costa, L. J., Ndinya–Achola, J. O., Piot, P., and Ronald, A. (1990). HIV infection among lower socioeconomic strata prostitutes in Nairobi. *AIDS,* 4, 139–144.

Smith, W. (1997) *Forced Exit: The Slippery Slope from Assisted Suicide to Legalized Murder.* New York: Random House.

Sourcebook of Criminal Justice Statistics. (1995). Available at www.albany.edu/sourcebook/1995/pdf/t41.pdf.

Suicide and Crisis Center. (2000). *Suicide facts & statistics*. Available at www.sccenter.org/facts.html.

Task Force on Life and the Law. (2000). *When Death Is Sought—Assisted Suicide and Euthanasia in the Medical Context*. Available at www.health.state.ny.us/nysdoh/consumer/patient.

UNICEF. (1997). *The State of the World's Children*. New York: UNICEF.

U.S. Department of Justice, Drug Enforcement Agency. (2000). *Drug use in the United States*. Available at www.usdoj.gov/dea/concern/use.htm.

Walker, G. (2000). *Venereal disease and sexual immorality in Victorian Britain*. Available at www.geocities.com/historicom/VD.htm.

Winick, C., and Kinsie, P. M. (1971). *The Lively Commerce: Prostitution in the United States*. Chicago: Quadrangle.

PART IV

RESPONSES
TO VICTIMIZATION

CHAPTER 16

A Constitutional Amendment for Victims
The Unexplored Possibility

Jennifer Eastman

Introduction

October 1995. The words "not guilty" stun the country. The verdict in the O. J. Simpson criminal trial for the murders of Nicole Brown, his ex-wife, and Ron Goldman made some spectators jubilant, others, angry and morose. All wondered whether the trial had been fair, particularly for the victims. But who were they? The African American community, the LAPD, or even Simpson? Or the Browns and the Goldmans, the families of the murder victims? Fred Goldman, Ron's father, did not believe the trial had been fair, and he stated after the verdict was announced that justice had not been served.

February 1997. O. J. Simpson is found liable for the wrongful deaths of Nicole Brown and Ron Goldman and ordered to pay their surviving relatives over $30 million. Again, the country is stunned, this time by the civil trial's verdict. Some again wondered whether the trial had been fair, particularly here to Simpson. Fred Goldman, now the victor, pronounced that justice had been done at long last.

Was the civil trial necessary to obtain this result? Did the fact that Simpson, protected by the Fifth Amendment, did not have to testify in the criminal trial but was forced to speak in the civil trial make a difference in the outcome? What if, in addition to constitutional safeguards for defendants, there had been a constitutional amendment in place for the victims? Would the history of the O. J. Simpson case have been any different? Would justice for all concerned have been served?

My way of answering these questions will be slightly circuitous, for responses can only emerge after a full exploration of the crime victim's role in the legal system itself. First, I trace the history of crime victims within various legal systems. I next explore the rights of victims in the United States with particular emphasis on those obtained during the last 25 years, paying close attention to the use of victim impact statements in sentencing, and the U.S. Supreme Court's role in advancing or inhibiting victims' rights. I focus on two Supreme Court cases, *Booth v. Maryland* and *Payne v. Tennessee*. Next, I make some conjectures about a constitutional amendment for victims and its potential advantages and disadvantages.

Legal Rights of Victims throughout the Ages

Since ancient Greece, where the Greeks paid death fines to the families of murder victims, there has been a history of compensation for the victims of crime. Under Anglo-Saxon rule in Britain centuries later, a criminal was fined, required to pay one portion to the victim's clan and the rest to the king for violating the king's peace (Frank, 1992). But it was in the intervening years, before any court system appeared and the king's power was firmly established, that the so-called golden age of the victim occurred. During this period, the victim of a crime established justice by engaging in feuds against the wrongdoer. "Victims and their relatives controlled the extent of retribution and consequently, the extent of their satisfaction with the punishment meted out to the offender" (McShane and Williams, 1992, p. 260). This resort to personal vengeance became such a threat to the well-being of society that eventually the state had to interfere. Criminal violations thereafter became violations against the king's peace, and save for the fines to which they became entitled under this system, the victim's role in meting out justice began to fade. Eventually even the fines were abolished and the victim was relegated to being merely a witness at a criminal trial (McShane and Williams, 1992).

Only rarely has the victim assumed a larger role in the criminal justice system since. In colonial America, for example, victims briefly assumed the prosecutorial role. They paid for the arrest warrants, investigated the crime, and hired a private attorney to draw up the indictment and prosecute the defendant (Davis, Kunreuther, and Connick, 1984). The goal of the legal system then was to compensate the victim. But gradually incarceration and punishment replaced restitution as a goal, and the victim's role as an instigator and financial support for the prosecution shifted back to the state. In part, the state was assuming its by-then traditional role of protecting society's peace. The state also took on the victims' tasks in an attempt to insulate the victim from the accused and to remove the burden of prosecution from the victim (Dolliver, 1987). After this time, the victim became a mere witness at the trial of the accused once more.

During the mid-twentieth century, victims tired of this passive role and wanted to change it. In the 1940s and 1950s, the science of victimology was recognized, and with it came recognition of the victims themselves (Carrington and Nicholson, 1989). And the victims? They were dissatisfied with a system which seemed to care more for defendants' rights than the wrongs endured by the victims. They were joined, if not led in these concerns, by political conservatives who in actuality cared more about limiting the rights of defendants than assuring that crime victims be heard (Davis and Smith, 1994). Whatever the motivation of those who clamored for victims' rights, the "victims' rights" movement soon became an integral part of the criminal justice system.

The first widely acknowledged right of victims was compensation. In the 1960s, the federal government began to fund programs which would compensate crime victims (Cuomo, 1992). In 1965, California became the first state to enact legislation to compensate victims of violent crime. In 1982, the federal government passed the Victim and Witness Protection Act, which allowed restitution for losses caused by criminal conduct. By 1988, at least 23 states had enacted legislation that permitted restitution in similar circumstances as the federal statute, and today, all states have some form of victim compensation legislation for criminal cases (Frank, 1992).

Rights other than compensation have been slower to receive recognition. In 1979, Wisconsin enacted the first Victim Bill of Rights (Carrington and Nicholson, 1989). In the next 10 years, 44 states prepared and passed similar bills. More recently, Rhode Island became the first state to amend its constitution to include victims in the criminal process. The amendment asserts that victims of crime have a right to be treated by officers of the state with dignity, respect, and sensitivity throughout the criminal justice process (Carrington and Nicholson, 1989). Other states have followed suit. One of the most extensive grants of victims' rights in existence today is in South Carolina. There, victims of crime have their own bill of rights protected by "law enforcement agencies, prosecutors, and judges in a manner no less vigorous than the protections afforded criminal defendants" (Hall, 1991, p. 239). These rights include making recommendations about pretrial release, making a victim impact statement regarding sentencing or any disposition hearing, and most unusual, having an attorney who shall have standing in the procedure to guarantee that a victim's right to due process is enforced, and the right to a speedy trial. A statute like this seems all encompassing, but it is seldom enforced to the fullest extent possible, and is the exception and not the rule.

The most noteworthy of the federal laws enacted for victims' rights is the Victim and Witness Protection Act of 1982, mentioned above. Part of the act provides for victim participation in sentencing. The federal law says that the victim statement at the time of sentencing shall include any financial, social, psychological, and medical harm (done to the victim) and shall give any other information that helps the court in determining the restitution needs of the victim (Posner, 1984). The main advantages in allowing such statements are that it gives the victim a role in the proceedings against her or his offender (other than as a mere witness at trial) and at the same time allows the court a "more rounded view" of the offense (Ashworth, 1993). Here, the participation of the victim can optimally create a more just result. The disadvantage comes when this participation may so inflame the jury that it becomes distracted from its task and may act too harshly when sentencing the defendant (Meek, 1992).

By 1987, 48 states had enacted legislation which allows for victim participation in sentencing (Davis and Smith, 1994). These statements, when allowed, generally include the following types of information: the circumstances of the crime, the identity and characteristics of the victim, the level of harm suffered by the victim, and the victim's opinion of the defendant and the sentence that should be meted out (Ashworth, 1993). The different states vary in terms of how much weight should be given to these statements. Some statutes require that judges take the victim's statements into consideration when passing sentence on the defendant, others, that judges merely consider statements along with other factors (Talbert, 1988). Some states, as in South Carolina, for example, as noted above, have gone further than just allowing the victim a say in the sentencing process. Overall, the right of the victim to make statements at sentencing is second only to their right to receive compensation.

The U.S. Supreme Court and Victims' Rights

During the last 25 years, the courts have played a mixed role in supporting this legislation and thereby, victims' rights. In a 1973 case, *Linda R. S. v. Richard D.*, the U.S. Supreme Court held that victims had no standing in criminal proceedings. This case concerned the mother of an illegitimate child who sought to enforce a criminal statute against the child's father for child support. The statute in question provided that only fathers of legitimate children were subject to prosecution. Therefore, the prosecutor refused to enforce the statute. Subsequently, the mother brought a class action suit on behalf of all mothers of illegitimate children. The Supreme Court held that while the mother doubtless has an interest in obtaining support for her child, such an interest would not be fostered if the statute were enforced: The statute mandated that the man go to jail. From that position, he obviously could provide no support for the mother or the child. The Court held that, because there was no connection between the relief sought and the result which would occur if the mother were successful in her prosecution, the mother (the victim, here) lacked standing to bring suit.

Ten years later, however, the Supreme Court, now with different members, expressed more interest in the position of victims in the case of *Morris v. Slappy*. Here, the victim, a young woman, left her apartment to go to the corner grocery store. At the store, she was accosted by the defendant, whom she did not know. She complained to the store manager and he told the defendant to leave. When the victim left the store, she found the defendant waiting for her outside, where he threw a beer bottle at her. She immediately went back into the store and asked the store manager to call the police. The store manager refused and told the victim just to walk away from the defendant. She started to head toward home, walking the long way back to her apartment building. There, she found the defendant waiting for her in the lobby. He forced her down to the basement, where he raped and robbed her. The victim managed to escape and fled to an all-night diner where she called the police. They arrested the defendant and charged him with five felonies.

The interaction between the defendant and his attorneys became the basis for the subsequent legal action. The defendant was first assigned to a public defender. Six days before trial, the case was reassigned to a more senior public defender when the first attorney had to undergo surgery. This second attorney declared that he was ready to proceed to trial. At the trial, the defendant was convicted of some counts, acquitted of others, and a mistrial was declared on the remaining counts. The mistrial led to a retrial, with the same senior attorney defending the accused. In this trial, the accused, apparently angered by the results of the first trial, refused to cooperate with his attorney. When the defendant was convicted, he appealed on the grounds that he had been deprived of his Sixth Amendment right to the effective assistance of counsel. The Court of Appeals agreed with the defendant by coining a new standard for attorney assistance. It stated that because of the short and rushed time in which the client and attorney had known each other at the first trial, they had not been able to establish a "meaningful" relationship. The court granted the defendant a third trial. The state appealed to the U.S. Supreme Court, which reversed the Appeals Court decision. More interesting than the reversal, however, were several observations made by the Court about the victim. These had not been solicited by any of the arguments before the Court. The Court stated that "in its haste to create a novel Sixth Amendment right [The Court had no patience with the very phrase "meaningful relationship"], the [Appeals] Court wholly failed to take into account the interest of the victim of these crimes in not undergoing the ordeal of yet a third trial in the case" (*Morris v. Slappy*, 1983, p. 14). Fearing that if the criminal justice system ignored the victims, they would hesitate to come forward with complaints in the future, the Court went on to say that it was not sure what weight should be given to the victim's ordeal of having to relive a humiliating and traumatic experience such as this had been, but that that factor should not be ignored by the courts in the future.

The Supreme Court has had no opportunity since *Morris v. Slappy* to decide what weight should be given to the victim's interest in this particular context. It has, however, addressed the problem of victim participation in sentencing in two cases, *Booth v. Maryland* (1987) and *Payne v. Tennessee* (1991), both capital cases in which the victims were allowed to express their opinions during the sentencing phase of the trial.

The facts in *Booth v. Maryland* were as follows. Allegedly John Booth and an accomplice, Willie Reid, entered the victim's home for the purpose of stealing money to obtain heroin. When Booth, a neighbor of the victims, realized that they could identify him, he and his accomplice bound and gagged the elderly victims, brutally stabbing them innumerable times in the chest with a kitchen knife. Booth was charged with and found guilty of the murder of Irwin Bronstein, aged 78, and his wife, Rose, aged 75.

The Bronsteins' son, daughter, son-in-law, and granddaughter contributed to the Victim Impact Statement during the sentencing phase of Booth's trial. The son stated that he currently suffered from lack of sleep and depression and was "fearful for the first time in his life." He believed that his parents were "butchered like animals." The daughter said that she also suffered from lack of sleep and, since the murders, had become withdrawn and distrustful. The granddaughter told how the death had marred the wedding of a close family member who, instead of going away on a honeymoon after the ceremony, had attended the funeral of the victims. The granddaughter herself received counseling for several months but then quit going when she became convinced that no one could help her. All of the witnesses testified to the exemplary character of the Bronsteins. The Victim Impact Statement concluded with the following:

> The murder of Mr. and Mrs. Bronstein is still such a shocking, painful, and devastating memory to them (the victim survivors) that it permeates every aspect of their daily lives. It is doubtful that they will ever be able to fully recover from this tragedy and not be haunted by the memory of the brutal manner in which their loved ones were murdered and taken from them. (*Booth v. Maryland,* 1987, p. 500)

Booth was sentenced to death for the murder of Mr. Bronstein and to life imprisonment for the murder of Mrs. Bronstein. Booth appealed his conviction and sentences on the grounds that the admission of the victim impact statement into evidence introduced an arbitrary and prejudicial factor into the sentencing process. He contended that the statement inflamed the jury by design, so as to divert its attention away from a decision based on reason rather than "emotion and caprice." In a five-to-four decision, the narrowest of margins, the Supreme Court agreed. It said that emphasis on the victim's character and the allowance of victims' statements from those who were particularly articulate, as were the witnesses here, resulted in arbitrary and unprincipled decisions in all cases. For example, in another case the victim's character might not be so praiseworthy or the surviving victims so articulate and cogent in their presentation of the impact of the crime. In such a case, and because of these factors, the jury might be more sympathetic to the defendant than it had been in *Booth* and decide in favor of life rather than death. To allow the introduction in all cases of these victim impact statements was to open the door to the arbitrary, emotional, and capricious decisions forbidden by justice in general, and in death penalty cases in particular, under the Eighth Amendment.

Four years later in 1991, in *Payne v. Tennessee,* the Supreme Court had the opportunity to review this issue again. The case concerned the actions of one Pervis Payne. On a Saturday in June 1987, Payne spent the day injecting cocaine and drinking beer. At three in the afternoon, he came to the Christophers' apartment, which was across the hall from his girlfriend's apartment. He started to make advances toward Charisse Christopher, aged 28, and when she resisted, he became violent. Neighbors heard screams and called the police. When the police arrived, they found the walls and floors of Christopher's apartment covered with blood. Charisse and her two children were lying on the kitchen floor. Charisse had sustained 42 knife wounds to her body; her daughter Lacie had sustained stab wounds to her chest, abdomen, back, and head. Both of them were dead. Her three-year-old son, Nicholas, despite sustaining knife wounds which went clear through his body, was still alive. After undergoing seven hours of surgery, Nicholas survived.

The police later apprehended Payne, who was then tried and convicted of two counts of first-degree murder and one count of assault with intent to commit murder in the first degree. At the sentencing phase of the trial, Charisse's mother spoke about how deeply affected Nicholas was by the loss of his mother and sister. When asked how Nicholas had been affected specifically, she said:

> He cries for his mom. He doesn't seem to understand why she doesn't come home. And he cries for his sister Lacie. He comes to me many times during the week and asks "Grandmamma, do you miss my Lacie?" And I tell him yes. He says "I'm worried about my Lacie." (*Payne v. Tennessee,* 1991, pp. 814–815)

In addition to this testimony from a relative of the victim, in his closing arguments, the prosecutor made lengthy comments about the continuing effects of the crime on Nicholas.

> Nicholas was in the same room. Nicholas was still conscious. . . . So he knew what happened to his mother and baby sister. . . . While there is nothing you can do for many of those associated with the crime, there is something you can do for Nicholas. . . . Somewhere down the road Nicholas is going to grow up, hopefully. He's going to want to know what

happened. . . . He is going to want to know what type of justice was done. . . . With your verdict, you will provide an answer. . . . (*Payne v. Tennessee,* 1991, p. 815)

The jury sentenced Payne to death. He appealed, claiming that the admission of such statements was prejudicial and violated his rights under the Eighth Amendment as applied in *Booth v. Maryland.* Given the decision in *Booth,* he certainly not only hoped but also expected that the Supreme Court would agree. It did not. Justice William Rehnquist, writing for the majority, stated that *Booth* had weighted the scales in favor of the defendant. Here, he and the rest of the majority wanted to tip back the balance in favor of the victim. Justice Antonin Scalia, who wrote a concurring opinion, argued that by admitting these statements, there was a parity achieved between the status of the defendant and that of the victim (*Payne v. Tennessee,* 1991, pp. 833–835). The majority believed that excluding such evidence placed the state at an unfair disadvantage and deprived the jury of essential information needed to determine the proper punishment, one of the advantages of the allowance in of such evidence mentioned above. The majority concluded that if the information contained in the victim's statement was too inflammatory, and thus overly prejudicial to the rights of the defendant, the judge could always intervene and decide to exclude it.

With *Payne,* the Court gave the admission of victim impact statements a much needed boost in both capital and noncapital cases. In terms of the sheer brutality of the murders, there was little to distinguish *Booth* from *Payne.* In the latter case, however, the Court, with new members since the decision in *Booth,* and a renewed sense of outrage against criminal defendants and compassion for the victims, allowed the statements. The Court believed that the admission of such statements would permit the victims to heal, and create a more just result. But over time, the Supreme Court has wavered in its support of victims' rights. Thus, one must ask if what the Court says makes much difference to victims.

Surprisingly, no. The very usefulness of such victim impact statements to help the victims believe that justice has been done and enable them to get on with their lives, both before and after *Payne,* has often been called into question. Some have said that the right to submit a victim impact statement may be high in profile, but low in creating genuine respect for victims (Ashworth, 1993). Others discuss how the victim impact statements are a relatively low-cost and noncontroversial way to involve the victim, but that they do little to create satisfaction with the justice system (Davis and Smith, 1994).

Those who consider victim impact statements mere window dressing on the entire issue of victims' rights believe that the criminal justice system knows nothing about the victims and does little to address their needs. For example, this side argues that the prosecutor may provide transportation so that the victim can testify, but does not consider that perhaps the victim needs counseling to recover from the trauma of the criminal event. Therefore, the prosecutor uses the victim's testimony as a means to an end with no genuine interest in how the crime continues to affect the victim. As has previously happened over time, the victim's role is once again reduced to that of mere witness (Erez, 1990).

Thus, far from feeling satisfied with their role in the criminal justice system, victims often feel frustrated and find that they are treated with little respect. Some have suggested that those within the system—the prosecutors, parole officers, and judges—need to be more sensitive to victim needs and that the statutory rights now extended to victims need to be more than just evidence that on occasion, the criminal justice system arbitrarily decided to be sensitive and sympathetic to victims (Eikenberry, 1987). As things currently stand, quite often victims feel frustrated because they believe they have something important to conribute that might affect the outcome of their case and then discover that no one is interested in listening to or considering their opinion (Erez, 1990). In all states at present, there are no enforcement mechanisms regarding victims and their rights. Thus, the victim has rights without remedies. This results in feelings of helplessness, lack of control, and further victimization (Davis and Smith, 1994). Victims' expectations are raised by statutory enactments and pronouncements by the courts, but seldom fulfilled. In many cases, consequently, the victims simply refuse to become involved in a system that does not care about them.

But an even more important factor in victim frustration is that victims often do not know what their rights are. One study has shown that the most important grievance expressed by victims was their lack of standing in the judicial process. A frequent complaint is heard: "I was the one raped (or beaten or robbed)—why didn't anyone consult me when the defendant was being prosecuted?" (Erez, 1990). Victims' rights as such currently exist in a no-man's-land. They are like defendant rights before the Miranda decision—the victim remains unclear that she or he has any rights and so the following statement becomes the norm: "If I don't know that I have rights under the law, I don't" (Wells, 1990, p. 27). When the defense in the O. J. Simpson trial diverted the jury's attention away from the alleged crimes of the defendant to the issue of alleged racism of prosecution witness Mark Fuhrman, what right did the highly offended Goldman family have within the courtroom to contest the diversion? None. Thus, even though the victim has been granted some statutory rights, in many instances these may not be upheld in a court of law (witness the contrasting results in *Booth* and *Payne*). In reality, the present victim rights are largely illusory.

Would an Amendment Work for Victims?

Would a constitutional amendment for victims solve this problem? Similar to the Supreme Court's vacillation concerning victims' rights, the popularity of even the suggestion of such an amendment has fluctuated with the times. Ronald Reagan was the first U.S. president to propose support for victims' rights and an amendment. During his first years as president, he established National Crime Victims Week in 1981 (Carrington and Nicholson, 1989). Then, in 1982, he established a Task Force on Victims' Rights. One of the recommendations of this body was a constitutional amendment that would extend rights to victims during criminal trials. Proposing that this amendment be attached to the Sixth Amendment, the task force wrote the following: "The victim has the right to be present and to be heard at all critical stages of judicial proceedings" (Roland, 1989). Congress took no action on the proposal. In 1986, the National Organization for Victim Assistance (NOVA) held a conference and suggested another amendment addressing the role of the victim in the criminal justice system. Here, proposing an entirely separate amendment, the organization wrote:

> Victims of crime are entitled to certain basic rights, including, but not limited to the right to be informed, to be present, and to be heard at all critical stages of the federal and state criminal process to the extent that these rights do not interfere with existing Constitutional rights. (Lambon, 1987, p. 130)

In its final vote at the conference, NOVA decided not to support either this proposed amendment or the task force's. One year later, a coalition of victims groups known as the Victims' Constitutional Network (Victims CAN) proposed yet a third alternative. This one varied slightly from NOVA's. It read:

> Victims of crime are entitled to certain basic rights including the right to be informed of, to be present at and to be heard at all critical stages of the criminal justice process, to the extent that these rights do not interfere with the constitutional rights of the accused. The legislature is authorized to enforce the amendment by appropriate enabling legislation. (Lambon, 1987, p. 132)

Nothing came of this proposal. Instead of working on a national level, Victims CAN urged its members to concentrate on making changes in state constitutions. Since 1987, there have been no new proposals or any action taken concerning a constitutional amendment for victims.

If established, what would an amendment for victims accomplish? First, to the extent that it is possible in our legal system, it would remove the issue of victims' rights from its dependence on a favorable political climate (Eikenberry, 1987). *Morris* occurred in 1983, a time when consciousness of victims' rights under the first Reagan administration was strong. *Payne* resulted in part because of a change in the membership of the Supreme Court. And, as was suggested earlier, the victims' rights movement may have been the product of conservatives' political will to begin with. During the presidential campaign of 1996, Bill

Clinton proposed passage of such an amendment. Once reelected, he said nothing more about it. In sum, the victim rights movement has been too subject to shifts in political priorities. A constitutional amendment might go far in insulating crime victims from having to depend on "a favorable political climate for their rights to be recognized" (Eikenberry, 1987, p. 49).

Second, a constitutional amendment might solve the question of standing, decided so emphatically against the victim in *Linda R. S. v. Richard D.*, and not addressed in most of the current statutes, in which most of the wording is subject to broad interpretation, such as one in Rhode Island requesting that victims be treated with dignity. How can such a request possibly be enforced or considered mandatory? The Victims CAN amendment proposal acknowledges this deficit when it talks about the enforcement mechanism. It leaves open, however, how such enforcement can come about.

Once removed from politics and granted legal standing, victims would still face the question of their rights versus the rights of the accused. *Payne* seemed to place victims on the same level as defendants, but in actuality as the Constitution currently reads, victims do not have the same rights as defendants. When the Bill of Rights was enacted, the writers, fresh from having thrown off the tyranny of the British government, feared oppression by any government. At that time, a person accused of a crime was at the mercy of a system weighted heavily in favor of the state (Eikenberry, 1987). Mindful that a defendant could be deprived of his liberty (if not his life) if found guilty, the authors of the Bill of Rights introduced the safeguard of due process to protect the defendant. It has been argued by some, that while the victim suffers from a variety of harms, loss of personal liberty in particular or sometimes life itself is not among them (Dolliver, 1987). Thus, there is some question whether the needs of the victim are as pressing as those of the defendant and should assume equal status under the Constitution.

Others believe that the criminal justice system has become so weighted in favor of the defendant that it is now time to redress the wrongs done to the victim by restoring some balance. These might argue that to be protected by the Constitution does not necessarily mean protection from a deprivation of liberty (Gewurz and Mercurio, 1992). Everybody, for example, is entitled to the protection of the First Amendment. The Supreme Court decisions in *Morris* and *Payne* aimed to equalize the rights of the victims and the defendants. In *Morris*, the Court said the victim should be considered; in *Payne*, Justice Scalia said that this decision brought the rights of the victims into balance with those of the defendants. But what does that balancing really mean? Both the NOVA and Victims CAN versions of the proposed amendment state that the rights granted to victims cannot interfere with those rights already guaranteed to defendants. If we suppose that such an amendment had been enacted prior to the O. J. Simpson trial, let us consider what might have taken place. The victims' families, the

Browns and the Goldmans, would have had the right to be present at trial and to be informed of the proceedings. This they had anyway. They might have had the right to be heard other than as witnesses only and even to object to evidence, such as the introduction of the issue of racism at trial. They could not, however, have forced O. J. Simpson to testify at the criminal trial. It was only at the civil trial in 1996–1997, where among other differences, O. J. Simpson did testify, that the Browns, Goldmans, and Simpson seemed to share the same level playing field. Given the phrasing of the current constitutional amendments as proposed, it is impossible to tell how parity between victim and defendant in the criminal justice system would be achieved. One commentator has examined the language of the proposed amendments with care and has found that each phrase is open to interpretation. He is quite critical of the proposals and their proponents and believes that the authors have not really thought through what they were doing to the extent that it could be seen just how much or how little such an amendment would change the criminal justice landscape in the United States (Lambon, 1987).

Another commentator has suggested a dire consequence of enacting such an amendment for victims. James Dolliver believes quite simply that such an amendment would reestablish a contest between the accused and the victim similar in nature to the blood feuds which existed during the supposed golden age of the victim. He contends that this possibility, instead of connoting progress, would be a regressive step, opening the door to a less civilized response to criminal behavior and society than we already have (Dolliver, 1987).

Conclusion

Blood feud and historical reversion, or moderate and temperate progress? Changes in the Constitution have always involved both. The Thirteenth, Fourteenth, and Fifteenth Amendments emerged from the bloody travails of the Civil War. Women's suffrage finally came after 60 years of struggles, setbacks, and upheavals (Flexner, 1959). Justice and notions of fairness always evolve from tumult and change. And what we have been talking about throughout this chapter is changing notions of fairness. It seemed fair at one point for the victim to seek personal vengeance against the wrongdoer. Then it seemed fair for the state to step in to prosecute the accused with ample safeguards to protect their rights against the power of the state, while insulating the victims from the process and further harm. Is it now time for the victims to enter the equation with a constitutional amendment which would promote a new, triangular form of justice between the state, the defendant, and the victim? This equation has not existed before. Are we prepared for or knowledgeable enough about the possible consequences of this new equation?

It is clear that, in the absence of constitutional and statutory protections which carry weight, whenever possible victims of crime can and will turn to the civil law to find some redress. The usual demarcations between criminal and civil law lose their distinction then, if the victims, such as the Goldmans and the Browns in the O. J. Simpson cases, can pursue justice in either court. As long as this possibility exists, the need for a constitutional amendment for victims of crime remains tenuous.

If this option of a civil remedy ceases to exist, then the questions raised here about the possibility of a constitutional amendment for victims of crime will reemerge and seek solution. But then, it is not at all clear that we will know the answers. Some people saw poetic justice in the O. J. Simpson criminal trial, in that there the police were seen as the culprits, whereas in the Rodney King trial that preceded it, the police were proved innocent of any wrongdoing. But such a view sees justice from a long-range and distanced perspective. Our aim as caretakers of the legal system should be to embody justice within our very institutions as they function within each case. Would a constitutional amendment for victims of crime make justice more real for all concerned—the O. J. Simpsons, the Browns, and the Goldmans, the criminal justice system and society at large? That is the important question, one that loses it import when it is only raised, as it is now, during presidential campaigns or celebrity trials. As long as the possibility of a constitutional amendment remains dependent upon such events, it is certain that a victims' rights amendment and the questions it poses will remain largely unexplored.

References

Ashworth, A. (1993). Victim impact statements and sentencing. *The Criminal Law Review*, 498–509.

Booth v. Maryland, 482 U.S. 496 (1987).

Carrington, F., and Nicholson, G. (1989). Victims rights: An idea whose time has come—Five years later: The maturing of an idea. *Pepperdine Law Review*, 17, 1–19.

Cuomo, M. (1992). The crime victim in a system of criminal justice. *St. John's Journal of Legal Commentary*, 8, 1–21.

Davis, R. C., Kunreuther, F., and Connick, E. (1984). Expanding the victim's role in the criminal court dispositional process. *Journal of Criminal Law and Criminology*, 75, 1–13.

Davis, R. C., and Smith, B. (1994). Victim impact statements and victim satisfaction: An unfulfilled promise. *Journal of Criminal Justice*, 22, 1–13.

Dolliver, J. M. (1987). Victims Rights Constitutional amendment: A bad idea whose time should not come. *Wayne Law Review*, 34, 87–93.

Eikenberry, K. (1987). Victims of crime/Victims of justice. *Wayne Law Review*, 34, 29–49.

Erez, E. (1990). Victim participation in sentencing: Rhetoric and reality. *Journal of Criminal Justice*, 18, 19–33.

Flexner, E. (1959). *Century of Struggle: The Woman's Rights Movement in the United States*. Cambridge, MA: Belknap Press of Harvard University Press.

Frank, L. F. (1992). The collection of restitution: An often overlooked service to crime victim. *St. John's Journal of Legal Commentary,* 8, 107–135.

Gewurz, D., and Mercurio, M. (1992). The Victims Bill of Rights: Are victims all dressed up with no place to go? *St. John's Journal of Legal Commentary,* 8, 251–279.

Hall, D. J. (1991). Victims' voices in criminal court: The need for restraint. *American Criminal Law Review,* 28, 233–256.

Lambon, L. L. (1987). Victim participation in the criminal justice process. *Wayne Law Review,* 34, 125–220.

Linda R. S. v. Richard D., 410 U.S. 614 (1973).

McShane, M. D., and Williams, F. P. (1992). Radical victimology: A critique of the concept of victim in traditional victimology. *Crime and Delinquency,* 38, 258–272.

Meek, E. A. (1992). Victim impact evidence and capital sentencing: A casenote on *Payne v. Tennesee. Louisiana Law Review,* 52, 1299–1311.

Morris v. Slappy, 461 U.S. 1 (1983).

Payne v. Tennessee, 501 U.S. 808 (1991).

Posner, A. K. (1984). Victim impact statements and restitution: Making the punishment fit the victim. *Brooklyn Law Review,* 50, 301–338.

Roland, D. L. (1989). Progress in the victim reform movement: No longer the forgotten victim. *Pepperdine Law Review,* 17, 35–59.

Talbert, P. A. (1988). The relevance of victim impact statements to the criminal sentencing decision. *UCLA Law Review,* 36, 199–232.

Wells, R. C. (1990). Considering victim impact: The role of probation. *Federal Probation,* 54 26–29.

CHAPTER 17

Police and Victims of Domestic Violence

Michael E. Buerger

Introduction

The police response to the problem of domestic violence, and their treatment of domestic violence victims in particular, has remained a thorny issue despite many advances in police education, training, and organizational reform during the last quarter of the twentieth century. Although the overall level of police services to domestic violence victims has improved, serious difficulties remain, often stemming from incidents of egregious deficiency in the police response.

This chapter revisits the issue conceptually, with four central (and testable) propositions, to suggest the need for a different research and policy focus.

1. Police officers and women's advocates define the problem of domestic violence from perceptions derived from their work, but they see two very different populations, which overlap to some unknown degree;
2. The stories that the advocates hear of egregious police conduct are true but not necessarily representative;
3. Overall, the police response to domestic violence is much improved over that of previous eras; and
4. It is possible that even achieving the maximum level of desired police service to victims of domestic violence will not fundamentally change the levels of repeat domestic violence, because in general the criminal justice option does not respond to victims' needs.

I write from a standpoint biased toward the police perspective, and derive material not from a purposive study or survey, but from a convenience sample of opportunistic encounters. The chapter does not report the results of a systematic study; it stems from observational research that includes a sustained participant–observation role with the Jersey City (NJ) Domestic Violence Crisis Intervention Teams (funded by the Office of Community-Oriented Policing Services) during the fall of 1997, and earlier participant–observation work with the Minneapolis RECAP (Repeat Call Address Policing) Unit from 1987 through 1990. The chapter reviews the recent history of domestic violence responses, addresses the main propositions in turn, and examines the policy ramifications of change.

Domestic Violence: History

The move to criminalize domestic violence was conducted in the political arena, part of a larger movement—then known as "women's liberation" and now called feminism—that sought equal treatment for women across a broad spectrum of legal and social dimensions. One specific goal was to eliminate the double standard in the application of criminal law regarding assault: the assumption that violence between intimate partners or family relationships was "a private matter" and not the concern of the state. Though felony-level violence usually was treated as such, and some misdemeanor violence led to arrest as well, the modal police response to so-called family fights was to either counsel the disputants and leave (sometimes with a threat that "if we have to come back, somebody's going to jail") or send one of them—usually the husband or boyfriend—out of the residence for a short time to "cool off."

The police saw domestic violence as an intransigent problem, beyond the power of the police to cure or change (see, e.g., Westley, 1970, pp. 60–61, and Wilson, 1968, pp. 132–138). From that perspective, the primary difficulty stemmed from the victim's refusal to do anything to change her situation. Either she actively interfered when the police arrested her batterer (e.g., Westley, 1970, pp. 60–61), or she withdrew her cooperation later, asking that charges be dropped or simply failing to appear in court to testify. (This is not a police view alone; prosecutors and battered women's advocates have observed, and lamented, the same phenomenon.)

Another element in the situation was the use of the term "domestic," through which the adjective used to describe the relationship between disputants took on the character of a noun. Unlike "Robbery in Progress" or "Disorderly Conduct" or "Burglary of Residence," in the language of dispatch codes, the term "Domestic" cued the officers to the relationship between the actors more than the type of event to which they were responding. Usually it was applied uncritically to the entire range of events that could occur in the relationship, from felony-level violence against a spouse, to loud disagreements between couples, to requests for help with a child's acting-out, to a request for police presence to prevent interference when one half of a couple attempted to leave or retrieve property. So many domestic calls did not involve violence that the violent calls blended in to the larger picture. In the police operational shorthand, "Domestic" became a synonym for "a persistent, irritating dispute, with no real solution, to which we will come back again regardless of what we do now." In the normal workplace environment, for many officers that was reason enough for doing as little as necessary.

Looking across their collective experiences handling domestics, officers concluded that victims did not want a formal justice system response; they just wanted the violence to end. Within that conceptual framework, the police response consisted of restoring order, either by minimal counseling or by sending one or the other party from the residence for a while. If the male was present, he was usually the one who left, unless the victim herself wanted to leave. Arrests were made in cases of serious violence, when the assault continued in the presence of the officers, or when the officers came under attack. In rare cases—if the victim was adamant about the arrest, either making a citizen's arrest or going to swear out a warrant—arrests were made for offenses that otherwise would have been ignored.

In addition to those actions, or if the offender was no longer at the scene, officers would advise the victim of the steps she needed to take to use her criminal justice system options (go to the courthouse tomorrow, swear out a warrant, bring it to the police station, testify in hearings and in the trial, etc.), and encourage her to seek additional support from family, friends, or social service agencies. If the victim would not cooperate with the police or criminal justice system, it was taken as further proof of the illegitimacy of the complaint (and of the police role in handling such "family matters").

In important ways, the requirements of law dictated the police response. Procedural law restricted police arrest powers: Officers could make an arrest on probable cause for a crime they did not personally witness only in the event of a felony. Misdemeanor arrests could be made when the act occurred in the officers' presence, but most domestic assaults were over by the time the police arrived. Unless the victim pursued the matter, there was no legal action the police *could* take in many cases. At times, despite assistance from the police, even aggressive pursuit of justice by victims failed: The inability to find a judge to issue a warrant or a restraining order late at night, or on weekends, was (and in some areas still is) a common experience for police officers. Challenged by women's advocates about their failure to treat familial or intimate violence on an equal footing with stranger assault, the police responded (correctly, if sometimes with crocodile tears) that "their hands were tied," as the law did not allow them to take the actions demanded by the advocates.

For many, of course, that was a convenient excuse: Most officers despised domestic calls, and they were often supported by sergeants who also had hated domestics when they were patrol officers. From the supervisory standpoint, "handle the call"—quiet the dispute—"and get out" (to be ready for calls considered more important) was the performance standard expected of officers. Taking their cue from those organizational priorities, many officers made informal policy decisions that effectively eliminated positive police response to the domestic call. Because on-scene supervision was rare, a common dodge was to recode the call GOA, or "Gone on Arrival," regardless of whether there was contact with an offender or victim. Delayed police response was a guild technique passed on to new officers during their informal orientation to the shift: drive slowly to the scene, in the hopes that "it will be over by the time we get there" and thus make enforcement action unnecessary (see, e.g., Reiss, 1971; Black, 1980, p. 146).

There were worse responses, too, although they tended to be individual rather than collective attitudes. Some (male) officers of earlier eras actively sided with the male, defending the masculinist right to use coercive violence within the relationship, and often refusing to aid the victim despite obvious need. (In recent years, too, the police establishment has begun to recognize, and deal with, the previously hidden problem of domestic violence *by* police officers, in part as a consequence of the passage of federal legislation requiring that persons convicted of domestic violence be deprived of their right to own and carry firearms.) Even as women entered the field as patrol officers, the anticipated change in attitude toward victims did not always materialize (though the author has never heard a woman officer defend the "right" of the male to beat his wife or partner, as he has sometimes heard from male officers). The old folk-caution about women jurors being less sympathetic to rape victims than men jurors has an analogy here as well: Women police officers, too, despair over the lack of assertiveness on the part of victims of domestic violence, and are equally prone to conclude that "there is little the police can do to help them if they won't help themselves."

CHANGES IN THE LAW

Women's advocates recognized the legal limitations on police powers, and lobbied for legislation that would change them. Arguing that the continuing nature of domestic violence required special recognition and consideration to protect victims, the advocates sought two main changes in the police response. The first was to give the police the power to make arrests based on probable cause for misdemeanor-level domestic violence (the arrest power usually was limited to a specific time period following the initial offense, which was four hours in the jurisdictions where the author has worked). The second was to remove or curtail the discretion to not make an arrest, a power that the advocates felt had been widely abused.

The new domestic violence laws of the late 1970s and 1980s actually expanded police powers of arrest, which victims' advocates wanted, and in almost any other area that would be viewed as a positive development by the police as well. However, that change simultaneously placed a substantially greater burden on police agencies, and limited officer autonomy in important ways. Furthermore, the new power had not come at the request of the police themselves, but was imposed on them from outside the police culture (indeed, from a group which often was publicly critical of the police), so the unanticipated end result was that many police officers regarded the change as a negative.

Misplaced in the debates about the efficacy and necessity of arrest was a recognition that the legalistic basis of the argument that "there's nothing we can do" was merely a convenient excuse. Samuel Walker (1999) speaks of "the myth of full enforcement" (pp. 197–198), an acknowledgment that the police cannot and do not enforce all laws equally and fully, but do so in discretionary fashion that stems from individual officers' "intuitive grasp of situational exigencies" (Bittner, 1970, p. 46). That "intuitive grasp," in the case of domestics, was the understanding that no matter how skillfully applied, the criminal justice option would not be pursued by most victims of domestic violence. Police attitude toward domestics was dictated by the cumulative weight of the individual behaviors they observed, not by the law. When the law changed, the underlying behavior did not, and thus the police attitude remained largely the same.

Legal elements alone (such as the "probable cause" standard) are not the determining factor in whether a police officer will make an arrest. Many scholars of the police have noted, directly or obliquely, that the police power of discretion is often exercised to not make an arrest, even in cases where legal factors present would justify the action. In one of the first modern studies of police behavior, Reiss (1971) found

> a high probability an officer will not make an arrest when he satisfies probable cause. Our observations of citizen initiated encounters with the police, for example, show that officers decided not to make arrests of one or more suspects for 43 percent of all felonies and 52 percent of all misdemeanors judged by observers as situations where an arrest could have been made on probable cause. Something other than probable cause is required, then, for the police to make an arrest.
>
> For the police, that something else is a *moral belief* that the law should be enforced and the violation sanctioned by the criminal-justice system. . . . All in all, an officer not only satisfies probable cause but also concludes after his careful observation that *the suspect is guilty and an arrest is therefore just.* (pp. 134–135; italics in original)

Black (1980) examined other elements in the decision-making process: The differential social status of the participants, the role of the complainant (including status, preference, and deference to the officer), and the seriousness of the offense all contributed to an essentially moral decision. The social distance between the complainant and the suspect, another of Black's arrest determinants, is the one most critical to domestic violence: The closer the relationship, the less likely the police are to arrest.

Police objection to handling domestics with anything more than a *de minimus* response was based on their assessment of victim behavior: If the victim was unwilling to participate in the criminal justice option, an arrest was not just. Many police officers also express a moral objection to probable cause requirements that are based solely on the victim's perceptions. They feel that victims' fear alone is simply not enough to justify an arrest. It is based not in actual conduct, but in a perception of future conduct—"I'm afraid of what he *might* do," a threshold of probable cause not accepted in other areas of the criminal law[1]—and seems to open the door for victims to illegitimately use the police as a tool for relationship management (Reiss, 1989; Mace, 1997). That objection is magnified when a more expansive definition of intimate violence is involved, including dating relationships, couples of the same sex, persons whose "relationship" lasted only long enough to conceive a child.

Another element in the issue was that of police autonomy. The same moral basis for not making an arrest was the basis for deciding to arrest. It is a point of pride in police culture generally that police experience bestows the power to sort the sheep from the goats: A police officer simply knows who deserves to be arrested and who does not. Any law, policy, or directive that trespasses on that sovereign power is resented, and mandatory arrest laws were a direct encroachment. Even "presumptive arrest" laws, which do not require arrest as a matter of statute, but require written documentation of why arrests were not made, are resented because of their symbolic expression of distrust. They are a constant expression of a social belief that the police officer cannot be trusted to do his or her job without constant oversight. In short, they are a continuing insult to the police self-image as a competent professional. That general rubric was intensified by the domestic violence laws, which in the minds of many police officers represented not a social consensus, but the particular agenda of a small, radical group that had inexplicably acquired political clout: the women's advocates.

Formal Organizational Responses

Despite some superficial similarities, a broad range of personalities do police work, although they are often more conservative than the proponents of social change or governmental restraint who foster the changes in the police working environment. Police administrators must guide the full spectrum of individual responses into a consistent set of responses that reflect the stated policy of the agency.

When the law changes, police agencies issue new operational directives, or alter existing ones, to reflect the new legal standard. Beyond that paper exercise are substantial issues of training, supervision, monitoring, and evaluation to ensure that the policies are actually being observed. Both individually and collectively, police officers have the capacity to ignore, subvert, and twist both the logic and the application of the law to suit their own interpretations of "justice." Consciously or subliminally, all police officers and executives know that several factors insulate them from any possible repercussions for noncompliance: (1) Full enforcement of all laws is not possible, and there is "wiggle room" in all but the most public of cases; (2) the low visibility of policing makes it extremely unlikely that any official version of events will be successfully challenged (the videotape of the beating of Rodney King is the rare exception that proves the rule); and (3) if the noncompliance is discovered, police actions are generally insulated from repercussions by a variety of structural mechanisms, of which the support of the department hierarchy is the most important.

In her study of management initiatives in the New York City Police Department, Elizabeth Reuss-Ianni (1983) observed that there once existed a

> street cop culture [with] a commonly shared ethos [that] unified the department through a code of shared understandings and conventions of behavior binding on everyone . . . the values of loyalty, privilege, and the importance of keeping department business inside the department. (pp. 5, 1)

That monolithic "clubhouse culture" has given way to a new "management cop" culture that works from different understandings and imperatives: "greater emphasis on accountability and productivity—on management processes and products that could be quantified and measured in a cost-effective equation" (p. 2). Whereas the top command in the old culture would protect the lower-ranking members, the new management cops are responsible for holding subordinates accountable for a broader range of behavior and responsibilities, including those relating to the treatment of women and minorities that directly contravene the old understandings of street cop culture.

Were the police merely "snappy operatives working under the command of bureaucrats-in-uniform" (Bittner, 1970, p. 53),[2] this chapter would be a short one. "The police command issued new directives to institute arrests in all domestic violence cases with probable cause, and render greater levels of assistance to victims. Line officers internalized the directives, made arrests, and provided services commensurate with those envisioned by the proponents of the new laws" would be the text. Nothing of the sort occurred, of course, for many reasons.

Many police agencies did indeed change their operational directives to be in nominal compliance with the new laws. Sherman and Cohn (1987) documented the degree of the changes early in the process, and there have been additional advances since that time. However, policies alone do not dictate behavior: Every police officer quickly learns which of the myriad policies enshrined in his or her Department Policy Manual are real, which were one-time responses to a spectacular screw-up,[3] and which are simply symbolic. In light of the persistent moral belief that domestic disputes should not be considered a police responsibility, the initial reaction to the new policies was to regard them as symbolic: necessary to protect the organization politically, but simply a device of "strategic rhetoric" (Manning, 1997, p. 46) without a functional imperative.

At the line and workgroup level, each change of the law creates not a new mandate, but a new variable to be assessed, and either capitalized on or neutralized, in the setting of the existing corporate culture's definition of "good work." The degree of acceptance that the changes enjoy depends on many factors, including the state of relations between management and workers (on which hinges the moral authority of the change orders themselves). In the case of the domestic violence laws, those factors were initially dominated by the old attitude.

That is not to say that police officers of the nation refused to discharge their new duties, because most did not. In some ways, an arrest and removal of the offender is a much simpler resolution than counseling, although it involves more time. For a time, the results of the Minneapolis Domestic Violence Experiment (Sherman and Berk, 1984) supported the advocates' views that arrest would reduce future violence in the relationships. That would also reduce police responses to repeat incidents involving the couple, and free officers from the onerous task of continually intervening in what had appeared to be an unresolvable conflict. For some officers, the mantra of "this will reduce BS[4] calls in the future" was sufficient reason for good-faith compliance with the new directives.

Despite its prominence as the first major randomized, controlled field experiment on the effects of police interventions, the Minneapolis Domestic Violence Experiment came under criticism for several potential shortcomings. Among them were a small sample size (only 324 cases were found eligible for inclusion), possible distortions of the treatment-as-delivered, and the relatively homogeneous population of Minneapolis compared to other major cities with much greater ethnic diversity. In response, the National Institute of Justice funded the Spousal Abuse Replication Project (SARP), a six-city attempt to confirm the Minneapolis findings in cities with widely disparate demographic profiles. When those results were published, the certainty about the efficacy of arrest for domestic violence was significantly diminished: Half of the cities reporting found a deterrent effect from arrest, while the others did not (the results are most cogently summarized in Sherman, 1992). Complicating the issue was the discovery of what Sherman termed a "backfire effect," whereby arrest for domestic violence initially deterred subsequent violence in the short term, but gave rise to greater violence within the year.

The impact of the Minneapolis Domestic Violence Experiment was immediate and wide-ranging. In addition to policy changes, the experiment's results were immediately enshrined in police training modules, and those initial offerings were not always amended to reflect the SARP results.

Police training modules for the new domestic violence laws were often written by the laws' advocates. Since the changes were imposed on the police, few internal resources existed for the development of training. Police could repeat the writ of the law for in-service training modules, but the rationale for the change was generally beyond them. The people who were brought in to justify the changes to the officers were often the advocates who had lobbied for the new laws—often against a backdrop of criticism of the older police practices.

In those training modules, the victims of domestic violence would often reflect the victims the advocates were seeing, and from whom they formed their concepts of the problem: women who were actively seeking to change their situation, either through counseling, negotiation, or escape. The models were "True Victims," women with horrific tales to tell, some of which involved the failure of the police to assist them. As heard by the police, the laws and the new policies were justified by their application to true victims, whom the police felt they rarely saw.

Informal Organizational Responses

Exasperation and grumbling aside, most police officers are professionals who immediately adapt their enforcement style to incorporate the new requirements of a given law. Although the public is constantly reminded of the exceptions to the rule, good-faith compliance with the law is the norm in police departments across the nation.

That is not to say that the response to the domestic violence laws was that of the "snappy bureaucrat," because it was not. There is a difference between adaptation and acquiescence, and to adapt does not require changing completely. In varying degrees, according to ability and interest, individual officers study and absorb the new set of rules—some by listening only to "the *Reader's Digest* version" that is presented in roll call, others by seeking the full text of the statute or court opinion (when it is published) and studying it in detail—and begin the process of distinguishing, determining just how much of their operational style must change. In cases where the outcome of the precedent case seems egregious, the police will individually and collectively seek alternative means to correct what they perceive to be an injustice.

On an individual basis, some (perhaps many) police officers resisted the change in the law regarding domestic violence even as their comrades attempted to enforce them in good faith. When departmental directives required arrest in all domestic violence cases where probable cause existed, the simplest form of resistance was to deny probable cause existed. Officers would handle the incident in time-tested fashion (that is, without an arrest), and radio in (or file a report) officially redefining the event as an argument: no violence involved, and hence no arrest required. The four-hour window for a probable cause arrest eliminated the utility of a delayed response, but the practice of clearing a call

GOA (Gone On Arrival) still constituted a reliable dodge. In one of the extreme cases known to the author, a two-officer team cleared a call involving a beating with severe facial injuries as GOA even though both parties were present (Goodmanson, 1987). An equally despicable practice reported by advocates, and confirmed by third parties, was the practice of cruising slowly by the address of the call, without stopping, and clearing GOA if no one was outside to flag down the police car. Some officers also express a deep resentment at being the instrument of someone else's "politically correct" ideas about how to handle domestic violence. In the field, this resentment can give rise to a form of monkey wrenching, the double arrest.

The dual arrest is a quick, efficient way to avoid the complexities of determining who was the aggressor, terminate the call as quickly as possible, and turn the victims' advocates' own efforts against them ("counting coup" on the moral plane, as it were). By applying to the batterers the new evidentiary standard intended to protect victims (accepting at face value "he said/she said" mutual accusations of assault), the police easily reach probable cause to arrest both the batterer and the victim. Any evidence or admission of self-defense by the victim is turned on its head, becoming probable cause to arrest the victim for domestic violence because she lifted a hand to ward off injury or to defend herself.

To victims' advocates, this is an outrage: The victim's supposed rescuers turn into another instrument of her oppression, giving moral and legal support to her tormentor. While there are times when a double arrest is appropriate, the phenomenon (where it occurs) seems to be a new reaction to external pressures by advocates to increase the police arrest response. However, the phenomenon itself is defined at this point largely by anecdotal evidence, backed by some local figures, and still in need of documentation. Where it occurs, it may well be the result of individual and small-group decision making, and is not likely to appear as a gross trend in agency-level statistics.

For the most part, those police officers who do shirk their imposed duties do so in the belief that what they are being asked to do is morally wrong, or a waste of time and police resources that should be devoted elsewhere.[5] They rely on past organizational practices and the local version of the Blue Wall of Silence to protect them, secure in the knowledge that the organizational commitment to the new rules is only superficial. As long as they "always have a story, always stick to that story, and do what the union guy tells [them]" (Donovan, 1996), the worst that is likely to happen to them is the discomfiture of being grilled by their superiors who suspect the truth, but have no independent source of evidence with which to impeach The Story.

For officers in that culture, even the grilling was viewed as a ritual, and their role in the ritual was to stick to The Story, thereby giving the organization "plausible deniability" with which to fend off external criticism. Since the organization was likewise shielded from adverse repercussions (for the most part), no incentive existed to push either for strict compliance with the new rules or for the truth about the handful of episodes which did not quietly fade into oblivion. Such was the initial reaction of many in law enforcement to the new requirements of the domestic violence laws, an attitude which worked until the lawsuit filed by Tracey Thurman changed the legal landscape.

THURMAN v. CITY OF TORRINGTON

Police scholars are well aware of the difficulties of direct supervision of patrol officer responses: The organizational tendency to rely on the responding officers' account of an incident is predicated on the necessary assumption that all members of the agency are "snappy bureaucrats." (There are severe repercussions for the agency if the reverse is true, and officers routinely are treated as though they were dishonest, incompetent, or moronic.) Even the most flagrant disregard for policy can be beatified by "creative report writing": Unless challenged with credible evidence—a rare event—the creative version of events becomes Official Truth, part of the agency's annual report and often another datum point in a social science study of police behavior.

The decision of *Thurman v. City of Torrington* was one of those rare events. The *Thurman* case was a claim of nonperformance or malperformance of police duties, the first successful federal case brought against a police department for failure to protect a battered spouse. It was an eight-month "pattern and practice" failure of the Torrington Police to take adequate steps to protect Tracey Thurman from her estranged husband, despite repeated threats (including some made in the presence of police officers) and acts of violence, including repeated violations of a restraining order. The violence finally ended on June 10, 1983, when Thurman's husband was placed under arrest after stabbing her and kicking her in the head at least twice, leaving her scarred and partially paralyzed. Though the case involved felony-level violence rather than a misdemeanor, it drastically changed the police response to domestic violence. While it stopped short of imposing direct consequences on individual officers, it created a new corporate responsibility for police agencies. The *Thurman* decision drastically eroded the protection of the existing Public Duty Doctrine, which had shielded police agencies and officers from liability by holding that the police duty to protect was a general one, and did not obligate the police to protect any single individual (Kappeler, 1997).

The multimillion-dollar judgment against the City of Torrington and its police department forced the attention of municipal risk management officers and police executives, spurring organizational changes in supervision and internal accountability: No longer could the new rules be ignored or passively resisted with impunity. Officer misconduct brought the administrative response under the microscope, and created a new climate of direct accountability for police malfeasance. The financial risks are now too great to permit the municipality or the administration to ignore officers' improper responses.

To justify the new ground rules, administrators framed them in terms meaningful to the street-level officer: The money the city or town pays in civil judgments cannot fund new hires, new cruisers, better radio equipment, or training. A few will reemphasize the new rules by intensification of the heavy-handed command and control techniques associated with the police version of quasi-military organizations.

Control techniques (which by definition are viewed as punitive by the officers subject to them) include new directives that require a comprehensive report to be filed in all "domestic" cases regardless of whether violence occurred, removing any incentive to reclassify a violent event into a "no-paper" one. Recognizing that street officers are more responsive to pressures from their immediate workgroup than those of central administration, a tactic that capitalizes on the shift supervisors' moral authority with their subordinates requires supervisors to respond to every domestic call and file an independent report. The burden on the supervisors creates an incentive for them to direct officers under their command to comply with the directives on domestics. Systematic recontact of victims by internal affairs or by supervisors from other shifts to validate the content of officers' reports eliminates (or at least increases the risk of) trying to "rug" a call through creative report writing.[6] And most departments, regardless of their place along the continuum of response, have been subjected to additional (often state-mandated) yearly in-service training about domestic violence.

Some jurisdictions have instituted "victimless prosecution" to thwart batterers' attempts to intimidate victims into withdrawing their complaints or dropping their restraining orders. Rather than place the burden for prosecuting the case on the victim, the state prosecutes the case on the strength of the police officers' investigation. Responding to advocates' assertion that it is the batterer's conduct rather than the victim's that should determine criminal justice policy, prosecution ensues even if the victim refuses to testify. The theory behind victimless prosecution is that there is no incentive for the batterer to engage in further violence if the victim has no control over the case. The evidence collected by the officers at the time of the initial call comprises the state's case, sometimes bolstered by evidence collected in its aftermath if the agency has a follow-up protocol. The officers testify to the statements made by the victim and any witnesses, and to the bruises or other evidence of injury. They also provide ancillary evidence, such as photographs of injuries or the physical condition of the home that was indicative of a violent struggle.

Victimless prosecution is a decision and a commitment made by the prosecutor's office in conjunction with the police agencies it serves. It places a greater responsibility on the responding officers to not just make an arrest, but to do a thorough investigation. In its own way, victimless prosecution places domestic assault on an equal footing with predatory stranger assaults, achieving at least a symbolic fulfillment of the advocates' original aims. What we do not yet know is whether victimless prosecution achieves the desired results and deters future violence, or whether it creates a longer-term "backfire effect" of greater violence after a short-term reduction, such as was found in Milwaukee by Sherman and his colleagues (Sherman, 1992, p. 18 and Appendix 2).

The Continuing Problem

At all points along the continuum of response, officers in the department will likely complain bitterly that the sole purpose of the training they must endure is shifting legal liability from the agency onto them (Buerger, 1998).[7] The complaint stems from the still-unresolved affront to their moral sense,[8] and a deeply held belief that arrest does not prevent or deter future violence. Most draw from the cumulative weight of their own experience, and the vicarious experience of their peers, which teaches a different lesson than the research-driven instruction of the mandatory in-service training modules. Despite repeated arrests, neither batterers nor victims change their behavior, and the police keep going back to their domestic squabbles and fights with monotonous regularity. When training instruction and experience are in conflict, street cops put their faith in experience.

(There are two flaws in the police experience, of course. Any negative feelings they may have about the police role in domestic violence—whether derived from personal experience or bestowed by socialization and war stories—are reinforced by selection bias: Officers see the intervention's failures frequently, and rarely the successes. The purported truth conveyed by the "war story" socialization process is both primarily anecdotal and usually devoid of external validity, save that it was said by another cop.)

Concurrent with their alternate perception of the efficacy of arrest is the moral belief that when victims have no intention of participating in the criminal justice process, an arrest is not just, and mandatory arrests are both a burden and a waste of system resources. In the police view, an arrest marks the entry into the criminal justice system, and is supposed to yield a system result, such as a plea bargain, an acquittal, or a conviction at trial.

Women's advocates have other perspectives on victim reluctance to go forward with criminal prosecution, of course. Along with a parallel string of anecdotal evidence of callous police behavior, advocates cite economic and emotional dependency, the various obstacles to participation created (sometimes inadvertently) by the criminal justice system, and the threat of or actual violence by the batterer to dissuade the victim from testifying against him in criminal proceedings (for a review of early materials, see Frieze and Browne, 1989).

The advocate position is also built on deeply held moral beliefs. Like the police worldview, it is composed of several complementary elements, held in varying degrees of intensity by persons who share the title of advocate. Foremost among them, and almost universally held, is the moral belief that an arrest for domestic violence is just, regardless of the victim's circumstances or intentions. The arrest has utilitarian value on a number of fronts, representing social condemnation of the act and a vivid demonstration that the batterer is wrong. Were that the only purpose served by the act of arrest (as it often seems to be), it would be justification enough. In the advocate's extreme view, the victim bears no responsibility for the battering; the decision to enact violence against another human being rests with the attacker alone, and the attacker bears sole responsibility. When the violence occurs, it is incumbent upon the state to avenge the act on behalf of the victim.

Whereas the symbolic purpose of arrest is universal, other justifications apply in some manner to some subsets of the abusing population. The arrest may get the attention of the batterer—through humiliation, shock value, deterrence, or any of a number of vehicles—and lead to his voluntary desistance. The arrest may empower the victim—the symbolic statement can apply as much to the victim as to the batterer—and by validating her position help the victim to take more positive steps to change her situation. In a smaller number of cases, the arrest is a utilitarian measure: The removal of the batterer by the police provides the opportunity for the victim to extricate herself (and her children) from the living situation, to seek safety in a shelter, with family or friends, or in rare circumstances to leave for parts unknown.

What has resulted, in many instances, is a tense standoff between two groups who rightfully should be allies in a common cause, but who are often separated by a gulf between moral principles. That gulf is generated, in part, by the two different groups of domestic violence victims that form the primary perceptions of the problem.

TWO GROUPS, TWO DIFFERENT PROBLEM DEFINITIONS

The definition of "victim" informs the two distinct worldviews of the police and the advocates. Advocates dealt primarily with True Victims, women who had taken at least a preliminary step toward changing their situation, perhaps as little as seeking information, or as radical as going to a shelter or seeking help formulating an escape plan.[9] The police deal with a broader range of victims, almost all of them "true" to the extent that they have suffered violence or intimidation at the hands of an intimate partner. As discussed above, however, the reaction of the majority of victims removes them from "true victim" status in the eyes of the police.

Even while observing the new duties created by reform laws, police officers continue to lament the unrealistic expectation of those laws. They grumble both about victims' failure to participate in the criminal justice system and about the portrayal of domestic violence in training materials, public assertions by members of the women's advocacy networks, and the domestic violence laws themselves. Trained to work within a linear system, in which their initial action (arrest) moves the case in a definite track toward a definite conclusion, the police generally are uninterested in, and unprepared to work in, a milieu that involves cyclical stages of change.

The activists and other helpers, however, work almost exclusively with the subset of domestic violence victims who have taken at least one definite step toward change, whether deliberately assessing and choosing their options or taking advantage of a shelter out of desperation. Although not all of the women who reach this stage will necessarily leave the relationship, they do present a more uniform set of personal resolve than the broad range of victims observed by the police.

This is not to say that there are no selection biases at work in the two groups of workers. For their part, domestic violence support workers are driven by a sense of mission. Some are themselves survivors of abuse, and they help train those who come to the work from other motives. They work more intensely with the women who have consciously chosen to either end the relationship, or change it; many (but not all) of those women have already had contact with police officers whose attitudes have been tepid or antagonistic. On the other hand, police officers are socialized by veterans of prior generations, who pass on a weird mix of collective experience and personal bias in the course of their instruction (and pass it on to rookie officers who receive it uncritically, as if it were gospel truth). A disturbingly large number of officers the author has worked with or around have expressed opinions sympathetic to the idea of masculine privilege and male dominance. Like their feminist opposite, they look for evidence that confirms what they already believe, and usually they can find it. This is not to cast blame on either side, but to recast the issue as a structural obstacle that must be recognized and dealt with. The two sides have different expectations of what the victim should want (and do), and different assumptions related to the capacity of the criminal justice system. Both of those expectations and assumptions may be missing the mark.

What the Criminal Justice System Offers

If we look at the seemingly broad range of options that the criminal justice system offers to victims of domestic violence, we find that most of them fall into a single category: sundering the relationship. Including the police interventions discussed above, the following are the options (legitimate and illegitimate):

Ignoring the Situation: Doing nothing is an illegitimate response, which does nothing for the victim. The relationship remains intact unless one of the principals chooses to leave, but the victim is left at a disadvantage if there is violence or intimidation. Ignoring the situation is predicated on a prescient belief (on the part of the police officer) that the long-term outcome will be no change whatsoever in the fundamental dynamics of the abusive relationship, and therefore any police actions are ineffective, essentially unjust, and unwarranted.

Counseling the Disputants: If there is no violence, and no intimidation, counseling the disputants is possibly a legitimate response by the police. Done properly, this involves providing information to the disputants about the options available, including the possibility of arrest, as a precaution against violence if the dispute continues (most of the options that would be explained are included below). Counseling preserves the relationship, although one or both parties could subsequently initiate a breakup.

Sending One Party: Formerly a legitimate option, the "Send" has fallen into disfavor with the advent of the mandatory and presumptive arrest laws. It temporarily sunders the domestic relationship, but presumes a quick reunification and a continuation of the relationship.

Arrest: The now-preferred option when violence has occurred, or threat or intimidation is involved, the arrest sunders the relationship on a temporary basis. Depending on how it is managed, the break may be as little as two or three hours, or as many as three or four days (arrests on a Friday evening of a holiday weekend, with no magistrates available). Like the "Send," the arrest creates a safety space where women who wish to extricate themselves from the situation—not necessarily the relationship—can leave with relative impunity. Unless victims elect to be the one to leave (under police protection) in the Send option, they are not likely to make any moves on their own. In an arrest situation, the victim's relocation may or may not be with police assistance, depending on the number of units available (city agencies often send two cars on domestics because of the potential for violence; smaller town departments often do not have that luxury, and the only car available must deal first with transporting the arrestee).

For advocates, the arrest creates the opportunity for the victim to leave the dangerous or demeaning relationship, and it changes the moral balance of that relationship. To the police, that change is too often more symbolic than substantive.

Temporary Restraining Orders/Orders for Protection: This is the first option that creates more than a short-term separation. In New Jersey, for instance, a temporary restraining order (TRO) can be obtained merely on the request of the victim, often facilitated by the responding officer. Though nominally carrying the full set of restrictions and components (financial support, child custody and support, etc.) of a permanent restraining order, the TRO is in practice a stay-away order. It has a specific expiration date (usually within 10 days to two weeks) unless both parties appear before the judge in a formal hearing to make the temporary order permanent. Although extensions are routinely granted if one or both parties fail to show up (many offenders are served with the order in jail or at the booking room, but those who depart the residence before the police arrive may evade service for a long time; technically, the TRO does not take effect until the defendant has been formally notified of the existence of the order by being served with his copy), they do not provide long-term protection without further positive actions by the victim.

The value of TROs is not universally recognized. To some, it is merely a piece of paper, a symbol, easily ignored by the batterer. In truth, a TRO does not stop bullets, and is no barrier to the dedicated offender bent on mayhem. However, in the less-than-worst-case scenarios, a TRO provides a legal basis for police removal of the offender *before* any additional violence occurs: When subject to a TRO, a domestic violence offender cannot claim the privacy of his own home, because he has been temporarily barred from it for cause. The victim and the police need not wait for another overt act of intimidation or violence before arresting the batterer. Sanctions are not universally applied; in some states, violation of a restraining order is a criminal offense, but in others—for instance, in some jurisdictions where TROs are issued by the family court rather than the criminal court—the penalties are merely civil in nature.

Permanent Restraining Orders: Obtaining a permanent restraining order usually announces that the relationship is over, though not always. The distance between the two primary members is formal, and extended under the terms of the order, which also may include support for minor children. For couples cohabiting without benefit of clergy or town clerk, the restraining order functions as a legal separation or divorce, effectively ending the cohabitation.

Legal Separation: Legal separation is generally a more civil separation arrangement between couples with a formal relationship. Though it does not end the legal marriage or civil partnership, it does distinguish the parties' legal obligations as individual rather than mutual. The legal separation is essentially a trial divorce (with each party trying isolation from the other as a means of determining whether to take the final step to formally end the relationship), but reconciliation is still a possible outcome.

Divorce: For married couples, divorce is the ultimate sundering of the relationship (although annulment is required in some religions, such as Roman Catholicism, that do not recognize divorce). Divorce ends the relationship on a permanent basis, civilly if not religiously. Whatever continuing responsibilities the former couple have to each other (alimony and child support, child custody) are mediated through the courts.

LIMITATIONS

Most of the instruments available to the legal system (civil and criminal) thus constitute a separation, in an ascending trajectory leading toward the permanent end of the relationship. (Informally, the frequently articulated expectation of many police officers is that if the victim does *not* seek to end the relationship, there is little or no legitimacy to her complaints.) A large portion of the domestic violence training and informational literature is derived from, and emphasizes, an assumption that the escape-and-terminate option is the ultimate solution. Whether the batterer is punished by society is less important than the future safety of the victim. My thesis has been that the advocates are much more likely to see women who have chosen that option than are the police, and so it is that frame of reference that informs their approach to the larger problem of violence within intimate relationships. The police see a much greater proportion of the vacillating victims, those in denial about their situation or incapable of making the decision to leave. That creates a different frame of reference for the police.

Since the passage of the modern domestic violence laws, the police focus has been the restraining order. A restraining order promises protection for the victim: One of the disturbing truisms of domestic violence has been that a woman is most vulnerable when she moves to end the relationship. It is then that her partner is most desperate, most violent, most likely to engage in stalking behaviors, and—if he is canny—completely "innocent" and beyond police sanction until he chooses to strike, often lethally. The restraining order allows the police to intercept and remove the once-and-probably-future offender before a fatal opportunity arises.

From the police standpoint, however, the restraining order has become a tool of relationship management. Officers report frequently responding to domestic calls at a residence where they have been before, arriving to find the batterer in the residence at the victim's request or permission, despite the still-active restraining order. A number of the calls are prompted by violence or threat of violence in the immediate situation; some others are without violence, but the victim requests the removal of the man from the residence (in accordance with the provisions of the restraining order) because their negotiations about the future of the relationship have come to an impasse, and he refuses to leave. In a small number of cases, that request comes after the man has been allowed to stay at the residence for a considerable amount of time (days and even weeks) despite the restraining order.

Police officers refer to this as the victim "self-violating" the restraining order, and are frustrated by the practice. In their view, if the victim—the person for whom the order was issued in the first place—invites the batterer in, the order should become invalid. Obviously the victim is not truly in fear of the man, so the order is not really necessary, just a tool to give her the upper hand in the management of the relationship. (Whether that is actually true, or whether any of the officers could appreciate the irony of the turn of the tables that it would represent it if were true, must be left for another discussion.)

Advocates find the police interpretation noxious. The restraining order is not taken out against the victim, and thus she cannot violate it. Its purpose is to curb the violent behavior of the batterer, and even though it is phrased as a stay-away order, that protection must remain in force even if the victim chooses to see her assailant again to renegotiate the terms of their relationship.

For police, who tend to define criminal justice goals narrowly, in terms of punishment, these patterns constitute a two-fold distortion of their mission. The first lies in the attempt to use the criminal justice system not as an end in itself, but as leverage for other social goals (though there are important exceptions to the rule, police officers tend to look on "social work" as the antithesis of law enforcement, and often define themselves as "not social workers"). The second lies at the individual level, in cases where it appears clear-cut that the woman is wielding the legal advantage of the restraining order as a cudgel and using the police as her personal servants.

The author is familiar with one such case in a large midwestern city, in which five separate calls were placed to the dispatch center asking for police assistance in removing the man (a live-in boyfriend, as it turned out) from the apartment. The first call was simply coded as a "Domestic" (no violence involved), and the request was simply to remove the man; the officers who responded found that his name was on the lease as was hers, and so he had as much right to occupy the apartment as she did. The officers advised the couple (correctly) that their dispute was a civil matter, and took no further action. Shortly after that, the woman made a second phone call claiming that the boyfriend had made threats against her after the police had left the first time; the third call was to report that he had hit her. The woman's fourth call was to allege he threatened her with a knife, and the fifth (and final) call claimed the threat had been at gunpoint. Each time, the police responded, investigated, and concluded that the new complaint was groundless, merely an extension of the woman's original request to remove her boyfriend. Each subsequent call upped the ante of the complaint, hoping to find the level at which the police would take some action to remove the *persona non grata*.[10]

On the last call, the complainant failed to replace the receiver properly, and the phone line stayed open, with the dispatch center's equipment recording the interior conversation from the time of the call until well after the police officers arrived at the scene. The tone of that conversation made it clear that there was no violence or threat of violence. The man was whining, pleading to be allowed to stay. The woman was a monotone example of the broken-record technique, saying "No" to everything.

When the knock on the door signaled the arrival of the police officers, the demeanor of both participants changed immediately, she complaining boisterously about the alleged assault and his continuing threats, he putting on a salesman's smile and voice, asking the officers if there was anything wrong (despite the fact that this was the fifth time in an hour that he'd seen those same officers) and denying up and down that there was any dispute whatsoever. The officers again told the complainant that there was no evidence of criminal behavior, and because the man's name was on the lease, he had every right to stay. (The shift sergeant also joined in, advising the officers and the dispatch center that because of the continuing nature of the false reports, there would be no more police response to the residence that night. There were no further calls to the police from that residence.)

This case of egregious pseudo-victim attempts to manipulate the system is probably as rare as the instances of truly egregious police misconduct. Once they occur, however, they become the polestar against which the entire debate is measured. Each side of the policy debate thus has its examples from the extreme ends of the spectrum, examples that become symbols of the dissatisfaction they feel for the other side's position and conduct. But, as with so many things, the core of the problem lies in the middle, well away from the inflammatory examples on the polar extremes.

In our language lies one clue: The language of the chapter, following the language of the policy debate, speaks of "the victim" and "her batterer" or "her assailant." The most neutral terms identify gender—the man, the woman—but behind that facade lies the recognition that it is the man who is the assailant, and the woman who is the victim. The policy debate effectively encapsulates the entire relationship in the dimensions of the assault, the threat, or the pattern of assaults.

The victim usually does not do so. Although there are some who will exit the relationship at the first violent act, many others remain emotionally committed to the relationship, confused by the violence, and uncertain what to do. The criminal justice response is engineered for the first group. If we can correctly infer that the latter group of victims do not want the relationship to end, but want it repaired, then the criminal justice system has much less to offer them.

Advocates argue that the sanctions of the criminal justice system are necessary to force the batterer to comply with court orders to seek counseling, or enter a batterers' program. To the extent that such programs are "the only game in town" for our ability to reach the assailant's behavior (as distinct from the victim's), they are correct. However, familiar problems with the criminal justice system's ability to deal with offenders come into play here as well: available programs; the limited number of effective programs; the limited capacity of batterers' programs overall (the good and the not-yet-good alike) compared to the population of offenders; the lack of an effective probation capacity to ensure compliance with the courts' orders; and the perpetual problem of "the light bulb has to *want* to change. . . . "[11]

What is needed is a mechanism for helping victims of domestic violence mend or reestablish their relationships on a more equal, less violent footing. All of the problems related to the victims' role remain: The batterer (the husband, the boyfriend, the co-parent) has the upper hand if the victim wants the relationship too much. Long-term interventions by the state encroach on the victim's privacy as well as the batterer's. Close scrutiny by the state may put the victim at legal risk if she uses contraband drugs, or spotlight poor parenting skills. But perhaps foremost among the problems facing any expansion of the victim-assistance role of the criminal justice system is the lack of new ideas and insights.

That is not to say that there is a lack of ideas; if anything, there is a surfeit of ideas that spring from moralistic wells, as the old polar opposites remain entrenched. Those who believe that no domestic dispute short of homicide should be a police matter exchange hurled mountaintops with those who believe with equal fervor that the male is always the aggressor and always at fault. In the middle are some who believe that the police response should be finite, especially if the victim voluntarily waives the protection of court orders to reestablish the relationship. This view essentially treats the relationship on a par with false intrusion alarms, and would withdraw police protection after a certain number of responses absent a positive demonstration by the victim that she is making strides toward altering her situation. Another perspective essentially treats the violent relationship as an attractive nuisance, and proposes a graduated series of sanctions leveled at the victim as well as the batterer, up to and including removing children from the household because of their status as secondary victims.

Clearly, none of these "solutions" is practical. Withdrawal of police protection, even in cases where the police are convinced that the victim is "crying wolf," is neither feasible under the concept of equal protection nor smart, particularly for those familiar with the ending of Aesop's fable. The number of domestic homicides amply demonstrates that at least in some cases, the wolf will someday appear, and the doctrine of liability for failure to protect is now well delineated in law. The civil liberties implications of "helping" a victim by imposing controls over her life as well as her tormentor's are ferocious, to say the least; also, there is no reason to believe the state could do a better job negotiating the relationship than the principals could—just a more expensive one.

Though we may very well end up with the same set of limited options now in place, a new dialogue needs to be constructed around documented realities of violence within relationships. Domestic violence creates an intersection of important precepts of law and social expectations: limited governmental intrusion into the private sphere, vindication of the innocent, punishment and correction of the offender, the sanctity of the bonds of marriage, principles of privacy and equality before the law, the interest of the state in protecting the innocent and curbing future violence. This generation has witnessed the replacement of the old moral code based on male privilege and dominance with a newer one based on equality of gender, and that moral force has driven the developments of law and practice. Moral precepts alone do not necessarily guide effective policy, however; moreover, moral positions are not monolithic, and different interpretations of moral rectitude often compete with one another in the social dialogue. When morality is driven by untested or imaginary suppositions, the policy errors that result both fail to achieve their desired moral ends, and produce unintended, potentially catastrophic results.

Acknowledgments

The author is indebted to Lawrence W. Sherman, Chief Tony Bouza of the Minneapolis (MN) Police Department, and to the members of the RECAP Unit (Lt. Alvah "Bid" Emerson, Sgt. David Niebur, Sgt. Duane "Skip" Goodmanson, Sgt. David Martens, David Rumpza, Steve Revor, and Cliff Johnson), as well as the staff of the Minneapolis Emergency Communications Center, for the opportunities and shared wisdom of the Minneapolis experience. Thanks are also owed to Chief Frank Gajewski of the Jersey City (NJ) Police Department, and to my collaborators on the crisis intervention project there: Robyn Mace, Michele Manspeizer, and Mannie Barthe, as well as to the staff of the Hudson County YWCA.

Endnotes

[1]Except in the realm of preventive detention, a concept which seems to enjoy the favor of the police when applied to gang members and others whose conduct is seen as being directly related to "real police work."

[2]Carl Klockars expands upon Bittner's definition a bit more colorfully, and more usefully, as "cogs in a quasi-military machine who do what they are told out of a mix of fear, loyalty, routine, and detailed specification of duties" (Klockars, 1985, 1991, p. 420).

[3]Such policies usually have the offender's name attached to them, at least informally ("Oh, that . . . that's The Buerger Rule"). They have an extremely short shelf life during which they must be rigorously and ostentatiously observed, and after which they can be ignored with impunity, in perpetuity.

[4]"Bogus Stuff," a euphemism for another less savory euphemism.

[5]Like any organization, police departments may have some employees who simply do not work, or do as little as possible to get by, but they are not the subjects of interest here.

[6]"Rug" as in "to sweep under the rug," obscuring the fact that the proper technique was not employed.

[7]A viewpoint not without some foundation, as the nation saw during the Simi Valley (CA) trial of LAPD officers Powell, Brisenio, Wind, and Sgt. Koon, where a primary focus of the trial was whether the officers' beating of Rodney King was, or was not, "within policy" of the Los Angeles Police Department.

[8]I am indebted to Stephen D. Mastrofski for his earlier observations about this phenomenon.

[9]Not every contact depends upon the victim's initiative, however; many assistance programs do active outreach. The Minneapolis Intervention Project/Domestic Assault Program (MIP/DAP) received police referrals on every domestic violence call handled by the Minneapolis Police. Wherever possible, MIP/DAP advocates would make a telephone call to the victim within 72 hours to offer additional support and information.

[10]The assertion that, in some neighborhoods, police will only respond to "man with a gun" or "shots fired" calls—and so all calls to the police claim a man with a gun, or shots fired, regardless of the actual need—has become a popular legend; it may also be that the victim expected that at least one of the calls would have a different car dispatched, with officers who were unaware of the preceding dispatches (see Buerger, 1994).

[11]The reference is to the old joke, "How many psychiatrists does it take to change a light bulb?"; the punch line is a play on the therapy professions' awareness that their work is often fruitless if the client does not make sincere efforts to change the things that make them unhappy. That motivation rarely applies to batterers, we are led to believe: They enjoy the dominance that their actions bring, and view their participation in classes as a punishment to be endured only long enough to be free of court supervision, whereupon they can return to their old ways.

References

Author's field notes, Minneapolis, MN 1987–1990.

Author's field notes, Jersey City, NJ 1996–1997.

Bittner, E. (1970, November). *The Functions of Police in Modern Society: A Review of Background Factors, Current Practices, and Possible Role Models.* National Clearinghouse for Mental Health Information. Chevy Chase, MD: National Institute of Mental Health.

Black, D. (1980). *The Manners and Customs of the Police.* New York: Academic Press.

Buerger, M. (1994). The problems of problem-solving: Resistance, interdependencies, and conflicting interests. *American Journal of Police,* 13 (3), 1–36.

———. (1998). Police training as a pentecost: Using tools singularly ill-suited to the purpose of reform. *Police Quarterly,* 1 (1), 27–63.

Donovan, E. (1996). Personal communication.

Duffy, J. J. (1995, February 27). *Domestic Violence: Police Response Guidelines.* Jersey City, NJ: Hudson County (NJ) Prosecutor's Office.

Frieze, I. H., and Browne, A. (1989). Violence in marriage. In L. Ohlin and M. Tonry (Eds.), *Family Violence, Crime and Justice: A Review of Research* (Vol. 11). Chicago: University of Chicago Press.

Goodmanson, D. (1987, August). Personal communication.

Guyot, D. (1979). Bending granite: Attempts to change the rank structure of American police departments. *Journal of Police Science and Administration,* 7 (3), 253–284. Reprinted as excerpt in B. Klockars (Ed.), *Thinking about Police: Contemporary Readings* (1991) (pp. 400–422). New York: McGraw-Hill.

Kappeler, V. E. (1997). *Critical Issues in Police Civil Liability* (2nd ed.). Prospect Heights, IL: Waveland Press.

Klockars, C. B. (1985). *The Idea of Police.* Beverly Hills, CA: Sage.

Mace, R. (1997). Personal communication.

Manning, P. K. (1997). *Police Work: The Social Organization of Policing* (2nd ed.). Prospect Heights, IL: Waveland Press.

Reiss, A. J., Jr. (1971). *The Police and the Public.* New Haven, CT: Yale University Press.

———. (1989). Personal communication.

Reuss–Ianni, E. (1983). *Two Cultures of Policing: Street Cops and Management Cops.* New Brunswick, NJ: Transaction Books.

Sherman, L. W. (1992). *Policing Domestic Violence: Experiments and Dilemmas.* New York: Free Press.

Sherman, L. W., and Berk, R. A. (1984). The specific deterrent effects of arrest for domestic assault. *American Sociological Review,* 49, 261–272.

Sherman, L. W., and Cohn, E. G. (1987). *Police Policy on Domestic Violence, 1986: A National Survey.* Crime Control Reports No. 5. Washington, DC: Crime Control Institute.

Skolnick, J. H. (1966). *Justice without Trial: Law Enforcement in Democratic Society.* New York: John Wiley & Sons.

Thurman v. City of Torrington, 595 F. Supp. 1521 (D. Conn. 1984).

Walker, S. (1992). *The Police in America: An Introduction* (2nd ed.). New York: McGraw-Hill.

———. (1999). *The Police in America: An Introduction* (3rd ed.). New York: McGraw-Hill.

Westley, W. A. (1970). *Violence and the Police: A Sociological Study of Law, Custom, and Morality.* Cambridge: Massachusetts Institute of Technology Press.

Wilson, J. Q. (1968). *Varieties of Police Behavior: The Management of Law and Order in Eight Communities.* Cambridge: Harvard University Press.

CHAPTER 18

Balanced and Restorative Justice
Reengaging the Victim in the Justice Process

Jennifer M. Balboni

Introduction

The traditional criminal justice system in the United States subjugates the victim's needs to those of the state. This adversarial system, pitting the offender against the government in a theoretically dramatic battle to maintain one's freedom and liberty, was born out of English custom developed after the Norman invasion in Britain in the eleventh century. Prior to this, crime was viewed as first a conflict between individuals, second a conflict against the state. The state subsumed the role of "victim," arguing that crime offended the king and disturbed the peace which he sought to maintain. At this time, the justice system fulfilled a utilitarian goal for the state: controlling the populace. Retribution became the primary focus, deterring other people with similar criminal propensities was secondary, and addressing victim needs peripheral. The U.S. justice system, built on this foundation, has continued the legacy of making the victim an afterthought. Recently, however, there has been some discussion to reengage the victim through a paradigm of "balanced and restorative justice." This chapter will discuss the traditional role of the victim in U.S. criminal justice, what the major tenets of "balanced and restorative justice'" are, and how this paradigm has the potential to reengage the victim in the justice process overall.

Victims in an Adversarial System

Maintaining the state as the primary legal victim in crime has created a category of victims wearing shades of opaque: Criminal justice professionals are aware of their existence but often look right through the victim to administer a less practical, more symbolic sentence. Victims are useful to the adversarial U.S. judicial system almost exclusively as a tool of evidence. Legal scholar Richard Abel (1998) writes, "The victim becomes an embarrassing anachronism—necessary to start the process but an inconvenience thereafter" (p. 448). This leaves the victim in a precarious position: If it were not for the initial victim's report to law enforcement, many crimes would go undetected, unaddressed, and unprosecuted. Once the process begins, however, victims have negligible control of how the case will be handled or what its result will be. The major criminal justice stakeholders (i.e., the police, prosecutor, defense attorney, and judge), not the victim, maintain the balance of control over particular cases.

Next, our current adversarial system focuses exclusively on *primary* victims, overlooking *secondary victimization* to the community. The idea that any particular crime has finite and clearly definable consequences is at best too narrow a view on crime and, at worst, a flatly false assumption. Although levels of secondary victimization vary in communities depending on the type of crime, the level of cohesiveness of the community, and other factors, there can be no question that crime causes ripple effects in many areas of a community's social life (Bazemore and Umbreit, 1998). For example, when a home is burglarized or a person is robbed in a particular community, the people within that neighborhood may experience increased levels of fear and anxiety after hearing about the incident. Unfortunately, the community has not been a direct stakeholder in the justice process[1] (Pranis, 1997a).

This disjunction between victims and the justice system eliminates the human elements of victimization for the offender, instead substituting perfunctory legal processes which obfuscate the true impact of crime. The adversarial process almost requires the employment of neutralizing strategies by the offender in the name of efficiency (Zehr, 1997). For example, the common practice of plea bargaining demonstrates how the state relieves the defendant (possibly because of a lack of admissible evidence) of partial guilt by lowering the charge to a lesser, often less distinct charge, or by dropping some charges entirely, thereby diffusing the offender's responsibility. Even if the accepted plea is deemed an "appropriate" charge, feelings linger that the offender received a bargain, particularly if victim input was never solicited or considered. Nolo contendere and Alford pleas, which indicate an offender's involvement but not complete culpability, allow offenders to creatively reconstruct the events of the crime, minimizing their accountability. The justice process instead becomes a gamble for the offender to "beat the system" by becoming more adept in evading responsibility (Walgrave, 1995). This process can revictimize the victim. The overall result has been an unsatisfied victim, an uninvolved community, and an unrepentant offender.

Within the last three decades, however, the role of the victim in justice has begun to change somewhat (even if it sometimes appears this change is moving at a glacial pace). An attempt to improve victim services in this country occurred in the 1960s through the victims' rights movements. Like other progressive social movements, the victims' rights movement attempted to galvanize a diverse group that had been systematically dismissed (Karmen, 1996). To a certain extent, the movement succeeded in putting victim needs and issues on the national agenda. Although progress can be seen in the hundreds of programs initiated to better assist victims through the criminal justice process, victim issues continue to be a peripheral concern after more traditional issues are resolved. There is no question that the proliferation of such programs has affected the community positively and helped many people; however, there still remain systemic inequities within the predominant paradigm in U.S. justice.

Defining Balanced and Restorative Justice (BARJ)

The paradigm of restorative justice, which attempts to bridge the gap between the victim, offender, and community, recently has received both scholarly and popular attention. In its most basic form, restorative justice first acknowledges the human impact of crime, then seeks solutions to repair the damage done by criminal behavior first to the primary victim, then to the community as a whole. Within the concept of restorative justice, many have come to include the concept of "balanced" justice (OJJDP, 1998). Balanced justice refers to addressing the needs of the victim and the community, and having the offenders develop skills in an effort to prevent future offenses. This paradigm, which has its roots in peacemaking criminology, has the potential to influence criminal justice philosophy significantly. Although the implementation of balanced and restorative justice remains at the preliminary stage in this country, its use in South Africa, Australia, New Zealand, and Canada promises hope for the American justice system (OJJDP, 1994; McElrea, 1996). This section explores the major tenets of the balanced and restorative justice philosophy.

The philosophies of balanced and restorative justice provide new hope for crime victions in a system that too often has failed them (Munn, 1993). The paradigm is as follows: Crime is viewed first as a conflict between individuals, second as an offense against the community (Umbreit, 1994). If retributive justice focuses on the act and rehabilitative justice focuses on the actor, then restorative justice focuses on the *scene:* how it was changed by the act and how it can be restored to its original form. This is a marked departure from traditional philosophies about crime prevention and deterrence. Problem solving, not establishing blame, becomes the primary concern (Umbreit, 1995). Lode Walgrave, a Belgian criminologist, defines restorative justice as a system which creates an "emancipatory" society on two fundamental principles: autonomy and solidarity between individuals (1995). In such a system, reparation and reconciliation replace the goals of force, hatred, and revenge (Walgrave, 1995).

By definition, the concepts of balanced and restorative justice originated separately, but recently have been combined. Restorative justice identifies a triad of participants in the implementation of justice: the victim, the community, and the offender (Bazemore and Day, 1996). Unlike the current system of justice, the victim and community's place is anything but perfunctory.

Balanced justice proposes a second triad of goals: accountability, competency development, and *community protection* (OJJDP, 1994). Because the concepts resemble popular terms which may also be used in the traditional models, the preceding components merit their own discussions.

Accountability. The first precept of a balanced approach to justice refers to the obligation that the offender has to the victim and to the community. At the very least, the victim deserves reparations for harm done. There are several proposed accountability interventions, all of which emphasize the human impact of crime (Umbreit, 1995). The first intervention requires financial restitution, with the victims' input. Unlike restitution in a retributive justice system, the restitution proposed here is agreed on among the victim, community, and offender, rather than the probation department or judge (Umbreit, 1995). The second component involves victim-directed community service work. The philosophy here is the same as the first intervention, but it stresses the harm done to the community by an offense. One example of this is the Genesee County (NY) diversion program. One offender, after his seventh drunk driving arrest, was ordered by the diversion program to perform community service for the Red Cross, attend Alcoholics Anonymous meetings, and participate in Mothers against Drunk Driving victim impact meetings. In a statement to the local newspaper, the offender stated, "I would like to apologize to the community of western New York for my conduct over the last ten years. I have finally turned my life around" (Laconte, 1998). It seems that such community work helped the offender make the human connection about the impact of his crime.

The third intervention is personal service toward the victim (Walgrave, 1995). This could be cleaning a vandalized garage or working for the victim to repay any costs that she or he may have suffered as a result of the victimization. This intervention, of course, must be used prudently so as not to revictimize the victim. Such intervention requires the victim to be comfortable with the accountability process.

The fourth intervention to help establish accountability requires victim–offender groups (Umbreit, 1995). Such groups may not include the specific victim involved in the offense, but may include victims of similar crimes. The groups should be facilitated by a skilled third party, and should include victims who are able to participate without the possibility of revictimization. Such groups enhance offenders' appreciation of the harm done by their criminal acts.

Probably one of the most important types of victim–offender groups is mediation, which may be the trademark for balanced and restorative justice. These sessions focus on holding offenders accountable and teaching empathy while restoring emotional losses (Umbreit, 1995). As opposed to other types of traditional mediation sessions, which tend to be agreement-driven, victim–offender mediation (VOM) groups tend to be dialogue-driven (Umbreit, 1998). In other words, the *process* of such meetings often is more important than the *product*. They allow for an exchange of information, interaction to express emotion, facilitating heightened understanding for all parties. In one research study of participants of victim–offender mediation groups in Alaska, the majority of participants viewed the program as successful (Flaten, 1996). Many offenders remarked that they learned how the offense had affected more than just the victim, and that the interaction in these groups made their victim "real" to them. One victim remarked that in the traditional (adversarial) system of justice, the offender could "hide" in the courtroom and never take responsibility for his or her actions (Umbreit, 1998).

In another study, the victims reported feeling reduced anxiety and feelings of vulnerability after the mediation (Umbreit, 1994). In a study done at the University of Minnesota, one victim commented that before he met with his offender, he had begun to see everyone around him as a potential criminal (Umbreit, 1998). Meeting the perpetrator helped to alleviate some of his fears. In contrast, the victim may never meet with the offender face-to-face in the traditional adversarial system. This seclusion facilitates victims in demonizing offenders, and often creates more fear and anxiety. With restorative justice, victims are afforded the opportunity (but never forced) to meet with the offender and ask the compelling questions that often plague them after the incident. In interviews with victims who had participated in victim–offender mediation groups at the University of Minnesota, several remarked that the process allowed them to ask the important question: "Why?" (Umbreit, 1998). Having the opportunity to ask these questions is often cathartic for victims, as they may find the responses less frightening than they had anticipated.

It is important to note that fear of crime can initiate individuals to withdraw from their community, in turn making the community less able to mobilize to collectively address their problems, thereby exacerbating the effect from the individual to the community. A highly interdependent community can address problems before they escalate, such as problem solving about an issue such as youth loitering, before it grows into a larger problem of youth violence or drug abuse. In this respect, the effect of reducing fear and anxiety in crime victims cannot be underestimated in its impact on both the individual and the community. However, considerable preparation is necessary for effective VOM groups. In this process, adequate preparation for all parties is seen as a critical element in determining success; all participants felt at least a year of preparation was needed after the offense to allow enough time for personal healing (Flaten, 1996).

In another study of mediation programs with juveniles in Albuquerque, New Mexico; Minneapolis, Minnesota; and Oakland, California, recidivism rates were significantly lower for those juveniles who participated in mediation (Umbreit, 1994). Only 18% of the experimental group accrued a new criminal charge within a year from the mediation session, while the control group averaged 27% (Umbreit, 1995). Of those offenses, the juveniles who participated in mediation tended to have committed less serious crimes than the control group (Umbreit, 1994). These findings seem promising, but their significance should be tested through replication of the study and further research.

Another popular variation of the victim–offender group is the sentencing or peacemaking circles, which combine principles from Asian and European communities (Pranis, 1997b). Such circles include the victim, mediator, offender, victim supporters, police, correctional representatives, defense counsel, community leaders, offender supporters, and a judge. Each person plays an integral role in contributing to the disposition of the offender and, in essence, the community (Pranis, 1997b). This process empowers communities to once again maintain a level of social control, illustrating the Durkheimian notion of self-regulation of healthy communities.

The voluntariness of each step in the process is important. Victims have individual needs and expectations, and not all victims will want to proceed within a balanced and restorative system (Bazemore and Pranis, 1997). A victim should never be coerced into participating in this process. Different crimes may necessitate differential handling. For instance, a serious personal offense involving violence may require significantly more preparation before the victim and offender can productively engage in a group setting, if at all. The preparation in such groups can be the most important aspect of the process; it cannot be reduced to a cookbook-type recipe where certain types of crime warrant a precise number of months of preparation. The key to success is the mediator's understanding and appreciation of the victims' emotional state and the offenders' maturity level (Levrant et al., 1999). Likewise, an offender who refuses to engage in the process should be remanded for more formal judicial proceedings (Walgrave, 1995). Before determining opposition to the restorative process, however, the system may require guidelines to ensure offenders are able to appreciate the opportunity of reparative justice at some functional level.

Competency Development. The second major component of the balanced approach is *competency development*. The premise is that the offender should leave the justice system with skills that enable him or her to participate in legitimate activities in society (OJJDP, 1994). This step assists the offender in developing self-identity. Competency development may include educational or vocational skills, or more basic skills, such as anger management or conflict resolution.

The impetus for competency development is that a person in the community who has a propensity for criminality and few legitimate skills is a liability. The community, then, must maintain a stake in the successful rehabilitation of the offender and therefore provide him or her with opportunities. The community's involvement, however, transcends charity. By helping the offender, they in turn benefit from the community service completed. The result is an improved quality of life among community members (OJJDP, 1994). Whereas competency development primarily addresses the needs of the offender, the benefit to the community is just as significant.

One example of a program stressing competency development with youth is the Eastern Oregon Homeless Project and Abuse Shelter Coalition. Both juvenile and adult probationers and parolees work within the community providing public works tasks. Among other accomplishments, offenders have constructed a homeless shelter and domestic abuse crisis center (Bazemore and Umbreit, 1998). Here, the offenders learn vocational skills, and the community receives the long-term benefits of their labor.

Community Protection. The third component of the balanced approach to restorative justice is community protection. The public has the right to be secure in their surroundings; thus, this model does not advocate for the abolishment of prisons or jails. In fact, balanced and restorative justice acknowledges the need to incarcerate violent predatory offenders (Bazemore and Umbreit, 1998). Their incapacitation, however, serves the goal of protecting society and the offender, and is not intended as a punitive measure (Laconte, 1998; Bazemore and Umbreit, 1998). Aside from these offenders, other less restrictive strategies may be employed to assist in the restoration process. Such alternatives include residential facilities, tracking and monitoring programs, day reporting centers, and other alternative sanctions. Each of these options maintains a level of supervision over the offender, but such tracking is an appropriate natural consequence of the offender's criminal behavior. Ideally, these programs should focus on using the person's time while in the community to do legitimate, constructive activities (Walgrave, 1995).

Once again, the role of the *community* in the goal of community protection is integral. The Office for Juvenile Justice and Delinquency Prevention (OJJDP) has begun to recognize the need for locally generated efforts to support community justice programs, through the proliferation of Title V Incentive Grants for Local Delinquency Programs (1997). Programs funded by such monies acknowledge that community regulation cannot be effective by coercive social control methods alone. As one criminal justice professional remarks, "One of the primary problems we face in our communities is that we have grown dependent on our social institutions to 'solve' crime" (Alford, 1997, p. 104).

The role of the justice system in the preceding components is unique. With retributive and rehabilitative justice, the system is a receptacle; in restorative justice the system is seen as one of many resources in the development of an ongoing process (Zehr, 1997). In the traditional systems, dispositions would *happen* to an offender. In restorative justice, dispositions *are made* with key actors: the victim, the offender, and the community. It is a system where the offender must actively engage in the restoration process. BARJ posits that the justice system should facilitate the healing process and teach skills to the offender and community that encourage restoration.

Will Victims and the Public Accept Balanced and Restorative Justice?

An important consideration in implementing such a justice system would be gaining acceptance from the public. Politicians often promulgate the interpretation that there are only two approaches to crime: "hard" or "soft" (McElrea, 1996). Because balanced and restorative justice is relatively new to this country, politicians fear that it may be perceived as the latter by their constituencies. Much to their surprise, however, there are preliminary signs of support for many of the precepts of balanced and restorative justice.

The most poignant endorsement of restorative justice principles comes from victims themselves. Studies have demonstrated not only a willingness by victims to participate in victim–offender reconciliation programs (VORP) (Walgrave, 1995), but satisfaction with the process after they have completed it. In a study done by Niemeyer and Shichor (1996) of the VORP in Orange County, California, the majority of victims expressed interest in meeting face-to-face with the respective offenders. Even in cases of serious personal crimes, 58% of victims desired to participate directly in the process and not through an intermediary source. Results from this study clearly give credibility to the viability of balanced and restorative justice. In cases where there was a joint meeting, 99% reached a mutually sponsored agreement. In those cases, only 3% of the agreements failed to be fulfilled.

Understandably, satisfaction with the present criminal justice system has dropped in the past two decades. In a public-interest survey done in Vermont, only 37% of the sample supported the current system of corrections in this state (Gorczyk and Perry, 1997). Such findings indicate that the public may be ready for change. For young nonviolent offenders, 91% of the sample favored community-based sanctions (Gorczyk and Perry, 1997). Other studies have found similar support for restorative methods of justice (Niemeyer and Shichor, 1996).

In the Vermont study, the public expressed several goals that they wanted a correctional system to achieve. From the offender, respondents wanted full acceptance of responsibility (no plea bargains) and acknowledgment of guilt, restitution, a commitment to never repeat the offense, and something beneficial to come out of the justice process (Gorczyk and Perry, 1997). Such findings indicate significant support for restorative justice principles. A study of burglary victims done by the Center for Development and Research at the University of Minnesota examined how victims defined "fairness" within a correctional system. One hundred percent of victims who participated in a mediation program and 90% of victims who declined participation expressed that rehabilitation of the offender was a foremost concern for them (Umbreit, 1994). The second most frequent concern regarding fairness for victims in this study was restitution, with the least commonly cited being incarceration (Umbreit, 1994).

The effects on rates of recidivism, however, are not as conclusive. One study done on the Genesee County restorative-based diversion program found that only 20% of the 150 felons were rearrested, a rate less than half of that for similar incarcerated offenders (Laconte, 1998). However, other studies have been done producing different results. Many studies report marginal decreases in recidivism, but their conclusions often remain statistically insignificant. Still, the preliminary anecdotal evidence promises a platform for honest change within a complex system.

By the beginning of 1996, 24 states had begun the process of adopting balanced and restorative justice precepts into their present juvenile-justice system (OJJDP, 1996). Maryland, in particular, has shown tremendous growth in this area. In 1997, the Maryland Legislature passed the Juvenile Causes Act, calling for significant reform in the state's juvenile system, with a focus on balanced and restorative justice principles. Although they appreciate the need to incarcerate a minority of offenders, this move decisively marks a shift toward targeting intermediate-level offenders and "at-risk" youth (Simms, 1997). Programs like Earn It, Justice in Cluster Education, and Project Attend focus on mobilizing community resources to collectively supervise the state's youth while making offenders accountable for their actions. Although these programs have not implemented all components of balanced and restorative justice (as described by Mark Umbreit earlier in this discussion), their existence marks a significant step in the direction of working with the community, victim, and offender collectively. Texas, Florida, Minnesota, Oregon, and Georgia have also integrated restorative components within their current system (Bazemore and Umbreit, 1998).

REALITY VERSUS UTOPIA: CAN THIS REALLY WORK?

As promising as balanced and restorative justice sounds, it is not without its critics. The difficulties with the new paradigm are either practical, legal, or both (Walgrave, 1995). Some criminologists question whether the existing justice system could uphold restorative justice principles. For example, the following quote examines the traditional system of justice:

> The means of intervention in both the rehabilitative and retributive systems are force and coercion. If the intention to rehabilitate is made part

of the justice system, it is precisely and solely because it uses the compulsive power of justice. . . . In both schemas, the power of the state is imposed from outside on the individual to bend him to the state's will, or to exclude him. Judicial rehabilitation is preretribution, or hidden retribution, which allows it to ignore legal guarantees which circumscribe over retribution. (Walgrave, 1995, p. 231)

Clearly, the present system is distinct from restorative justice; thus, consonance within such a system may be difficult to facilitate. The use of force may either thwart legitimate efforts to establish a balanced and restorative system or provide a backbone to make such a system work. In other words, a justice system without any inherent coercion may be quixotic; implementing restorative principles in the existing system, however, could provide the best of both paradigms.

In addition to the complex use of force which is implicit in the present justice system, one fundamental criticism lies in the belief that such a system simply could not peacefully coexist in an adversarial system. If it is first necessary to establish evidence of guilt beyond a reasonable doubt before engaging in restorative principles, many offenders will be excluded from the process. In this manner, the state intervenes before a conflict of individuals can be resolved. What about an offender who was found with stolen property, but whose Fourth Amendment rights were violated during an illegal search and seizure? Under customary practice, the "fruit of the poisonous tree" would be excluded in judicial proceedings. Additional problems with plea bargaining may cause complications in the balanced and restorative model. This issue leaves many unresolved questions about how to effectively implement restorative justice (Ashworth, 1993).

Despite these theoretical obstacles, the New Zealand Youth Court, which employs both adversarial and restorative principles, has maintained this balance for many years (McElrea, 1996). Although they have many due process safeguards, once guilt has been established, restorative principles dominate the juvenile-justice process. The success of the New Zealand Youth Court, then, diffuses the theoretical ammunition that the two models cannot peacefully coexist (McElrea, 1996).

The second basic criticism made against restorative justice is the potential lack of predictability in sentencing. By involving victims and communities in the restoration process, it is likely that dispositions will reflect great disparities, not only between regions, but even among similar cases (Ashworth, 1993). For instance, a victim in one case may harbor great hostility toward the offender for any number of reasons; another victim may wholeheartedly endorse restorative principles. It is easy to see how similar crimes potentially could yield very different results. Similarly, one offense may have multiple victims. Balancing all of the victims' concerns into a reasonable sentence may not be an easy task (Bazemore and Pranis, 1997). Some critics argue that such disparity could constitute a violation of the right to equal protection under the law. One response suggested to alleviate potential disparities would be to construct general guidelines for minimum and maximum dispositions (Bazemore and Umbreit, 1998) that could provide a framework for reasonable sanctions under the law. To combat this issue, the New Zealand Youth Court has court officials who ensure a broad range of equity (McElrea, 1996). Furthermore, this court maintains that differences in sentencing are not inherently bad. They propose that similar crimes do not always merit like dispositions (McElrea, 1996).

A third criticism of restorative justice lies in the language of the paradigm. Implicit in the premises of balanced and restorative justice are the concepts of victim and offender as separate entities (Ashworth, 1993). How would the paradigm change if victims and offenders were members of the same family? To further complicate the issue, how would this system be affected by a parent–child relationship? Crime between intimates complicates the process, but it does not necessarily negate the precepts of the model.

Aside from these considerations, misconceptions threaten to impede further the progress of this model. One of the dangers of restorative justice lies not within the model itself, but in misunderstood language. For instance, a particular justice agency may use the terms "accountability" or "community protection," but may try to implement the goals in a retributive fashion. Under the traditional correctional system, the term "accountability" is quite often used; however, it does not refer to the victim or community. It refers directly to the state, and it unmistakably equates to punishment (Zehr, 1997). Furthermore, the term "balance" does not define a balance between punishment and rehabilitation in the restorative model (Bazemore and Pranis, 1997). The definition of community service also takes on a whole new meaning in balanced and restorative justice. Although it presently is used often as a punishment, in a balanced system, community service serves a reparative goal (Bazemore and Maloney, 1994). Such confusion in language threatens to marginalize restorative effects, masking goals from the retributive system (Bazemore and Umbreit, 1998).

Another common misconception involves equating restorative justice with outlawing incarceration entirely, which has understandably created doubts about the utility of restorative justice. Few, if any, criminologists advocate this extreme position (Laconte, 1998). On the contrary, there appears to be near universal acceptance that some offenders require confinement, not only for the safety of society, but for their own safety as well (Munn, 1993). Their incarceration, however, is more a protective measure than a punishment (Bazemore and Umbreit, 1998).

Conclusion: Paradigm Shifts in U.S. Justice

Our justice system was built upon centralizing the role of the state rather than the primary victim, but it is still a dynamic system with room to evolve. Currently, there are several competing philosophies vying for support. These include rehabilitation, retribution, and restorative justice. The hope of rehabilitation for offenders, lauded by many in the 1960s and 1970s, was dashed only a few years after it had been implemented because of its failure to reduce crime on a macro scale. Some question whether the perceived failure of rehabilitation transpired because it inadvertently modeled itself after the traditional justice system in the United States by excluding the victim and community—neither the retributive nor the rehabilitative models engaged these two in the justice process.

The traditional retributive model continues to hold significant appeal for politicians and policymakers. The evolution and growth of the retributive model, particularly since the 1960s, is quite significant; retribution now encroaches on areas where it previously had not. This is in part because of the decline of informal levels of social control which occurred in the 1960s (Pranis, 1997a). To fill the vacuum left by retreating informal social control, the government began to exert its power on a level not seen before. A sense of community, and all of the informal control exerted by it, largely dissipated (McElrea, 1996). The government's involvement in "picking up the slack" of social controls had unforeseen effects on the concept of community. As Durkheim had astutely predicted two hundred years ago, an area of space which loses its sense of community loses the ability to define norms, identify abhorrent behavior, and ultimately to regulate itself. The more its members are connected and invested in a community, the more likely they are to restrain impulses which are socially defined as deviant (Pranis, 1997a). Many speculate that the consequence of increased government interaction was a rise in violent crime. The problem, some maintain, is that the government begrudgingly usurped a role it was ill equipped to fulfill. In combination with the numerous other social factors, this effort largely failed (Bazemore and Day, 1996). The result has been an overreliance on retributive philosophies in the correctional/penology field. "'Three strikes and you're out," mandatory sentencing, and the resurrection of the chain gang are the outcome of such policies. All of the aforementioned responses to crime had marginal effects in reducing crime. In fact, such implements have been counterproductive in reducing recidivism and actually may exacerbate racial and social class tensions. There have been long-lasting effects; society has become compartmentalized and family units insular from their communities. For victims, this has translated to less formal and informal support in their communities.

The public, as a financial contributor to criminal justice and social service agencies, is justified in being disgruntled with the justice system's efficacy. The public is misguided, however, in believing that emphasizing one model (retribution) over the other (rehabilitation) will be successful.

The most promising proposal probably lies with neither the retributive nor rehabilitative model. Neither adequately addresses the victim in their sense of justice; the focus either advocates punishing or treating the offender, both of which alternatives inherently fail to engage the perpetrator or the victim

(Umbreit, 1995). The offense becomes lost in a due process obstacle course, encouraging offenders to engage in the adversarial dance and shirk their responsibility (Zehr, 1997). In short, there is little in the criminal justice process which encourages an offender to appreciate the harm he or she has done to the victim or community. Neither system adequately addresses the human impact of crime.

Although the retributive model may temporarily quell people's fears about crime, this model lacks efficacy in the goals of preventing crime, reforming offenders, or servicing victims and communities. While the public embraces this philosophy after the news of a particularly egregious violent crime, the reaction amounts to another "quick fix" panacea destined to fail in addressing a complex problem.

Balanced and restorative justice, however, provides a more realistic approach. It appreciates that any crime is more than the act and more than the actor. It recognizes the complex interplay between the offender, victim, and community. These ideas, however, are quite new to the U.S. justice system. Undoubtedly, any change that requires such a complete paradigm shift will be difficult. The implementation of such a system will take both time and intelligent planning, but it has worked tentatively well in limited sections of this country and consistently well in other countries. Critics who say this design lacks the insatiable appeal of the "just desserts" policies underestimate the U.S. public. Justice requires looking at those most affected by crime—the victims—and addressing their needs. Balanced and restorative justice may be the vehicle to do just that.

Endnote

[1] Of course, one could argue that the community makes its voice heard through electing officials that represent their perspective on justice. However, the community is rarely a direct stakeholder in the routine justice process (e.g., speaking directly to a judge, prosecutor, or police about an appropriate sentence for an offender, etc.).

References

Abel, R. (1998). Torts. In D. Kairys (Ed.), *The Politics of Law: A Progressive Critique* (3rd ed.), (pp. 445–470). New York: Basic Books.

Alford, S. (1997, December). Professionals need not apply. *Corrections Today,* 59, 104–108.

Ashworth, A. (1993). Some doubts about restorative justice. *Criminal Law Forum,* 4, 277–299.

Bazemore, G., and Day, S. E. (1996, December). Restoring the balance in the response to youth crime: Juvenile and community justice. *Juvenile Justice,* 3 (1), 3–14.

Bazemore, G., and Maloney, D. (1994, March). Rehabilitating community service: Toward restorative service sanctions in a balanced justice system. *Federal Probation,* 58, 24–35.

Bazemore, G., and Pranis, K. (1997, December). Hazards along the way. *Corrections Today,* 59, 85–128.

Bazemore, G., and Umbreit, M. (1998). Balancing the response to youth crime: Prospects for a restorative juvenile justice in the twenty-first century. In A. R. Roberts (Ed.), *Juvenile Justice* (pp. 371–408). Chicago: Nelson-Hall.

Flaten, C. L. (1996). Victim–offender mediation: Application with serious offenses committed by juveniles. In B. Galaway and J. Hudson (Eds.), *Restorative Justice: International Perspectives* (pp. 387–402). New York: Kugler.

Gorczyk, J. F., and Perry, J. G. (1997, December). What the public wants. *Corrections Today, 59,* 78–83.

Karmen, A. (1996). *Crime Victims: An Introduction to Criminology.* New York: Wadsworth.

Laconte, J. (1998, January/February). Making criminals pay. *Policy Review, 87,* 26–31.

Levrant, S., Cullen, F. T., Fulton, B., and Wozniak, J. F. (1999). Reconsidering restorative justice: The corruption of benevolence revisited? *Crime and Delinquency, 45* (1), 3–27.

McElrea, F. W. M. (1996). The New Zealand Youth Court: A model for use with adults. In B. Galaway and J. Hudson (Eds.), *Restorative Justice: International Perspectives* (pp. 69–83). New York: Kugler.

Munn, M. (1993). Restorative justice: An alternative to vengeance. *American Journal of Criminal Law, 20,* 299–302.

Niemeyer, M., and Shichor, D. (1996, September). A preliminary study of a large victim/offender reconciliation program. *Federal Probation, 60* (3), 30–34.

Office of Juvenile Justice and Delinquency Prevention. (1994, October). *Balanced and Restorative Justice: Program Summary.* Washington, DC: U.S. Department of Justice.

———. (1996, July). Balanced and restorative justice project (BARJ). Fact sheet #42. Washington, DC: U.S. Department of Justice. Prepared by Peter Freivalds.

———. (1997, July). Mobilizing communities to prevent juvenile crime. Washington, DC: U.S. Department of Justice. Prepared by Donna Bownes and Sarah Ingersoll.

———. (1998, December). *Guide for Implementing the Balanced and Restorative Justice Model.* Washington, DC: U.S. Department of Justice.

Pranis, K. (1997a, March/April). From vision to action: Some principles of restorative justice. *Church and Society,* 32–42.

———. (1997b, December). Peacemaking circles. *Corrections Today, 59,* 73–122.

Seymour, A. (1997, December). When staff are victimized. *Corrections Today, 59,* 90–93.

Simms, S. O. (1997, December). Restorative juvenile justice. *Corrections Today, 59,* 94–114.

Umbreit, M. S. (1994). *Victim Meets Offender.* New York: Willow Tree Press.

———. (1995, Spring). Holding juvenile offenders accountable: A restorative justice perspective. *Juvenile and Family Court Journal, 46,* 31–42.

———. (1998). *Victim Offender Mediation Programs* [Videotape]. St. Paul: University of Minnesota.

Walgrave, L. (1995, August). Restorative justice for juveniles: Just a technique or a fully fledged alternative? *Howard Journal of Criminal Justice, 34,* 228–249.

Zehr, H. (1997, December). Restorative justice: The concept. *Corrections Today, 59,* 68–70.

Index

A

Abel, Richard, 371
Achille Lauro, 162
ACLU (*see* American Civil Liberties Union)
Acquaintance rape, 65 (*see also* Date rape)
Addiction (*see* Substance abuse)
Advertising, violence and sexuality in, 78–79
Advocacy Committee for Women's Concerns, 316,
   317
Afghanistan, 160
Africa, AIDS in, 314
African Americans:
   and attitude towards police, 206, 208
   black-on-black crime, 18
   and hate crimes, 189, 190, 191
   racial profiling and, 207–212, 214–215
   serial killers, 18–19
   in "wrong" neighborhood, 209
Age, and violence, 261–262
Aggravated assault on campus, 268
AIDS prostitution and, 314
Al Qaeda, 160, 187
Alcohol (*see also* Substance abuse)
   addiction and, 317
   and binge drinking, 271
   campus violence and, 262–263
   and disease, 319–320
   and drugs, 316
   prohibition and, 318–319
   and rape, 38, 43, 45, 47
   statistics on, 317
   as vice, 319
Alcoholics, high-risk lifestyle of, 28
Alfred University, 270
American Academy of Pediatrics, 83
American Civil Liberties Union, 210, 319, 320
American Family Association, 82
American Medical Association, 119
American Psychological Association, guidelines, 59
Amin, Idi, 169–170
Amnesty International, and torture of children, 21
*An Inquiry into the Effects of Ardent Spirits upon
   the Human Body and Mind* (Rush), 316

Animal House (movie), 264
Arab League, 179–181
Armstrong, Eric, 19
Asian Americans, 198, 212, 214
Assault and battery, 34
Assessment, Lethality of the Batterer, 123–124
Assisted suicide, 323–327
   case law and, 325
   disabilities and, 326
   harm of, 326–327
   legislation and, 326
   in Oregon, 324, 326
   prevalence of, 323–324
   public opinion and, 325
   state law and, 325
Athletes, 264, 270, 271, 292
Atlanta, Georgia, child killings in, 18–19
Attention deficit–hyperactivity disorder, 243
Ayala, Richard, 17

B

Balanced and restorative justice, 370–382
   acceptance of, 377–378
   community protection and, 376–377
   competency development and, 375–376
   criticisms of, 378–380
   definition of, 372–373
   dissatisfaction with, 377
   mediation programs and, 374–375
   misconceptions about, 380
   in New Zealand, 379, 380
   in other countries, 372
   public goals of, 377–378
   recidivism and, 378
   rehabilitation and, 376
   and search and seizure, 379
   sentencing disparities and, 379–380
   supervision and, 376–377
   victims' support for, 377
Barnes, A., 192
Battered woman syndrome (BWS), 103–104, 105
   (*see also* Domestic violence)

Battered women's movement (*see also* Domestic violence)
  history of, 118–119
  shelters for, 118–119, 134
Batterers (*see also* Domestic Violence)
  group treatment, 130
  lethality assessment, 151
  potential for change, 133, 135, 155
  probation, 143
  support for, 139, 140
Bayley, J. E., 252
Bayog, Dr. Margaret Bean, 65–66
Bean, J., 286, 287
Berk, R. A., 354
Best, C. J., 37, 104
Bias crimes (*see* Hate crimes; Nonbias crimes)
Bill of Rights (*see* U.S. Constitution)
Bin Laden, Osama, 160, 187
Bird, James, 189
Black, D., 350, 351
Blackstone, William, 324
Blazer, D., 38
Blind Eye (Stewart), 22
Bloom, B., 102
Bogan, J. B., 223
Boston, hate crimes in, 193, 202
Bowker, L. H., 223
Browne, Dr. Angela, 129
Bruised Inside (National Association of Attorneys General), 242
Bryant, Jennings, 76
Bullying, 249–252, 305
Bundy, Ted, 16, 28
Bureau of Justice Statistics, 101, 102
Burt, M. R., 42
Bush, President George W., 160

C

Caffrey, Dr. John, 94–95
Calhoun, Commander Alfred, 12
Campus Security Act of 1992, 267, 278–279 (*see also* Clery Act of 1998)
Campus violence, 258–279
  age and, 261–262
  aggravated assault and, 268
  desensitization and, 261
  dormitory life and, 263, 268
  gender and, 263, 276–277
  hazing and, 270–272
  murder and, 275–276
  prevalence of, 270–271
  reporting of, 260, 263
  sexual assault and, 259–260
  and stalking, 268–270
  statistics of, 260, 261
  student groups and, 264, 271
  teachers and, 267
  victims of, 265–266, 269–270, 272, 274–275, 277
Cardinal Mindszenty, 172

Case law (*see also* U.S. Supreme Court)
  Anthony's Pier Four v. HBC Associates (1991), 294
  Baker v. McCollan (1979), 295
  Bernstein v. Aetna Life & Casualty (1988), 285
  Blare v. Husky Injection Moulding Sys. Bos. Inc. (1995), 304
  Booth v. Maryland (1987), 334, 338–339, 340, 341
  Burlington Industries v. Ellerth (1998), 285, 288–289, 303, 304
  Busby v. Truswal Systems Co., (1989), 301
  Byrd v. Richardson–Greenshields Securities, Inc. (1989), 294
  Castaneda v. Partida (1977), 290
  College-Town v. MCAD (1987), 301
  Commonwealth v. McAfee (1871), 118
  Commonwealth v. Welansky (1944), 305
  Cremen v. Harrah's (1988), 302
  Faragher v. City of Boca Raton (1998), 286, 289, 303, 304
  Foley v. Polaroid (1987), 296
  Foster v. The Loft (1998), 299
  Harris v. Forklift Systems, Inc. (1993), 285–286, 291, 303
  Harrison v. Edison Brothers Apparel Stores, Inc. (1989), 300–301
  Highlander v. KFC National Management Company (1998), 285
  Henson v. Dundee (1982), 299
  Jane Doe v. Purity Supreme (1994), 283–284, 286–287, 293, 296, 303
  Johnson v. Transportation Agency, Santa Clara Cty. (1987), 290
  Karibian v. Columbia (1994), 299–300
  Linda R. S. v. Richard D. (1973), 337, 343
  Lipsett v. University of Puerto Rico (1988), 297
  Lopes v. McDonald's (1987), 299
  Mary M. v. City of Los Angeles (1991), 299, 300
  Melnychenko v. 84 Lumber Co. (1997), 292
  Meritor Savings Bank, FSB v. Vinson et al. (1987), 284–285, 289, 291, 299, 301, 303
  Morris v. Slappy (1983), 337, 342, 343
  Munford v. James T. Barnes & Co. (1977), 297
  Newport News Shipbuilding & Dry Dock Co. v. EEOC (1983), 290
  O'Connell v. Chasdi, 293
  Oncale v. Sundowner Offshore Services, Inc. (1998), 286, 290, 292
  Parent v. Spectra Coating Corp. (2000), 304
  Payne V. Tennessee (*1991*), 334, 338, 340–341
  Reeves v. Sanderson Plumbing Products (2000), 304
  Rideout v. Crum & Forster, Inc. (1944), 292
  Ruiz v. Estelle (1980), 225
  Seminole Point Hosp. Corp. v. Aetna Casualty & Sur. Co. (1987), 296, 297
  Thurman v. City of Torrington, 357–359
  Tolbert v. Martin–Marietta Corp. (1988), 284, 302, 305
  Vacco v. Quill (1997), 325
  Washington v. Glucksberg (1997), 325
  Wilkins v. Maryland (1988), 210
  Wisconsin v. Mitchell (1993), 191

Worcester Insurance Co. v. Fells Acre Day School, Inc. (1990), 292, 296
Yunker v. Honeywell, Inc. (1993), 300
Zurian v. Wohl Shoe (1994), 299
Celebrities
  as authorities, 70
  sexuality of, 78–79
Centerwall, B. S., 80
Chao, B. S., 103
Checklist of Abuse, 123
Child abuse, 89–99
  adult criminality, 103
  adult threats of, 91
  burning and, 95
  child labor and, 93
  community impact of, 96
  data on, 93, 97, 98–99
  Department of Justice and, 98
  domestic violence and, 133
  emotional symptoms of, 95–96
  families and, 92, 98, 246
  fear of disclosure and, 91, 96, 98
  gang members and, 107–112
  gender and, 93
  government agencies for, 97
  history of, 93–94
  physical symptoms of, 94–96
  prostitution and, 315
  reaction of children to, 90–91
  recognition of, 92
  runaway youth, 105
  society's apathy and, 91–92
  socioeconomics of, 92–93
  support for victims of, 97–98
Child labor, 93
Child Protection Act of 1984, 99
Children (*see also* Juvenile violence)
  aggressive behavior of, 242–243
  characteristics of, 242–245
  domestic violence and, 126, 127, 132, 133, 152–153
  early childhood problems of, 242
  media and, 72–74, 80–83
  moral development of, 80–81
  as murderers, 69–70
  nature versus nurture, 242–243
  serial killers, 11, 20–21
  sex abuse of, 327
  torture of, 20
  TV violence and, 80–83
Chronicle of Higher Education (CHE), 274
  1999 Annual Report on the Freshman Class, 262, 271
Civil Rights Act of 1964, Title VII, 284–285, 286, 290, 291
Civility code, 291
Clemmer, D., 222
Clepper, Gregory, 18
Clery Act, 264, 269
Clery, Jeanne, 259, 260
Clinton, President Bill, 55, 56, 215–216, 343
CNN, 16

Cocaine, 316 (*see also* Drug use; Substance abuse)
Cohn, E. G., 353
College students, and serial killers, 11
Columbine High School tragedy, 239, 247
Comprehensive Drug Abuse Prevention and Control Act of 1970, 318
Conflict management, 268
Consent, 34–36
Contract killers, 12
Cook, S. L., 39, 47
Coombs, Cindy, 161
Corll, Dean 21, 27
Corona, Juan, 21
Cosgrove, S., 78
Covenant House, 55
Crime control strategies, 205–216
Crime victims (*see also* Victims)
  in criminal justice system, 25–28, 335, 337–338, 341, 343, 370–372
  lifestyles of, 25, 27–28
Criminal justice system:
  accountability and, 373–375
  as adversarial system, 371
  beating the system and, 371
  changes in, 380–382
  community protection and, 373
  crime reduction and, 381
  dehumanization of, 371
  diversion programs and, 373
  domestic violence and, 361–363
  mediation and, 374
  plea bargaining and, 371
  and presumption of innocence, 35
  primary victims and, 371
  rehabilitative model of, 381
  retributive model of, 381, 382
  secondary victims and, 372
  social control and, 381–382
  social goals and, 365
  victims and, 25–28, 335, 337–338, 341, 343 370, 371–372
Criminal law, 25
Crouch, B. M., 224, 225
Cults members, 27–28, 72, 162
Culture war, 82–83
Cunanan, Andrew, 24
Cuomo, M., 335

D

Dahmer, Jeffrey, 24, 27
Dana Farber Cancer Institute, 324
Danks, Joseph, 22
Date rape (*see also* Acquaintance rape; Rape)
  alcohol and, 39, 43, 45, 47
  physical setting (location) of, 39–40, 45, 48, 49
  on college campuses, 260–261, 265
  consensual foreplay and, 46, 48–49
  definition of, 36
  female use of alcohol and, 45, 47–48
  female verbal resistance and, 46, 48

Date rape (*continued*)
  legislation and, 319
  male character types and, 39
  male use of alcohol and, 45
  nonreporting of, 260, 264, 265
  physical isolation and, 39
  physical resistance to, 46, 48
  prior sex and, 45
  relationships and, 45, 47
  substance abuse and, 320
  survey of, 41–49
  threat of force and, 46, 48
  victims of, 37–38
  women's perception of risk, 38–41, 45–46, 47–49
Date-Rape Drug Prohibition Act of 2000, 319
Dating situations, 34
De Plessis, Y., 309–310, 327
Decriminalization drugs and, 320–321
Defoe, D., 312
DeMause, L., 93
Depression, and delinquent behavior, 243
Desensitization, 261
Designer ("club") drugs, 319
Developmental psychology, and TV, 85
Diagnostic and Statistical Manual of Mental
      Disorders, 252, 322
Dietz, M. L., 12
DiIulio, J. J., 225
Dikko, Umaru, 164–165
Dinero, T. E., 37
Disabilities:
  and consent, 35–36
  hate crimes and, 189
Disease Concept of Alcoholism, The (Jellineck), 319
Divorce, 363
DNA evidence, 19
Doctor–patient sexual relationship, 56–57, 61
  as criminal offense, 62–64, 65
  doctors defense of, 58–59
  laws by state, 62–63, 64
  legal remedies for, 62–65
  therapeutic relationship and, 59–61
Domestic violence, 115–159 (*see also* Battered
      women's movement)
  abusive behaviors and, 123, 124, 149–150
  advocate's role and, 135, 136, 137–138
  "blame the victim" mentality and, 127–128
  business programs against, 139–140
  causes of, 127–128
  checklists for, 123, 149–150
  children, 126–127, 132, 133, 152–153
  civil liberties and, 367
  college students and, 268
  community issue and, 140–142, 146
  as control issue, 121
  counseling and, 129–130, 142
  as a crime, 130, 133, 135–136
  criminal justice system and, 118–119, 135–139,
      361–367
  definitions of, 121–122, 123
  delinquent youth, 126–127, 246
  divorce and, 120–121, 129, 363
  economic issues and, 132
  equality wheel and, 123, 148
  false complaint and, 365–366
  as family issue, 125, 126–127, 132–133, 348–349
  fear and, 131–133
  fear of reporting, 121, 135
  gender and, 119, 366, 367
  in history, 118, 348–367
  homicide and, 367
  indicators of, 123–124
  injury and, 124
  intervention and, 125, 133–135, 142, 366
  jealousy, possessiveness and, 124
  law enforcement and, 122, 135–139, 143,
      347–367
  legal separation and, 363
  marriage (couples) counseling and, 129–130
  medical intervention and, 133–134, 154
  medical profession and, 121
  mental illness and, 128
  mentoring programs and, 145
  model programs on, 141–145, 146
  myths about, 127–130
  obstacles to separation and, 131–133, 154
  personal change and, 133
  power and control wheel, 12, 147
  predictability of, 129
  prevalence of, 119–121
  prevention of, 122, 145–146
  probable cause and, 350–351
  public education about, 140–141
  reform of laws, 350–364
  and refusal to press charges, 348, 350–351
  relationships and, 366–367
  resources about, 155–156
  restraining orders and, 122, 129, 138, 139, 142,
      155, 362–363, 364
  social costs of, 121
  as social issue, 131
  socioeconomic causes of, 128–129, 130
  stalking and, 124
  state as prosecutor and, 358–359
  student programs about, 139–140, 145–146
  substance abuse and, 127
  support for victim of, 139–140
  terrorism and, 166–167
  threats to kill and, 124
  treatment for victims of, 154
  underreporting of, 120, 121
  victim rights and, 137–138
  victim's safety and, 133, 136, 143, 154–155
  and women's movement, 350, 352, 359–360, 361,
      364
Domestic Violence Intervention Project (Duluth),
      123, 147–148
Dreamworlds (film), 78
*Driving while Black: Racial Profiling on Our Nation's
      Highways* (Harris), 209
Drug dealing, 320
Drug Enforcement Agency, 316
Drug enforcement, 318–319
  "schedules" and, 319

Drug use (*see also* Substance abuse)
   addiction and, 105–106
   on campus, 262–263
   and date rape, 319
   and designer (club) drugs, 262–263
   patterns of use, 317
   race and, 216, 217
   violence and, 320–321
   youth and, 105–106
   women and, 105–106
Drugs and terrorism, 162
Durkheim, E., 381

E

Eagan, Margery, 128
Eastern Oregon Homeless Project, 376
Ecstasy (drug), 262–263
Edgework, 71
Egger, S., 11, 13, 14–15, 27
Elderly, and serial killers, 10, 11
Electronic media, 69, 80, 82 (*see also* Television)
   physical violence and, 70
   reform of, 83
   socialization and, 70
EMERGE (Cambridge, MA), 155
Employers Practices Liability Insurance, 293, 297
Ephross, P. H., 192
Equal Employment Opportunity Commission
   (EEOC) Title VII guidelines, 285
Eron, Dr. Leonard, 72
Erotomania ("pathological love"), 78–79
Estrich, S., 35, 63, 65
Ethnicity:
   hate crimes and, 189, 192, 195
   in workplace, 192
Everyday Violence (Stanko), 238–239

F

False imprisonment, 295–298
Families, 245–247
   child abuse and, 90, 96, 246
   disciplinary practices of, 245–246
   domestic violence and, 125, 126–127, 132–133,
      348–349
   protective factors of, 246–247
   as victims of murder, 30
   violence and, 84
   and violent youth, 245–247
Farais, Hillory J., 318–319
Farber, Stephen, 65, 76
Farrell, Mairread, 183–184
Federal Bureau of Investigation, 18, 22 (*see also* Law
   Enforcement)
   and domestic violence, 120
   and terrorism, 160, 182
Feinberg, J., 311
Female youth gangs, 107–113 (*see also* gang violence)
   Criminality of, 109–112
   peer support in, 112–113
   victimization and, 106–107

Females, vulnerability of, 28
Feminism and domestic violence, 118, 361 (*see also*
   women's movement)
*Forced Exit: The Slippery Slope from Assisted
   Suicide to Legalized Murder* (W. Smith),
   326–327
Ford Motor Company, 306
Ford, David, 26
Foreseeability, 299
Fortune, 84
Fossey, R., 264
Foundation for Research on Sexually Transmitted
   Disease, 17
Fox, J., 27
Fox, James Alan, 22
Fox, R., 91
Frasier, J., 74
Freeman, L., 57–59, 60–61
Freud, Sigmund, 56, 59
Fulton, B., 375
*Fungible Woman and Other Myths of Sexual Harass-
   ment, The* (Korn), 284, 292, 293, 302, 305

G

Gacy, John Wayne, 27
Gallup Poll:
   and assisted suicide, 325
   attitude towards police, 208
   racial profiling, 207
Galtung, J., 79
Gambling, 321–323, 328
   as pathology, 322–323
Gang violence, 250–252, 255 (*see also* Female youth
   gangs)
Gays and lesbians (*see* Homosexuals)
Gender equality, 367
Genesee County (NY) diversion program, 373,
   377
Geralds, Hubert, Jr., 17–18
Gibbs, J. T., 253
Green River killings, 15–16, 17
Guillen, Tomas, 16
Gun control, 84

H

Hannibal Lecter, 9–10
Harris, Sim, 173
Harrison Act of 1914, 318
Hartogs, Dr. Renatus (*see* Roy–Hartogs case)
Harvard University, 258
Hate crimes 189–202, 274–275 (*see also* Nonbias
   crimes)
   age and, 195, 274, 275
   and campus violence, 272–275
   as community problem, 197, 202
   as compared to nonbias crimes, 189, 190–191,
      195–196, 202
   definition of, 189, 272–273
   diversity and, 273
   education level and, 195

Hate crimes (*continued*)
  emotional reactions to, 192
  gender and, 192–193 195, 274
  group attacks and, 196, 201
  homosexuality and, 192–193, 198, 274–275
  household income and, 195
  immutable characteristics and, 191
  legal definition of, 272–273
  legislation on, 189–190
  location of, 194–195, 201
  multiple offenders and, 201
  nature of, 196–197
  in New York City, 191
  prevention of, 197
  psychological reactions to, 192, 193, 198–200
  race and, 189, 190, 191, 198
  religion and, 191
  reporting of, 197–198
  secondary victimization, 190–191
  study of, 193–202
  victim interchangeability of, 190, 191
  victims of, 274–275
Hawn, Stacy, 19
Hazing, 270–272
Hearst, Patty, 171–172
Henkoff, R., 81, 84
Henley, Elmer Wayne, 21
Herek, G., 192
Heroes, 9–10
Heroin, 316, 317 (*see also* Substance abuse)
Heyman, G. M., 319, 320
Hickey, E., 18, 24, 28
Hispanic Americans (*see also* Minorities)
  and racial profiling, 207–208, 215
HIV (*see* AIDS)
Homelessness:
  and serial killers, 10, 13, 22
  street youths and, 105
Homicide, 281 (*see also* Serial killers)
Homosexuals (*see also* Gays and lesbians)
Hood, S., 261, 275
Hopkins, Sir Anthony, 9–10
Horney, Karen, 56–57
Hoyt, D. R., 33, 38, 48
Human Sexual Inadequacy (Masters and Johnson),
  62

I

Igarashi, Hitushi, 182
Illingworth, Patricia, 60–61, 66
Indianapolis, gay murders in, 26
Infanticide, 91
Infants, media influence on, 80
Insurance companies, 305–306
  and liability rider for employers, 292–293,
  303–306
INTERPOL, 161
IQ and delinquent youth, 243, 247
Iqbal, Javed, 20

Irish Republican Army (IRA), 165, 168–169,
  183–184, 185

J

Jack the Ripper, 15
Jacobs, J., 190
Jacobson, J. L., 314
Jellineck, E. M., 319
Jenkins, Brian, 160
Jersey City (NY) Domestic Violence Crisis
  Intervention Teams, 348
Jews, hate crimes and, 191
Jhally, S., 74
Joe, K. A., 106
Jones, Paula, 55
Journal of the American Medical Association, 80
Jung, Carl, 56
*Juvenile Offenders and Victims: 1999 National
  Report* (Snyder and Sickmund), 240
Juvenile violence, 69–70, 81–82 (*see also* School
  violence; Violent youth)
  American culture and, 248
  bullying and, 241–242
  causes of, 242–248, 250
  data on, 126–127
  gender and, 240–241
  IQ and, 243
  media and, 248
  mediation programs and, 375
  murders and, 240
  physical appearance and, 252
  physical fights and, 241
  race and, 250
  rural and urban, 241
  statistics on, 240–242
  teachers as victims of, 242
  theft and, 241
  weapons and, 241

K

Karmen, A., 11, 12, 372
Katz, B. L., 38
Kaufer, Steve, 281
Kearney, Patrick, 22
Kennedy, Justice Anthony, 301
Kennedy, Senator Ted, 177, 178–179
Keppel, Robert, 12, 28
Kervorkian, Dr. Jack, 324
Khomeini, Ayatollah, 182–183
King, Rodney, 206
Kinsie, P. M., 314
Klinghoffer, Leon, 171
Kochanska, G., 79, 80
Konopka, G., 251
Koop, E. C., 83
Korn, Jane, 284, 292, 293, 302
Koss, M. P., 33, 37, 38, 47, 48, 50
KQED (TV station), 75

Kreidler, M. C., 88, 89
Ku Klux Klan, 190

L

Laqueur, Walter, 161
Larcom, B. E. K., 192
Lautenberg, Senator Frank, 177–178
Law enforcement (*see also* Police)
    credibility of victim, 64–65
    date rape and, 65
    domestic violence and, 122, 135–139, 143
    investigations of, 206
    "less dead," and, 28–29
    and minorities, 198
    and professional sexual misconduct, 65, 67
    psychological approach to, 25–28
    public attitude towards, 206
    and racial bias, 206
    serial killers and, 16, 17–18, 19, 22, 28–29
    stereotypes and, 29–30
    stressful situations, 185
    terrorism, 161
    victimological approach to, 26
Law, function of, 66–67
League of Women Voters of Minneapolis, 118
Legal separation, 363
Lehigh University, 259
Lesbianism, 57 (*see also* Homosexuality)
"Less-dead," 10, 13–15, 28–29, 30
Levine, L., 261, 265
Lewinsky, Monica, 55
Libya, terrorism and, 175–181
"Lifestyle liberalism", 82–83
Lifestyles, high-risk, 27–28
Lightfoot, L. O., 47
Lockerbie, Scotland (Pan Am flight 103 explosion),
    171, 173–175, 175–181
Logistic regression, 232–233, 234
Lopez, Pedro, 20–21
Lotteries, 323
Lovemaps (Money), 74
Lovesickness, 59–60
Lozano, Paul, 65–66
Lunde, D.T., 12

M

Machismo and media, 72
McVeigh, Timothy, 167
Maghan, J., 11–12
Magruder, B., 37, 38
Majors, Orville Lynn, 22–23
Maloney, Rep. Carolyn, 294
Marijuana, 316, 317, 320 (*see also* Drug use;
    Substance abuse)
Marquart, J. W., 224, 225
Marriage (couples) counseling, and domestic
    violence, 128–130

Massachusetts Coalition of Battered Women's
    Service Groups, 118, 119
Massachusetts Medical Society, 133
Massachusetts Supreme Judicial Court (SJC), 283,
    284
Massachusetts Victim Bill of Rights, 137–138
Massachusetts, hate crimes in, 272–273
Mattman, Jurge, W., 281
Media (*see also* Electronic media; Movies;
    Television)
    and cultural norms, 75–77
    as cultural training ground, 71
    defenders and critics of, 71, 83
    desensitization to violence and, 73–74, 261
    domestic violence and, 120
    double messages of, 71–72
    family responsibility and, 84
    image management and, 70
    serial killers, 77–78
    and sexuality as violence, 74, 78–79
    violence data on, 81–82
    and women as victims, 70
Mediation programs, 374–376
Medved, M., 73, 75, 76
Migrant workers, and serial killers, 11
Mill, J. S., 312
Miller, James, 28
Miller, L. C., 48
Minneapolis RECAP (Repeat Call Address Policing),
    348, 354
Minorities (*see also* African Americans; Asian
    Americans; Hispanics; Homosexuals)
    police and, 198
    preferential treatment of, 273
    and violence on campus, 273
Minority communities, and serial killings, 17–19
Miranda decision, 341
Missing children, and serial killers, 11
Missing persons, 27
Monahan, J. L., 48
Money, J., 74, 90, 91
Moore, Joan, 106, 107
Moos, Jeanie, 16
Morrison, Helen, 12
Movies:
    Basic Instinct, 74
    Burning Bed, The, 73
    marketing of, 72–73, 76
    pre-teens and, 72
    Raiders of the Lost Ark, 73
    and serial killers, 9, 10
    shock value of, 75–76
    Silence of the Lambs, 9–10, 73, 75
    violence and 73, 74, 75–76
    violent sexual behavior, 264
    and women as sex objects, 74
    and women as victims, 70
MTV, 72, 73, 79
Mueller, E., 104
Mugford, S., 70

Murder on campus, 275–276
Murder: No Apparent Motive (HBO documentary)
    77

N

National Association of Attorneys General, 242,
    250
National Center for Missing and Exploited Children
    (NCMEC), 97
National Center for Victims of Crime, 268–269
National Child Abuse Hotline, 98
National Clearinghouse on Child Abuse and
    Neglect, 97
National Coalition Against Domestic Violence, 118
National Commission on the Causes and Prevention
    of Violence, 83
National Crime Victims Week, 342
National Household Survey on Drug Abuse, 316,
    317
National Institute of Justice, Spousal Abuse
    Replication Project (SARP), 354
National Institute of Mental Health (NIMH), 103
National Institute of Occupational Safety, 276
National Organization for Victim Assistance
    (NOVA), 98, 342, 343
National Organization on Male Sexual Victimization,
    98
National Resource Center on Child Abuse and
    Neglect, 97
National Resource Center on Child Sexual Abuse,
    97
National Resources Center on Domestic Violence,
    119
National Rifle Association, 79
National Safe Workplace Institute, 282
National School Safety Center, 240
National Transportation Safety Board (NTSB),
    182
National Victims Center, 265
Native Americans, and serial killers, 10
Neft, N., 261, 265
Negligent entrustment, 298
Negligent hiring, 298–305
Negligent retention, 295, 296
Netherlands, 320
Nevada, gambling in, 322
New York *Times*, and serial killings, 17
Nichols, John, 167
Niemeyer, M., 377
Nonbias crimes (*see* Hate crimes)
Nonviolence, 140, 148
Norfolk County (MA), 133
Norris, J., 39, 40, 48
Nurge, D. M., 106

O

O. J. Simpson case, 128, 333, 341, 343, 344, 345
O'Malley, P., 70, 104
O'Toole, M. E., 243–245, 246

Office of Juvenile Justice and Delinquency
    Prevention, 105
Office of National Control Policy, 319
Okolo, J. E., 165
Olweus, D., 249, 250, 252
On Liberty (Mill), 312
Operant-defiant disorder, and delinquent behavior,
    243
Oregon, assisted suicide in, 324, 326
Organized crime, 322
Oskamp, Barbara, 326
Owen, B., 103

P

Packwood, Senator Robert, 55, 56
Pakistan, serial killing in, 20
Palestine Liberation Front, 162, 165
Paludi, M. A., 265, 266
Pam Am Flight 103 Witness to Justice Act,
    175–181
Peacemaking (sentencing) circles, 375
Penn, Alvin, 209–210
Persaud, R. D., 78, 79
Personality disorders, 33
Philadelphia, D., 250
Picarelli, J. A., 47
Pines, A. M., 102, 105
Pizzey, Erin, 118
Player, Michael, 22
Poland, James M., 161
Polaroid, 131
Police and domestic violence, 348–349 (*see also*
    Domestic violence; Law enforcement; Police)
    arrest powers and, 349–350, 351, 352, 362
    attitude towards, 349–350, 351–352, 354, 360–361
    counseling the disputants, 363
    discretion of, 353
    double arrest and, 356
    GOA ("Gone on Arrival"), 350, 355–356
    masculine rights and, 350, 361
    and new laws, 350–356, 364–365
    and resistance to enforcement, 355–357, 360–361
    selection bias and, 359
    slow response to, 350
    state as prosecutor, 358–359
    training for, 355
    women's movement, 350
Police:
    beliefs of, 351–352, 360–361
    "Blue Wall of Silence", 356
    clubhouse culture of, 353
    and community relations, 208, 215–216
    control techniques and, 358
    goals of, 348
    malperformance of duties, 357–359
    management processes of, 353
    perception of minorities of, 214–215
    social change and, 352–353
    women and, 350
Political assassination, 162

Post-traumatic stress disorder (PTSD)
   and rape, 38, 49
   and terrorism, 171
   victimization and, 103, 104, 105
Power and Control Wheel checklist, 123
Predatory stranger offenses, 27
Prejudice, 29–30
Pre-teens (*see also* Children)
and media, 72–73
Print media, 69
Prison, 222–223 (*see also* Prison inmates)
   "BT" system (building tender model), 225, 226
   control model, 225, 226
   deprivation model, 222–223
   importation prison model, 223
   integrated model, 223
   literature about, 222
Prison Community, The (Clemmer), 222
Prison inmates (*see also* Prison; Prison inmate study)
   gangs and, 225
   mental health of, 226
   perception of prison safety, 225–226, 229–232
   vulnerability of, 223, 224–226
   methods, 226–228
   inmate age and, 229, 230, 231, 232, 233, 234
Prison inmate study, 226–235
   arrest records, 228, 231, 234
   education of, 228, 231
   non-participation, 227
   perception prison violence, 226–235
   prison records, 228–229, 231, 232
   race/ethnicity and, 229, 232, 233, 234
   regression model, 234
   sampling for, 227–228
   Spanish speaking inmates, 228, 233
   survey questions and, 230, 231, 234
   time served, 231
Professional sexual misconduct, 55–67 (*see also* Doctor–client sexual relationships)
Prohibition (of alcohol), 318–319
Prostitution:
   arrest statistics for, 313
   child abuse as cause of, 102–103
   criminalization of, 314
   decriminalization of, 309, 310
   harm and, 314–316
   high-risk lifestyle and, 28
   history of, 313–314
   media coverage of, 14–15, 17
   preconditioning factors of, 315–316
   prevalence of, 313
   prohibition of, 313–314
   psychological consequences of, 315
   runaway youth and, 105
   serial killers and, 10, 11, 13, 14–20, 25
   society's opinions of, 14, 16
   in South Africa, 309
   STD and, 312, 314
   substance abuse and, 315
   as victimless crime, 327–328
   violence and, 315

Prostitution Education Network, 315
Protective-order statute, 119
Psychiatry:
   and professional sexual misconduct, 55, 56–59, 60–61
   and therapeutic relationship in, 59–62
PTSD (*see* Post-traumatic stress disorder)
Public executions, 75
Punitive damage settlements, 306

Q

Quincy (MA) Court Model Domestic Violence Program, 141–145

R

Rabin, Yitzak, 162
Race (*see also* African Americans; Minorities; Racial profiling)
   drugs and, 216, 217
   hate crimes and, 189, 191, 195
   industrial accident and, 293
   serial killers and, 18–19
   workplace violence and, 290
Racial profiling (*see also* Traffic stops)
   African Americans and, 207–208, 214–215
   and contraband, 214–215, 216
   in Connecticut, 209–210
   evidence of, 208–212
   in Florida, 216
   international data on, 212
   legislation and, 216
   in London, 215
   in Maryland, 210–211, 214
   in New Jersey State Police and, 209, 211–212, 214
   in New York, 212, 214
   politics and, 215–216
   public opinion and, 207
   social costs of, 206–208
   statistical data on, 210–211, 216
   stop and frisk laws and, 212
   U.S. Customs Service, 214
Radecchi, Thomas, 76
Rape (*see also* Date rape)
   on campus, 264
   consent and, 33–36
   disabilities and, 35–36
   gender and, 37
   "loss of control" and, 321
   prevalence of, 265
   prevention of, 38–39, 50, 265
   public attitudes toward, 253–254
   resistance to, 33, 36, 44
   revictimization and, 252–254
   risk factors and, 38–40, 50
   school violence, 252–254
   statistics on, 265
   substance abuse, 36, 320–321
   victims of, 37–39, 265–266

Rape *(continued)*
    workers' compensation, 302
    workplace violence, 283–284, 298
Rape myth acceptance (RMA) scale, 42, 43, 45, 46
Rape, case of "Jane Doe," 283–284, 286–288, 293,
        294, 297–298, 299, 303, 305
Rapists, 33
Reagan, President Ronald, 341–342
Reardon, Christopher, 96
Recidivism:
    and balanced and restorative justice, 378
    and mediation programs and, 375
    in states, 377
Regression therapy, 66
Rehnquist, Chief Justice William, 325–326, 340
Reid, Samantha, 318
Relationships, 61–62
    and domestic violence, 366–367
    and rape, 45, 47
Religion:
    hate crimes and, 191
    terrorism and, 162
Reno, Attorney General Janet, 78, 205
Research studies, hate crimes, 193–202
Respondeat superior, 298
Restitution (compensation), 334
Restorative justice (*see* Balanced and restorative
        justice)
Restraining orders, 362–363, 364
Reus–Ianni, Elizabeth, 353
Revenge of the Nerds (movie), 264
Revictimization, 105–106
Richards, D. A. J., 312, 313, 314, 316, 318
Rifkin, Joel, 16–17, 27
Ritter, Father, 55
Rock music, lyrics of, 77, 82
Rodney King case, 345
Rohypnol (drug), 319
Rose, Dr. Jeremy, 303
Rothenberg, David, 89–90
Roy, Julie (*see* Roy-Hartogs case)
Roy-Hartogs case, 57–59, 60–61, 62, 65, 66
Runaways, and serial killers, 10, 13
Rush, Benjamin, 316
Rushdie, Salmon, 182–183
Rwanda, serial killing in, 20

S

Sadat, Anwar, 162
Sagarin E., 11–12
San Diego and domestic violence program, 122
Sanborn, J. B., Jr., 42
Saunders, B. E., 104
Scalia, Justice Antonin, 340, 343
Scherman, A., 50
*School Shooter, The: A Threat Assessment Perspec-
        tive* (O'Toole), 243–245, 246
School violence, 69–70, 238–256 (*see also* juvenile
        violence)
    bullying and, 249–252
    and delinquent youth, 247–248
    in elementary schools, 241–242
    in high schools, 241–242
    media reports of, 239
    prevalence of, 240
    rape and, 252–254
    sexual harassment and, 254–255
    student perception of, 239–240, 250, 255
Schuh, J. H., 261, 275
Scott, G., 313
Scream Quietly or the Neighbors Will Hear (Pizzey),
        118
Sears, Charles, 22
Seattle Times, 16
Self-esteem, hate crimes and, 192
Sentencing (peacemaking) circles, 375
Serial killers, 11, 12–13
    charisma of, 28
    childhood of, 12
    children and, 18–19, 24, 28
    empathy of, 28
    families of, 30
    fiction about, 9–10
    homosexuals and, 25, 27
    identification with victims and, 12, 13
    in Latin America, 20–21
    law enforcement and, 16, 17–18, 19, 22,
        28–29
    location of crimes of, 24–25, 27–28
    media coverage of, 16, 17, 77–78
    medical profession and, 22–23
    mobility classification and, 24
    in other countries, 14
    psychology of, 28
    race and, 18–19
    rage of, 11–12
    relationship with victims and, 13
    sensationalism of media, 77–78
    sexual abuse and, 28
    statistics on, 13, 14–15
    street smarts of, 15
    survivors of, 30
    victims, information about, 26
    victims, and their killers, 13, 27, 28
    victims, vulnerability of, 26–28
    women and, 24, 27–28
Sexual abuse:
    and female offenders, 102, 104
    gang members, 107–112
    and runaway youth, 105
Sexual aggression (*see also* Rape)
    on college campuses, 259–260, 263
    definition of, 37
Sexual harassment, 38, 266
    abusive language and, 285–186
    as constitutional issue, 293
    construction industry and, 303
    employer knowledge of, 297–298
    employment and, 300–301
    gender-related jokes and, 286
    hostile environment, 285–286, 288, 289,
        303
    in schools, 254–255, 266–267

legislation on, 294–295, 296
liability for, 294
prevalence of, 266–267
public policy and, 301
quid pro quo, 285, 289
race and, 267
same-sex, 290, 291, 292
severe or pervasive, 285–286
socializing and, 291
statute of limitations and, 295, 297
supervisor/employee sex and, 299–300, 301, 302, 303
by teachers, 267
of waitresses, 303
in workplace, 285
Sexual orientation (*see* Homosexuals)
Sexual sadists, 12
Sexually transmitted disease (STD), 312, 314
Shaken baby syndrome, 94–95
Sharkansky, J., 38
Sherman, L. W., 353, 354, 359
Shott, Steve, 22
Silence of the Lambs, The, 9–10, 75
Simpson, O. J. (*see* O. J. Simpson case)
Smith, Carlton, 16
Social skills and delinquent youth, 247, 251
Socialization, and electronic media, 70
Society of Captives, The (Sykes), 222
South America, street children in, 20
Spielman, Sabrina, 56
Spitzer, Eliot, 212
Stalking, 78–79, 268–270
   domestic violence and, 124
   prevalence of, 269
   victims of, 269–270
Stanko, E., 238, 239
Stereotypes, 29–30
Stewart, James B., 22
Stockholm syndrome, 172–173
Street people, and serial killers, 10
Stress related physical disorders and terrorism
   (*see also* PTSD), 166–167
Student organizations and violence, 271
Substance abuse, 316–321, 327–328 (*see also* Alcohol; Drug use)
   addiction and, 317–318, 320, 321
   adults and delinquent youth and, 245
   child abuse and, 315
   and domestic violence, 127
   harm of, 319–320
   prostitution and, 315
   and rape, 320
   statistics on, 316–317
   victims of terrorism and, 166
Summers, R. W., 275, 276
Swango, Michael, 23
Symbionese Liberation Army (SLA), 171–172

T

Teachers, sexual harassment by, 267
Television vs. America (Medved), 75, 76

Television, 69
   and developmental psychology, 85
   protests against, 78
   violence and, 73, 76–78, 80–83
Temperance movement, 327
Temporary restraining order (TRO), 122
Terrorism, 159–187, 160–162, 163 (*see also* Victims of terrorism)
   in Africa (Rwanda, Uganda), 162, 166–167, 169–171
   on airplanes, 169, 171–182
   assassination as, 164
   attacks against U.S., 162
   in Beirut, 183
   cyclical nature of, 183
   definitions of, 163, 165
   economic sanctions and, 177–181
   in Great Britain, 159–160, 168, 172–173, 185–187
   history of, 161–163
   in Iran, 172–173
   legislation and, 168, 175–181
   media coverage of, 166, 167, 173
   in Nigeria, 164–165
   Northern Ireland, 163, 165, 183–184
   number of attacks, 165–166
   in Oklahoma City, 162, 166, 167–168, 171
   and Palestinians, 165, 169
   piracy as, 163
   prosecution of accused, 176–177
   religion and, 165, 182–183
   rescue workers and, 167
   response to, 183–184
   revenge and, 184
   state-sponsored, 162, 164–165
   Stockholm syndrome, 172–173
   stress reaction to, 184–185, 186–187
   TWA Flight 800, 181–182
   warnings of, 173–174
   World Trade Center (9–11), 159, 166, 187
Terrorism Research Center, 163
Terrorists, as victims, 183–184
Thatcher, Prime Minister Margaret, 169
Therapeutic relationship and, 59–61, 65–67
Third-party lawsuits, 295
Thomas, Allannah, 17
Title V Incentive Grants for Local Delinquency Programs, 376
Torricelli, Rep. Robert, 179
Toufexis, A., 77
Toxic shame, 88
Traffic stops (*see also* Racial profiling)
   criteria for, 213–215
   race and, 211, 213–215
   stop and search data, 211–212, 216
Transference, 59, 61
TV Guide, 84

U

U.S. Bureau of Statistics, 120
U.S. Constitution:
   Bill of Rights, 343
   Fifteenth Amendment, 344

U.S. Constitution (continued)
First Amendment, 275, 343
Fourteenth Amendment, 283, 344
Nineteenth Amendment, 318
Thirteenth Amendment, 344
U.S. Department of Health and Human Services, 97, 98
U.S. history, 344
racism and, 18
serial killers in, 9–10
U.S. society (culture)
and delinquent youth, 248
desensitization to violence and, 261
and image management, 70
mobility of population, 12, 28
U.S. Supreme Court, 301, 325–326, 340, 343
(see also Case law)
and victims' rights, 336–341
U.S. Surgeon General, report on violence in media, 76
United Nations World Conference for Women, 144
University of Minnesota, 374

V

Vagrants, and serial killers, 11
Victim and Witness Protection Act, 335
Victim Bill of Rights states and, 335, 336
"Victim blaming" techniques, 194
Victim groups and terrorism, 174
Victim rights, 336–341
compensation for, 334–335, 336
constitutional amendment for, 333, 341–345
criminal justice system and, 337–338, 341, 343
and domestic violence, 137–138
history of, 334–336
rights of accused and, 343
sentencing statement and, 335–336, 338–339
U.S. Supreme Court and, 336–341
victim impact statement and, 338, 339–341
Victim shield, 63
Victim, credibility of, 64–65
Victim's Bill of Rights, 278–279
Victim's status, 10
Victimization:
poor people and, 328
adult offenders, 102, 104, 109–112, 114
psychological consequences of, 103–104
street life and, 104–105
Victimless crime, 305–328 (see also Gambling, Prostitution, Substance abuse)
definition of, 310–311, 327
harm caused by, 311, 312
legislation and, 327
list of, 310
public morality and, 312
social reform and, 327–328
Victimless Crimes: Two Sides of a Controversy (Schur), 310
Victim-Offender Mediation (VOM), 374

Victims:
compassion for, 10
families of, 30
revictimizing of, 371–372
criminal justice system, 371–372
Victims of campus violence, 260, 265–266, 269–270, 272, 274–275, 277
Victims' Constitutional Network (Victim CAN), 342, 343
Victims of domestic violence:
criminal justice system and, 349–350
future safety of, 364
noncompliance of, 364
refusal to press charges and, 348, 350–351, 364
Victims of hate crime, 274–275
behavioral reactions of, 198
feelings of safety of, 200
negative experiences of, 200–201
and offenders, 196
psychological reactions of, 198–200
responsibility for, 196–197
vulnerability of, 201
Victims of rape, 37–38, 265–266
and psychological effects, 287
revictimization of, 253–254
and substance abuse, 266
Victims of school violence, 249–256
Victims of serial killers, 11–12
Victims of sexual harassment, by teachers 267
Victims of terrorism, 163–171
and forgiveness and justice, 183
individuals as, 171–173
legal rights of, 167–168
legislation and, 177–181
nations as, 168–171
psychological/social problems of, 166–167, 171
support groups for, 174
survival of, 183
Victims of workplace violence, 282–283, 305–306
Villeponteaux, L. A., 37
Violence:
children and, 69–70
civic responsibility and, 84–85
as cultural norm, 78–80
glorification of, 248
prevention of, 277
in schools, 69–70
Violence against women, Congress and, 268–269
Violence and drugs, 320–321
Violence and media, 69–85
Violence and substance abuse, 320
Violence as public health emergency, 83–84
Violence in prison (see also Prison inmates)
and age, 224
in North Carolina, 223–224
race and, 223, 225–226
self-report data on, 223
statistics on, 221, 224
in Texas, 224–228
Violence research, 238
Violent sexual behavior, and movies, 264

Violent youth:
    family characteristics of, 245–247
    personality traits of, 243–245
    programs for, 247–248
    school characteristics and, 247–248

W

Waite, Terry, 171, 183
Wald statistic, 232
Walgrave, L., 371, 372, 373, 375, 376, 377, 378–379
Walker, Lenore, 103–104
Walker, N., 198, 199
Walker, Samuel, 351
Weapons, and media, 81–82
Wilkins, Robert, 210–211
Wilson, A. E., 49
Winick, C., 314
Witches, and serial killers, 10
Women (*see also* Women's movement)
    campus violence and, 260–261, 264
    crime rate of, 101–102
    and drug addiction, 105–106
    in workplace, 281
Women offenders, rates of victimization, 102–103
Women police officers, 350
Women, as victims of sexual aggression, 33
Women, images of in media, 71–72, 78–80
Women's movement and domestic violence
    advocates for reform and, 352, 359–360, 361, 364

Women's suffrage, 344
Workers' Compensation, 292–295
    exclusivity provision and, 293–294, 295
    legislation on, 294–295
    Massachusetts and, 294, 296
    rape and, 302
    sexual harassment and, 294–296
Workplace violence, 281–306
    conservative politics and, 305–306
    economic cost of, 282
    employer retaliation and, 282–283
    and gender, 281, 290, 291
    high–risk businesses and, 299
    prevention programs and, 282
    punitive damage and, 306
    race and, 290
    statistics on, 282
    victims of, 305–306
    women and, 281, 290
World War I, 162

Y

Yates, Robert, Jr., 19–20
Youth gangs, 106–107 (*see also* Female youth gangs)
Youthful runaways, 104–105, 107–108

Z

Zupancic, M. K., 88, 89